TIN-GLAZE POTTERY

TIN-GLAZE POTTERY
in Europe and the Islamic World
The Tradition of 1000 Years in Maiolica, Faience & Delftware

ALAN CAIGER-SMITH

FABER & FABER
3 Queen Square
London

First published in 1973
by Faber and Faber Limited
3 Queen Square London WC1
Printed in Great Britain by
W & J Mackay Limited, Chatham
Colour plates by
The Curwen Press, Plaistow
All rights reserved

ISBN 0 571 09349 3

139626

CONTENTS

ILLUSTRATIONS

COLOUR PLATES

London Museum. (Photograph, A. C. Cooper Ltd.).

T. CHARGER painted with the royal yacht. Probably Lambeth, about 1668. *On loan to the Bristol City Art Gallery from an anonymous collection.* (Photograph, Derek Balmer).

U. BLUE-DASH CHARGER with tulip decoration. Probably Lambeth, late 17th century. *Ashmolean Museum, Oxford (Warren Collection).*

V. (a) MALLING JUG, opaque blue glaze with silver mounts. Probably London, about 1600. (b) WHITE PITCHER with rope-twist handle. Probably Ansbach or Nürnberg, late 17th century. *Both from Gerald Reitlinger Collection.* (Photograph, Fine Art Photography Ltd.).

W. LARGE BOWL painted in lustre, by the author. (Photograph, Fine Art Photography Ltd.).

X. 'ALTARPIECE' by Vlastímil Kvétensky, Karlovy Vary, Czechoslovakia, 1970.

MONOCHROME PLATES
at the end of the book

1. SMALL BOWL painted with the maker's name. Mesopotamia, 9th century. *Keir Collection, London.* (Photograph, Cecilia Gray).

2. SMALL BOWL. Mesopotamia, 9th century. *Kenneth Malcolm Collection.* (Photograph, Cecilia Gray).

3. BOWL painted with a fire altar. Mesopotamia, 10th century. *British Museum.*

4. POLYCHROME LUSTRE BOWL. Mesopotamia, 9th–10th century. *Keir Collection, London.* (Photograph, Cecilia Gray).

5. LUSTRE DISH. Mesopotamia, 9th–10th century. *Keir Collection, London.* (Photograph, Cecilia Gray).

6. SMALL LUSTRE BOWL painted with a bird. Mesopotamia, 9th–10th century. *Private Collection.* (Photograph, Cecilia Gray).

7. SMALL BOWL AND JUG painted in lustre. Mesopotamia, 10th century. *British Museum.*

8. SMALL BOWL painted in blue. Mesopotamia, 9th–10th century. *Collection, the Hon. Robert Erskine, London.* (Photograph, Cecilia Gray).

9. BOWL painted in lustre. Mesopotamia, 10th century. *Musée du Louvre.*

10. BOWL painted with figures in lustre. Mesopotamia, 10th century. *Keir Collection, London.* (Photograph, Cecilia Gray).

11. BOWL painted in lustre with a warrior. Mesopotamia, 10th century. *Keir Collection, London.* (Photograph, Cecilia Gray).

12. BOWL painted in lustre. Egypt, 10th century. *Islamic Museum, Cairo.*

13. JAR painted with a hare in lustre. Egypt, 10th century. *Keir Collection, London.* (Photograph, Cecilia Gray).

14. BOWL painted with cockfighters on red lustre. Egypt, 12th century. *Keir Collection, London.* (Photograph, Cecilia Gray).

15. BOWL painted with a bird in yellow lustre. Egypt, 12th century. *Islamic Museum, Cairo.*

16. DISH painted with a mule and rider in lustre. Egypt, 11th–12th century. *Keir Collection, London.* (Photograph, Cecilia Gray).

17. FRAGMENT OF A DISH painted in lustre with Christ in Glory. Egypt, 12th century. *Islamic Museum, Cairo.*

18. BOWL painted with a hare in lustre. Egypt, 12th century. *Musée du Louvre.*

19. BOWL painted over flowing glaze. Egypt, 11th or 12th century. *Islamic Museum, Cairo.*

20. BOWL painted in lustre. Rayy, 12th century. *Victoria and Albert Museum.*

21. BOWL painted with a horseman in lustre. Rayy, late 12th century. *Victoria and Albert Museum.*

22.   EWER painted in lustre. Kashan, about 1200. *Collection of Mr. and Mrs. Raymond Ades.* (Photograph, Victoria and Albert Museum).

23.   SMALL JUG painted in lustre. Rayy, later 12th century. *British Museum.*

24.   LUSTRE DISH with figures. Kashan, dated 607 A.H./1210 A.D. *Metropolitan Museum of Art, New York.*

25.   MINAI DISH signed by Abu Zeyd. Kashan, dated 584 A.H./1187 A.D. *Metropolitan Museum of Art, New York.*

26A,B.   SMALL MINAI BOWL painted with figures and riders. Kashan, late 12th century. *Musée du Louvre.*

27.   LARGE DISH painted with fishes in lustre. Persia, 13th century. *Fitzwilliam Museum, Cambridge.*

28.   UNGLAZED PAINTED JAR. Almería, Spain, 13th century. *Museo Arqueológico, Madrid.*

29.   Two ALBARELOS painted in lustre and blue. Málaga, late 14th century. *Instituto de Valencia de Don Juan, Madrid.*

30.   Two JUGS painted in blue. Málaga, 14th century. *Instituto de Valencia de Don Juan, Madrid.*

31.   Three aspects of the 'GAZELLE VASE'. Málaga, late 14th century. *Museo Arqueológico, Alhambra, Granada.* (Photograph by courtesy of Don Manuel Casamar).

32.   Detail from Plate 31. (Photograph by courtesy of Don Manuel Casamar).

33.   Detail from Plate 31. (Photograph by courtesy of Don Manuel Casamar).

34A,B.   Two aspects of the collar of the 'GAZELLE VASE'. (Photograph by courtesy of Don Manuel Casamar).

35.   JUG painted with a huntsman in red lustre. Málaga, late 14th century. *Instituto de Valencia de Don Juan, Madrid.*

36A,B.   LARGE BOWL painted with a ship in lustre. Málaga, late 14th century. *Victoria and Albert Museum.*

37.   DISH painted with a cross design. Paterna, 13th–14th century. *Valencia, Museo Historico.*

38.   DISH painted with mock-kufic letters. Paterna, about 1400. *Palacio Nacional, Barcelona.*

39.   DISH painted with a figure and two fishes. Paterna, 14th century. *Palacio Nacional, Barcelona.*

40.   BOWL painted with a girl's head. Paterna, 14th century. *Palacio Nacional, Barcelona.*

41.   JUG painted in blue. Manises, late 14th century. *Palacio Nacional, Barcelona.*

42.   ALBARELO painted in blue. Probably Manises, about 1400. *Instituto de Valencia de Don Juan, Madrid.*

43.   SHALLOW DISH painted in blue. Manises, about 1400. *Palacio Nacional, Barcelona.*

44.   DISH painted with an armed rider. Paterna, about 1300. *Museo Historico, Valencia.*

45.   DISH painted with a boar. Paterna or Manises, mid 14th century. *Museo Historico, Valencia.* (Photograph, F. Perez).

46.   DISH painted in yellow lustre and blue. Manises, early 15th century. *Victoria and Albert Museum.*

47.   Back of an ARMORIAL DISH, painted with an eagle. Manises, first half of the 15th century. *Museo Arqueológico, Madrid.*

48.   DISH painted with a castle in lustre. Manises, mid 15th century. *Museo Arqueológico, Madrid.*

49.   SMALL VASE painted in silvery lustre. Muel, about 1500. *Palacio Nacional, Barcelona.*

50.   'EARED' BOWL painted in silvery lustre. Muel, about 1500. *Palacio Nacional, Barcelona.*

51.   TALL JAR with inscriptions. Teruel, about 1400. *Palacio Nacional, Barcelona.*

52.   DISH painted with a dog and a hare in lustre. Manises, about 1500. *Instituto de Valencia de Don Juan, Madrid.*

53.   ALBARELO painted in lustre and blue. Manises, 15th century. *Musée du Louvre.* (Photograph, M. Chuzeville).

54.   SMALL BOWL painted with an angel in lustre. Manises, mid 15th century. *Museo Historico, Valencia.* (Photograph, F. Perez).

55. DISH painted with a bull in lustre. Manises, about 1500. *Gerald Reitlinger Collection.* (Photograph, Fine Art Photography Ltd.).

56. SMALL DISH painted with an owl in lustre. Valencia, about 1700. *Collection of Mr. and Mrs. Cawthra Mulock.* (Photograph. Mark Mulock).

57A. LARGE LUSTRE PLATE with a cross design. Valencia, second half of 17th century. *Victoria and Albert Museum.*

57B. SMALL BOWL. Sicily, 13th century. *Gela Museum, Sicily.*

57C. 'ARCHAIC' PEDESTAL JUG. Early 14th century. *Museum of Montalcino, Siena.*

58. 'ARCHAIC' JUG. Orvieto, 14th century. *Musée du Louvre.*

59. DRUG-JAR decorated in relief blue. Florence, about 1430. *Victoria and Albert Museum.*

60. ARMORIAL DISH with lions and hounds. Florence, about 1450. *Musée Céramique, Sèvres.* (Photograph, R. Lalance).

61. THE VISITATION, Luca della Robbia. About 1460. *Chiesa S. Giovanni Fuorcivitas, Pistoia.*

62. SPOUTED DRUG-POT. Florence or Faenza, mid 15th century. *Musée Céramique, Sèvres.* (Photograph, R. Lalance).

63. DRUG-JAR painted with a girl's head. Faenza, late 15th century. *Musée du Louvre.*

64. SATIRICAL PLATE. Deruta, early 16th century. *Musée du Louvre.*

65. PLATE painted with St. Jerome, attributed to Maestro Benedetto, Forli, dated 1510. *Victoria and Albert Museum.*

66. DISH painted with the Rape of Proserpine, attributed to Nicola Pellipario. Fabriano, about 1527. *Victoria and Albert Museum.*

67. ARMORIAL DISH. Venice, about 1530. *Germanisches Nationalmuseum, Nürnberg.*

68. URN with Papal arms, painted in lustre and blue. Deruta, about 1525. *Victoria and Albert Museum.*

69. DISH painted with animals and *putti.*

Deruta, early 16th century. *Reproduced by courtesy of the Trustees of the Wallace Collection, London.*

70. PLATE painted with Cupid Bound. Giovanni Maria, Casteldurante, about 1510. *Victoria and Albert Museum.*

71. LARGE PLATE painted with a battle. Pesaro, mid 16th century. *Victoria and Albert Museum.*

72. CRUET with armorial emblems. Patanazzi workshop, Urbino, about 1570. *Victoria and Albert Museum.*

73. HERALDIC MARRIAGE-PLATE. Urbino, second half of the 16th century. *Reproduced by courtesy of the Trustees of the Wallace Collection, London.*

74. POPULAR DISH. Montelupo, about 1630. *Palazzo Venezia, Rome.*

75. ARMORIAL DISH. Deruta, early 17th century. *Victoria and Albert Museum.*

76. PHARMACY JAR from the Escorial. Talavera, about 1570. *Instituto de Valencia de Don Juan, Madrid.*

77. DRUG-JAR. Lyon, about 1550. *Fitzwilliam Museum, Cambridge.*

78. TILES from the Vyne, Hampshire. Antwerp, about 1520. *Reproduced by kind permission of the National Trust.* (Photograph, Fine Art Photography Ltd.).

79. SPOUTED DRUG-POT. Nîmes, about 1580. *Victoria and Albert Museum.*

80. DISH painted with riders and landscape. Talavera, second half of 17th century. *Instituto de Valencia de Don Juan, Madrid.*

81. PLATE painted with a man's head. Seville. 17th century. *Palacio Nacional, Barcelona.*

82. DISH painted with the Virgin and Child. Nürnberg, dated 1530. *Germanisches Nationalmuseum, Nürnberg.*

83. STOVE-TILE. Bavaria, first half of the 16th century. *Germanisches Nationalmuseum, Nürnberg.*

84. PITCHER with relief decoration. Annaberg, about 1570. *Fitzwilliam Museum, Cambridge.*

85. INSCRIBED DISH decorated with coloured

glazes. Silesia, dated 1607. *Germanisches Nationalmuseum, Nürnberg.*

86. OWL-JUG with relief ornament. Bavaria, about 1535. *Germanisches Nationalmuseum, Nürnberg.*

87. INKWELL. Winterthur, about 1650. *Germanisches Nationalmuseum, Nürnberg.*

88. DISH with Oriental decoration. Portugal, early 17th century. *Victoria and Albert Museum.*

89. VASE painted with Old Testament scenes. Nevers, about 1630. *Victoria and Albert Museum.*

90. LARGE PLATE painted with Europa and the Bull. Nevers, mid 17th century. *Musée du Louvre.*

91. KETTLE or TEAPOT. Nevers, about 1650. *Fitzwilliam Museum, Cambridge.*

92. BANQUET PLATE. Rouen, about 1710. *Victoria and Albert Museum.*

93. JUG. Rouen, dated 1729. *Fitzwilliam Museum, Cambridge.*

94. LIDDED JUG painted with birds and sprays. Sinceny, about 1750. *Victoria and Albert Museum.*

95. TEAPOT. Northern France, mid 18th century. *Fitzwilliam Museum, Cambridge.*

96. LARGE OVAL DISH painted in the style of Bérain. Moustiers, about 1740. *Musée Céramique, Sèvres.* (Photograph, R. Lalance).

97. POT-POURRI JAR painted in enamel colours. Strasbourg, about 1770. *Victoria and Albert Museum.*

98. PLATE with trellis rim, painted in enamel colours. Strasbourg, about 1770. *Museum für Kunsthandwerk, Frankfurt.*

99. REVOLUTIONARY PLATE. Nevers, dated 1791. *Fitzwilliam Museum, Cambridge.*

100. PLATE painted in enamel colours. Veuve Perrin factory, Marseilles. *Musée Céramique, Sèvres.* (Photograph, R. Lalance).

101. PUZZLE-JUG. Nevers, dated 1780. *Fitzwilliam Museum, Cambridge.*

102. FLASK with pewter mounts. Probably Holland, dated 1570. (Photograph by courtesy of Sotheby's, London).

103. PLATE with polychrome decoration. Holland, early 17th century. *Fitzwilliam Museum, Cambridge.*

104. PLAIN WHITE FLAGON. Probably Delft, about 1650. *Victoria and Albert Museum.*

105. PLATE painted by Frederik van Frytom, Delft, about 1660. *The Hague, Gemeentemuseum.*

106. THREE PITCHERS with pewter mounts and *chinoiseries.* Delft, about 1680; Frankfurt, late 17th century; Hanau, late 17th century. (Photograph by courtesy of Christie's, London).

107. WALL-PLAQUE with winter scene. Probably Delft, early 18th century. *Collection of Dr. and Mrs. Fairbairn.*

108. VASE with lotus-flower decoration. Delft, late 17th century. *Victoria and Albert Museum.*

109. WINE-COOLER. Delft, early 18th century. (Photograph by courtesy of Christie's, London).

110. SMALL BOWL with polychrome painting and gilding. Delft, about 1710. *Reproduced by kind permission of Nijstad Antiquairs, Lochem N.V., Lochem, Holland.*

111. LARGE DISH by Lambert van Eenhoorn. Delft, about 1700. *Fitzwilliam Museum, Cambridge (Glaisher Bequest).*

112. POPULAR DISH. Friesland, 18th century. *Fitzwilliam Museum, Cambridge (Glaisher Bequest).*

113. PLATE with free leaf-decoration. Delft, mid 18th century. *Museum für Kunsthandwerk, Frankfurt.*

114. TILE PANEL. Probably Delft, first half of the 18th century. *Victoria and Albert Museum.*

115. DZBÁN with pewter lid. Moravia, dated 1593. *Private Collection in Prague.*

116. DISH with the arms of Matthias Corvinus of Hungary. Faenza, about 1476. *Victoria and Albert Museum.*

117. PLAIN PLATE. Slovakia, dated 1702. *Narodni Museum, Prague.*

118. HABANER CASK. Slovakia, about 1650.

Herman Landsfeld Collection, Stráznice, Czecho-slovakia.

119. HEXAGONAL TILE. Slovakia, about 1650. *Herman Landsfeld Collection, Stráznice, Czecho-slovakia.*

120. SLOVAK DISH, dated 1707. *Victoria and Albert Museum.*

121. PITCHER with blue glaze and tin-white painting. Slovakia, 17th century. *Narodni Museum, Bratislava.*

122. PITCHER painted with a lion. Slovakia, dated 1775. *Narodni Museum, Bratislava.* (Photograph, J. Lietavec).

123. Pieces from a dinner service. Holič, Slovakia, second half of the 18th century. *Narodni Museum, Bratislava.*

124. PITCHER. Slovakia, dated 1831. *Narodni Museum, Bratislava.*

125. PITCHER with flower decoration. Slovakia, 19th century. *Narodni Museum, Bratislava.* (Photograph, J. Lietavec).

126. POTTER'S SIGN from Velka Leváré, Slovakia, dated 1732. *Museum of Applied Art, Budapest.*

127. DISH with running glaze decoration. Modra, Slovakia, 19th century. *Herman Lands-feld Collection, Stráznice, Czechoslovakia.*

128. JAR with a handle over it. Slovakia, dated 1883. *Narodni Museum, Bratislava.* (Photograph, T. Valékova).

129. DRUG-JAR. London or Antwerp, late 16th century. *W. W. Winkworth Collection, London.* (Photograph, Fine Art Photography Ltd.).

130. MUG. London, dated 1630. *London Museum.*

131. SMALL JUG, London, about 1600, and plain ointment pot. London, about 1650. *W. W. Winkworth Collection, London.* (Photograph, Fine Art Photography Ltd.).

132. DISH painted with Susannah and the Elders. London, dated 1648. *Colonial Williams-burg, U.S.A.* (Photograph, Delmore Wenzel).

133. WHITE POSSET-POT. London, second

half of the 17th century. (Photograph by kind-ness of Sampson and Seligman, London).

134. LARGE DISH with landscape decoration. London, dated 1657. (Photograph by courtesy of Sotheby's, London).

135. SPOUTED DRUG JAR. London, dated 1669. (Photograph by courtesy of Sotheby's, London).

136. DISH with tulip decoration. London, about 1650. *Bristol City Art Gallery.*

137. POSSET-POT with lid formed as a crown. Brislington, about 1670. *Bristol City Art Gallery.*

138. FIGURE OF NO-BODY. London, dated 1675. *Fitzwilliam Museum, Cambridge.*

139. CHINESE PORCELAIN FIGURE. Late 17th century. *Victoria and Albert Museum.* (*Ionides Bequest*).

140. PLATTER with bust of Charles II. Bris-lington, dated 1682. *Bristol City Art Gallery.*

141. BOWL painted with mounted figure of William III. Probably London, end of 17th century. *Reading Museum (Blatch Collection).*

142. DISH with freely painted landscape. Probably Bristol, mid 18th century. (Photo-graph by kindness of Sampson and Seligman, London).

143. PUNCH-BOWL painted after Hogarth. Bristol, about 1740. *Private Collection.*

144. PLATE painted with a theatre scene. Bristol, about 1755. *Gerald Reitlinger Collection.* (Photograph, Fine Art Photography Ltd.).

145. PLATE with *bianco sopra bianco* decora-tion. Bristol, about 1760. (Photograph by kindness of Sampson and Seligman, London).

146. PLATE painted with figures in a land-scape. Bristol, about 1760. *Ashmolean Museum, Oxford (Warren Collection).*

147. JAR decorated in a Chinese manner. Liverpool, about 1770. *W. W. Winkworth Collection, London.* (Photograph, Fine Art Photography Ltd.).

148. THE 'FLOWER' PUNCH-BOWL. Bristol, dated 1743. *Ashmolean Museum, Oxford (Warren Collection).*

149. FLOWER-BRICK. Bristol or Liverpool, about 1760. *Reading Museum. (Blatch Collection).*

150. PUNCH-BOWL painted with the ship *Wigelantia*. Bristol, dated 1765. *Manchester City Art Gallery.*

151. FOUR TILES. Puebla de los Angeles, Mexico, second half of the 17th century. *Victoria and Albert Museum (Maudsley Bequest).*

152. JAR painted with a chariot and horses. Puebla, Mexico, late 17th century. *Reproduced by courtesy of the Hispanic Society of America.*

153. PUEBLA DISH. Mexico, about 1900. *Victoria and Albert Museum.*

154. PLATE painted with a soldier. Talavera or Triana, late 17th century. *Instituto de Valencia de Don Juan, Madrid.*

155. LOBED DISH painted with *chinoiseries*. Frankfurt, about 1720. *Germanisches Nationalmuseum, Nürnberg.*

156. JAR painted in hazy blue. Frankfurt, late 17th century. *Fitzwilliam Museum, Cambridge (Glaisher Bequest).*

157. Two PITCHERS with *hausmaler* decoration. Frankfurt faience, painted in Nürnberg, late 17th century. *Germanisches Nationalmuseum, Nürnberg.*

158. TANKARD painted in enamel colours. Ansbach, dated 1736. *Germanisches Nationalmuseum, Nürnberg.*

159. FIGURE OF A HORSE AND RIDER. Potsdam, about 1740. *Germanisches Nationalmuseum, Nürnberg.*

160. CRUET-BASKET. Marieberg, Sweden, 1768. *Nationalmuseum, Stockholm.*

161. ROCOCO TUREEN. Rörstrand, Sweden, about 1770. *Nationalmuseum, Stockholm.*

162. DISH painted with a lady's head. Barcelona, mid 17th century. *Palacio Nacional, Barcelona.*

163. JAR painted in deep blue and purplebrown. Portugal, late 17th century. *Museu Nacional de Arte Antiga, Lisbon.*

164. BARREÑO painted with an amiable bull. Níjar, Almeria, mid 19th century. *Private Collection.* (Photograph, Fine Art Photography Ltd.).

165. JAPANESE ASH-JAR. About 1800. *W. W. Winkworth Collection, London.* (Photograph, Fine Art Photography Ltd.).

166. *Faience fine* DINNER PLATE designed by Felix Braquemond. About 1864, France. *Musée des Arts décoratifs, Paris.*

167. PITCHER painted by Duncan Grant. Tunisia, about 1911. *Reproduced by kind permission of the artist.*

168. SMALL POT with clay-slip decoration, by Michael Casson, 1958. *Reproduced by kind permission of the artist.*

169. LARGE DISH painted with Europa and the Bull, by William Newland, 1952. *Reproduced by kind permission of the artist.*

170. DISH painted by Anne Clark, 1971. *Reproduced by kind permission of the artist.*

171. MOUNTED RIDER. Picasso, about 1955. *Victoria and Albert Museum. Reproduced by permission of the Victoria and Albert Museum and S.P.A.D.E.M., Paris.*

172. DISH by Picasso, painted in white slip and tin-glaze. Vallauris, 1948. (Photograph, the Arts Council of Great Britain. *Reproduced by permission of S.P.A.D.E.M., Paris*).

173. PAINTERS AT WORK, from Piccolpasso, *Arte del Vasaio.* (Photograph, Victoria and Albert Museum).

174. SKETCHES OF PLATE DESIGNS from Piccolpasso, *Arte del Vasaio*, (Photograph, Victoria and Albert Museum).

175. DRAWING OF A KILN from Piccolpasso, *Arte del Vasaio.* (Photograph, Victoria and Albert Museum).

176. FIRING A LUSTRE KILN, from Piccolpasso, *Arte del Vasaio.* (Photograph, Victoria and Albert Museum).

177. DIAGRAM OF THE MUFFLE, from Piccolpasso, *Arte del Vasaio.* (Photograph, Victoria and Albert Museum).

178. TILE-PICTURE of the Bolsward factory, Friesland, dated 1737. *Rijksmuseum, Amsterdam.*

179. DIAGRAM OF A KILN from Gerrit Paape, 1794. (Photograph, Victoria and Albert Museum).

180. DIAGRAM OF A KILN from the French *Encyclopédie* of 1756. (Photograph, Victoria and Albert Museum).

FIGURES

MAPS

PREFACE

This book has grown from my own experience of living by the making of tin-glaze pottery. While my livelihood depended chiefly on English patrons, I was especially struck by the reactions of people from other European countries and by their recognition of the work. Gradually I began to realise that painted tin-glaze pottery is probably the strongest and most lasting influence in all the European pottery traditions. Slipwares, stonewares and porcelains are found in most parts of Europe, the last two increasingly so in recent times, as new materials and equipment become easily available. But painted tin-glaze pottery and its near relation, painted slipware, were made for centuries in almost every part of Europe, beginning in Spain and extending to Scandinavia and the Balkans, and the attitude of mind they express still exists even where the tin-glaze potteries have been replaced by modern industries.

The tradition is of course originally Islamic, and some of the most beautiful examples were made in the Middle East at a time when European pottery was still restricted to crude and humble purposes.

The attempt to make this book was a threefold process: a discovery of the long and fascinating sequence of the tradition I had chanced upon; an act of homage to men whose achievements underlie the work of the present day, even though I had not known it before; and above all the recognition that the technique is the main European and Mediterranean tradition of pottery, a district family of ceramics, passed on continuously from people to people over a thousand years from Kashan to Cordoba, from Belfast to the Black Sea.

A full study could only be made by a regiment of scholars, and the mass of detail might break the thread and lose the joy. I write only as a devotee whose interest has been captured and drawn along by the variety and richness of the pottery itself, by the ideas and assumptions of the men who made it. There must be many gaps and defects, but I believe the theme is vivid enough to make up for them.

One omission, at least, is deliberate, and this concerns tiles. Many millions of tin-glaze tiles have been made, so many that they really need a study to themselves, and I have merely been able to mention tiles occasionally and illustrate a few examples. Although tiles were an important part of tin-glaze ceramics, the omission seems justifiable because in the chief centres of manufacture they were made by special factories, not by potters, and the ideas and techniques they involved were often very different from those of the makers of vessels.

I have depended not only on the writings listed in the bibliography but on a great deal of direct, personal help, for which I am deeply grateful. I wish especially to thank Mr.

Michael Archer of the Victoria and Albert Museum for his generous encouragement and
help in general and specific matters, particularly with the literature on the English wares
and with engravings from early technical books, and for the benefit of his knowledge of
public and private collections. I wish also to thank Mr. Robert Charleston, Keeper of
Ceramics at the Victoria and Albert Museum, for his general advice at the early stages
of my work, for his detailed comments on my manuscript as it neared completion, and
for helping me to fill out much of the background with the aid of his experience and wide
learning.

I have been privileged to study and handle examples of tin-glaze wares in many public
collections, and have gained substantially from conversations with people who have the
care of them. For this my thanks are extended in particular to Mr. Ralph Pinder-Wilson
of the Department of Oriental Antiquities, British Museum, to Mme. Waffiya Izzi and
Said Abdul Rauf Yusuf of the Islamic Museum, Cairo, to Sr. Jaime Benét of the Palacio
Nacional, Barcelona, to Mr. Eric Stanford of the Reading Museum, to Mr. James Allan
of the Ashmolean Museum, Oxford, and to Mr. J. R. K. Cooper of the Bristol City
Art Gallery.

I have received most valuable help with the chapter of Moravian and Slovak wares
from Mr. Oldrich Ašenbryl and Miss Dora Sebestová, and from Mr. Herman Landsfeld
of Stráznice, who has given me the benefit of much unpublished material from his own
researches and excavations and taken me to Habaner sites in Slovakia, as well as allowing
me to study his own collection. To each of them I am grateful for the considerable time
and energy they have given.

Some of the most interesting tin-glaze vessels are in private collections, and I wish to
thank Mr. Gerald Reitlinger, Mr. Edmund de Unger, Mr. W. W. Winkworth, and Miss
E. Godman for their kindness in allowing me to handle pottery in their collections and
for conversations about it from which I have learnt a great deal, as well as for permission
to illustrate certain pieces. Similarly, I thank also Miss Kate Foster of Sotheby's and
Mr. Hugo Morley-Fletcher of Christie's for advising me about important pieces coming
into the salerooms, for valuable discussions, and for illustrations.

I am particularly grateful to Mr. David Castillejo for his tireless help in Spain, which
enabled me to add considerably to the text and illustration of the chapters on Moorish
and Hispano-Moresque wares.

To each of the following my thanks are due for help on some particular aspect of the
study of tin-glaze pottery, past or present: Mrs. Esin Atil of the Freer Gallery of Art,
Washington; Miss Mavis Bimson of the British Museum Research Laboratories; Mrs.
P. M. Burdett, Librarian of the North Staffordshire Polytechnic; Don Manuel Casamar
of the Alcázar Museum, Málaga; Mr. Kenneth Clark; Said Hamid El-Sadr; Sr. Luis
Llubiá y Munné; Mlle. Petiet of the Musée des Arts Décoratifs, Paris; Mr. Bradford L.
Rauschenburg of Old Salem, Inc., North Carolina; Mr. Hugh Wakefield of the Victoria
and Albert Museum; and Dr. David Whitehouse, of the British School in Rome, Director
of the Excavations at Siraf.

My thanks are due also to the private collectors and museum authorities who have
given permission for examples from their collections to be illustrated. Their names appear
in the caption to each illustration.

Finally, I wish to thank Miss Melody Cooper for her expert help with the typing and correction of the manuscript, and my wife for drawing the maps, for helping with the sketches and drawings in the text, and for listening to sections of this book at all hours of the day and night over several years.

Shalford, All Hallows' Eve, 1971   ALAN CAIGER-SMITH

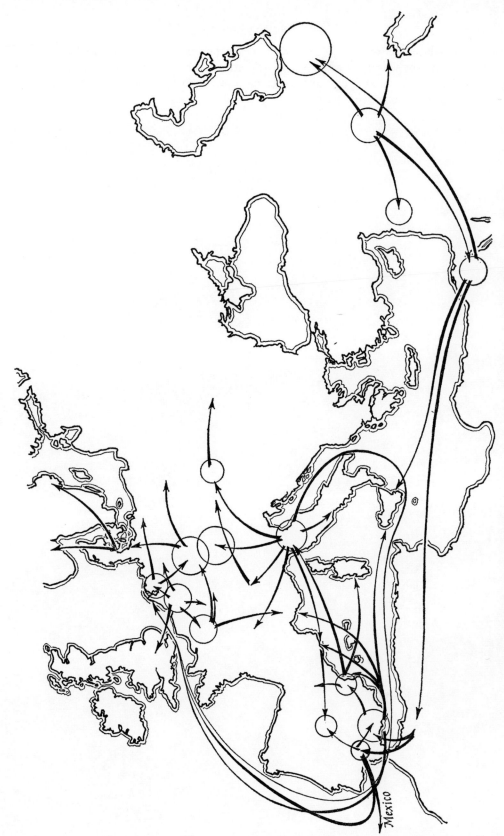

Map 1. Map showing the principal centres of tin-glaze pottery and their main connections, 900–1900.

I

MESOPOTAMIA

Traditions are like rivers. The main river can be mapped and measured. Tributaries feed it and cities with names are built along it. Some men use it for their delight, some ignore it, and some live by it. Finally, the river widens and is merged with the sea. Its source is often unknown. Are there perhaps several sources? Has the idea of a beginning any meaning except as a theoretical point on a map? So it is with the tradition of tin-glaze ware: the main tradition is clear but the beginnings are lost in uncertainties. The earliest sherds belonging to a recognisably continuous production originated in the Middle East, probably in Mesopotamia, about the ninth century A.D., but none of the old kiln-sites have yet been recognised. It is also difficult to know which of the surviving sherds are the oldest or where they were made, for the early vessels were highly valued and frequently travelled as gifts or merchandise far from their place of origin. Tin-glaze potteries are thought to have existed at or near Baghdad, Susa, Rayy and Fostat (Old Cairo), but who can say that there were not others as yet undiscovered? Thus any account of the beginnings of the long tradition is inevitably interpretation rather than established fact.

By the ninth century the empire of Islam stretched from India to the Atlantic and encompassed all the Middle East except Asia Minor. Because of their nomadic background the Arabs themselves had few arts and little knowledge of building, but once the empire was established they used the skills of their subjects to build extravagantly and satisfy their newly-acquired delight in luxuries. Trades and manufactures began to flourish again as they had not done since the height of the Roman Empire, and the needs of the new aristocracy challenged the skills of the many races of craftsmen living under its rule. Islam brought together many cultural traditions, Roman, Greek, Egyptian, Persian and Tartar, which gradually merged into forms that are now recognised as Islamic.[1]

In the first hundred and fifty years of Arab rule there was a remarkable development of glazed vessels. In theory, glazes could have been used extensively in the Middle East long before. Some beautiful blue glazes were made in Egypt and Syria under the Romans, and simple green and yellow lead glazes were widely used from the first century A.D. onwards; however, the glazing of earthenware remained the exception.[2] During the ninth century the use of glazed vessels rapidly became much more general, and many

1 The following books relate to the whole scope of this chapter: R. L. Hobson, *Guide to the Islamic Pottery of the Middle East* (London, 1932), M. S. Dimand, *A Handbook of Muhammedan Art* (New York, 1944), and Arthur Lane, *Early Islamic Pottery* (London, 1947).
2 R. J. Charleston, *Roman Pottery* (London, 1955), p. 30 *et seq.*

different types and colours of ware were developed and traded throughout the Middle East. They were used as luxuries, and the best of them also followed up the imaginative and poetic side of glaze and ornament in its own right in a way which had hitherto only occurred in China.[3]

Glazed ware needed more technical skill than simple terracottas, and the desire for it must have affected the routine of potteries and the knowledge and status of craftsmen. Unglazed pots are relatively simple to handle as they can be set one within another in the kiln, and the larger pieces can be used as supports, while glazed vessels have to be carefully placed and must be protected from ash and grit, and the temperature of the firing must be more carefully judged. In potteries making glazed ware there must have been at least a few men working with more responsibility and skill than had been required before. Once a workshop achieved this, new technical and artistic possibilities came within range. In a few generations some master-potters must have experimented systematically to arrive at the complex glazes and special clay bodies which were the beginnings of the tin-glaze tradition.

Discoveries whose details are unknown are often attributed to chance. It is easy to underestimate the methods used before the scientific era, or to assume that there were no methods. Any potter who has compounded his own white slip from natural materials and fitted it to a clay body, or who has devised a tin-glaze frit which neither boils, bubbles, crazes nor crawls, will agree that such things do not happen by blind trial and error. Was it simply coincidence that new pigments and glazes were developed under a civilisation that included in its learning the first studies of chemistry?

Despite many statements to the effect that glasses and glazes in the ancient world were opacified with tin oxide, recent analyses have shown that it was seldom if ever used for that purpose. The usual opacifier was romeite (calcium pyroantimoniate, $Ca_2Sb_2O_7$). Many opaque Egyptian glasses contain this material as do the glazed bricks of the Assyrian palace of Nimroud (ninth century B.C.). So, in all likelihood, do the white and opaque coloured glazes of the pottery and mural paintings of Ashur (c. 1400–700 B.C.).[4]

Although tin had long been used for making bronze, it was uncommon, and the sources from which it was obtained are uncertain. Some may have been mined in North-West Persia, some in Cornwall, and some may have been dug from alluvial deposits near the mountains of Keswran in Syria.

By the ninth century A.D. there were already trade connections between Islam and China.[5] Until this time, glazed pottery had developed independently in the Middle East and Far East. Now, pottery began to travel in both directions between the two empires.

3   A great Arab victory in 751 is said to have led to the capture of 30,000 prisoners. The skills of these men are thought to have speeded the advance of Islamic pottery and other crafts.
4   For the chemical analyses, see W. E. S. Turner and H. P. Rooksby, 'A study of the opalising agents in ancient opal glasses', *Glastechnische Berichte, V. Internationaler Glasskongress*, 32K (1959), Vol. VIII, pp. VIII/17–28. For the ceramics of Ashur, see W. Andrae, *Coloured Ceramics from Ashur* (London, 1925). Andrae assumed that tin was used as an opacifier in these marvellous ceramics, but his samples were not analysed because they were held up in Lisbon during the Great War. Later analysis of associated ceramics from Nimroud suggest that the Ashur glazes probably contained romeite, not tin oxide.
5   Hobson, op. cit., p. xiv, and Basil Gray, 'Persian influence on Chinese art from the 8th to the 15th centuries', *Iran, Journal of the British Institute of Persian Studies*, vol. 1 (1963).

Islamic pottery had almost as much impact in China as Chinese pottery in Islam, though the Chinese had certainly developed further. The T'ang potters had achieved two kinds of ware which evidently impressed the ruling classes of Mesopotamia: a hard, yellowish-white stoneware, and an off-white and slightly translucent ware, the first porcelain.

White pottery was unknown in the Middle East and the whiteness alone of this T'ang porcelain and stoneware would have made it famous. The porcelain was exquisitely thrown, and the pearly-white glaze was extremely beautiful. It was the ware that inspired the first tin-glaze earthenware, which was probably made for the Caliph's court in Baghdad.

T'ang porcelain is praised in several Arabic writings of the 'Abbasid period, and fragments of porcelain have been found at Samarra, Ctesiphon, Nishapur and elsewhere. A remarkable record, made famous by Arthur Lane, describes the arrival of this porcelain in the Middle East. It comes from a book written in 1059 by Muhammed ibn al-Husain (Abu 'l Fadl) Baihaki.

'Ali ibn-Isa, governor of Khurasan, sent as a present to the Caliph Harun-al-Rashid 'twenty pieces of Chinese imperial porcelain the like of which had never been seen before at a Caliph's court' in addition to two thousand other pieces of porcelain.[6]

Harun-al-Rashid was Caliph of Baghdad from 786 to 809 and presided over one of the most cultivated and luxurious courts of all time. There the examples of T'ang porcelain must have been admired, for soon the Islamic potters were imitating them. They did not have materials for high-temperature porcelain. Instead, they used a finely prepared yellowish earthenware clay covered with a cloudy-white alkaline tin glaze with a semi-matt surface. If they never achieved forms as subtle as those of T'ang porcelain, the attempt to follow Chinese forms is clear from the earliest plain white vessels—small bowls with sides pressed into lobes and rims out in cusps in the Chinese manner. No earthenware could equal the hardness of porcelain, but to the eye the resemblance was fairly close. This was the first white-glaze pottery to be made outside the Far East.

Tin-glaze sherds were found amongst other pottery excavated during the First World War from the palace of Samarra, about fifty miles north of Baghdad.[7] Samarra was an extravagant complex of buildings erected by Caliph Mu'tasim, son of Harun-al-Rashid, in about 836, and it was used as the seat of the Caliphate until 883. The sherds were assumed to date from the same period as the palace itself, but actually they need not have done so, for the palace continued to be used for other purposes after the Caliph returned to Baghdad and the sherds could therefore be of later date. However, excavations at Siraf (in progress since 1966) have shown that at this medieval port a provincial version of the kind of pottery found at Samarra was already being made by the first half of the ninth century. So that the dating of the tin-glaze fragments from Samarra to the end of the eighth or beginning of the ninth century appears to have been correct, though for the wrong reasons.[8]

6   Lane, op. cit., pp. 10–11.
7   Excavated by F. Sarre and E. Herzfeld. See their 'Archäologische Reise im Euphrat- und Tigris-Gebiet', I (1911) and IV (1920).
8   I am indebted to Dr. David Whitehouse for this information, details of which will be published in his reports of the Siraf excavations.

Some of the Samarra sherds are plain white, some are painted with blue and green pigments, and some are from pottery and wall-tiles decorated in lustre, a technique entirely new to ceramics. Where this white luxury pottery was made is uncertain. It was probably produced in or near the Abbasid capital of Baghdad, which was a centre for many kinds of manufacture, or at Basra or Kufa.[9]

Most of the early tin-glaze vessels that survive today are small bowls with turned-out rims. They were only used by the wealthy, and were probably drinking-vessels. A number of such bowls were decorated in cobalt blue, and they are the first of the long succession of wares painted in this most powerful and stable of all ceramic pigments. At that date cobalt blue was not being used anywhere else, not even in China.[10] The presence of signatures on a number of the blue-painted bowls, sometimes on the upper surface, sometimes under the foot, shows that they were regarded as something special when they were made, since common wares were not signed [1].[10a]

At first the colour was used formally, and the painted designs would seem rather tentative but for their simplicity. Some examples have symmetrical patterns constructed on a central star or flower device, with squares or cusped motives emphasised by hatched lines and blobs of solid colour [8]. A curling leaf or palmette design appears quite often and the rims of the bowls were frequently decorated with lunettes [2; Colour Plate A]. Some of these designs resemble earlier relief-decorations which were cut into clay moulds and used for moulded or stamped ornament. This may explain why in some of the geometrical designs the brush was used like a pen or an incising-tool rather than as a supple instrument. Other designs contrast starkly with the roundness of the bowls: the painting was done in the same way but without any intention of pattern-making [3]. Instead it draws out an emblem that crosses the curve of the bowl. The meaning may once have been familiar; it is now cryptic. In all these bowls the blue is a slate blue with a dark inner grain caused by the impurities in the cobalt ore. Bright blues were not obtainable for many centuries.

Tin-glaze ware was only produced in small quantities in the ninth century; however, there are signs that the technique spread fairly quickly to Rakka in Syria, and also to Cairo. In both places the painting was mostly done in green and brown from copper and manganese, the clay body being coarser, and the fritted glazes less finely ground and with a harsher texture.[11] Copper and manganese are both fusible pigments which tend to blur in the firing, so that painted motifs did not develop the clear line that could be achieved in the cobalt blue painting of Baghdad.

9   As so often with questions of origins, there is little certainty. A. U. Pope gives a summary of different opinions in *Survey of Persian Art* (New York, 1939), vol. II, p. 1490, note 1, as does A. W. Frothingham, *Lusterware of Spain* (New York, 1951), pp. 3–4. However, R. L. Hobson op. cit., p. 10, refers to Karabacek, 'Zür Muslimischen Keramik', in *Monatschriften für den Orient*, Dec. 1884, No. 12, as follows: 'Summarising the results of his literary researches, he mentions as famous for pottery in the ninth century, Hims in Syria, al-Kufa, al-Basra, and above all Baghdad in Irak.'

10   The Chinese probably learnt of cobalt blue from imported Islamic pottery, and called it Mahommedan Blue.

10a   References to the black and white plates are given thus.

11   A fritted glaze is one whose ingredients are fused together to bring the soluble constituents (usually soda and potash) to an insoluble form before application to the ware.

There are some blue-painted bowls whose brushwork is more rhythmical than the types just described, made perhaps in Northern Iraq or Syria in the tenth or eleventh century. They usually have localised decoration of closely-grouped broad strokes suggesting leaves or flowers [Fig. 1]. The glaze is less matt and was either higher fired or contains more flux than the Baghdad glazes. The pigment appears to have erupted as the glaze began to melt, and later re-settled, leaving a blurred contour.[12]

Figure 1.   Leaf-palmette.   Figure 2.   Lunette.

Around Baghdad small bowls with everted rims were painted not only in cobalt blue and copper green, but also in lustres, which required a different technique. Since the same shapes with the rare tin glaze were used for both these kinds of decoration, one might have expected some close connection between the painted designs. However, the lustre wares are based on a completely different idea. There are enough occasional similarities, such as the lunettes [Fig. 2] round the rim and the use of cross-hatched frames, to indicate that they come from the same source. Otherwise they have unexpectedly little in common.

Nearly all the earliest lustre painting was done on small bowls or wide, shallow dishes. The painted designs extend over the entire surface of the vessel. They are also remarkable for being in polychrome lustres, yellows, browns, greenish-browns and silvery-greens (all derived from silver), with the occasional appearance of deep ruby reds from copper. The vessels are sometimes so densely painted that the first impression is of a confused abandon of indeterminate shapes filled in with contrasting filler-patterns, dots, zigzags, herring-bone ornament, spirals, and hatching. One has to look carefully to see that behind this apparent disorder there is a coherent scheme. Most of the bowls are painted on a theme of garlands and flowers, with occasional suggestions of trees and fountains, and they have some affinity with late Roman garland-ornament [5].[13] The herringbone patterns suggest the veins of leaves, and the blobs and spirals and circles are fruits and flowers. The abandon is really abundance, amplified by the diversity of the colours introduced by the firing. Except for some tiles decorated with cocks, found in the ruins of Samarra, no figurative decoration seems to have been attempted on the earliest lustres.

It is at first sight surprising that the earliest lustres should have been polychrome. The technique is hazardous, and polychrome might well be thought to increase the uncer-

12   This is a characteristic of calcium compounds in earthenware glazes. Cobalt and manganese pigments are especially affected.
13   R. L. Hobson, op. cit., p. 3, fig. 7, shows a basin with patterns springing from a six-pointed star. The garland idea is very clear.

tainties. So it did, but it also had the advantage that of the two, three or four pigments employed, at least one or two would develop satisfactorily in the special firing. To take several risks at once can sometimes be safer than taking one at a time. That is not, of course, the reason why polychrome lustres were undertaken in the beginning. Almost certainly the idea came from the use of silver and copper stains on glass, which was practised in Cairo in the eighth century if not even earlier.[14] The glass was admired in Mesopotamia, and there the technique was adapted to the decoration of ceramics. The earliest lustre sherds found in Egypt are all imports from Mesopotamia.

Stains of silver and copper could be applied to a ceramic glaze and could, in certain conditions, give a deeper colour and stronger reflection than could be obtained on glass itself. The lustre technique used at this period was never recorded; it can be guessed at from the appearance of the lustres themselves and from the techniques of later times.

The silver and copper stains were probably mixed with ochre and sulphur and would have been finely ground. This mixture may have been stored for a while in vinegar or some other organic acid, which would dissolve most of the metallic compounds and also make the pigment fluid so that it could be applied with a brush or quill. The pots were painted over the already-fired glaze and were then fired to a low red heat sufficient to soften the glaze slightly. In the early stages of the firing the dissolved metallic part of the pigment would become oxidised; later, at a higher temperature, the sulphur would reduce the oxides, bringing them almost to the state of pure metal. This reduction was probably intensified by restricting the supply of air to the fire. If the reduction coincided correctly with the softening of the glaze, a film of pure or nearly pure metal would be deposited and fixed on the surface of the glazed pot. Unless the temperature rose too high, the ochre which had carried and diluted the pigments could be rubbed away when the wares were taken from the kiln, revealing the metallic film.

It seems likely that the early polychrome lustres either were fired at very low temperature, or depended for reduction principally on the sulphur in the mixture rather than on reduction by the fire, for they were not entirely reduced to the pure metal, but remain as compounds protected by the glaze. The question arises whether the different colours were fired all at once, or in succession at progressively lower temperatures. My own experience suggests that the various colours could have been obtained from different concentrations of silver and copper, all fired at the same time.

Lustre-painted pottery was quite new. The manufacture might have spread quickly to other centres if the technicalities had not been difficult. Apart from the knowledge of the composition of the lustre pigments and the glaze, both of which were probably kept secret, the difficulty lay especially in the judgement of the kiln temperature and the control of the fire. It was not just a matter of knowledge but one of actual practice, which would vary from one kiln to another. Thus, although examples of lustred earthenware were much admired and travelled to many places, the practice itself did not. Throughout the ninth century it seems to have been known only in the region of Baghdad.

14 The Islamic Museum in Cairo possesses a small glass goblet with an inscription painted in silver stain, including a date in the eighth century. See G. T. Scanlon, 'Fustāt Expedition: Preliminary Report 1965, part 1', *Journal of the American Research Centre in Egypt* V (1966), p. 105 and fig. 15.

From this centre, lustre were travelled to the extremes of the Islamic world. Lustred tiles were sent in 862 to Tunisia to be set in the walls of the Great Mosque of Kairouan, where they still are. Excavations at Fostat have revealed many sherds of Baghdad lustre that are distinguished from Egyptian lustres by their finer clay body and their alkaline glaze. Fragments of polychrome lustre have also been found on the sites of ruined palaces as far distant as Eastern Persia, Medina-Azzhara near Cordoba, and Brahminabad in Sind, India.[15] In the tenth century lustre began to be made in Cairo and at Rayy. In the eleventh century Rakka in Syria and Kashan in Persia became important lustre centres, and Sultanabad produced lustreware after about 1200.

At some time in the tenth century polychrome lustres were discontinued. The usual explanation is that the technique was too hazardous to be worth sustaining. That is implausible because actually many of the lustres came out extremely well, and in fact the polychrome effect was less of a risk than the firing of single-colour lustres, which could fail completely if the firing temperature were not quite right. It is more likely that the single-colour lustres succeeded polychrome not so much to simplify the process but because the process had at last proved sufficiently controllable to allow the risk of single colours to be taken. Designs painted in lustre were well diversified by the varied reflections, without being further confused by polychrome effects. Furthermore, the old garland type of design was gradually being superseded by stronger designs with figures of birds, animals and human beings [6, 7, 8]. The new designs were concentrated in a single central image instead of dispersed into overall pattern, and they did not lend themselves to polychrome.

In relation to the new figurative designs, it is worth repeating what has many times been said before, that the Moslem faith and religious law did not forbid all kinds of imagery. Though images tending to idolatry were forbidden, imagery in general is not prohibited in the Koran. There is such a prohibition in the *Hadith*, or Traditions of the Prophet, but these teachings were not generally accepted as obligatory. The Abbasid caliphs, and the Ummayads of Damascus before them, had not feared to represent living creatures in other arts such as wall-paintings and manuscripts. It is true that they were famed for their secular luxury rather than for piety, but they were not breaking any absolute religious precept by enjoying imagery. Considering the vast amount of figurative designs there are in Islamic art, it is surprising how persistent the idea is that all kinds of representations of living creatures were strictly avoided. The only place where this really held true was the mosque.

The figurative designs were painted in single-colour yellow or yellowish-green lustre. With their formalised figures of birds, hares, lions, bears, camels and human beings, they are most remarkable. Although the strong outlines, the severe economies of drawing and characterisation, utterly without sentiment or personality, have some chance resemblance to *avant-garde* drawings of the modern era, they came into being in a very different way. The subjects of the lustre vessels were drawn thus not as a personal style nor as a process of deliberate selection, but to bring out the character of the image. That was what mattered, and the nature of the drawing was largely incidental. Some of the figures resemble textile designs and mural ornament in stucco; in such a remote epoch

15 Hobson, op. cit., p. 8.

it is difficult to know which came first. Other designs appear to be original [10, 11].[16]

The earliest examples are probably those of birds. The bird is often drawn round a central circle with a solid dot inside it, looking rather like a target [7]. Sometimes this circle appears in the tail. The circle had also appeared in some of the older garland patterns. One can only speculate about its meaning. The wing and tail and the various divisions of the bird's plumage could be indicated with a motley of the old filler-patterns, hatchings, herringbones, 'eyes' and dots, which tend to disguise the bird in a way which was perhaps not fully intended. Soon they were left out of the figures and used only for the background. A small jug in the British Museum shows the two features in combination: the upper part is painted with the old eye-and-dot pattern, while the lower zone has a rhythmical pattern of stylised peacocks [7].

Not long afterwards, more powerful images appeared: the running hare and the winged lion; the palmette, signifying fire, honour, and achievement; the royal wing-ornament that had formerly been used by the Sassanian kings; and the figures of two birds in the tree of life, a symbol of immemorial antiquity that appears in the mythology of many lands. One famous fragment is painted with a camel carrying a flag and a domed litter or 'qubbah' which housed a sacred object, symbolising the tribal leader or the Prophet.[17]

One of the most striking of all the emblems, ancestor of the great figure-painted bowls of Kashan, was the figure of a seated or enthroned man who looks to modern eyes like a magician. Sometimes he appears to be a king; sometimes he is certainly a musician; some of the images are said to represent a wandering dervish.[18] However the image was intended, it certainly suggests a man of some special power or authority. Just as the fragment with the camel and flag has been shown to have had a meaning, these other images also must have had one.

There is probably some connection between these remarkable images and the tribesmen of Northern Persia, whose weaving and metalwork and slip-decorated pottery was rich in patterns and emblems, themes which evoked fables, legends and intimations which words can often not describe. Some of the tribesmen, the Buyids, became progressively more and more powerful, and eventually, in about the middle of the tenth century, took over control of the greater part of the caliphate, allowing the Caliph in Baghdad to remain as a mere figurehead. To the East, in Khurasan, the Samanid tribesmen established themselves independently of Baghdad, and their city of Nishapur became a rival capital.

The ancient, powerful image-making tradition of decoration touched the tin-glaze pottery of Baghdad but two generations before the magnificent era of the Abbasid dynasty came to an end. By that time the painted white pottery had been sent abroad

16   For the general historical-artistic background see R. Pinder-Wilson, chapter III, 'The Empire of the Prophet', in *The Dark Ages*, ed. D. Talbot-Rice (London, 1965).

17   The meaning of certain images is investigated by R. Ettinghausen in 'Notes on the Lusterware of Spain', *Ars Orientalis*, vol. I (1954), p. 133 *et seq.* For the camel, see pp. 136–7.

18   E. Grube, *The World of Islam* (London, 1968), p. 42, fig. 19, shows an incised slipware dish of the tenth century from the Garrus district of Persia. Grube interprets the image as a representation of Dahhak, son of Mardas and King of the Arabs, who invaded Iran, defeating and killing Jamshid Shah, making himself Shah of Iran. A. U. Pope, *An Introduction to Persian Art* (London, 1930), p. 74, suggests the dervish.

as presentations and in trade to far distant places, and the objects themselves and the craftsmen who could make them, were sought after in other places whose star was in the ascendant. With the end of the Abbasids, some of the craftsmen migrated to Cairo, taking their tradition with them to reappear in a different mood in the beautiful ceramics of the Fatimid dynasty.

2

EGYPT

During the Great War some areas of original stucco ornament were discovered on the arches of the mosque of Ahmed ibn Tulun in Cairo. They consisted of palm and leaf motifs, intricate interlacing forms and geometrical figures, carried out on arch after arch of the vast courtyard, without any pattern being repeated.[1] This plaster-relief has the same type of ornament as was painted on the early polychrome lustre pottery of Baghdad; in fact it is clearer than on the pots themselves, for on the great arches the patterns could be laid out with geometrical accuracy, and the main forms could be distinguished from the small-scale inner patterns in a way that was impossible on a small dish. It is scarcely surprising that such patterns became confused when translated to pottery.

The present interest of these patterns is that they show the deliberate recreation in Cairo of the fashions of Baghdad. Ibn Tulun's mosque was built about 879 and is thought to have been copied from a mosque near Samarra where he grew up. Ibn Tulun came to Egypt as the governor appointed by the Caliphs of Baghdad. He was a man of enormous energy and talent, and soon established himself as an independent ruler. His artistic ideals remained those of his homeland, and the craftsmen who worked for him and his nobles were either brought in from Baghdad, or were taught the conventions which belonged to that city. These styles appear in Egyptian architecture, metalwork, carved woodwork and sculpture of the ninth and tenth centuries.

Tulunid lustreware is only known from excavated fragments dating from the tenth century. They belong to the later Baghdad style in which stylised figures of men and animals accompanied the older type of formal patterns and plant-forms. Tulunid lustre would be difficult to distinguish from that of Baghdad but for the difference of the clay body. In place of the hard, yellow 'Samarra body' of Mesopotamia, the Tulunid wares were made of a coarser sandier clay, necessarily more thickly thrown, and rather less carefully finished [12, 13]. The lustres are mostly brown, yellow or olive-green. There are few signs of polychrome lustre, which was already being discontinued in Mesopotamia itself, though it is possible that it was also made in Egypt.

Tulunid lustreware is scarce and fragmentary. Its interest is principally that it was made on Egyptian soil, and that it provided the foundation for the famous lustre pottery of the Fatimid dynasty.

The Fatimids originated in North Africa where they ruled an area roughly corres-

1 See K. A. C. Cresswell, *Burlington Magazine*, vol. XXXV, pp. 180–5 (1919.) Most of the patterns visible today are restorations based on original fragments. Similar stucco patterns of the same period are in the sanctuary of the chapel of the monastery of Dei-as-Suryani, Wadi'n Natrun.

ponding to that of Tunisia and Algeria today. After a number of ill-starred attempts to wrest Egypt from the governors who held it in the name of the Abbasids, the capital was taken in 969 by Jauhar. A new city known as al-Kahirah, 'the Victorious', was soon begun by the Caliph al Muizz-li-din-Illah. Some of his city still stands today in the old part of Cairo surrounding the mosque-university of the Azar. A vast building programme was undertaken, needing the work not only of architects and masons but of many other craftsmen who could furnish the important buildings with wooden fittings, wall tiles, textiles, books, paintings, pottery and architectural and domestic metalwork.[2] Some of the projects were too enormous ever to be finished, such as the mosque of the second Caliph, al-Hakkim, the arcades of which are standing today, still awaiting their plaster facing.

The Fatimids profited from the over-extension of the Abbasid empire whose far-flung frontiers could no longer be maintained. The taxes and trading dues that had formerly helped to fill the coffers of Baghdad were now directed to the new Cairo. Under the Fatimids there was not only a military struggle with Baghdad; there was also a religious schism. The Fatimids claimed to be the rightful leaders of Islam on the basis of their supposed descent from the Prophet's daughter Fatima, and they regarded the Abbasids as usurpers of the spiritual and secular authority. The Abbasids saw the Fatimids as rebels and heretics, for they had not only invaded the Abbasid empire, but had endangered the Faith by championing heresies known as Shi'a doctrines.

Cairo being at enmity with Baghdad, ideas and art forms of purely Egyptian character began to appear for the first time since the beginning of Islam.[3] With the exception of the strange second Caliph, al-Hakkim, the Shi'ite Fatimids were tolerant in matters of race and religion and some at least of the vigour of the artistic activity of their time stemmed from the freedom allowed to minorities within the varied population of their capital.

The pottery of the Fatimids is closely related to their other arts, masonry, wood-carving (often on a monumental scale), textiles and book-illustration. Almost every design idea or motif appearing in one of these crafts finds an equivalent in the others, and the same mood of elegance and cultivated enjoyment underlies them all.

Except for the dishes used for mural decoration in Italy (see page 41) nearly all the examples of Fatimid pottery known today have been excavated from the ruins of Fostat, a locality whose importance for Islamic pottery deserves some explanation, as it was both a centre of manufacture and later the site of many important excavations.

Fostat today is a flat, grey waste land of half excavated ancient walls and pavements and wells, its fine, sun-dried soil laden with sherds of pottery and glass and the powdered residue of many centuries. It lies two miles south of modern Cairo and the city which the Fatimids built around the Azar. About half a mile to the north-west of Fostat is 'Old

2 The building activity belonged especially to Cairo, so the secondary effects were felt only by the city craftsmen working there. Alexandria, which might well have produced fine pottery, seems to have produced little or none until the Mamluk period (late thirteenth and fourteenth centuries). Much Mamluk pottery has been excavated at Kom-el-Dekka near Alexandria.

3 See Dr. Gamal Mehrez, Introduction to Catalogue of an Exhibition of Islamic Art in Egypt, 969–1517 A.D. (Cairo, 1969).

Cairo', with its enclave of ancient Christian churches which have always been the focus of the Coptic Christians. The new city begun by al-Muizz became the natural centre of government and learning and the home of public servants and professional men. Fostat and Old Cairo, which were already very old towns, were inhabited mostly by traders and artisans. Most of the glazed pottery of the Fatimid era was made at Fostat, where the potters were gathered in one district. Some vessels are signed and marked 'made by . . . in Misr', referring to the potters' quarter of Fostat.[4]

In 1171 Cairo was taken by Salah-el-Din (Saladin) as he consolidated Islam against the Christian crusaders. The heretical Fatimids were deposed, and the city passed under the rule of Saladin's family, the Ayyubids, whose firm and half military rule differed much from that of their predecessors. During the conquest Fostat was burnt to the ground, and much of it was never rebuilt.[5] It became a rubbish tip for both the old and the new cities which bordered it to the west and the north. The wells and pavements were covered, and century after century the debris accumulated till the ancient walls were buried and the refuse reached above the level of the former roofs. Thus, after being a centre of pottery manufacture, Fostat became a pottery cemetery. Wood, metal and stone could be used again, but broken pottery accumulated and Fostat has produced a vast quantity of sherds of many kinds, from Roman and Coptic pottery to T'ang porcelain and Sung celadons, medieval Syrian, Persian and Egyptian, Spanish and Turkish wares, and even English factory pottery of the eighteenth and nineteenth centuries.

Beneath the debris have been found kilns dating from the thirteenth and fourteenth centuries A.D., and traces of Fatimid kilns, together with wasters from kiln-sites of the twelfth century.[6]

Fatimid tin-glaze pottery was primarily lustre-painted ware, the most famous luxury pottery of its time. Other techniques were used during the same period in much larger quantity:[7] a hundredweight of sherds from Fostat might contain only a few fragments of tin-glaze lustreware. The lustreware was made with imagination and care and was valued by its owners beyond all other pottery except perhaps the celadons imported from China [12].

The forms of Fatimid tin-glaze vessels received considerably less attention than the painting. There is no direct evidence to show whether the throwing and the painting were done by the same men or by specialists, but there was probably already a division of labour, in which the throwers were artisans engaged in relatively repetitive work, providing the painters with shapes to embellish. This division of labour occurred almost inevitably throughout the tin-glaze tradition because the technique lent itself so readily to painting. The painting required a special expertise and was slower work. Having provided the painters with enough to work on, the throwers often turned to unglazed or plain-glazed wares which made up the bulk of the production. If the division of

4   Misr is an alternative name for Cairo, and can also mean the district around it.
5   Fragments of pottery flasks used as hand-grenades have been found; they were filled with oil and rags, then lit and hurled into the town.
6   See Hamid al-Sadr, *Madinet el Fukhaar* ('Town of the Potteries') (Cairo, 1960, in Arabic).
7   Unglazed pottery was, of course, the most extensive manufacture. The commonest glazed pottery of the period had a coloured transparent lead glaze, usually green or brown, over grey or pink clay, sometimes with and sometimes without decoration in clay slip and sgraffito drawing.

labour permitted time and care to be lavished on the painting, it could also make the painters insensitive to the vessel forms, while the men at the wheels might become careless or unimaginative unless the two groups had a good understanding of each other.

On the whole, the painting of Fatimid pottery does show sympathy between painter and thrower: the feeling of the form as a whole is seldom denied, and the painters worked with an assurance which shows that, although they may have been specialists, they still had within them the awareness of the spinning clay assuming forms on the potter's wheel. The forms themselves, however, remained conservative and relatively unrefined.

The commonest types of vessel were bowls and jars, such as were used for serving or storing food in the houses of the well-to-do, and which would look decorative and pleasing in wall racks round the room when not actually in use. Even luxurious rooms probably had little furniture, and their painted pottery had an importance seldom equalled in the West until the Renaissance. The largest bowls are about eighteen inches wide, and were used for ornament; many pieces are shallow bowls about twelve inches wide for serving food, and there are a large number of small bowls for spiced and sweet delicacies accompanying the main dish.

The painting of the lustreware is best described as of four principal types, that were usually quite distinct in the earlier part of the Fatimid era, but seem to have become mixed together by the twelfth century.[8]

1. Predominantly geometric ornament, much of which is derived from patterns in architecture or from inlaid wood mosaics, a technique which was much used on panelling and other interior fittings. Some of the pottery patterns were very ingenious: they consist of interrelated forms of varied character, mostly formed by the interaction of squares, circles and rectangles. The eye explores the network, discovering the half-concealed patterns within it, and forms make and remake themselves as the mind plays with them.

2. Stylised plant-form ornament such as the palmette, half-palm, tree of life, spiral stem with leaf and flower, and various kinds of interlace and interweaving forms. Some of these patterns appear also in textiles and in architectural ornament.

3. Patterns dominated by kufic lettering, often fancifully floriated [Figs. 3, 4]. The lettering is usually an invocation of prosperity and happiness, occasionally a mark of ownership, and sometimes is simply a repetition without any meaning in words [15].

4. Figures of men and animals or birds, often against a background of contour panels, small spirals or leaf and stem interlace [Figs. 5, 6]. The images which had appeared in late Mesopotamian and Tulunid lustres were formal, with little suggestion of the movement and joie de vivre which belongs to most of the Fatimid figures. In Fatimid lustreware the most popular figures were musicians, usually playing the lute; dancers; and the seated figures of beautiful young men and women [Fig. 7]. The animals, which pottery shared with carved wood and textiles and metalwork, seem to have been chosen for their vigour and their associations with good fortune: hares [18], gazelles, griffins,

8   By far the richest collection of Fatimid lustreware is in the Islamic Museum in Cairo. For examples of the types of pattern described in the text, see Lane, *Early Islamic Pottery* (London, 1947), plates 22B–29.

winged lions, horses, harpies, cocks, peacocks, eagles, doves and fishes. These animals had appeared earlier in textiles and carvings, but once they came into pottery they acquired a delight in movement and a humorous fantasy which had not been seen before. They fantasticated themselves into leaping, dancing, acrobatic forms; they leaped over lettering and entwined themselves in scrolls and leaves and interlace. Sometimes they appear singly (especially in the earlier pieces), sometimes they form groups or chase each other in borders. So far as can be told from surviving pieces, the painters improvised their designs with great ease, and preferred to introduce variations rather than to repeat standard patterns.

The figures do not seem to be drawn from life; they incorporate characteristic movements and postures which come from remembered observation. They are a convention, and a convention coming from experience rather than from abstract forms. Peculiarities

Figures 3, 4.   Floriated kufic letters.

Figures 5, 6.   Animals from Fatimid lustre bowls.

Figure 7. Human heads from fragments of Fatimid lustreware. *Islamic Museum, Cairo.*

of hair, fur and feathers are sometimes suggested, and there is a feeling of particularity about each figure. They have a Greek or Mediterranean spirit of realism, and sometimes also of humour, that was notably lacking in the Baghdad convention. Some of them, such as the popular theme of pairs of birds on the Tree of Life, the fish, the rabbit or hare, and the winged lion, may have had a symbolic or allegorical origin. but in Fatimid art they are light-hearted and predominantly decorative. They were not decorative in the modern sense of 'interior decoration'. The painted pottery was conceived not so much as something to take its place in an overall scheme, as for each piece to be a focus of attention, a world-in-itself, like a song or a poem which asks not simply to be heard, but to be listened to [16].

One of the most unusual of the animal pieces is the famous late tenth century bowl painted with an elephant, a combination of remembered observation, character drawing, humour and decorative ingenuity.[9] It is probably a fairly early piece, for the elephant fills most of the bowl and the leaf decoration is merely a device occupying an otherwise vacant area. The lobed decoration on the inner edge and the cursory circles and dabs on the outside directly follow the convention of Baghdad.

Later in the Fatimid era, the painting of pottery tended to become more elaborate, with ever closer inter-relation between the figures and the pattern work. The movement towards delicacy and femininity is, perhaps, not surprising since many of these pieces would have belonged to the women's quarters of a house or palace, the most lavishly appointed part of the establishment. In the course of the refining process the painters' overall approach to their work began to change. Instead of devising motifs to occupy the form as a whole, the form became subdivided into zones, trefoils, quarters, roundels and other areas, and the painting explored and filled them, making rhythm and movement within the form as a whole, repetitions with variations, like a dance.

A remarkable group of lustre-painted dishes stands apart from the rest. Perhaps the finest is a bowl painted with a man and a woman with fighting cocks.[10] The background to the figures is a rare soft copper red lustre [14]. The drawing is more searching than those of more purely decorative vessels: in fact, the motive behind this piece is as much descriptive as decorative. A few other pieces of very similar character are in the Islamic Museum in Cairo: a dish depicting a noblewoman attended by a musician and a servant giving massage;[11] a scene with two men wrestling; a small dish painted with a porter carrying a heavy load; and a dish showing two men fighting a sporting contest with sticks. Each subject is carefully drawn against the solid lustre background in a manner slightly reminiscent of Greek vase painting. The group is so distinct that these vessels may have originated from the same workshop, possibly from the same hand.

These unusual vessels are a reminder that Cairo was a city of many races, a meeting point of many traditions, some of which were only Islamic in the sense that they were

9   Lane, *Early Islamic Pottery*, plate 22A and pp. 21–22.
10   R. J. Charleston, *World Ceramics* (London, 1968), plate 24. See also plate 211 which shows a lustre dish of similar style with a drawing of a hawk attacking a water-bird.
11   Lane, op. cit., plate 27B.

ruled over by Islam. The painters themselves may well have been Greeks or Copts, or have come from Byzantium or Asia Minor or the Western Mediterranean. Under Fatimid rule, non-Moslem craftsmen were freer than for centuries to come.

The Copts, whose isolated Christian community had survived in Egypt from the early days of the Church, were famous for their work in metals, jewellery, weaving and pottery. The Coptic area of Old Cairo lay hard by the kilns of Fostat, so it is perhaps not strange that some specifically Christian 'Islamic' lustreware still survives. An example is the sherd painted with the striking figure of Christ in Glory [17]. Another fragment in the Islamic Museum depicts the Baptism of Christ. One of the most delightful of all Fatimid lustre vessels is the small bowl painted with the figure of the Coptic priest with the censer to one side and the *Ankh* or Key of Life cross to the other [Colour Plate B]. This piece is signed by Sa'd, whose manner contrasts with the scene paintings described above. Sa'd's drawing is free and imprecise; the details of the hands and face are suggested rather than described. There is no sense of figure structure, yet the design and rhythm is so consistent and unified that it established a world of its own—a world in which representation and fantasy play equal parts.

Sa'd's signature appears on several other vessels and some sherds, all painted in the same easeful, rhythmical manner with generous use of fine scratched pattern within the areas of solid painting. His style and the material of his vessels suggest a date in the first half of the twelfth century.

Fatimid lustre pottery was quite frequently signed. The elephant bowl bears the signature '. . . Ibrahim in Misr'. A dish inscribed with the name of a general and the name of his caliph, al-Hakkim[12] (996–1021), is signed by the painter Muslim, whose name is found also on several sherds. Other signatures are bin-Assaji, g'afar al-Basr (from Basra in Mesopotamia), Atabib, whose individuality is further emphasised by the fine kufic lettering in which he wrote, and 'Alawi and Sayad. One remarkable sherd bears the signatures of both g'afar and Atabib.[13]

Islamic pots were not usually signed, and no signatures have yet been found on other Fatimid vessels. These signatures indicate that the painters were not merely talented craftsmen; they were individuals whose personal styles were recognised and valued.

The Egyptian clays varied a good deal in colour. Most of the tin-glaze lustre pieces are made of a grey or buff body, but yellow, pink and sometimes red clays also occur. The custom was probably (as it is to-day) to blend the slimy, fusible Nile clays, which fired white, with the coarser red clays found in villages South of Cairo which gave stability to the body for throwing and prevented the ware from deforming too easily during the firing.

The soft glazes used over these clays were sometimes lead-based and sometimes alkaline. Lead-based glazes were most often employed for whitening with tin oxide, and were used for transparent glazes over slipware. Alkaline glazes were used in the twelfth

12   A fragment of this dish is shown in Lane, op. cit., plate 25A. Recently another piece of the dish has been found. It has now been repaired and reassembled, and is shown entire in Yusuf, *Art and Techniques of the Fatimid Potters* (Khazafoun misr Alasr Alfatimi was Asaleibihim Alfannyah) (Cairo, 1962), (in Arabic), Plate 1A.

13   Abd-el-Rauf Yusuf, op. cit. (many plates of signatures on pots and sherds).

century for lustre over white slip, for they helped the development of red lustre from copper. They were also used over underglaze painting.

None of the Egyptian glazes were aesthetically so pleasing or technically so well-behaved as their Mesopotamian equivalents. They were usually shinier and liable to run if over-fired or thickly applied. Many bowls have pools of glaze inside and beads of glaze gathered around the footring. The Tulunid and early Fatimid tin-glaze pots are mostly glazed all over, but later Fatimid examples are unglazed on and inside the foot, and sometimes the outside of bowls is left bare on the lower quarter of its surface. The reason for this custom was the likelihood of the glaze flowing on to the supports and spoiling the fired vessel.

Until about 1100 lustre painting was always done on white tin glazes. About this time three variants began to appear. Sometimes the tin glaze was made light green by the addition of about two per cent of copper compounds. This green glaze began as an attempt to imitate the green of Chinese celadons, which were admired in Egypt and are well represented among the sherds of Fostat. A great variety of plain green glazes based on lead had been made in the eleventh century, and the combination of copper-green with tin oxide was a good attempt to achieve the milky green of celadon, although it could never have been mistaken for it. Unfortunately it could give a light bright green which nowadays is avoided by all but the most innocent art-potters. However, some of these greens made an excellent background for yellow or tawny orange lustres with their flecks and iridescences, especially for the close-wrought leaf-scroll and interlace patterns which were popular in the twelfth century.

The second variant probably originated in Syria, which was then, as at most times, closely connected with Egypt. It consisted of lustre painted on a plain transparent alkaline glaze over a white slip, or on an unslipped light-coloured clay. It was a cheaper version of the Fostat lustres, for it left out the tin oxide, which was a costly material then as now. It had the special advantage that it favoured the development of red and orange lustre from copper, though copper-lustres had to be fired slightly higher than silver compounds, and wasters show that there was considerable likelihood of the pigments volatilising or dissolving in the kiln vapours, and successful copper-red lustres are rare.[14]

The third variant needs some technical explanation. The glaze on most Fatimid pots is crazed. It was almost inevitable because of the low firing temperatures which had to be used. Nearly all low-fired glazes are rich in fluxes and therefore have a cooling shrinkage greater than that of the clay they cover, with the result that, as they cool, they craze and consequently the vessels are porous and not very strong. The only sure way to overcome the tendency was to change the composition of the clay so that it would harden at low temperatures and shrink more than the glaze as it cooled. This was done around the year 1100 at Fostat.

A mixture of white or grey clay with additions of flint or quartz and alkaline fluxes

14   A fine twelfth-century bowl painted in orange-red lustre on alkaline transparent glaze with the figure of a seated youth is in the Victoria and Albert Museum (C48–1960). It was found near Aleppo, in Syria. The Islamic Museum in Cairo has sherds of some very poor copper lustres, perhaps wasters, which show that difficulties were encountered.

would harden easily and shrink on cooling, putting a soft glaze under compression and thus allowing it to cool without crazing. Such a body was a kind of very soft paste porcelain, much harder than ordinary earthenware. If made with fine materials it could also be whiter than any natural clay and could become slightly translucent. Its discovery, or re-discovery, was the closest the Middle East came to the true procelains of China. Many fortified clays of this type are found amongst Egyptian sherds of the twelfth century,[15] though natural clays continued to be used for the cheaper wares and for cooking and storage pots.

In Egypt the fortified clays, or frit-pastes, were normally used with a white slip and an alkaline glaze for red lustre, but they were also quite often used under opaque lead and tin glazes for the yellow or green lustres derived from silver. The technique passed to Persia, where it was perfected and became the standard body for use with an opaque tin-glaze in the luxury wares of Rayy and Kashan, which are described in the next chapter.

In the Fatimid period tin glaze was used principally for lustre-painted pottery; however, other tin-glazed wares were also made, though they are of less importance. One centre of manufacture appears to have been in the Fayum area to the north-west of Cairo. The tin glaze was painted in the normal manner while it was still powdery after being poured on the once-fired biscuit ware, and in the second firing the colours fused into the glaze. Fayum faience was usually painted with strong, simple strokes in manganese brown and copper green. Cobalt blue and antimony yellow came into use in the late thirteenth century, and some pleasant if unremarkable floral and leaf-scroll patterns were painted on tin-glazed Mihrab tiles and mosque lamps and other cere-monial and religious vessels.

The clay of the Fayum wares was usually buff but was sometimes pink or reddish. The bowls painted in brown and green were as a rule glazed only on the inside. The soft, fusible glazes were thickly applied and sometimes moved considerably during the firing, carrying the painted pattern with them, forming a thick pool in the middle of the bowl and making strange curling shapes out of the broad brushwork [19].[16] The effect looks accidental but was probably deliberate. The bowls were obviously admired in their own day, for a number of them found their way to Italy and appear together with Fatimid lustre dishes let into the walls of buildings to make a decorative frieze. A con-siderable number of them were incorporated in the Abbey tower at Pomposa, for in-stance, when it was built in 1063. The remarkable fluidity of the glaze probably came about because of its high lime content. Lime in glazes can lead to a pleasant crystalline mattness, and was perhaps the cause of the matt texture of Mesopotamian tin glazes. However, if the glaze is overfired the lime rapidly becomes an active flux and the 'matt' glaze becomes runny and shiny. (Lustre painting, being done on the already-fired glaze, was unaffected by this characteristic.)

15 A sherd of this material, signed by Sa'd, is in the Victoria and Albert Museum. See Lane, op. cit., p. 23.
16 Fayum faience is little represented in public collections, probably because most of it was used till it was broken. A few small examples are in the Victoria and Albert Museum, and a slightly wider collection is in the Islamic Museum in Cairo.

A finer tin-glaze ware, mostly painted in green, brown, or blue, was produced in Syria during the Fatimid period. The manner of painting came from Mesopotamian blue-painted pottery. Small bowls are the commonest articles, and were chiefly painted with simple rhythmical patterns abstracted from the earlier leaf-spray ornament. In many of these bowls the edge of the colours, the blue especially, is attractively furred by the bubbling and resettling of the glaze during the firing. A few noble pieces survive, such as a remarkable vase painted with a two-headed eagle.[17]

By the end of the twelfth century the blue, green and brown painted tin-glaze wares had given way to pottery painted in underglaze pigments on white slip, covered by a transparent glaze. Here the flowing of the glaze was less likely to destroy the painted motifs, although they could easily become blurred. Underglaze painting on white slip gives effects rather similar to tin-glaze, and could be called its first cousin, and from this time forth the two were often practised in the same areas.[18] In Egypt, however, the demand for luxury wares with tin-glaze seems to have fallen off after the deposition of the Fatimids. Lustre-painted pottery became infrequent in Egypt after about 1200, though this was the time of its greatest glory in Persia, and tin-glaze painting gave way to underglaze painting, which remained the dominant technique for glazed domestic wares under the Ayyubid and Mamluk caliphs.

Finally, one might ask: how much did the Fatimid rulers themselves have to do with the artistic activity of their time? The court was beset with intrigues and was chronically unstable after the period of the first two caliphs, and it is difficult to conceive of new or dynamic impulses originating from it. Only the first two caliphs, al-Muizz and al-Hakkim, seem to have been active patrons of artists and craftsmen; their influence was primarily through large-scale building, which resulted in work for craftsmen concerned with the inside of the buildings.

Perhaps the greatest contribution of the Fatimids to the arts was that, by establishing Cairo as a free capital, they gathered into it money and skills that had hitherto been drained away to Baghdad. Furthermore, since the Fatimids were regarded as heretics by the rest of Islam, they were enabled, and to some extent even forced, to have dealings with the Christian crusaders in the Holy Land and Syria, and to look to the West, especially Spain and to the Norman Kingdom of Sicily,[19] for commercial, cultural and military connections. Saladin deposed the Fatimids principally for this reason.

The pottery of the western Mediterranean bears traces of their contact, though little is known of the way the Fatimid influence spread. The shapes and motifs of the pottery of the Moorish kingdoms of Spain owed much to Egypt: the tin-glaze wares of Paterna shared much of their imagery and decorative conventions with Egypt, and the archaic tin-glaze ware of Sicily and southern Italy was partly of Egyptian and Syrian inspiration. There still exist many dishes that were taken back to Europe by people returning from

17   Victoria and Albert Museum.
18   Most of the painted 'white' pottery of the Middle East from the early thirteenth century onwards, and almost all Turkish painted pottery, is decorated on white slip under a transparent glaze.
19   See Grube, *World of Islam* (London, 1966), plate 28, for paintings by Fatimid artists in the Capella Palatina, Palermo.

the Holy Land; for instance, the bowl painted in the style of Sa'd with a young man in a long-sleeved robe, built into the wall of the twelfth-century Church of S. Sisto at Pisa, another in the wall of the Hotel de Ville of St. Antonin in the South of France, and a lustre bowl painted with birds on a tree, found in Sicily.[20] There remain some hundreds of other dishes with lustre or polychrome decoration embedded in the walls of buildings in Northern Italy, a form of decoration which was especially favoured between about 1050 and 1200. Three of the walls of the Torre Comune of Pavia, for example, retain the Fatimid dishes which were mortared into place when the tower was built about the end of the eleventh century.[21]

The pottery which was taken abroad in this and other ways bore with it something more lastingly suggestive than a specific technique or any particular image; it brought an idea, a taste, a mood, a concept of painted pottery which was so deeply absorbed by the West that it influences much of our expectations about what is pleasing and decorative in ceramics even today.

20 Lane, op. cit., plate 28A; same as plate 31 in Rivière, *La Céramique dans l'Art Musulman* (Paris, 1913), which shows several pictures of Fatimid pottery, complementing the illustrations in Lane.

21 I am grateful to Dr. David Whitehouse for this and other information about the setting of bowls and dishes into walls. In many cases the buildings can be dated, thus providing some means of dating the pottery, whose date would otherwise be highly uncertain. Much material remains to be gathered, and it is to be hoped that Dr. Whitehouse will be able to fulfil his hopes of publishing it.

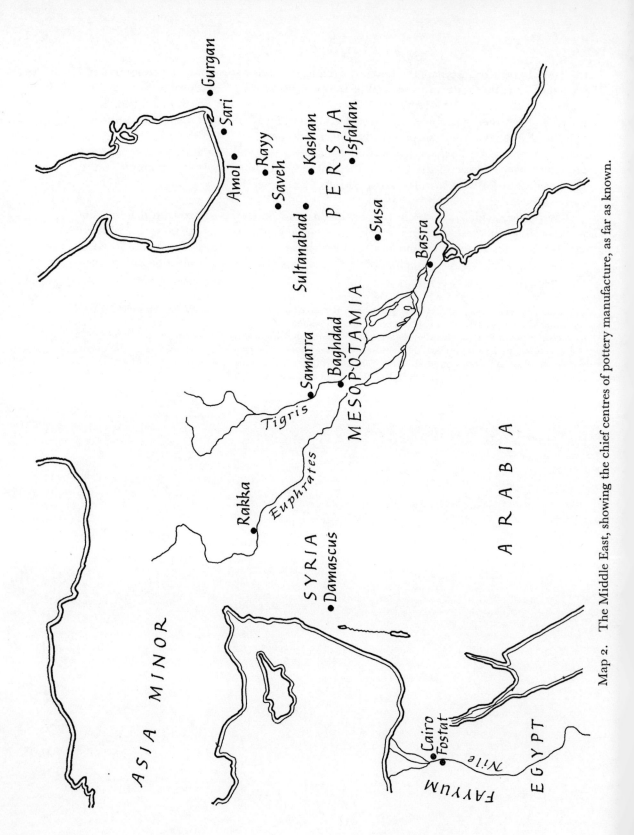

Map 2. The Middle East, showing the chief centres of pottery manufacture, as far as known.

3

PERSIA

A few decades before the fall of the Fatimid dynasty in Egypt, one of the most creative periods of all ceramic history began in the north-west of Persia under the Seljuk Turks. The Seljuks had been semi-nomadic tribesmen and warriors in Central Asia. In the eleventh century they spread westwards and conquered Persia, Iraq, and part of Armenia and Anatolia. Their warrior-aristocracy revitalised the cultures of the conquered peoples, and through their firm administration trade and liberal pursuits flourished. Architecture, painting, metalwork and pottery all witness their lavish tastes and artistic judgement, and the round faces of Seljuk warriors, huntsmen, musicians and courtesans appear again and again in pottery decoration of the twelfth and early thirteenth centuries.[1]

The Seljuk empire became fabulously wealthy under the rule of the great Malik Shah (1072–1092).

The vast extent and sound economic condition of the Seljuk Empire are epitomised in the oft-told anecdote, recorded by Mustaufi, about Nizam-al-Mulk, Malik-Shah's Vizier. The great prime minister paid boatmen, who had ferried troops across the Oxus River, with a money-order on Antioch. He was demonstrating that resources on the Western edge of the Empire formed the basis for negotiable paper on the Easternmost frontier. The private wealth of some people at that time is revealed through various episodes recounted by historians, some showing such vast liquid resources that they seem scarcely credible. Thus it would be hard to believe that, during the reign of Malik Shah, a governor of Hamadan could pay, on one week's notice, 700,000 old gold dinars, were the fact not attested by the Royal Treasurer, Anoushirvan Khalid, who himself went to Isfahan to collect the money.[2]

The most important pottery centres were Rayy and Kashan. Rayy was a very large city even by present standards. Throughout the Seljuk period, roughly 1040–1220, the Rayy potteries were prolific producers of painted, incised, carved and relief-decorated wares, mostly made of artificial frit-pastes similar to those used in Egypt, and glazed with blue, turquoise, green and white glazes. Until about 1160 the dominant influence was Chinese. Many of the leaf-motifs and emblems of pottery decoration were suggested by Chinese porcelains and stonewares, which were quite well known, for the empire stretched almost to the Chinese frontier. Frit-paste vessels with white tin glaze, often with moulding resembling the exquisite Ting ware, or with perforations and 'windows'

1 Arthur Lane, *Early Islamic Pottery* (London, 1947), gives a general survey of the entire field covered by this chapter.
2 Quoted by Mehmet Bahrami, *Gurgan Faiences* (Tehran, 1949), p. 19, from Hamdallah Mustafi, *Tarkh et Gozide*, ed. J. Gantin (Paris, 1903), p. 218.

filled by translucent glaze, came as close to the character of porcelain as is conceivable with non-porcellanous materials.

After about 1160 painted wares seem to have become especially fashionable.[3] Tin glaze was used in two distinctly different types of ware, first for lustre-painted pottery, and soon afterwards for enamel-painted wares, known as *minai*, which are described later in this chapter. Together they became the most coveted of all the luxury-pottery of the time.

The painted lustre and *minai* wares marked a change from all that had gone before, for they were suggested by western Mediterranean traditions. The close resemblance between the brushwork and figure-decoration of early Rayy lustres and those of twelfth-century Egypt [21] suggest that craftsmen from Cairo were being attracted to Persia at the time of the fall of the Fatimid dynasty, and perhaps before. As the Fatimid rule weakened, other craftsmen seem to have travelled westwards to north-west Africa and Spain, implanting the artistic and technical traditions of Cairo there also. Considering the great distance between Rayy in Persia and Málaga in southern Spain, the affinity between some of their brushwork and decorative themes is remarkable, and the departure of pottery-painters from Cairo to both regions would account for it.[4]

The Seljuk lustres [Colour Plate C] and *minai* enamels [Colour Plate D] belong to the brief period about 1160–1220, roughly a lifetime, a flowering which was abruptly ended by the Mongol invasions. They represent one end-point of the tin-glaze tradition. Partly for this reason, and partly because of the use of tin glaze over frit-paste, which distinguishes this school from the further development of the technique in the West, these wares are sometimes regarded as separate from the main tradition. They are not really so, for they expressed an extreme of decorative refinement that earlier tin-glaze earthenware had sensed but not reached; they are a distillation of special sensibilities which were never surpassed anywhere else but were to affect Europe in later ages in many ways. Although these wares were little known in the West until the eighteenth century, their influence was exerted like that of a beautiful dream beyond precise recall, all the more suggestive for being impossible to define or copy. Indeed, it is hard to see how the late styles of Rayy and Kashan under the Seljuks could have evolved further, even if there had been no Mongol invasions. Their pottery has the feeling of the last exquisite days of a beautiful summer—which seem timeless but cannot last. Much the same thing happened in Moorish Spain before the Christians reconquered the kingdom.

There is an interesting gradation of style between the products of Rakka in Syria, Rayy in Western Persia, and Kashan in Northern Persia. At Rakka a tawny-green lustre pigment was most often used on a transparent glaze, seldom over tin glaze. Over the greyish glaze surface which resulted the lustre had a sombre reflectancy, agreeing well with the heavy, juicy strokes of the brush characteristic of Syrian painted pottery. At Rayy the decorative concepts and motives were similar, but were transposed into a

3 The earliest piece with a dated inscription is the ewer in the British Museum, dated 575 A.H. (1179 A.D.).
4 Arthur Lane, op. cit., p. 37, thought that the lustre pottery of Rakka and Rayy was started by migrant craftsmen from Egypt. He points out that there is no sign of an experimental stage in Persian lustre, and shows the affinity between certain Egyptian and Persian examples.

higher key. If the deep, tawny-green lustre pigment was still used, especially in the earlier lustres [Colour Plate C], the brushstrokes are finer and more articulate, and are enlivened by the white tin glaze that underlies them [Colour Plate C]. Rayy had a preference for pictorial subjects, riders, huntsmen, travellers, musicians, ladies in converse stories and romances [20]. The later Rayy lustres are usually a soft yellow-gold. Rayy designs of the late twelfth century are as it were feminine counterparts of Rakka themes, and their lightness of key is emphasised by fine throwing seldom found at Rakka, where the clay was coarser and relatively fewer luxury pieces were made. Many of the Rayy forms were based on jugs, cups and ewers of beaten metal [22, 23]. Quite possibly the potters at their wheels, and the painters too, had actual metal examples in front of them as they worked. The same process of derivation from metal vessels was to occur in Italy during the Renaissance.

Kashan developed as a pottery centre towards the end of the twelfth century. It was the focus of a group of pottery-making towns including Gurgan, Amol, Saveh and others whose names are no longer known. They all appear to have produced painted tin-glaze lustreware as well as plain white vessels, and they worked in frit-paste similar to that of Kashan, but the Kashan paste was the hardest and whitest of all. The workmanship of Kashan was more delicate yet than that of Rayy, both for shapes and for glaze and lustre quality.

Frit-paste was mentioned in the previous chapter (page 38). But a little more needs to be said here, since it was the normal material for all the Persian luxury pottery. A frit-paste is a plastic clay to which a glassy flux or frit has been added. The clay and the glass fuse during the firing and become hard and semi-vitreous on cooling. The flux normally used in the Middle East was a fusible alkaline frit similar to the glaze. Frit-pastes also incorporated some form of silica, sand or powdered flint or quartz to stabilise the mixture as it fused, and to reduce the risk of warping. Additions of five to ten per cent of flux and silica would appreciably fortify a natural clay and would also discourage glazes from crazing. Frit-pastes were a great improvement on the natural clays which had hitherto been used in the Middle East, and which were still used for coarse ware. They could also be made whiter than natural clays. Their disadvantage was that they were laborious to prepare and could be difficult to work with, and therefore they were only used for luxury wares.[5]

Chinese porcelain and stoneware must have been a constant incentive to the Persian potters to improve their clay-bodies. Frit-paste was a highly ingenious way of making pottery harder without raising the firing temperature, and its origin is not known. Probably it started in Egypt under the Fatimids; it was adopted at Rakka by the mid-twelfth century, improved at Rayy, and virtually perfected at Kashan by about 1200. Because of its hardness it could be thrown more thinly than natural clays, and at Rayy and Kashan especially some very light and delicate pottery was made from it.[6]

5   The French ceramist Theodore Deck of Sèvres loved Persian pottery and experimented for years with frit-pastes based on Persian wares. His recipes for glazes and clay-bodies are given in his book *La Faience* (Paris, 1887), pp. 245–58. See also H. E. Wulff, *Traditional Crafts of Persia* (Cambridge, Mass., 1966), p. 165.
6   It is described in the remarkable treatise of 1301 by Abu'l Qasim of Kashan, cited by Lane, op.cit.,

Frit-pastes could be made plastic enough to be thrown on the wheel; however, even the least plastic could be formed in moulds of ready bisque-fired clay to make figures or tile-slabs. Warped pots and wasters show that the firing temperature was fairly critical. Over the white of the finest pastes, coloured glazes gave deep, luminous colours, and tin glazes gave a dense, semi-matt white surface. White tin glazes were often used together with glazes of deep cobalt blue; the backs of bowls and the insides of jars are frequently blue, while the visible surface is white.

The lustres of Rayy have affinities with Egyptian and Syrian decoration, for instance the practice of representing figures against a solid lustre ground. At Rayy the decorative rather than the 'observed' element in the theme was developed, following the later Fatimid custom. The solid background was ornamented with incised patterns of flowers and palmettes or scrollwork, leaf-pattern and interlace, while the figures were given patterned robes and head-dresses, painted in fine brushwork or quill-drawing on the reserved white. The combination of a 'solid' background with a reserved figure, the one ornamented with incised pattern, the other with painted pattern, became a standard theme at Rayy and later at Kashan [20]. It was a wonderful way of fitting figurative themes into vessel forms: the subject remained distinct; the patternwork, now colour on white, now white against colour, spread over the form as a whole. The only undecorated parts of the design were the hands and faces—the faces 'beautiful as moons' as they are described in poems and stories. They were chiefly drawn with a few deft strokes, almost as simple as a modern strip-cartoon, but because of the contrast with the surrounding ornament the expressions and gestures of the figures dominated the design.

The whole was more than a style; it was a mood, an expression of a courtly ideal of living, depicting human relationships against backgrounds of twining leaves and sprays of flowers which idealise the beauty and abundance of nature, and also suggest the metaphysical background of emotions and ideas which interpenetrate each individual's corporal life. They are decorative, but they are very much more than decorative. The decoration is a vehicle for this inner quality [24].[7]

Such poetic ornament first became famous at Rayy. But its most exquisite examples were made at Kashan around 1200. By this time Kashan was overshadowing Rayy. Some of the later Rayy lustre-painting looks hurried. The drawing of figures sometimes became trite, and though the general impression may be satisfactory the details are often disappointing. They ceased to be coherent on the small scale. A feature of later Rayy drawing was the excessively short legs of men and horses; horses intended to be cantering or rearing often look as if they are about to slither backwards.

---

p. 32. The treatise contains a description of the materials used for ceramics, instructions for making frit-paste bodies, glazes, enamels, and lustre pigment. It has recently been translated into English by Mr. James Allan of the Ashmolean Museum. Extracts are given in chapter 14.

7   E. Grube, *The World of Islam* (London, 1966), shows such a piece in colour plate 18, a beautiful lustre plate painted by Sayyid Shams al-Din al-Hassani of Kashan in 607 A.H. (1210 A.D.), telling part of a story in which a royal groom falls asleep while guarding his master's horse, and has a strange dream. See Lane, op. cit., plate 64B, for the same in black and white.

The Kashan potteries excelled in detail. There the painters tended, if anything, to lose the coherence of the larger scale. The forms of the pots were in danger of being swamped by the intricate painting and incised ornament. The painted design, often similar to miniatures and chased metalwork, became virtually a ceramic picture, rather as occurred in Italian maiolica in the early sixteenth century. The Kashan painters were most versatile and they never lost the sense of vessel forms, nor the special touch and other requirements of ceramic painting, although their subject matter was elaborated to the very limit. Some of the finest painting is to be found on hexagonal tiles and star-tiles where the lustre-painter could work almost as if he were illuminating a book.

Some of the luxury vessels, particularly the bowls and wide shallow dishes, seem to have been specially made as commissions or gifts, and were painted with scenes from historical romances and fables, or with scenes honouring notable men, and other illustrations. The inscriptions and the care lavished upon the painting, show that they were important possessions. Though fine pieces were regular articles of merchandise, some of them were evidently made regardless of time and cost. Independent owners of small workshops would have needed to consider the cost and risk of manufacture, but a craftsman enjoying the direct patronage of a great noble would have been free of such anxieties. Above all, his concern was to enchant and astonish his patron.

Some dishes with finely painted scenes are inscribed with dedications and poems and are dated and signed. A number of the poems are love verses. The feelings might be the painter's own, or they could be merely the supposed emotions of his patron. Dr. Mehmet Bahrami has described one such dish in detail.[8] The deep bowl is painted inside with four people conversing, surrounded by flowers and leaves, sitting beside a pool in which six fishes are swimming. On the outside of the bowl is a design of circling vine-tendrils, and within them are groups of birds. Part of the surviving bands of inscription on the outside are translated thus:

> Like a candle, if you had suffered separation,
> You would have been destroyed by deep sorrow.
> Transformed into a bright lamp by your Love's fire,
> You would have burnt the beloved and yourself have died.

The reference is to the moth who flies to the candle. Moth and candle are traditional symbols in Persian poetry for the lover and the beloved. The fire of the beloved draws the lover, who flies around it until he is burnt up. Then the candle 'cries' or melts because the lover is destroyed. They are united in death.

These verses could be given a romantic or a metaphysical interpretation, and were perhaps intended in both senses at once. Apparently Sufi mystical imagery occurs fairly often in inscriptions on Persian pottery. The courtly emotions of many poems and inscriptions are close to the idea of chivalry in medieval Europe and seem far-removed from the system of male pre-eminence for which the Islamic world has often been reproached in the West.

The inclusion of dates, place of manufacture and the painter's signature in Islamic

8   Mehmet Bahrami, 'A Master-Potter of Kashan' (*Oriental Society Transactions*), vol. 20 (1944–5), pp. 35–40 (in French).

pottery is nearly confined to special pieces made in Cairo under the Fatimids and to this last period of Seljuk rule in Persia, where the convention was quite common. It implies that the painter (though not the potter) was regarded as an individual artist rather than as a skilled artisan. It was well deserved by such painters as Sayyid Shams, Abu Zeyd, whose signature appears in twenty surviving examples, and Muhammad bin Abī Tahir, a great painter of tiles, for such men were not only supreme performers with brush pen; they were inventive illustrators and calligraphers who seldom if ever repeated and themselves despite a sustained pressure of work over many years. They had strong personal styles and their ideas were starting points for others.

Amongst the most famous works of the two last-named painters were the moulded lustre tiles of the tomb chamber of the Imam Ridha of Mashad, by Muhammad, and the tomb of the Imam-Zadeh at Qumm, where the two men collaborated.

The tiles of magnificent buildings carried the fame of Kashan far and wide. Tiles were in fact known by its name, as *kashis* or *kashanis*, a name which is still current in the Middle East, signifying painted tin-white pottery generally. In the same way Faenza later bequeathed its name to *faience*, and Delft to *delftware* and Málaga may have been the origin of the word *maiolica*.

Kashan tiles were moulded in large sections to form a wall-covering in semi-relief with columns and niches and dados—a structure within a structure—translating the load-bearing masonry that they covered into a shimmering world of colour and light and movement, in which all the technical and thematic devices which had already been evolved on pottery vessels, were used with a new, monumental effect. Any area could be picked out or contrasted with an adjacent area without interrupting the flow of pattern and rhythm which ran through the whole design. Immense wall decorations made in Kashan were erected in many parts of Persia under the Seljuks and later under the Mongols, and they are really a study on their own. Nonetheless, it is remarkable how closely they relate throughout their history to the pottery vessels of the same time, and it seems as if the same potters and painters must have worked on both. Even the moulded plant forms and arabesques of the tiles are a direct translation into a larger scale of the relief-patterns which had appeared on moulded pottery all through the twelfth century.

Like the stained-glass convention in the West, the great tile-schemes are essentially an interior art. The impact is concentrated, in both a physical and an emotional sense. The embellished wall as a whole becomes the world in miniature, making 'one little room an everywhere', a symbol of all creation. The detail and ornament become its life, its variety, always unique, always inseparable from the underlying rhythms which interweave throughout the whole.

These great tile-schemes seem to have been started at Kashan quite suddenly about 1203 (600 A.H.). The idea was not new in a general sense. Rayy had made large quantities of tiles, and the tiling of mosques and palaces was long established as a successor to stone facings. However, the Kashan painters brought to interior tiles a poetry and delicacy they never had before, and the use of tiles was taken far beyond the mere repetition or permutation of standard units. In the Kashan schemes, each tile-panel has a unique combination of moulding and painting. Incidentally, virtually all the tiled interiors were carried out in tin glaze.

A.   Bowl with everted rim, painted in cobalt blue and copper green. Mesopotamia, 9th–10th century. 25 cm wide. The earliest tin-glaze bowls were probably made in imitation of T'ang porcelain, but they were often painted. Some of the designs were dramatically simple. The colours were probably painted directly on the unfired clay, and penetrated the glaze when it melted. *The Hon. Robert Erskine. See page 24.*

B. Small deep bowl with the figure of a Coptic priest and censer and a tree in the form of a Coptic Cross. 24 cm wide. Cairo, early 12th century. Signed by the painter S'ad. As lustre was painted on an already-fired glaze, the pigment could be incised with a pointed stick. S'ad's signature also appears on several other pieces decorated in this way. The gradations of colour in the lustre were caused by uneven heat in the kiln, the cool side becoming yellowish, and the hotter side dark red-brown. This bowl is actually not tin glazed, but has a white clay-slip over buff clay, which is only evident when one examines the footring. The effect is so like tin glaze that it is included with the excuse that it shows how similar the two techniques could sometimes be. *Victoria and Albert Museum. See page 37.*

E. Small dish decorated in areas of white tin glaze, opaque cobalt blue, and transparent iron-brown glaze. 23 cm wide. Probably Seville, about 1500. Juxtaposed coloured glazes were first used in Egypt about 1100, but the colours were apt to run together in the firing. The Moorish potters of Andalucia separated the colours with a line of ochre mixed with oil or fat. In the kiln the fats fired away, leaving a dry line like a cord between the glazes, from which the method got the name *cuerda seca*. It was only suitable for fairly flat surfaces, and was most commonly used on tiles. It was absorbed into Spanish tradition in the 15th century. The dish was probably made by Moorish potters in or near Seville. Is the breaking of the symmetry deliberate, or an unplanned happening? Either way, it indicates the Moorish potters' way of working, and their disregard for logical dispositions. *Instituto de Valencia de Don Juan, Madrid. See page 55.*

F.   *Albarelo* painted in cobalt blue and lustre. 38 cm high. Manises,
Valencia, early 15th century. On jars of this kind Hispano-Moresque
painters lavished the wealth of the treasury of traditional patterns,
with geometric, calligraphic, floral and interlace patterns, direct and
reserved pattern, all combining to make one of the most dramatic
effects ever achieved on pottery. Few of the patterns were newly-
invented: they reappear, differently combined, on many other kinds
of vessels. *Victoria and Albert Museum. See page 70.*

G. Large dish painted in cobalt blue and lustre. About 37 cm wide. Manises, Valencia, first half of 15th century. A fine example of positive and negative, male and female pattern, beloved by Islamic tradition. The two are united by interlacing lines and rhythms. *Museo Arqueológico, Madrid. See page 70.*

H. Large plate painted in lustre with the arms of Castile-Leon and Aragon. About 48 cm wide. Manises, Valencia, about 1430. A sumptuous armorial dish, early enough for the decoration to be still almost completely Moorish. At this period the princes and prelates of Europe first came to regard pottery as something worth possessing, instead of assuming that it could never be more than a menial craft. The line decoration includes *alafia* pattern and tree of life motifs and was probably done with a quill. A curious feature of the design (quite common in Moorish ornament) is the repeat of five units round the coat of arms, bordered by a repeat of seven, resulting in a shifting relationship between the features of each area. *Musée National, Sèvres. See page 75.*

Such monumental work might have been foreseen as the natural outcome of the tendencies of Kashan pottery vessels to become free of any limiting forms and extend without restraint into the preserves of the architect, the painter and the illuminator. Some at least of the Kashan pottery-painters may well have been also mural painters or book illuminators or scribes. Painting, drawing and writing on the fired glaze surface with lustre pigments would not have required nearly so much technical expertise as would be necessary for painting on the unfired glaze, the traditional maiolica painting technique of Europe. It would have been but a small step from painting on vellum or ivory.

Technically, the tile mural achievements are extraordinarily impressive. The process of lustre-firing must have been controlled to a high degree, for the units of tile compositions were hard to replace if spoilt in the kiln; yet the rarity of glaze and body faults in the finished work is remarkable, and the consistency of the lustre colour hardly suffers at all from the inevitable irregularities of heating in the reduction firing by which the lustre was developed and fixed. Kashan must also have excelled in factory organisation to make the great number of moulds needed for big murals, prepare the fine materials in bulk, and fire, transport and erect the finished work—often far from the place where it was made. From the nature of their work one might guess that Kashan 'factories' were a good deal larger than most potteries in Renaissance Italy.

At the other end of the scale, Kashan potteries specialised in *minai* ceramic illumination. The technique depended on the embellishment of an already-fired plain tin-glazed vessel with enamels. The enamels were fixed to the foundation glaze in a third firing at low temperature in an oxidising atmosphere. There could be further firings if the enamels were to be laid over one another. The enamels were soft, fusible glasses. Much stronger colours could be obtained than in ordinary glazes fired at normal glazing temperatures. The technique as developed at Kashan in the later part of the twelfth century was almost a new invention, and it opened up new possibilities of extremely fine drawing and ornament on pottery [26; Colour Plate D].

Minai vessels were made from a hard frit-paste and were nearly always very thinly thrown, and the details of rims and footrings were finely finished. *Minai* ware mostly feels like an extremely thin shell, but, alas, it is considerably more brittle. At first the glaze was a plain white tin glaze, usually slightly yellowish, with a somewhat matt surface. The majority of examples are small bowls, cups and containers. There must have been considerable danger of cracking large pieces in the third (enamel) firing.[9] In this firing the foundation glaze was not fully melted; as with lustre, it reached only the first stages of softening, so that it would receive the softened enamels without any blurring of the delicate lines of the drawing.

On the earlier *minai* pieces the foundation glaze was white, but the technique was fashionable and new variations were soon developed. First, copper was mixed with the tin glaze to make a soft turquoise colour, and later a deep cobalt blue was devised, known as *lajvard*. The coloured grounds were chiefly embellished with white, black, yellow, red and green enamels, most often in patterns of dots and flowers. If these coloured grounds

9 A famous exception is the great dish painted with a battle-scene, now in the Freer Art Gallery, Washington, reproduced in Lane, op. cit., plate 70C.

were an interesting variation of the new *minai* technique, they did not offer the same possibilities for delicate line and colour, and white remained the most usual ground glaze.

Minai pottery was almost always decorated with episodes from romances and legends, frequently with scenes of remarkable encounters or courtly dialogues and hospitalities, and many of the compositions have stock figures of attendants, travellers and angels, and trees in the background. The first drawing was done in a dark umber enamel, which was then fired. Next the drawing was filled in with strong coloured enamels which shone out against the dark contour drawing. The effect was like manuscript illumination, and it is possible that manuscript painters also worked on these ceramics. Gold leaf was often used in the decoration. Lustre, however, seldom occurs in *minai* painting, which is strange because the same miniaturist drawing is found in both techniques, and the lay-out and details of trees and horsemen in the painted scenes are often alike.

Abu Zeyd, famous for his painting in lustre, signed a charming *minai* bowl, painted with a man travelling on a donkey, accompanied by attendants and guardian spirits. The piece is dated 1187 [25].

Minai vessels were an extreme, aristocratic, romantic, exclusive, in which the treasures of the rugged world were gathered into the small compass of an enchanted space. Like all miniatures, *minai* pieces have their own inner space. But one cannot see it until, like Alice in Wonderland, one has eaten of the right side of the mushroom and quietened oneself down to the right scale. Until then *minai* can be looked at but is not seen. Perhaps this was always part of their appeal—that they make this pleasing demand on all who care for them?

Such was its popularity that in the end the *minai* technique began to caricature itself. The drawings became more and more diminutive until they became precious. The late vessels were often given elaborate relief moulding and window-piercings as well as polychrome decoration, and were sometimes fired again and again to build up incrustations of enamel. In time the cusped rims and elaborate flutings of late examples came to be given finishing touches in gold leaf. The intricacies of moulding and surface ornament tended to cancel each other out, and the forms of the vessels became weak. Eventually the fine enamel ornament had nothing coherent to belong to.

Minai is about as far removed from the ideals of most modern ceramists as can be conceived. Some have said that it is simply 'not pottery'. By the standards of modern purists, able to choose from a wide range of refined materials, it could be called a misuse of material. However, this is judgment by hindsight. There was no material available in Persia in the twelfth century which could achieve the hardness of true porcelain, and the *minai* potters were simply doing what men have always done, taxing the available material to the limit to give form to their imagination. More than five hundred years later the early Meissen enamellers under Böttger were to encounter many similar problems. European enamellers probably never realised that they were having to rediscover technicalities whose secrets had been lost long before in the Mongol invasions.

Within a few years of the making of the Rayy vessels we see today, their ancient parent-city with its vast, varied population, its thousands of mosques and minarets, its wealth, skills, its far-flung trading contacts, its intricate web of human relationships, was little more than mounds of rubble and charred timber. How strangely different are the

time-scales of creation and destruction! The city was partially rebuilt, but it was sacked
again by Tamerlaine in 1404 and its ruins have been preyed on by treasure-seekers and
excavated by archaeologists for a long time, and are still rich in antiquities and are only
partly recorded. Rayy was ravaged in 1223, and what remained was pillaged several
times over in the next decade. Gurgan, once a prosperous sister-city to Kashan, was
sacked in 1220 and has remained more or less deserted ever since. Only in the last twenty
years have archaeologists discovered how important it used to be.[10] From Gurgan have
come some of the very few undamaged pieces of medieval Persian pottery, found still
buried in sand in great terracotta jars, in which someone hid or abandoned them long
ago.

Kashan survived the Mongols and continued to make large quantities of tiles and some
pottery under their rule until the fourteenth century. The mood of painted decoration
changed in response to Mongol taste. Most of the work is tighter, more geometric and
less lyrical than that of the Seljuk period [27]. The Persian branch of the tin-glaze
tradition had already reached fulfilment by the time the Mongols appeared, and was
beginning to lose its vigour in the proliferation of ornament.

It is time now to follow those craftsmen who left Egypt but did not go to Persia and
migrated west to Tunisia, Algeria and Spain, where a long future awaited tin-glaze
pottery.

10   See Mehmet Bahrami, *Gurgan Faiences.*

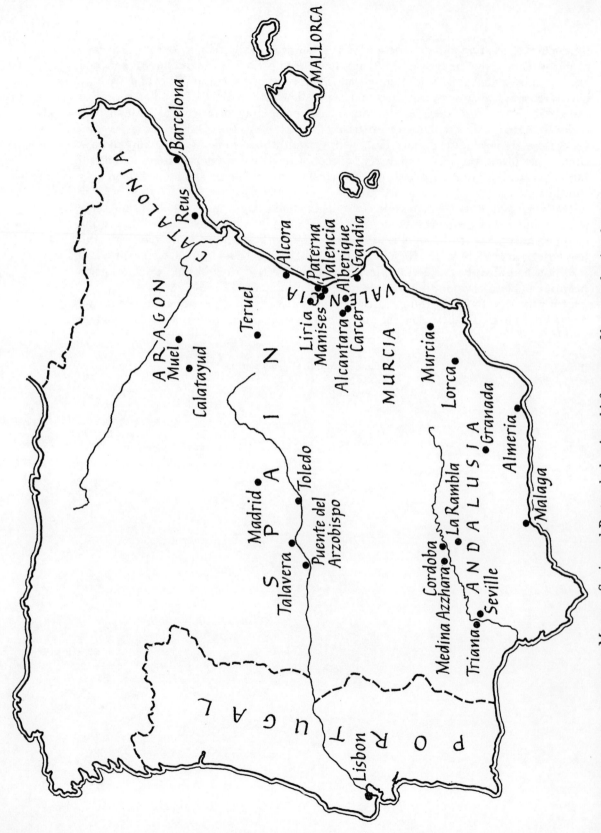

CATALONIA

Barcelona

Reus

ARAGON

Muel

Calatayud

Teruel

SPAIN

Alcora

Paterna

VALENCIA

Valencia

Alberique

Gandia

Liria

Manises

Alcantara

Carcer

MURCIA

Murcia

Lorca

Granada

Almeria

Malaga

MALLORCA

Madrid

Toledo

Puente del
Arzobispo

Talavera

Cordoba

Medina Azzhara

La Rambla

ANDALUSIA

Seville

Triana

PORTUGAL

Lisbon

Map 3. Spain and Portugal, showing chief centres of lustre and painted pottery.

4

MOORISH SPAIN

The Arab conquest of Spain (711–719) seemed to be a disaster for Christendom. Within a few generations Islam expanded to include the whole of Mesopotamia, Persia, North Africa and most of the Iberian peninsula, and was only prevented from engulfing much more of Christendom by Charles Martel, who held back the invading hosts at a battle near Poitiers in 732. Actually, the conquerors brought Europe benefits beyond her imagination. The Ummayad caliphate of Cordoba lasted from the eighth to the early twelfth century, and in its golden age it equalled Baghdad itself in learning and architecture and science, in the luxuries of art and fine craftsmanship. Through the Ummayad culture Europe regained much of the philosophy, science and mathematics of ancient Greece, and Moorish music, poetry and applied arts introduced Christians to aspects of Islamic culture that took such deep root that eventually they came to be thought of as purely European.

The Hispano-Moresque tradition of ceramics was one of the fruits of this mixing of cultures. From Spain the technique of painted tin-glaze pottery spread into every part of Europe, becoming the dominant mode of European pottery for three or four hundred years. Islamic influence went far beyond technique; it led to a recognition that clay, glazes and fire could reveal new worlds of form, colour and poetry. From the fall of Rome until this time, European pottery had been limited to mundane purposes and a small range of techniques. The earthy dignity of medieval pottery is acknowledged today in all those 'advanced' communities which have been surfeited with highly-coloured commercial novelties. It seldom excited the imagination of medieval people, however, and most vessels were left to the scullery-hands. The discovery that pottery could be beautiful and uplifting grew by degrees, as Egyptian and Syrian pottery came into the hands of crusaders, as traders revealed the painted slipwares of Isnik and Damascus, and as Persian and Far Eastern ceramics percolated into Europe. But the strongest impact came through the pottery of Moorish Spain.

Searching for beginnings, people's minds are apt to be clouded by excitement and wishful thinking. At one time the first Spanish tin-glaze wares were thought to be certain lustre-painted sherds found in the ruins of the palace of Medina Azzhara, the 'City of the Flowers', built by Caliph Abdul Rahman III (912–961) as a gift for a beloved concubine. One of these sherds, painted with the head of a camel, must be one of the most famous pieces of broken pottery in the world, and many theories have been based on it. One of them was that the Spanish lustre tradition began in the tenth century. The fragment is now recognised as a type of luxury pottery made in Mesopotamia, and it probably came to Spain as a gift.[1]

1   See Alice Wilson Frothingham, *Lusterware of Spain* (New York, 1951), pp. 2–4. Also R. Ettinghausen, 'Notes on the Lusterware of Spain', *Ars Orientalis*, vol. I, 1954, p. 133 et seq.

Another kind of lustre sherd, made of coarser clay, also found in Andalucía, has likewise been claimed as native manufacture, but these pieces have been shown to come from Persia or Syria.[2] In fact it is unlikely that any tin-glaze lustre was made in Spain until the early thirteenth century, when lustre was certainly being made at Málaga and perhaps in one or two other places. By this stage the tin glaze had already been used for some time with other simpler, methods of decoration.

The first tin-glaze pottery definitely made in Spain is probably represented by fragments unearthed at Medina Azzhara. Most of the pottery from this site is a white slipware painted in brown and green, covered by a clear glaze. It is known as Elvira pottery. A few sherds, however, have an opaque white glaze, also painted in copper and manganese. Both types of sherd are made of local pinkish-buff clay, still used in the region today. The ornament on the slipware and tin-glaze ware is very similar, and consists mostly of trefoils, palmettes, rope-twists, kufic lettering and birds. As the palace was begun in 936 and took about forty years to build, and was inhabited for less than a hundred years before being sacked, these tin-glaze fragments can be dated about 1000 A.D.[3]

In the eleventh and twelfth centuries, when the Ummayad government was collapsing, Moorish Spain broke up into separate principalities and the making of fine pottery and other luxuries became relatively rare. Enough survives, though, to show that where centres of order remained, the legacy of the Ummayads was not quite lost.[4]

Common wares of unglazed clay, plain or painted with slips or decorated with impressed ornament, continued to be made [28]. There were also slipwares with underglaze painting and a clear glaze. Some pottery had a honey-brown transparent glaze with sweeping lines painted over it in manganese brown. More sophisticated vessels, often very big ones, such as wine and water jars, pitchers and well-heads, had moulded ornament and an opaque copper-green glaze overall. Painting on white tin glaze also continued. To begin with it had little advantage over slipware, but in time the white became denser and the painting made better use of the white ground.

Some green and brown tin-glaze wares were painted in a way that eventually led to the *cuerda seca* or 'dry cord' technique, and they deserve a short digression. The design was first drawn in manganese brown mixed with oil or fat so that it would resist overlain glaze or pigment. The areas thus reserved were filled with white glaze and stained with copper and manganese pigments. When the pot was fired small areas of coloured glaze remained, separated by the lines of the resist. In the eleventh and twelfth centuries this technique was used to make intricate jewel-like patterns which had some resemblance to mosaics. Later the process was used for bowls and finials for buildings, and especially for tiles. Gradually the areas defined by the resist became larger and more definite and were filled with glazes of plain white, black, opaque blue, and orange-brown. When the firing was good the 'dry cord' of resist prevented the glazes running together as they melted.

2   M. Gomez-Moreno, 'La Loza dorada primitiva de Málaga', in *Al-Andalus*, vol. V (1940), pp. 383–398, and especially *Ars Hispaniae*, vol. III (Madrid, 1951), pp. 310–322, where some of the fragments are interpreted as Spanish and are reproduced.

3   The sherds are in the Museum on the site of the ruins. A. J. Butler, *Islamic Pottery* (London, 1926), p. 93, mentions similar tin-glaze sherds painted in green and brown, dated to the tenth century, excavated at Tlemcen, Algeria.

4   For a general survey of this period, see Luis M. Llubiá, *Ceramicá medieval española* (Barcelóna, 1967).

The technique was started by the Moorish potters of Andalucía in the early Middle Ages. Later, through the potteries of Seville and Triana it passed to Toledo and Talavera and Puente del Arzobispo, where some very good bowls and tiles were made in the fifteenth and sixteenth centuries [Colour Plate E].[5]

To return now to the main development of tin glaze, the arrival of cobalt ore in the early thirteenth century was an important advance. Painting in cobalt emphasised the whiteness of the glaze and some beautiful cloudy blue pigments were developed. Blue was as yet unknown in European pottery. Being both new and beautiful it soon superseded the traditional brown and green pigments, especially on ceremonial vessels. The cobalt usually seems to have been painted on the raw clay, below the glaze. Being a strong colour, it penetrated the glaze during the firing, staining it with graded tones which varied from sky-blue to indigo.[6]

The white glaze for special vessels was soft enough to carry lustre pigments, that were fixed to it by a third firing at low temperature in reducing conditions. Yellow and brown lustres came from silver pigments and reds and golds from copper. Silver and copper together gave varieties of orange-gold. Yellowish lustre was the most frequently used. From some time in about the middle of the thirteenth century onwards these lustres were regularly employed with cobalt blue.

The lustre and blue pottery can be attributed with certainty to Málaga, Murcia and Almería, and possibly also to Granada—and it may have been made in other places also.[7] Within a few years the manufacture of this kind of pottery developed beyond the needs of the Moorish nobility, and began to be sold abroad, in Aragon, Catalonia and further afield. The techniques of throwing, painting and firing developed to a high degree and the difficulties of the third firing that developed the lustre were mastered in a surprisingly short period of time.

It was probably no coincidence that the potteries of Málaga developed when Ibn Ahmar established the Nasrid kingdom of Granada by uniting Granada, Málaga and Jaen into a single, powerful state. Ibn Ahmar[8] exploited the rivalries of the Christian kingdoms to the north and profited from his position as intermediary between them and the Almohades of North Africa. He achieved periods of peace in which manufactures and trade developed and his people benefited from their commerce with the Christian kingdoms. Under him Granada became the cultural capital of the Spanish peninsula; the beautiful palace of the Cuarto Real was built, and he began the building of the

5   The most extensive collection of these rare pieces is in the Instituto de Valencia de Don Juan, Madrid. See Balbina Martinez Caviro, *Catalogo de cerámica española* (Madrid, 1968). There must surely be some connection between *cuerda seca* and the earlier use of coloured glazes in Egypt, where no divisions were made between the glazes, which therefore tended to run together. The type of glazes and general idea were very similar to *cuerda seca*. See M. Gomez-Moreno *Ars Hispaniae*, vol. III, p. 323. *Cuerda seca* wall-facings were being made in Persia and Syria by the late fourteenth century.
6   These pots are all fairly rare. The most important collections are those of the Alcázar in Málaga, the Museo Arqueológico of the Alhambra, Granada, and the Museo Arqueológico, Córdoba.
7   The only kiln of this period yet discovered is at Almería, but excavations and written records show that Málaga was the most important place of manufacture. See also Arthur Lane, 'Early Hispano-Moresque Pottery; a Reconsideration', *Burlington Magazine*, vol. 88 (Oct. 1946), pp. 246–252.
8   Abu Abdullah Muhammad ibn Al Ahmar, originally prince of Jaen.

Alhambra, the citadel and symbol of his realm. Of the giant vases which take their name
from this palace, one has never left it, and eight others are still in existence. The palace
walls still retain some of the tiles and *alicatados* made for them in the thirteenth and
fourteenth centuries.[9]

Málaga, Almería and Murcia are ports, and a good deal of their work was sent abroad.
The lustre and blue pottery was shipped to Spain, France and Italy, to the Almohade
kingdoms of North Africa, and even to Egypt, where it has been found at Fostat. The
trade extended to England. In 1289 pottery from Málaga was landed at Portsmouth for
Queen Eleanor of Castile, the first wife of Edward I: '42 bowls, 10 dishes and 4 earthenware jars of foreign colour'. A list of pottery imported at Sandwich in 1303 included
thirty bowls and pitchers of 'Malyk'.[10] A large Málagan dish, now in the Victoria and
Albert Museum, was found in the bed of the Thames. Other pieces have been excavated
in the City of London, at Winchester, and at Lesnes Abbey in Kent, and two jugs have
been recovered from the sea off the north German coast.

A record dated 1297 from the port of Collioure, near Perpignan, shows different rates
of duty for three classes of Málaga ware: pieces painted only in lustre paid the highest
rate, lustre and blue paid a middle rate, and pottery with blue decoration paid the same
duty as the green and brown wares of Barcelona.[11]

Some Arabic writings of about 1300 include praises of the 'golden ware' of Málaga
and remark on its popularity abroad.[12] Twenty-three Moorish bowls intricately painted
in yellow-gold lustre and blue are still in position in the walls of the church of San Am-
brogio Nuovo at Varazze, near Savona, where they were set when the walls were built,
about 1350. Such was the fame of lustreware that even in the fifteenth century it was
still being described in Valencia as 'obra de Malequa', even after Manises had been
making it for more than fifty years.

Considering the acknowledged repute of Málagan pottery, it is strange how little of it
is apparently to be seen in collections today. The reason is that much of it is attributed to
Manises, which began to make lustre and blue pottery in the fourteenth century and
superseded Málaga about 1400. The pottery of this town became so well known to collectors that till recently almost any good piece of lustre from Spain was automatically
attributed to Manises, and the importance of Málaga was forgotten.

It is often difficult and sometimes impossible to distinguish between Málaga and
Manises pottery, because Manises itself was probably started by potters from the Moorish
kingdom, and some wholly Moorish work has been found on the sites of its old kilns.
Not until after about 1400 did Manises work begin to become distinct. Correct attribu-
tion is made still harder by the fact that Málagan pottery going to Catalonian and

9   These are distinguished and dated by Llubiá, op. cit., p. 110. *Alicatados* are small, shaped tiles with
coloured glazes. The shapes fit together to make ingenious patterns.

10   The descriptions of the pots are 'xlij scutellis, x salariis, et iiij ollis terreis extranei coloris', by which
last may be inferred lustre or blue colours, then unknown to European potters. The description of the
second importation is 'xxx soldatis discorum et pitcherorum de Malyk'. See G. C. Dunning, 'A group of
English and imported medieval pottery from Leshes Abbey, Kent; and the trade in early Hispano-
Moresque pottery to England', *Antiquaries Journal*, vol. XLI (1961), p. 8.

11   Llubiá, op. cit., pp. 93–96.

12   Llubiá, op. cit., pp. 96–97.

Figure 8.   Shapes of Málagan pottery:
(1–4) large bowls, about 40 cm. wide;
(5) small cup, 10 cm. high; (6) jar with
twist handle, 12 cm. high; (7) flask with
ring handle, 15 cm. high; (8–9) two-handled
jars, about 17 cm. high; (10) spouted
ewer, 20 cm. high; (11) *albarelo*, about
28 cm. high.

French ports was usually carried in Moorish ships only as far as Valencia, where it was re-shipped for the second stage of the journey.[13]

Nonetheless, there are certain distinguishing features. The most fundamental is the material itself. The clays of Andalucía mostly contain more calcium than those of Valencia. As a result the fired clay of Málaga tends to be lighter in weight and paler in colour. The shapes of the pots are also some guide to their origin, as is the quality of the throwing. Málagan shapes were nearly always made with a finer touch than any of the Valencian pottery, and their rims, handles, spouts and footrings were more carefully worked. One of the commonest early shapes was the two-handled pitcher, made in many varieties, some of which are very graceful [Figs. 8, 9]. Often the handles have a small bead that springs upwards from the highest point, emphasising the upward lift of the shape. Small drinking bowls with splayed feet are fairly common, too, and so are flasks with lips for pouring and large, slightly flattened ring-handles. A few elegant spouted vessels for wine have been found, resembling metal ewers from Persia. Málagan *albarelos* mostly have almost straight sides, a flared foot, and a flared collar [29]. Oil-lamps on a tall shaft springing from a wide saucer are also fairly plentiful in excavations of Moorish sites. Many kinds of bowl were made, most of which have a heavy rim and a flared foot-ring. A certain kind of large bowl with a strong rim, tapering steeply to a small deep base, is now recognised as Málagan, not Valencian.

1   2

Figure 9.   Shapes of Málagan pottery: (1–2) two-handled pitchers, 30 cm. and 12 cm. high.

In general the definition of the base of vessels is a good guide. The Moorish potters had a preference for a splayed footring or a small pedestal foot which made even every-day pottery slightly ceremonial [30]. Valencian pots usually have a base which is less certainly formed; they are relatively bottom-heavy, and when the pedestal foot was made in Valencia it was apt to be bulbous and out of proportion.

Certain painted motifs appear again and again in Málagan work, like a hallmark. Amongst these are knot patterns and interlace, kufic letter patterns, devices based on the tree of life, the Nasrid blazon, and a certain kind of trefoil [29]. The placing of painted

13   M. Gomez-Moreno, *Cerámica medieval española*, pp. 57–58.

ornament was more assured at Málaga, and the designs have a general character which is rather different from that of Valencian pottery.

Before lustre and blue pottery began in Málaga it was only made in the Persian and Syrian potteries around Rayy and Kashan and Rakka. Pottery from those areas was imported into the Nasrid kingdom, and fragments have been found at Granada. They could therefore have suggested new techniques to the potters of Andalucía. This is really only a theoretical possibility, however, for things seldom happen in that way: it has almost always been the craftsmen themselves who have travelled, bringing their traditions with them. The knowledge of lustre is particularly unlikely to have travelled except through the migration of individuals. The 'secrets' of masters of lustre lay not only in the recipes and materials but above all in the construction and handling of the special kilns, and in judging the temperature and duration of the reduction-firing which developed the colour. The use of cobalt blue and lustre at Málaga in the early thirteenth century suggests the arrival of skilled men from somewhere in the Middle East. It is the more likely because the fall of the Fatimids in Egypt in 1171 left many craftsmen without work, while the Mongol invasion of Persia and Syria reduced large areas to chaos only a few years before Ibn Ahmar established his capital at Granada.[14]

Málagan and Middle Eastern earthenwares resemble each other in the frequent use of knot patterns and interlacing stems and foliage and intersecting geometrical figures [Figs. 10, 11], as well as certain emblems and creatures, particularly hares, gazelles, peacocks and fishes. Málaga's closest connection may have been with Syria, for Syrian designs were more formal and geometrical than the Persian, and Málagan decoration, also, was formal and lacked the romance and fable that featured so much in Persian pottery. Moreover, the frit-paste which was normally used for all luxury pottery in Persia was not used at all in Spain. Had there been a close connection with Persia it would surely have been known.

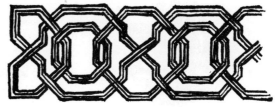

Figure 10. Knot pattern from Moorish lustre bowl. *Berlin Museum.*

Figure 11. Interlace pattern from Moorish ware excavated at Granada.

14 A. W. Frothingham, op. cit., p. 23, mentions earlier connections between Persia and Southern Spain, including the statement by the thirteenth-century geographer Ibn Battuta that some Persian dervishes chose Granada as their home because it resembled their native land.

A characteristic of Málagan pottery is the use of signs and emblems, that occur on every kind of tin-glaze vessel, large and small. The emblems are sometimes alone, like the *Khams* or Hand of Fatima sign on two of the Alhambra vases,[15] or like many versions of the Tree of Life symbol [Figs. 12, 13]. Sometimes they are worked into a pattern

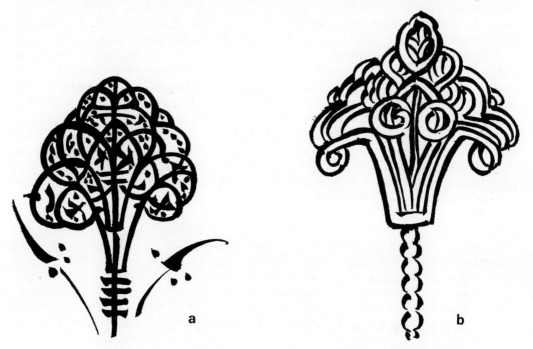

Figure 12a, b.   Variations on the Tree of Life pattern.

Figure 13.   *Khams* or Hand of Fatima.   Figure 14.   *Alafia* pattern.

15   One in the Hermitage Museum, Leningrad, and one in the Archaeological Museum, Madrid. This emblem belongs especially to Egyptian and Moorish-Spanish pottery. Roughly, it means 'God with us'.

sequence, but in such a way that the emblem still remains recognisable. Even when they are most closely worked into an overall pattern they are still obviously signs and symbols. Themes such as the *alafia* pattern (based on the inscription of the word 'Providence' or 'Blessing'), the knot, the star, the pinecone, and so forth, are all decorative but they are present as charms and protective signs just as much as for the pleasure they give to the eye [Fig. 14]. In most pottery traditions the basic language of signs and emblems generally becomes modified in the course of time as it is repeated and varied by a long succession of craftsmen, and the old tribal or religious signs eventually dissolve into a general pattern-convention. Málagan pottery pattern did not do this. Improvisation was very unusual.

Painters adapted all their emblems to suit particular shapes and placings, as was ingeniously done on the Alhambra vases, but each theme kept its own character; interlace patterns, for instance, never merged with patterns of kufic lettering. Leaf and scroll patterns remained distinct from the palmette and the Tree of Life, as if the painters felt meanings in them, and were not interested merely in making pretty effects. Only around 1400, when alien Gothic themes occasionally crept in, did the painters begin to depart from their traditional repertoire.

The clarity of its ancient emblems gives Málagan pottery a somewhat archaic character. In more sophisticated art or craft the emblems tend to become softened into more simply decorative effects. Moorish pottery was decorative but it was also magical: it was painted with signs to bring health and fortune and to protect from accident or evil influences on the object itself and on the owner. Behind this convention lay an attitude to objects that differed greatly from modern man's attitude to his expendable possessions.

It is difficult to understand an attitude of mind so removed from the assumptions of today, but it is still possible to catch the feeling. The following quotation from an authority of Islamic art applies well to Moorish Spain. The writer refers to formalised lettering, which is often regarded by Europeans as just a pleasing pattern.

The Orient has at all times considered script as something mysterious, conveying some magic virtue, hence its extensive use in all industrial arts and the seriousness and admiration with which it is universally regarded.[16]

Many of the world's most famous 'decorative' emblems have a magical or sacred origin. One may well question the common modern assumption that 'decoration' is merely a secondary contrivance added to give aesthetic pleasure or to 'emphasise the form.'

Perhaps aesthetic completeness on the one hand and magical protection on the other, are only different views of the same thing. The completeness of an interlace ornament or a leaf-scroll returning upon itself, and the suggestion of eternity in continuous patterns and linking rhythms, satisfies the eye and the mind at one and the same time. It brings to mind the psalmist's verse, 'One day telleth another, and one night certifieth another'. Few pots are so rich in metaphysical suggestion as the Alhambra vases, the most ambitious of all the works of the Moorish potteries [31–34].

16 Quoted by A. W. Frothingham, op. cit. from Samuel Flury in A. U. Pope, *Survey of Persian Art* (New York, 1938).

Nine of these vases still exist. They were not necessarily all made for the Alhambra, although its name is associated with them. Some of them certainly belonged to the Alhambra, and the palace grounds have yielded fragments of others. All the vases carry designs which also occur in the plastered walls and the woodwork of the palace itself.

The vases were probably made in Málaga. No trace of the manufacture of any pottery approaching their size has been found in Granada, and the local potteries seem to have made only small domestic ware. These immense pots, skilfully built in sections made of a specially blended pink sandy clay, finely painted in blue and lustre, requiring three firings, could only have been made by potters of high experience, using large kilns which must have been expertly controlled. To glaze and fire them at all was a considerable achievement. Most of them show signs of technical difficulties, such as areas where the glaze has been too thickly applied and has run in the firing, obscuring some of the cobalt blue painted underneath it. There are also places where the lustre pigment is but lightly reduced and is pale because of the unevenness of the draught in the kiln.

The variations of shape and painting in the surviving vases suggest that they are a fairly small proportion of those originally made. Those that survive span a period of about a hundred years. The generally agreed dating is as follows.

1. Vase in the National Museum, Palermo: end of the thirteenth century.
2. Vase in the Instituto de Valencia de Don Juan, Madrid: about 1300.
3. Vase in the Hermitage Museum, Leningrad: beginning of the fourteenth century.
4. Vase in National Archaeological Museum, Madrid: early fourteenth century.
5. Vase in the National Museum, Stockholm: second half of the fourteenth century.
6. Fluted vase from Hornos, Jaen, in the National Archaeological Museum, Madrid: late fourteenth century.
7. Vase in the Archaeological Museum of the Alhambra (handles lost and surface badly damaged): late fourteenth century.
8. Gazelle vase in the Archaeological Museum of the Alhambra: late fourteenth century.
9. Vase in the Freer Art Gallery, Washington (missing collar and handles): about 1400.

Three collars also survive from vases now lost. They are in the Archaeological Museum of the Alhambra, the Hirsch Collection, New York, and in the Collection of the Hispanic Society of America. A fragment of another vase, found at Fostat, is in the Victoria and Albert Museum in London.

In the four earliest vases the horizontal zones of painting are emphasised and contain large, distinct features. The Palermo and Institute vases have central zones with formalised kufic inscriptions which dominate the whole design. The vases in the Archaeological Museum of Madrid and in the Hermitage have bands of floriated kufic lettering which do not contrast so much with the rest of the painting. These two vases have the *Khams* emblem of the hand painted in the upper angle of the handle. The fluted vase from Hornos stands alone because of its vertical ribbing and the resulting vertical panels of painting: the narrow base of its collar and the outward turn of the upper part of the wing-handles are totally different from the earlier vases. The vases in the Alhambra and the Stockholm vase have a relatively bulbous shape; the painting on them is overall and diffused, and the necks flare distinctly outwards from the collar. Their forms are less subtle than those of the earlier vases, and the painting on them lacks the interplay of positive and negative pattern, though it is assured and ingenious.

The vases are almost the height of a man. They appear to have had no function and to have been simply monumental palace ornaments. The forms are derived from the traditional Andalucían wine-storage jar, the *tinaja*, which has a nearly spherical body and a short collar with two handles, but between the two there has been a transformation of the whole concept.

There may be some connection between the strange handles and the ancient Sassanian wing-ornament, that was originally a symbol of supernatural authority, and may underlie the imagery of angels as winged beings. The idea may seem fanciful when written down, but it agrees with the impressions of a man standing beside one of these giant forms, sensing the magic of its presence, absorbing the silence and movement of its unending patterns. If there is any truth in what has been said about the emotional content of Moorish emblems, then these vases are not less than treasuries of beneficent signs and symbols.[17]

Many of the painted designs of the Alhambra vases reappear in simpler form on regularly produced, functional vessels. For example, the lustre bowl in the Berlin Museum is painted with interlace and leaf-scroll pattern that is remarkably close to some of the designs on the vase in the Hermitage.[18] The gazelles on the vase in the Alhambra reappear on many plates and dishes, and patterns from the collars of the vases occur on domestic pottery throughout the fourteenth century. A good example is an *albarelo* in the Victoria and Albert Museum (almost certainly from Málaga), that incorporates four broad bands of patterns which could have been taken directly from the vases.[19]

Part of the attraction of the simpler Moorish pottery lies in the informal brush-strokes which give a rhythmical verve to the most ordinary designs. They appear again and again in a collection of small bowls found in the church at Pula in Sardinia, now in the Museum of Cagliari. These bowls seem to have been used as patens for the Holy Bread at Extreme Unction. The best bowls a family possessed would be employed, and once they had served this purpose people felt that they must be put aside in the church.[20] The patterns on these bowls are clear and basic. Had they been painted with geometrical precision they would have been rather dull. But in each example the formal pattern has been changed by unexpected movements which come from the spreading and folding of the loaded brush and the rapid motion of the painter's hand. This brings the pattern to life and makes a series of unique variations, rather as each leaf on a tree varies from the ideal pattern of the species.

17   And wall-niches in the Alhambra and in a Moorish palace near Málaga are inscribed in praise of the vases which formerly stood in them 'in metaphors appropriate to a bride'—Arthur Lane, op. cit., p. 249.
18   This bowl has a mark painted inside the footring, of which the Arabist M. Gomez-Moreno has said cryptically, 'Si se lee mal, dice Málaga' ('Badly read, it says Málaga').
19   M. Gonzalez Martí, *Cerámica del Levante Español*, vol. 1 (Barcelona, 1944), colour plate XII. A number of the illustrations in this fine book show pottery which would today be ascribed to Málaga rather than Manises.
20   The bowls were once thought to be Italian. A. van der Put attributed them to Manises, Martí to Paterna, and Llubiá says they are from Málaga. They are shown in Martí, op. cit., figs. 416–441. See also pp. 332–334.

Far removed from these simple vessels painted with standard motifs are a few pieces with highly individual subject decoration that were probably specially commissioned, perhaps by Christian patrons, for some examples have European details in the representations. A fine example is a lustre jug painted with large figures of a huntsman in European dress, with birds and trees against a background sprinkled with small dots and dabs of lustre [35]. The magnificent bowl painted with a ship is another example [36a, b]. It has the same two-dimensional, drawn quality as the huntsman, a superb disposition of figurative silhouette, 'readable' as a representation and as an abstract design. Incidentally, this bowl has often been called Manises work, with the comment that the shape and certain motifs are typical of Andalucía. A similar bowl has been excavated at Málaga. Both were probably made there.[21]

From about the middle of the fourteenth century onwards, potters from the Kingdom of Granada began to move northwards to take employment around Valencia. They may have been encouraged to move by agents of the Buyl family, who had a commercial interest in the Manises potteries. Hitherto, Málaga and the Andalucían potteries had enjoyed a monopoly of the trade in lustre and blue pottery, and it was inevitable that merchants further north would not rest content with buying and re-shipping the ware, when with some negotiation it might be made on their own land.

By the late fourteenth century the Nasrid kingdom was suffering from the rivalries of the leading nobles. The central government was weakening, and the growing sea-power of the Aragonese deprived the kingdom of much of its vital trade and shipping. Patronage shrank, and the quality of ceramics and other manufactures began to decline. One of the last fine works is the famous 'Fortuny tablet' made for Yusuf III (1408–1417) with an inscription in his honour, set round a design of interweaving peacocks and dragons with leaf and scroll patterns, centring on the Nasrid blazon three times repeated.[22] This lovely tablet symbolises the cultural contribution of Granada to Spain. It has a feminine charm, but little vigour compared with the older Moorish work. It belongs to the end of the line. Yet it also stands for the order, poetry and delicacy of touch which were such an important part of the legacy of Islam to Spain, in architecture and many subsidiary arts as well as pottery.

That quality lived on in the potteries of Valencia and Catalonia, to which many Moorish potters moved. Even after the conquest of Granada by the Catholic Kings in 1487, the Moorish element in Spanish pottery remained very strong, as the next chapter will show, and Moorish influence remained a leaven in Spanish design until the leaders of the Catholic Counter-Reformation became ashamed of it and legislated against Moorish customs in the later sixteenth century. Finally, in 1610 the Moorish population was expelled to North Africa, and Spanish lustreware never recovered from the loss.

21   Llubiá, op. cit., p. 99 and fig. 144.
22   The tablet is in the Instituto de Valencia de Don Juan, Madrid. It is painted in tawny-silver lustre.

5
HISPANO-MORESQUE POTTERY

Despite intermittent warfare between the Christian kingdoms of Leon and Castile and the Moorish kingdoms of the South, the cultures of Islam and Christendom interacted more closely in Spain than anywhere else, except perhaps in Byzantium itself. Scholars, traders and craftsmen were able to move around in tolerable security and until the reign of Philip II (1556–1598) there was little of the religious fanaticism or racial suspicion that divided the cultures elsewhere. The names Mozarab and Mudejar came into existence to describe people who belonged to both cultures: the one signifying Christians living under Moorish jurisdiction, the other, Moslems living under Christian rule. Mudejar craftsmen were sought after in Christian Spain. Their ingenious workmanship and their intricate patterns appear in Spanish architectural façades, manuscript illumination, metal and leatherwork, painted woodwork and carvings, and especially pottery.[1]

The principal pottery centres in Christian territory were the areas around Valencia and Barcelona, both of which had been making pottery from Roman times or earlier. The most important Valencian centre was the small town of Paterna, which produced a great deal of unglazed and plain earthenware but was known particularly for its tin-glaze pottery painted in green and brown. Nearby, Manises became yet more famous in the later fourteenth century for its fine pottery decorated in blue and lustre. Together, these two small towns formed the heart of the Hispano-Moresque pottery industry.

Around Valencia a number of other small centres also produced pottery from about the year 1400, such as Mislata, Manresa, Liria, Alberique, Alcantara, Carcer and Gandia. They enjoyed abundant natural clays and easy transport for their products by sea, river and land. Inland, some sixty miles up the river Turia, Teruel became a prolific centre from the late fourteenth century onwards, borrowing many of the forms used at Paterna, and subsequently developing methods and decorative motifs of its own.[2]

To the north, the Catalonian coastal area, and Barcelona especially, were important producers of pottery. The early wares resembled the brown and green of Paterna, and

---

1   See Frances Spalding, *Mudejar Ornament in Manuscripts* (New York, 1953). ' . . . these examples of Islamic ornament in church service books stand as unpretentious records of the cultural tolerance between Muslims and Christians in their joint devotion to the arts.'
2   Generally, see the following:
    Manuel Gonzalez Martí, *Cerámica del Levante Español* (3 vols.), (Barcelona, 1944 and 1952).
    Alice Wilson Frothingham, *Lusterware of Spain* (New York, 1951).
    J. Ainaud de Lasarte, *Cerámica y Vidrio, Ars Hispaniae*, vol. X, (Madrid, 1952), (especially for sixteenth and seventeenth centuries).
    Luis M. Llubiá, *Cerámica Medieval Española* (Barcelona, 1967).
    For Teruel, see Martí, op. cit., p. 623 et seq.

later the potteries adopted the use of cobalt blue and lustre from Manises. Partly because of their access to Provence and Italy the Catalonian potteries continued to flourish in the sixteenth and seventeenth centuries whilst those of Valencia were in decline. Muel, and later Reus, made some remarkable bright lustreware from the fifteenth to the seventeenth centuries. Calatayud, near Zaragoza, also produced much tin-glazed, painted and lustred pottery in the same period. From about 1600 a great deal of tin-glaze pottery was made in and around Talavera and Seville and up the Eastern side of Spain from Granada to Catalonia. Most of such work, however, lies outside the scope of this chapter because it owed more to Italian polychrome pottery than to Hispano-Moresque tradition. Examples of some of the later wares are included in the illustrations.

To return to Paterna and Manises: Valencia and the whole of Aragon was under Moorish rule until 1232, and all the pottery of the area had Islamic features which distinguished it from the traditional pottery of the rest of Christendom. By the twelfth century Paterna was already using a semi-opaque white glaze with decorations of manganese brown and copper green painted on the clay surface and penetrating the glaze from beneath in the firing. Though the forms of the vessels were crude compared with those of the Middle East, they reflected in a provincial way the imaginative details of handles, collars, lips, spouts, footrings and other features that made so much Islamic pottery gracious and articulate. Above all, there survived at Paterna a tradition of Islamic imagery and a feeling for rhythm and movement in brushwork. Plates, bowls, cups, jars, pitchers, flasks and candlesticks and other domestic objects were thrown from a blend of red clay and whitish marl and river sand. The clay was fired at about 960–980° Centigrade. Most of the pots were quickly and simply made, and the potting was fairly coarse, but fluent. The vessels were outstanding for their painted decoration and the ease with which designs of various types were intuitively fitted to different shapes. The painting was rapid and even nonchalant, it seldom failed to discover some way of subdividing the pot-surface in a manner that was dramatic without being contrived. The designs were painted in strong manganese brown, filled in with broader strokes of dilute copper which gave an acid grassy green.

Cursive motifs of Islamic origin were most in evidence, palmettes, spirals, cusps, arabesques [Fig. 15], and contour panels; also patterns based on Kufic script [38], and themes such as the Tree of Life, the roc or castle flanked with trees or pine cones, the six-pointed star, fantastic birds, gazelles, lions, hares and fishes, and renderings of the human face and figure—some of which are distantly reminiscent of finer versions from Persia and the Middle East [39]. Mixed with these motifs were geometrical themes that may have come from Visigothic or Iberian traditions before the Arab conquest, net patterns, zigzags, swastika forms, key-patterns [37]. Certain other themes were distinctly European, such as naturalistic leaf patterns, and versions of the human figure akin to Christian manuscript illumination and wall-paintings [44].[3]

3 For a short, well-illustrated account of Paterna and some of the work of Manises, see Llubá, op. cit., and José Martínez and Jaime de Scals Aracil, Cerámica del Museo Municipal de Valencia (Valencia, 1962). The most extensive collection of Paterna pottery is in the Museo Municipal (Palacio del Marques de Dos Aguas), Valencia, and in the Palacio Nacional, Barcelona. The latter includes good collections of comparable work from Teruel and Muel.

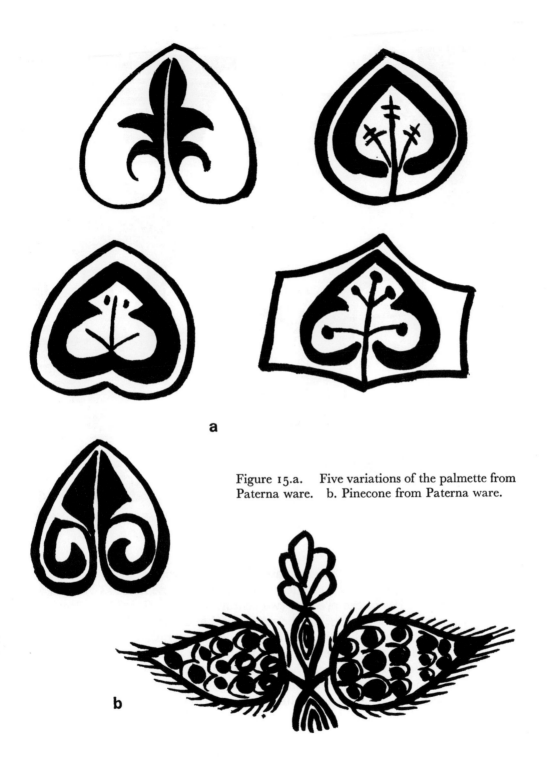

a

Figure 15.a.   Five variations of the palmette from
Paterna ware.   b. Pinecone from Paterna ware.

b

Figure 16.   Shapes from Hispano-Moresque pottery: (1) 'Citra', about 24 cm. high; (2) 'Greallet', 10 cm. high; (3) 'Librell', 28 cm. wide; (4) 'Terraç', about 50 cm. high; (5) 'Jarro', usually about 30 cm. high.

Except for the *albarelo* and the winged vase, the thrown forms of the great Hispano-Moresque ware of the fifteenth century derive largely from those made at Paterna and other Aragonese potteries in the previous two centuries. [Figs. 16, 17] The deep, flat-bottomed dishes with broad rims which became grand and ceremonial in the fifteenth century derive from a type of plate that had been made by generations of Paterna potters. The *lebrillo de ala*, a deep steep-sided bowl with brim or flat broad rim, likewise became celebrated in the great days to come. The *cuenco de orejas* or 'eared bowl' with two flat ear-like handles, sometimes elaborated, moulded and painted, lent itself particularly well to later Hispano-Moresque decoration in lustre. A jug form with a pedestal base, almost spherical belly and long straight neck, became adapted in the fifteenth century for ceremonial urns and vases.

Figure 17.   Shapes from Hispano-Moresque pottery: (1) *albarelo*, about 30 cm. high; (2) *'alfabeguer'*, 28 cm. high and more.

Altogether the Paterna patterns made a repertoire of immense richness. Some of the painted themes remained current over many generations but no version is an exact replica of another. The basic patterns took on a life of their own as they were repeated, and they were seldom if ever referred back to the literal detail of a prototype or a pattern-book (a practice that took the life out of many a good design in continental tin glaze of a subsequent era). As with popular songs which are learnt by heart, variations developed spontaneously and unselfconsciously while the pots passed in their thousands through the painters' workshops. If the forms and painted themes were sometimes crude, they were seldom inharmonious, always boldly alive, and they grew from a sense of movement rather than from calculated visual planning, and little or no critical after-thought was expended on them. To be in a room of Paterna pottery is to experience the fertility innate in the hand and body, a force that in the right conditions flows effortlessly through men, making each one an artist, and like other basic instincts such as sex and appetite is always impersonal, always individual, never totally to be explained.

About 1350, some bowls were made with decoration in cobalt blue, a material hitherto only used by Moorish potters in Andalucía. The blue-painted bowls were glazed all over, whereas the traditional green and brown wares were left unglazed on the backs. At the same time new pattern elements appeared that were more articulate than the old motifs, and showed a remarkable sensitivity of placing too. Amongst them were a number of pieces painted with animals which seem to have been observed at first hand, slightly humorously, and their character was captured in adroit brush-drawings [45].

From this time onwards Moorish names appear more and more frequently in pottery contracts, and there is little doubt that the changes in the work of Paterna were brought about by Moorish craftsmen. As early as 1326 two brothers, Abdalazic and Abrahim Almurci (the Murcian), were working at Paterna.[4]

4   A. van der Put, *Valencian Styles of Hispano-Moresque Pottery* (New York, 1938), p. 22.

At some time around 1350–1370 there was another surprising development, which has never been fully accounted for, at the town of Manises, lying on the southern side of the river, only a mile or two from Paterna. This small town began fairly quickly to produce pottery decorated in blue, and lustreware, of a much more elaborate and refined character than anything ever made at Paterna. In fact, the shapes and the decoration of the early pottery of Manises were so close to the pottery of Málaga as to be virtually indistinguishable [43; Colour Plate F].

Figure 18.   *Ataurique* device.

The Moorish decoration of Manises was far more definite than the old Paterna themes, and it was carried out with much more care and a sense of contrasting scales, large and small features interacting like a theme and a refrain, that indicate not only a different origin but a different manner of setting about any given piece of work. In it appeared details for which Paterna had no precedent but which can be exactly paralleled with Málagan designs. Such are the use of geometrical interlace, versions of the Tree of Life or 'hanging lamp' device, intricate palmette patterns, cursive interlace, trefoil patterns, *atauriques* [Fig. 18], *alafia* ornament, kufic script, and the use of white reserves with lustre background, to name but a few. (See figures.) The larger pieces have a complex overall design of lustre and cobalt blue incorporating a great diversity of detail [46]. The blue part of the design was usually painted directly on the raw clay, and penetrated the glaze from below when the piece was fired. The areas to be painted in lustre had to be foreseen, for the lustre painting was not added until later.[5] The actual execution of much of the work shows the same fertile invention as the work of Paterna, but at Manises it was controlled by a highly developed feeling for intricate composition and balance, and by a capacity for restraint [Colour Plate G].

The sustained production of fine pieces at Manises during the years 1380–1430 is without parallel in the history of ceramics. Many of these vessels will keep their place amongst the world's finest pottery for ever, regardless of changes in taste and outlook.

How did all this happen within so short a space of time? Since there can be little doubt that the early Manises work was by Moorish potters and painters, how is their arrival to be explained?

5   Martí, op. cit., vol. 1, p. 193 and p. 551 says that at Manises and Paterna the blue, green and brown were painted *under* the glaze, and came through from below, whereas in Teruel the painting was done on the surface of the unfired glaze, in the way which became customary in Italy and the rest of Europe.

They were probably encouraged or even persuaded to settle by the de Buyl family, the landlords of Manises. The family had provided the court of Aragon with ambassadors to several Moslem principalities, and they would have had first-hand knowledge of the skill of Moorish craftsmen and the esteem of ceramics in the Moslem world. Probably they would have conveyed special examples of this work from one court to another as gifts and been aware of the impression such things made on Christian princes and noblemen. They would also have known of the difficulties besetting the Moorish south in the fourteenth century, and of the readiness of the craftsmen to seek new employment. It seems possible that they deliberately re-settled Moorish potters on their own lands.[6]

The flowering of the Hispano-Moresque tradition in the period around 1400 may therefore be directly attributed to the commercial enterprise of the de Buyl family whose arms appear quite often in fifteenth-century dishes. The landlords reserved the right to a tenth of the value of the annual sales of pottery. The value of this right is indicated by a receipt that survived by chance in the files of a Valencian notary, in which Caterina Boyill, then Lady of Manises, acknowledged receipt of 3,000 sueldos, the royalties on sales of pottery for the first six months of 1454, equivalent to the wages of 3,000 men.[7] It is likely that some members of the family, courtiers or diplomats, may have played a central part in promoting Manises pottery in high society and encouraging its use as gifts of state. Without some such intermediaries, it would be hard to explain the astonishing number of noble coats of arms which were painted on Manises lustreware in the first two generations after its beginning.

The famous description of the potteries by Franciso Eximenez of Gerona, supposed to have been written in 1383, was probably a patriotic interpolation of about a hundred years later, not, as used to be thought, evidence of a fabulously rapid growth of the lustre industry; but it does describe its standing in the fifteenth century.

The communal industry of Paterna and Caceres is the making of fine jars, jugs, bottles, chargers, plates, bowls and tiles, and like desirable objects. But the beauty of the golden ware of Manises excels them all, painted in masterly manner, which with good reason has made all the world its admirer, so that the Pope himself and the Cardinals and Princes of the world all covet it, and are amazed that anything so excellent and noble could be made from common clay.[8]

Nevertheless, some important commissions were undertaken at an early date, such as the making of tiles for the Papal Palace at Avignon by two Manises potters, Juan Albalat and Pascasio Martin, in 1362. The potteries became really famous, however, in the first half of the fifteenth century when work was done for the royal and noble families of Aragon and Castile, Navarre, Savoy, Burgundy and many others in Italy and Sicily, as well as for important ecclesiastical patrons, including the Borgias, who came from near

---

6   Martí, op. cit., vol. 1, pp. 213–220.
7   A. van der Put, *Valencian styles of Hispano-Moresque Pottery* (New York, 1938), p. 9.
8   Translated from the quotation in A. van der Put, *Hispano-Moresque Ware of the XV Century* (London, 1904), p. 9. The passage is suspected of having been interpolated into the printed edition of Eximenes' description of Spain, dated 1499. (See Arthur Lane, 'Early Hispano-Moresque pottery,' *Burlington Magazine*, vol. 88, p. 251.)

Valencia. The special attraction of Manises ware lay in the lustre, hitherto known only to a few, and the fine quality of the intricate painting. The European aristocracy had not been even remotely interested in pottery until now. Through Manises the accumulated experience and aesthetic wealth of centuries of Islamic pottery flooded into the courts and palaces of Western Europe. At first the potters and painters drew almost exclusively on their established repertoire of patterns and figurative drawings [42, 53], but as time passed they responded to the requirements of European taste. By the middle of the fifteenth century the shapes of vessels and the painted designs had become distinctly different from those of the pure Moorish tradition.

One of the important requirements was for small-scale repeat patterns that would form a resonant and scintillating background for the dominant European motif of a coat of arms or crown or other emblem, or religious inscription or sacred monogram. The motif had to be repeatable but not facile. The best of such patterns, and certainly the most popular, was the vine leaf and stem painted in alternating lustre and blue. Another was the 'hojaflor', or leaf-flower, a beautifully simple, ever changeable series of rhythmic strokes; another was the repeated spur pattern that occurs sometimes as an overall dazzle-pattern on important pieces, and on small pieces as a dominant pattern in its own right. Other motifs were based on the leaves of parsley and thistle, and the 'sliced orange' was based on the marguerite flower.

There are no direct records of the lustre technique used by these potters, but it can be inferred from later records, and must have been in essentials similar to that used long before in the Middle East (described in chapter II). In his great treasury of pictorial and documentary records, *Cerámica del Levante Español*, Don Manuel Gonzalez Martí includes a drawing of a lustre kiln that is based on lustre kilns excavated at Manises [Fig. 19]. In principle it is not unlike the traditional updraught kilns used at that time, and still used in Spain, for the firing of ordinary ware except that the draught is choked back by the floor of the kiln and the inlets in the centre and corners of the chamber are arranged to distribute the smoke, making the air flow evenly amongst the lustre-painted pieces. The principal requirement (confirmed by the writer's own experience) appears to have been a much slower draught than that of an ordinary firing. Lustre was fired at a very low temperature, and it was crucial to hold the fire back to prevent the overheating of the projecting or exposed parts of the pots.

In kilns of the type, it would be hard to avoid overheating some pieces and underfiring others. The pots near the floor of the kiln would inevitably get hotter than those higher up. Careful examination of Manises pieces shows that this did indeed happen. Some pieces are only just lustrous, and the dominant colour is a soft chestnut brown. These have been slightly overheated, and the copper and silver pigments have begun to combine with the glaze, losing some of their metallic reflection. Other pieces have lost some of their lustrous surface by abrasion or exposure to acids in the soil. On these the lustre surface may originally have been very bright, but because it adhered but lightly to the glaze it was easily removed. Other pieces have merely a pale lustre because of insufficient reduction in the firing: the metals have remained on the glaze partly in the form of oxides, which, of course, lack the metallic, reflecting surface. Martí illustrates a few pieces where the lustre is said to have been eroded away and nothing but the blue part of the design

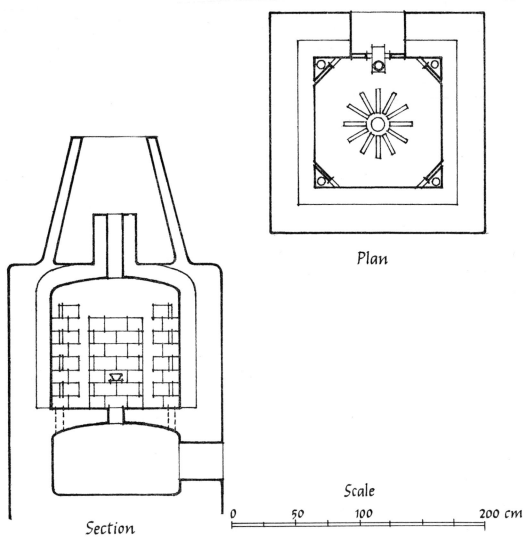

Plan

Scale

0   50   100   200 cm

Section

Figure 19. Diagram of lustre kiln excavated at Manises. (From Martí, *Cerámica del Levante Español*, vol. I. p. 323.)

remains. Possibly the lustre never took to the glaze surface at all because of a combination of underfiring and under-reduction.

The fusible buff clay traditionally used at Paterna and adopted also at Manises was specially suitable for lustre because it could be covered by a glaze that could be fired at a low temperature and yet would not craze because of the considerable shrinkage of the clay body in cooling.[9]

9   See Chapter 13 on the technical basis of tin-glaze pottery.

The Moorish lustres were usually compounded chiefly of silver, and gave a finished surface of yellow or amber, and, if very low fired, of greenish-brown. Many celebrated Málagan lustre pieces, such as the Alhambra vases and the Fortuny tablet, were done in this kind of pigment, and most of the early Manises lustres were similar. Towards the end of the fourteenth century, however, some copper red lustres were tried at Málaga, though there were signs of technical difficulties, particularly volatilization of the copper and greying of the glaze.[10] The reddish-gold lustres seem to have been developed at Manises to a degree never achieved in the south. Some early fifteenth-century *albarelos* carry an astonishing deep red that was often contrasted with a strong blue. Until the last quarter of the century, however, the most common Manises lustre was an orange-gold such as would be produced by a silver pigment with about a tenth part of copper. The oxides of the metals were dissolved in vinegar and mixed with ochre in a proportion of about one to four. Then they were painted on the fired glaze with a brush or feather, or a quill-pen, and fired at about 600–650° Centigrade. As soon as this temperature was reached, the air-inlets to the firechamber were almost closed and resinous brushwood (rosemary, juniper, etc.) was thrown into the fire to make a great deal of smoke. That probably lasted for about an hour, after which time the metallic oxides would have been reduced to the state of more or less pure metal, deposited on the glaze surface while it softened. Once the pottery was withdrawn from the kiln, the ochre was rubbed off the surface, revealing the film of lustre beneath.

In 1785 the following lustre-recipe was sent to the mayor of Valencia in reply to an enquiry about the methods used at Manises:

In the composition of lustre pigment there are five ingredients, namely, copper, which is better the older it is; silver, which is likewise better when it is old; sulphur, almazarron, which is called here almagre, and strong vinegar; each mixture from the above ingredients is formed in the following proportions: copper, three ounces; silver, one peseta; sulphur, three ounces; almazarron, twelve ounces, and vinegar, half a gallon (una azumbre), which is here understood as half a quarter, and to all this is added three pounds of twelve ounces of the dirt or ochre which is left by the ware after firing, the pots being cleaned in a tub of water in which this deposit gathers.[11]

The recipe dates from a decadent period in Manises lustre, by which time it had become brash and brassy, but it is probably similar to the earlier recipes. The finished effect depends as much on the composition of the glaze as on the lustre pigment, and by this late date the Manises glazes were poor. On a glaze with more tin, and some alkalis, such a recipe would have given much subtler lustre.

A number of detailed records of contracts and sales of Manises lustreware, including the special names of different types of pots, were published by the Duke of Osma in 1908. The following commission is dated 1414:

Agreement by Çahat Almale 'serracenus', master-potter of Manises, to supply Joan Bou [Boil?] of Valencia with one dozen alfabeguers [plant-pots on a pedestal base] of earthenware with Malequa [Malaga] gold, four jars of Paterna ware, four dozen lustre dishes, well and

10 Examples of defective red lustre are in the Archaeological Museum of the Alhambra, Granada.
11 Translated from the text published by Martí, op. cit., vol. 1, p. 321.

soundly made and as big as they can be, and a dozen made in his own style of working; thirty-two dozen in all lustred scudelles grealenques [bowls with a pedestal foot], lustred eared bowls, golden tiles of the middle size, that is to say flat paving tiles, greallets dauratos [lustred goblet-cups with a handle], and four dozen large basins of the same shape as dishes of white silver.[12]

Commissions such as this were by no means unusual, and the making of lustreware at Valencia must have been a commercial scoop of a kind only equalled by the demand for porcelain in the eighteenth century. Perhaps the most important attribute of lustre was its ability to arouse admiration to the extent of obsession. There is something about the reflecting surface of lustreware which fascinates beyond reason: it can never be defined because it is ever-changing with the light and the position of the observer; one moment it 'disappears' into mere colour, the next it flashes into life with unexpected hues and iridescences, and yet has changed again before it can be closely seen or described. Lustre has the same power as jewels and women to awaken immoderate desire.

The mysterious richness of lustre was perhaps most fully brought out in the intricate Moorish designs combining gold or silvery-yellow lustre and deep blue, used on dishes and albarelos around 1400, designs at once complex and lucid, like a rich musical chord, densely patterned, and vibrant with changing colours. The great heraldic dishes, however, were mainly painted in lustre alone, as were three famous dishes made in 1428, one with the arms of Blanche of Navarre, one with the arms of Maria of Castile [Colour Plate H], and one with the arms of Philip the Good of Burgundy. Each is dominated by the coat of arms in the centre, but the blazon disperses itself into the background pattern that extends over the full sweep of the form. The background is geometrically disposed but is built up of a variety of organic forms, knots and interlace, spirals, palmettes, leaves and stems, radial panels of the kufic alafia letter-pattern, all carried out in small quill-drawn motifs [Figs. 20, 21]. The painting on these dishes can be seen in different ways, according to the units the eye dwells on. The decoration became something more than decorative. The dish is merely a dish; however, it can also be felt as an enchanted circle, a microcosm or little world.

A few years afterwards, about 1440, the backgrounds of the armorial dishes became smaller in scale and more mechanical and repetitive. Established recipes for background patterns were developed, probably because of the many demands being made on the potteries, especially from Florence, for whose nobility many of the dishes were made. If some of these dishes were beautifully painted, they lack the unity of mood and form which had been achieved before. The coat of arms sometimes seems isolated, as if painted by another hand, and is sometimes haltingly rendered in comparison with the easy, ingenious patterns of the background. The background emphasised the arms themselves, but actually the heraldry is often the least interesting part of the design. In contrast, the reverse side of many armorial dishes is painted freely and dramatically. The eagle on the reverse of many Hispano-Moresque dishes is one of the most famous of all European pottery emblems [47] ,and it was perhaps this mixture of formal freedom and

12   From Don G. J. Osma, *Apuntes sobre Cerámica Morisca* (Madrid, 1908), and Van der Put, *Valencian Styles of Hispano-Moresque Pottery* (New York, 1938), p. 20. Van der Put establishes the meaning of many of the strange pot-names used in the original documents.

Figure 20.　Leaf and scroll patterns from Hispano-Moresque pottery.

Figure 21.　(1) Spur pattern and cross-hatching. (2) Vine-leaf pattern.

inner coherence that prompted a distinguished Japanese potter (Hamada) to call it the best brushwork in Europe.

The *albarelo*, or drug jar, like the bowls and chargers, was a utilitarian form which in time became ornamental. The clean sweep of the slightly waisted, tall body, coming to an abrupt change of direction at the foot and shoulder, made a clearly defined area for the painter to explore with his brush. Some of the early fifteenth-century *albarelos* with Moorish panel patterns and borders of Kufic lettering have a heavy richness without equal in the world's pottery [Colour Plate F]. The lighter and more disciplined vine-leaf and bryony patterns were more easily placed amongst conventional possessions; they were popular in Italy in the fifteenth century and were, in fact, copied in Florence and Faenza. In the later part of the century came a variety of free patterns which covered the whole body of the pot with sinuous leaves and scrolls, Moorish in their rhythm, Spanish in their weight and grandeur. The blocked leaf designs were frequently incised after the pigment had dried, ornamenting the leaves with inner patterns of curved ribs that were balanced by light line-and-point patterns on the white areas between the leaves. The same technique had been used by the Egyptian lustre-painter Sa'ad in the twelfth century.

The ceremonial vessels represent only one facet of the Hispano-Moresque tradition. Unpretentious pieces were being made every day, counted by the dozen—jugs, plates, bowls, tiles, pitchers, and the like. Relatively few of these simpler pieces were sent out of Spain, and since they were for use, most of them were used to destruction. In them the fluency of the Spanish pot-throwers is most clearly felt, a sense of balance which made even thick vessels seem light by gathering weight at the rims, a rightness of proportion which made handles, spouts and other features harmonise with the forms and invite the touch. Such things were not so much designed as felt by the potters, and they evolved as much through constant repetition as by planning. Actually, until modern times, remarkably little importance was attached to the functional performance of pottery, whereas its appearance mattered very much. In Spain the throwers' skill was taken for granted. Then, as now, Spanish throwers were regarded as no more than artisans, of less importance than the painters. Their sensibility is felt in their work but it was not challenged or fully developed. The shapes served as carriers of decoration whose quality they were not expected to equal.

One of the most pleasant of all the simple repeat patterns was called the *escudilla de monja*, or 'nun's bowl', painted in a series of simple strokes that built up to form the figure of an angel with outstretched wings and a stylised head and bust which are suggestively human [54].

Ordinary pieces of the kind were the routine life of the potteries and they made the grand ceremonial pieces possible. They were the repetition wares on which each generation of apprentices was brought up. They were the wares that filled the kilns once the special pieces were in position, and could be relied on to cover costs when large things were cracked or damaged in the firing.

About 1470 Manises began producing dishes with moulded panels, in all probability suggested by chargers of beaten metal. The raised ribs, made with applied coils of clay, sub-divided the dish into panels in a way that had hitherto been done by painting. The raised surface inhibited bold or cursive brushwork and forced a return to smaller patterns with intricate reflecting surfaces such as had been used on the great charger of Ferdinand and Isabella,[13] but without the noble simplicity of its plain surfaces. The dishes with applied clay ornament mark the beginnings of a decline: there was a certain contradiction between the surface of the pot and the painted ornament, and the painting itself became more a matter of the multiplication of small units instead of a design conceived in the large and carried out with living brush-strokes.

Towards 1500 the dishes with applied ornament were replaced by forms made over a mould that gave a swelling, gadrooned surface, something like a large catherine wheel. The convex surfaces of the gadroons and other shapes of this period usually received a sumptuous application of deep red lustre patterns with clever modulations of scale. From a distance the effect is magnificent; on closer inspection the details are often facile. The decoration seems to try too hard for effect, rather than allowing an effect to come naturally from the quality of the work put into it.

Was it merely coincidence that these dishes were made at the time of the first serious commercial threats to the Valencian potteries? The Florentine nobility, who over two generations had brought Manises some of her most valuable commissions, were turning their patronage to their own potteries, and already the Italian ceramists possessed a versatility and technical enterprise which Manises could not equal. Above all, they were developing painted themes in harmony with the Renaissance ideals expressed in the fine arts, using line drawings and a wider range of colours than Manises had ever known,

13   Victoria and Albert Museum, ref. 1680–1855.

and introducing classical subject-matter that had no place in the Hispano-Moresque tradition. Perhaps the over-dramatic feeling of many of the Valencian show-pieces of this time represents an attempt to recapture a dwindling market. For the sophisticated market the Valencian potters failed in one cardinal quality: they were not modern, and their Moorish background prevented them from becoming classical. Lustre was not out of fashion; in fact, the Italians were at pains to develop it, but the whole feeling of Hispano-Moresque lustre was too Islamic for the Humanist tastes of Italy.

The Spanish lustre potteries remained active throughout the sixteenth century and were described admiringly by several travellers, notably by Lucio Marineo in 1539 and Martin de Viciana in 1564, but now they were praised as the best potteries in Spain rather than the best in the world. If the inability to classicize the designs was a commercial loss, it was perhaps a cultural asset because it enabled the lustre tradition to respond to the consistent tastes of a more local public, and the best of the work has outlasted the twists and turns of fashion right up to the present day. Such, for example, is the lustre dish in the Victoria and Albert Museum which is said to date from as late as the middle seventeenth century, painted in heavy masses on a floriated cross design, with dramatic use of small areas of reserved background [57A]. The dish painted with a bull is an example of vigorous Valencian lustre of about 1500 [55]. It is a theme which was painted in a number of free renderings at about this time, and shows a vitality which had, to a large extent, been bred out of the more formal, armorial dishes.

During the fifteenth century a number of lustre masters appear to have moved further north to Catalonia, where lustre was made after about the middle of the century. A contract survives from 1461, in which a master-potter of Mislata agreed with a citizen of Barcelona to work in Barcelona initially for a year, together with his son and his nephew and one slave. The citizen was to provide the house and workshops and all necessary equipment, and to take charge of marketing the work, and the profit would be divided equally between him and the potters.[14]

Another definite record of a Barcelona potter is the remarkable notebook kept by Nicolau Reyner between 1514 and 1519, now preserved in the Cathedral archives at Barcelona. Reyner was a Catalan master-potter, and in this book he kept details of his business dealings, the organisation of his workshop and his three assistants and the boy who minded the kiln. It records purchases of clay, the firing of kilns, agreements to rent the kilns of neighbouring potters for large orders, and the purchase of faggots of heather and rosemary for fuel, and the practical arrangements that lay behind the making, selling and exportation of pottery at this time. It is remarkable how small Reyner's establishment was. Had the diary not been written in Catalan with many mis-spellings and contracted words, all in an almost illegible hand, it might long ago have been published.[15]

Catalonian lustre includes many pieces painted in a silvery yellow. If the firing were done at very low temperature (little above 600° Centigrade) greenish-brown resulted, with iridescent sheens of blue, purple, green and crimson.

Catalonia also produced much tin-glaze ware painted in blue, on which a strong informal brush decoration was used. By the time this ware developed, the area was feeling

14   Martí, op. cit., vol. 1, p. 231.
15   See A. W. Frothingham, op. cit., p. 237, for a fuller description and further references.

the influence of Italian pictorial decoration. This was only half assimilated, and the resulting blend of Italian idea and Hispano-Moresque touch is sometimes very pleasing. The most popular themes on dishes include stylised ladies wearing long dresses and hats, young men with hawks, sun-faces, fishes, rabbits and birds, a kind of castle or tower, 'urns' with bursting flowers, and geometrical patterns. Most of the dishes were intended for hanging on walls, and have two small holes at the top for fixing [162].

Some lively lustreware was produced at Muel, near Zaragoza in the fifteenth and sixteenth centuries. The feeling and the technique of this work are extraordinarily Moorish.[16] They are most evident in the spiky Mudejar patterns and thistle devices resulting from the kind of strokes the long brushes naturally tended to make. The designs were only half planned: the general types of pattern must have been pre-arranged, but the details and edges were left to the brush itself. Thus, even when there was symmetry, it constantly varied in diverse illogical formations of a kind completely different from those the mind conceives beforehand [49, 50].

Muel used both silver and copper lustres with a striking brilliance, which may have been caused by a low firing temperature and an extremely fusible glaze. They are little known outside Spain.

A great deal of lustre of orange-gold hue was produced at Reus, near Barcelona, in the seventeenth century. The standard signature pattern of Reus is a long-tailed bird, generally haltingly drawn in a sectional manner, with simple units and extensions suggesting a child's construction kit, a kind of gauche folk-emblem, notable principally for its lack of rhythm, imagination and meaning. How could such a device result from the Hispano-Moresque tradition?

The event explaining this degeneration more than any other is the expulsion of the Moors in 1610. From the kingdom of Valencia some 134,000 people were deported to North Africa, despite the fact that for some two hundred years Moorish craftsmen had worked amongst Christians with surprisingly little friction. Amongst them were families who were really the life-blood of the Valencian potteries, especially of the lustre technique, people whose techical skills were just as great as their artistry.

Almost immediately after the expulsion, the quality of lustre pottery began to decline. The thrown shapes, the composition of the glazes and the standard of painting deteriorated steadily. The long chain of practical knowledge and skill that had passed through generations of masters and pupils was broken. A few craftsmen migrated Northwards to Narbonne in France, and a few may have lingered in parts of Catalonia, but to all intents and purposes their skills were now lost to Spanish pottery.

Lustre continued to be made in Spain abundantly until the late eighteenth century [56]. Thereafter only small quantities were made until recent times, when the industry was revived and began to produce so-called facsimiles of old designs. The similarity is superficial, for the glazes and lustre pigments are cheap and have nothing but their reliability to commend them. The vitality of the old Moorish brushwork has not been

16 A. van der Put, *Hispano-Moresque Ware*, p. 19. note 1, quotes a 4½ year contract of apprenticeship from Calatayud in 1507 between a Moorish master, Muhammad ben Suleyman Attaalab, and a pupil, Abdallah Alfoguey. It is one of many records which indicate that lustre remained mostly in the hands of Moorish masters.

recaptured, and probably cannot be, for its roots are deeper than matters of technique or stylistic convention or skill. They lie in what people are in themselves, and in what they feel about what they do, and they are as deeply hidden as the roots of all poetry, whether of word or line and colour. The real import of Hispano-Moresque pottery lay in its emotional undertones, its life and its joy. It is seldom perfect: one cannot easily find pieces that are not marred by some technical or artistic imperfection, yet they have a magnanimity which is one of the highest achievements of ceramics in the Western world.

What is it in a tradition that enables such feelings to come to the surface through what are, after all, mere lines and shapes painted on a simple glaze? Why does one piece have an inner content, whereas another, very similar, is only decorative? What is it that men pass down from one to another in a living tradition that makes that tradition more than the sum of its technical processes and skills?

After about 1600 the soft silver-yellow lustres were rarely seen again. They were superseded by bronze or red-copper lustres which behaved reliably, and gave a powerful but relatively brash surface reflection. Some of the later designs, such as the feathery lily or carnation flower, were effective and well suited to repetition by artisan painters, but they did not equal the older work. By this time potters and painters were no longer artists as well as artisans. The potters fell back to the place of mere manufacturers, as they had always been thought of before the arrival of the Moors.

Some memories of Hispano-Moresque tradition have lingered on in the popular polychrome pottery which had flourished in different regions of the Iberian peninsula from the late sixteenth century to the present day [162, 163, 164]. Perhaps because of this element, Spanish and Portuguese pottery has always retained a feeling for movement and dramatic brush-painting and a sense of two-dimensional pattern and background belonging particularly to pottery, and is totally different from line drawing and picture-painting. However, the later wares with their predominantly figurative themes were as much Italian as Spanish in inspiration. Even before the expulsion of the Moorish communities, Spanish pottery had lost the special spice that comes from a sense of doing something new.

Though at one time Italian pottery had borrowed directly from Spanish examples, its development was strangely different, and it responded to influences unknown to the Moorish masters, and entered worlds they had never dreamed of.

6

ITALIAN MAIOLICA

In little more than a hundred years Italian tin-glaze wares developed from an unpretentious craft to an applied art that found an honourable place in courts and palaces. By the late fifteenth century the finest work in ceramics was occasionally referred to, even by Lorenzo de' Medici himself, as equal in artistic merit to the work of the jeweller and silversmith.[1] People expected to be astonished by the jeweller: that they could also be astonished by painted pottery was indeed notable. It would not have been extraordinary in the Far or Middle East, but in Europe it was, for Christian patrons were accustomed to regard clay as a base material whose very nature denied it nobility unless it were used on a monumental scale in architecture or sculpture. The colours on tin-glaze vessels undoubtedly helped to raise their esteem, for good colours were still rare and mysterious and were associated with secret skills, above all the durable colours of glass, enamel and ceramic pigments. It was no accident that the first pottery to be highly regarded in Europe was painted tin glaze. Consequently, maiolica craftsmen were able to undertake increasingly ambitious and expensive projects and develop their technical resources, while simpler, purely utilitarian pottery remained almost unchanged for hundreds of years.

The development of maiolica lay above all in the exploration of drawing and colour and subject-matter on the white glaze: it was essentially painter's pottery. The change from the simple designs of about 1430 to the complex compositions and colour schemes for important subjects by about 1530 was phenomenal. The shapes were secondary to the painted decoration and they seem to have been left mostly to the artisan clay-workers and throwers. There were some neat and ingenious ideas, such as the screw-stoppers, basket-moulds and modelled ornaments illustrated by Piccolpasso in his remarkable book the *Arte del Vasaio* (described at the end of this chapter), but these ideas seem to have originated from the men on the workshop's earthen floor rather than from the studio; they involved no radically new concepts equivalent to those which were introduced in ceramic painting. Painting on maiolica became almost a new art form. Only when the adventure of painting had run through its primal vigour, around 1550, were any signal changes made in the forms of pottery vessels, and even then they were mostly adaptations of shapes that already existed in metalwork.

The collectors' pieces that are famous today give a false impression of their times.

1   Letters of Pope Sixtus IV and of Lorenzo de' Medici, dated 1478 and 1490 respectively, express this estimate of painted pottery. See G. Liverani, *Five Centuries of Italian Maiolica* (London, 1960). For the social background of maiolica in the Renaissance, see also J. Giacomotti, *La Majolique de la Renaissance* (Paris, 1961). For a general survey, see Bernard Rackham, *Italian Maiolica* (London, 1952).

Map 4. Italy, showing the principal maiolica centres.

They have survived because they were treasured. Ironically, the everyday pottery is as rare now as the fine work because it was used until it was used up, and the surviving examples come mostly from excavations and from the bottoms of wells [Colour Plate L].

As will be seen in the later part of this chapter, Italian workshops were technically very advanced, and they depended on mills and manpower, tools and materials, amounting to a high capital value. Most of the techniques which were to be used three hundred years later by industries supplying a mass market were already known in principle to Italian potters who lived before Shakespeare was born. The capital behind Italian workshops opened the way to many new developments; it also subjected the pottery tradition to new and unsettling influences, and some of the fine ceramics of the *cinquecento* raise misgivings while they compel admiration.

The early Italian tin-glaze wares are much earlier than is usually supposed. The use of tin glaze may actually have started earlier in Italy than in Spain. It was made in both the northern and the southern parts of the land, but the wares were distinctly different, and do not seem to have had a common origin.

Tin-glaze pottery painted in green and brown was being made for local demand in a number of centres in Tuscany and Umbria by the beginning of the thirteenth century. It is usually known as 'archaic maiolica' or 'Orvieto ware' because it was early noted in that district, though Orvieto was only one amongst several centres for it. Tin glaze was being used at Pavia in the early twelfth century, for a wall in the Torre Comune, built not later than 1110, contains bands of locally made bricks with tin-glazed surfaces, and a wall in the church of S. Lanfranco in Pavia is ornamented with *bacini*, tin-glaze dishes with animal and geometric ornament and some elaborate borders. This wall and the dishes date from about 1150.[2]

'Archaic' ware decorated in brown and green was also made in and around Pisa, Viterbo, Florence, Montalcino, Siena and Ravenna by the fourteenth century and probably earlier, decorated in a wide variety of plant forms, geometric devices and animals, some of which are weird and fantastic. The range of things made was equivalent to that of Paterna in Spain, although the vessel-forms and the painted designs were distinctly different. If there are signs of Islamic influence in some of the designs, it is far less evident than in Paterna ware. There must surely have been some connection or perhaps a common origin between the two. No one has yet shown what it was.

From about 1300 onwards the 'archaic' maiolica tended more and more towards line drawing rather than to the broader brushwork used at Paterna [58]. The painters began to distinguish between the dominant emblem and the rest of the design by cross-hatching the background. The brush-pencil and drawn line basis of Italian ceramic painting, which underlay all the maiolica of the Renaissance, was already evident two hundred years before.

In Sicily and Southern Italy tin-glaze pottery was being made by 1200, and was made in many places by 1250. The kingdom of Sicily had a considerable Moslem population, and Moslem craftsmen from Tunisia may have been employed there for building

2   For the Torre Comune, see Francesco Aguzzi, 'La decorazione ceramica dell' antica cathedrale di Pavia', in *Atti, III Convegno internazionale della ceramica* (Albisola, 1970), p. 281. For *bacini* generally, see Liverani, op. cit. p. 13 et seq and illustrations.

and painting and for making pottery. Simple themes with Islamic affinites were painted on many of the pots—figures of warriors, horsemen, dancers, animals and sometimes tall cypress trees. They were painted in brown and green, but to these were added yellow and soft blue, colours which were not used in the north. The glaze contained about 5 per cent of tin oxide and the painting was often rough to the touch. The outsides of bowls and dishes were usually left unglazed, for economy. These wares are known as 'proto-maiolica'. Examples have been found in the Peloponnese, in Cyprus, and at several places on the east Mediterranean coast, notably in the castle at Atlit in Israel, to which they were taken by pilgrims and other travellers.[3]

The influence of the four-colour 'proto-maiolica' extended to workshops in Naples by the thirteenth century, and to Rome by the fourteenth or earlier. It was no less important than the 'archaic' maiolica of the North in providing a seed-bed from which Renaissance maiolica evolved, though the important developments which took place in the fifteenth century occurred mainly in the northern centres.

Many of the late medieval Italian shapes were similar to those of Hispano-Moresque pottery—but never quite the same—such as the *albarello* and the *tondino*, a small bowl with a rounded well and a wide flat rim (an invitation to any painter), and the *tagliera*, a flat-based dish with steep shallow sides opening to a wide rim. Other shapes seem to have been specially Italian, like the pear-shaped jug on a rounded foot with deep indentations on either side of the lip, the pedestal jug and the common *panata*, broad, footless jug with a large applied spout [Figs. 22, 23, 24]. Italian jugs and pitchers generally have a wide, strap-like handle springing from the neck of the vessel and descending almost vertically to the shoulder, a curious convention that lasted for centuries despite its awkwardness in the hand. A specially Italian form of drug-jar had two handles starting from the upper part of the shoulder and returning to the belly of the pot [59]. This was later refined by being given a pedestal-foot, a lid, and more elegant handles, turning into a ceremonial urn.

For nearly two hundred years after the first tin-glaze vessels were made in Italy, the bulk of Italian pottery was still incised slipware, in which the pattern was cut through a white slip into the underlying red clay, with blotches of green and honey-brown reinforcing the incised pattern. Tin-glazed vessels remained uncommon and were probably used only by merchants and by others with money to spare. The tin glaze was often applied merely on the visible surface of the vessel, the inside and the base being made impervious with ordinary transparent glaze to save expense. The fine tin-glaze pottery was still only available from Spain.

About 1420–1440 there appeared in Florence a number of large dishes painted in the traditional green and brown, not in the old, clear-cut heraldic manner, but in a more elaborate and poetic style [60]. A dish in the Louvre is painted with an heraldic lion with a curiously small head, carrying in his right paw a banner bearing the *fleur-de-lis* of Florence, against a background sprinkled with small leaves and flowers, resembling tapestry. A dish in the Victoria and Albert Museum represents a hare standing by a

3 See David Whitehouse, 'Medieval glazed pottery of Lazío', *Papers of the British School at Rome*, vol. XXXV (new series, vol. XXII) 1967, for a description of the sequence of 'proto-maiolica' and 'archaic maiolica'.

formalised teazle, probably also an heraldic emblem. The treatment is more formal, with suggestions of modelling in the animal itself and in the indented leaf ornament of the background and the border. The indented leaf was a favourite Florentine ornament of the period. It comes from the spiky 'mudejar' leaf-patterns of Valencia, but instead of being painted in solid colour with incised veining, the leaves were first drawn with a fine brush and were then filled in with graded toncs of colour which emphasised the suggestions of depth in the drawing. The elaborate idea and gentle mood of these dishes leaves the pottery of the archaic period far behind. Each is a carefully devised individual piece and is intended not simply to carry a decorative feature but to be a focus of attention.

Figure 22. Italian pedestal-jug, usually about 30 cm. high.

Figure 23. Traditional *panata* jug shape, usually about 12 cm. high.

Figure 24. Italian two-handled jar, from about 23 cm. high.

The well-known Florentine 'relief blue' oakleaf jars and pitchers of the mid-fifteenth century were decorated with freely drawn birds, animals or emblems, against a background of formalised serrated leaves and stalks [59]. The drawing of the fine lines of purple-brown is blocked in with a deep blue-black, made of impure cobalt ore and a flux. Because the cobalt was refractory the pigment stands out from the body of the pot. The relief wares are not so different from the fine green and brown pottery as they seem at first sight. Despite the crude, heavy blue, the design is still a drawing filled in with colour.

The relief blue jars resemble Valencian pottery. Florentine workshops were also actually copying Valencian *albarelos* with the popular vine-leaf decoration. In both it is striking how they ignored the positive-negative balance of flat pattern and background because they were really more interested in the line drawing.

Pursuing this interest they made simple drawings which agreed perfectly with the restricted colour palette of the time, as they did with the simple forms of traditional vessels. They were full of life but did not overload the pottery shape, and their fresh-ness suggests that they were newly devised, not copied from prints, as became general practice in the next century [64].

The coloured drawing remained a popular type of ceramic painting throughout the next hundred years. It was perpetuated by the custom of making presentations of pottery to celebrate betrothals and marriages and the birth of children, and to express affection. Pottery painted with the head of a girl accompanied by a scroll with her name on it was a present given during courtship or betrothal, known as *cope amatorie*, 'love-pottery' [63; Colour Plate J].

The well-known Cafaggiolo plate, painted with a young couple having their likeness drawn on a dish,[4] is a remarkable record of a common custom. Some of the heads on dishes are so individual that it seems they are lightning sketches from life trimmed up after the sitter had left.

It was customary for visitors to call on women after childbirth, bringing pottery called *boli da puerpera*, or sets of dishes called *tazze de impagliata*, with gifts and light refresh-ments.[5] These pots would often be painted with the arms or badge of the family, set against a back-ground of flower patterns.

The best potteries were no longer dusty workshops centring on their kilns, surrounded by the equipment and waste-products of manufacture. Painters had to be able to work apart, undistracted, and their work had to be safely stored before going to the kilns. As it took longer to paint a vessel than to fashion it on the wheel, the painters came to outnumber the throwers and other artisans. Some part of the premises must have been kept in good enough order to receive clients, to record their instructions, show samples, and estimate costs. The artistic and social side of pottery-making was becoming as important by the late fifteenth century as the basic techniques of manufacture.

Old traditional potteries made a limited range of serviceable objects. There was no point in asking the owner for something special or different: it was simply not in his line. But the more versatile of the maiolica potteries were open to a new pressure: the imagination of their clients. They were asked for pottery for some specific use, for a certain occasion, or for a particular place in a certain building, and many of these ideas were found to interest other people too. Any designer will recognise what an enormous flood of new ideas this opened up. So many things are suggested almost accidentally by the private purposes of individuals in their ordinary lives, which even the most imaginative designer would never think of. These ideas now impinged, free of charge, on the maiolica potteries because they were adaptable. 'To him that hath, shall be given.'

The colouring of drawn designs on pottery led naturally to a development of the colours themselves. By the 1470s and 1480s Florence and the rapidly developing potter-ies of Faenza had achieved a rich palette which supplemented the basic copper green and manganese brown with several shades of cobalt blue, yellow and orange from mix-tures of antimony and iron, olive greens from copper and antimony, a turquoise blue from copper and soda, a mauve-purple from cobalt and manganese, and a variety of intermediate tones, all of which together enabled painters not only to colour line draw-

4 *World Ceramics*, plate 426.   5   M. Bellini, *Maioliche del Rinascimento* (Milan, 1964), pp. 25–27.

ings and patterns but to simulate relief and to achieve colour gradations and contrasts that opened up possibilities the Hispano-Moresque potters had never explored [Colour Plate K]. They made feasible the evolution of the full *istoriato* convention of the next century, but first they were put to the test in a variety of emblems and floral patterns, usually known as the 'Gothic-floral' style.

Once again the development came through line drawing. The stems of the plants were turned into spirals and arabesques, circles and other figures, to which formalised leaves and flowers and fruits were attached. The stems and some of the leaf patterns and garlands gave movement, and the flowers and fruits punctuated the rhythm with mass and colour. The motifs varied from stylised daisy-like flowers and lines and curling leaves reminiscent of some Persian decorations, to highly abstract forms such as the broad-leaf and split-leaf patterns which were special features of Faenza [62]. The floral motifs could easily be intermixed with other designs such as the Persian palmette and peacock feather pattern that appeared in Faenza pottery about 1470, and the wavy ray pattern associated with San Bernadino of Siena. Altogether the various elements were infinitely versatile and could be used as background or border to any line drawing on special pieces, or alone and in their own right on less important pots. The painters adapted them easily to any kind of shape and scale.

It is not surprising that the Gothic-floral convention became one of the most enduring of all influences on European pottery. It was a treasury of suggestions, many of which were followed up in the showpieces of the next century; yet it was also simple enough to become a long-lived pattern convention for standard decorative wares and to be adopted in countries whose potteries were not advanced enough to attempt line drawings or subject painting. Flemish, Dutch and English tin-glaze pottery of the seventeenth century all borrowed patterns from this Italian convention of a hundred and fifty years before. Later, in the peasant potteries of Central Europe, the fruit and flowers took on a new robust and fantastic life in swelling gourds and curling vine tendrils and the half-abstract forms of bursting flowers, lacking the control of the Italian originals, but still based on the moving line and static mass and enlivened by bright colours. The mood of these later versions was established by the potter-painters of Faenza and Florence. It is so familiar that we tend to take it for granted; however, it underlies the general European expectation that pottery decoration should be colourful, cheerful, encouraging, and be associated with pleasant life-giving experiences.

In Italy itself in the first three decades of the sixteenth century the Gothic-floral style underwent almost continuous change, particularly when it was associated as background or border with 'fine' ceramics including figure-subjects or scenes by an individual ceramic painter. Oriental blue and white porcelain was imported into Italy through Venice from the late fifteenth century onwards, and the Italian ceramists were, as one would expect, fascinated by a treatment of flower and leaf patterns which had much in common with their own. Venice and Faventine potteries began to produce intricate flower and leaf patterns in a palette limited to tones of blue, a direct reflection of the Far Eastern convention, known as *alla porcellana*. Some of these are amongst the most pleasing examples of all Italian maiolica. They achieved great delicacy without denying the form of ceramic vessels, and without becoming pretentious. The Italians absorbed the Chinese manner and married it to their own tradition. The result was a mode of painting that remained moving and alive, distinct from the affected *chinoiseries* of later times.

Another influence came from Turkish Isnik wares, that were also imported into Italy in considerable quantity. They already shared a common ancestry with the Gothic-floral style, and borrowings came naturally and easily. They are most clearly seen in Venetian and Paduan pottery in the elongation and refinement of leaves, in abstract designs based on flowers and seed-pods and in the further development of strong colour, which the Italians were already well able to pursue.

The third influence was that of the grotesques, that became a feature of many Italian decorative designs from about 1500 onwards and especially after the discovery of the ancient grotesques in the Golden House of Nero, which were used by Raphael[6] and made known by engravings of his work by Marcantonio Raimondi. Grotesques included exotic animals, masks, birds, mermaids, dolphins, canopies, cornucopias and garlands, and virtually any fantasy which came into the mind. The motifs of Gothic-floral style were made to twist and curl and twine in sympathy with the rest of the grotesque design. This had an effect on leaf and flower patterns even when they were used alone: after the coming of grotesques they became mannered and florid, rounded with the excess of autumn rather than the promise of spring. It became the standard mood of the leaf and flower decorations of the late sixteenth and seventeenth centuries, and appeared often in the painted tin-glaze wares of Savona and Castelli [72, 73].

All the decorative pottery just described, and the fully-painted ceramics of the early sixteenth century, have an underlying characteristic radically different from the Hispano-Moresque and Islamic tin-glaze wares from which they developed. It is the clarity of concept, the reasoned design, that underlies Italian work from the simplest repeats to the most elaborate special pieces. It shows itself in the rational arrangement of the painted design into zones or panels or other subdivisions of the total surface. But this is found in Hispano-Moresque wares also. In Italy the planning extended to minute subdivisions of subsidiary areas to a control of brushwork and colour that virtually eliminated any impromptu stroke, and to a methodical approach to the whole interplay of base-glaze, drawn design and polychrome painting. Even the line drawings of late fifteenth-century wares and the individual figures or *istoriato* paintings on sixteenth-century pottery seem to be carefully planed before a single stroke was made. Such mental clarity was never a feature of Hispano-Moresque work. The potter-painters of Spain were not disturbed, for instance, at juxtaposing painted zones, the one based on a sixfold repeating unit and the other on a repeat of four, entailing irregular references between them, and a central device with a repeat of three. In general, where Hispano-Moresque painters judged by eye, the Italians measured; where the former repeated a movement, the latter repeated the actual motif; where the former

6   In his paintings in the bathroom of Cardinal Bibbiena's suite in the Vatican. The word 'grotesque' comes from the 'grottoes' in which Roman paintings were discovered at about this time. The rooms where they were found lay underneath so much later building and rubble that they seemed like caves. See Peter Ward-Jackson, 'Some main streams and tributaries in European ornament from 1500 to 1750', Victoria and Albert Museum *Bulletin*', vol. III (1967), pp. 58–71.

started from an idea, the Italians followed a clear design.[7] Thus the Italians built up a method, a delicacy of composing and drawing, which the Hispano-Moresque potters never dreamed of.

The ingeniously planned hexagonal tiles of the church of San Petronio, Bologna, are examples of what has just been said. They were also a foretaste of things to come. They were made in 1487 in the workshop of Petrus Andrea of Faenza. There are more than a thousand unique tiles in this pavement, constituting a rich encyclopaedia of ideas and designs. Each tile has a central device surrounded by an elaborate border: masks, trophies, musical instruments, weapons, shields, badges and sacred emblems, fabulous beasts and weird fantasies. In them can be seen two of the main characteristics of Renaissance ceramics—painting on flat surfaces with the illusion of relief, achieved by clever use of tone, and the dependence of pottery-painting on themes from architecture, sculpture and painting. Both were essential attributes of the *stile bello* and the *stile istoriato*, terms which mean, broadly speaking, *maiolica* with striking and carefully designed decoration, and *maiolica* decorated with stories, allegories and historical scenes. The kind of painting that appeared first on the flat tiles of San Petronio was soon afterwards being done on the curved surfaces of all kinds of pottery.

The result was a new category of ceramics. The traditional forms and basic types of vessels became sometimes little more than a conventional vehicle or 'canvas' for fine ceramic painting. The luxury wares of the early sixteenth century belonged to a different family from even the most luxurious pieces of earlier ages, for they were intended to be collectors' pieces, furnishings for palaces and noble houses, objects of *virtù*, carriers of elevating themes, quite as much as to serve their nominal function.

It is true of many types of Italian maiolica, particularly so of large plates and dishes whose place in contemporary life is partly explained by the older convention of setting roundels and large tile-panels into walls in buildings. Mention has already been made of the custom of setting Islamic decorated dishes into architectural settings at a time when Italy herself produced nothing suitable for the purpose. Some of the most important commissions to Faenza workshops in the later fifteenth century were for commemorative decorated discs that could likewise be set into the walls of an important building honouring the founder or a benefactor. These discs often bore a coat of arms or an illustration of some religious subject, and some had only the pictorial theme, such as the medallions made in the della Robbia workshop in 1450–56 for the ceiling of the study of Piero de' Medici, now in the Victoria and Albert Museum.

Things which are set into walls are supposed to last for ever and require unique decoration of some special merit. The mural medallions were really very like large dishes. It was but a small step to change the idea to moveable plaques, and hence to decorated dishes proper, hung on the wall or supported on ledges. From this followed the show-piece-dish with important *istoriato* painting on it to embellish the interior of a private establishment. Some surviving dishes have letters or numbers on the back, showing that they belong to a series. Although they are pottery they are paintings as much as vessels, for they are descended from the decorated pictorial wall-tablet. They reached their greatest popularity between about 1510 and 1540.

7   Piccolpasso's *Arte del Vasaio* includes sketches of such designs. (See note 19.)

Because their importance was aesthetic, not functional, and because of the patronage they commanded, the painting of showpieces, dishes and other things could be done without regard to time or expense. The dominant historical, symbolical or poetic themes might take weeks to complete, and even the borders of grotesques, trophies, musical instruments or flower-and-leaf patterns were given a degree of attention which would have been unthinkable for the most ceremonial wares of earlier times.

Certain new qualities were expected in showpieces. Their designs should be more complex than ordinary pottery, their secrets should not be readily discovered, they should be enjoyable in large and in detail and the interest should grow with time. The work should also require a high degree of skill: it should be unique, impossible to reproduce. The conception should be original, dramatic and invigorating, both in its subject and in its execution. Above all, the themes should have the right overtones and affinities, such as could uplift or refresh or amuse the sensibilities of those whom Piccolpasso called 'men of lofty spirit and speculative minds'.

The classical Graeco-Roman heritage, its mythology, history and allegory, was therefore highly suitable subject-matter for generations who felt themselves to be spiritually the heirs of Greece and Rome. Christian imagery was also, of course, unexceptionable. It was usually 'classicised' by being set in landscapes or cities suggesting the ancient world. Scenes from popular life were also acceptable in a pastoral or idealised form, suggesting the solaces of carefree labour and the vitality of innocent minds. Though this list is over-simplified, it covers nine out of ten of the subject paintings on ceramics between 1500 and 1550.

Artists themselves were, of course, influenced just as much by the prevailing ideas as were their patrons. Potters, or rather pottery-painters, responded to these canons of taste not only to please their patrons but because their own aspirations led the same way. As often occurs in times of change, the way forward consists partly of stepping out of all the associations of the immediate past, and for ceramic painters of the year 1500 this meant going beyond repetition, utility and simplicity, and entering the world of the unique, imaginative work of art, backed up by technical skill and refined materials beyond those of popular ceramics. A man's dignity in his own eyes, as well as his future prosperity, might depend upon taking this jump.[8]

To do so, the potter or painter had to refer to themes and imagery which were not part of his background. Traditional religious imagery was familiar to him, and there were plenty of examples in mural paintings and sculptures. Classical mythology was not accessible except from engravings, books and privately owned paintings or sculpture. Hence it tended to be borrowed rather than re-created by the painter's own imagina-

8 Sir Anthony Blunt refers to the contemporary '. . . belief in superiority of the intellectual over the manual or mechanical, which corresponds to the desire of artists at this time to shake themselves free from the accusation of being merely craftsmen, manual labour being considered in the society of the Renaissance as ignoble as it had been in the Middle Ages. The pride which artists took in not being involved in much manual labour appears in the contrasted description which Leonardo gives of the sculptor and the painter. The former goes through an exhausting labour with hammer and chisel, is covered with dust and sweat so that he looks like a baker and not like an artist, whereas the painter sits in great comfort before his work, well dressed and wields his light brush loaded with lovely colours.' *Artistic Theory in Italy* (Oxford, 1940), pp. 54–55.

tion.[9] From this period begins the long history of derived designs, which dominated fine European ceramics until the early twentieth century. At first it was a necessity; later it became a habit, leading the painters to borrow designs from pattern books, engravings, mural painting and oriental pottery, instead of exercising their own imagination. By the mid nineteenth century the custom had become stagnant. Except for 'vulgar' and peasant pottery, almost everyone, potters and public alike, assumed that any decoration worth having must be derived from some work which was already admired. This had many ill effects, but it was not entirely a loss, for it introduced a wider range of figurative and decorative designs than pottery might otherwise have known, and it aroused the interest of a large public, much of which might otherwise not have reacted at all. Without such interest, many technical developments of porcelain, enamels and stonewares might never have come about, and pottery might have been relegated to the position of a humble craft, technically almost static, hardly touched by the ideas or needs of the rest of society.

Until about 1500 Italian tin glaze was dominated by Florence and Faenza. The workshops of Faenza devised the finest, whitest and most durable smooth and semi-matt tin glazes ever known, as well as a rich and reliable palette of subtle ceramic colours. They also devised the famous rich 'Faenza blue' glaze, and white and yellow pigments which were dense enough to be painted on this dark ground.

The Faenza potteries attracted artists whose working conditions allowed them to design and carry out special pieces quite outside the range of normal repeat wares. These painters began to initial or to sign their works, to inscribe them with some record of the time and place of completion. The practice was new in Italian pottery. It coincided with the appearance of the *stile bello* and indicates the value placed on individuality.

The skill and knowledge accumulated by the ceramists of Faenza seem to have reached bursting point by about 1500. Within a few years other workshops in many other towns were in active production, using materials and artistic styles that only a few years before had been virtually confined to Faenza and Florence. Some of these masters are known to have come from Faenza, and many others are thought to have done so. Maestro Benedetto di Giorgio, of Faenza, began working at Siena in 1503, and Giovanni Maria, formerly of Faenza, was using Faenza techniques and mannerisms in Casteldurante by 1508. Maestro Giorgio Andreoli, who became famous for his ruby and pearl lustres, is thought to have left Faenza for Gubbio in 1498. By the early years of the sixteenth century, fine tin-glaze wares were in full production in Cafaggiolo, Siena, Pisa, Casteldurante, Deruta, Gubbio and Venice, as well as in Faenza and Florence themselves.

Not more than a few of the Italian potteries were able to adapt themselves to the making of collectors' pieces, and these are the centres that are remembered today. Many potteries must have been too fully committed to production in quantity to make the change to the new aristocratic forms of painted pottery. For example, Orvieto, Viterbo and Ravenna had been well known for their potteries for several centuries, but they never became known for their showpieces. By contrast, the famous pottery in the Castle

9 The works of a large number of painters and engravers were used by pottery-painters. Amongst the most popular were Bramante, Mantegna, Raphael, Raimondi, Burkmair, Dürer and Schongauer.

of Cafaggiolo, administered by Pier Francesco de' Medici, was established about the year 1500 principally for producing wares of high prestige. Many of its artisans were gathered from the old-established potteries around the clay-beds of Montelupo. The painters and draughtsmen were probably drawn from Florentine workshops and were re-trained by the Fattorini family who managed the factory. As a result, the range of Cafaggiolo pottery styles was extensive and few common wares were made there.

The little town of Gubbio, which had produced serviceable domestic pottery for centuries, might never have become famous but for the arrival of Giorgio Andreoli, who set up the pottery which was to become one of the two great centres of Italian lustre ware. The fame of this town depended almost entirely on his initiative, which was acknowledged by special privileges and tax exemptions accorded to him first by the Duke of Urbino in 1498 and again by Pope Leo X in 1519, 'in consideration of the honour which redounds to the city, and to his overlords, and to the community from the popularity of these wares, in whatever land they are taken, and in consideration of their great profitableness and revenue.'[10] The same was true in other famous pottery centres also, although it was never so generously acknowledged.

The number of towns celebrated for their pottery remains bewildering. It may be helpful to give a list of the principal pottery centres of the period 1440–1650, with a brief description of their work:

Orvieto   Centre of a medieval pottery area; well known in the fourteenth and early fifteenth centuries for tin-glaze wares painted in green and brown in Gothic and Near Eastern styles. Maiolica was produced in later times, but seldom achieved originality or renown.

Siena   Active pottery centre from the thirteenth century until modern times. Flourished particularly in the first half of the sixteenth century, and was famous for delicately painted tiles and pavements. Siena developed a light, delicate decoration of flowers and grotesques, often on coloured grounds, which was used either alone or with religious and other figures to decorate pottery vessels.

Florence   Pottery was made from at least the fourteenth century onwards. Finely painted green and brown wares (*c*. 1420–50) and 'relief blue' jars and pitchers led to the development of the polychrome Gothic floral style and line drawings on pottery, reaching its finest expression about 1480, but continuing in the fifteenth century. The della Robbia workshop in Florence probably influenced potteries towards undertaking individual pieces with unique figurative designs. Ordinary wares made in Florence are hard to distinguish from those of the whole area around the Montelupo clay-beds.

Cafaggiolo   A centre for early Tuscan tin-glaze wares. From about 1495 a workshop controlled by Pierfrancesco de Medici specialised in fine maiolica. Under the Fattorini family Cafaggiolo made some of the most richly coloured and designed pictorial wares with historical, allegorical and religious themes, and grotesques, but by 1550 the work was no longer distinctive.

10   G. Liverani, op. cit., pp. 46–47.

Faenza   Green and brown tin-glazed pottery was produced by or before 1400, similar to that of Orvieto and related to the work of Paterna. Faenza workshops developed rapidly around the middle of the fifteenth century, and by 1470 had become the most prolific of all Italian producers. The last quarter of the fifteenth century saw immense technical developments in Faenza, above all the perfection of pigments and opaque glazes, both white and coloured. Faenza led the way with many new decorative conventions such as the famous peacock-feather eye pattern, palmette and flower patterns, figures of men and animals, classical features from architecture and sculpture, and the first examples of the *istoriato* style. The most famous of its many workshops was Casa Pirota, which excelled in *bianco sopra bianco* on a blue ground. Piccolpasso referred in 1558 to Faenza as 'occupying the first place for its pottery'. It is an important centre today.

Padua   Pottery was produced during the fifteenth century, mostly common wares, *sgraffiato* slip ware, but probably also green and brown painted tin-glaze wares. Continued as a minor pottery centre in the sixteenth and seventeenth centuries, producing some *istoriato* ware and floral decoration derived from Isnik originals.

Deruta   A pottery centre from medieval times to the present day. Flourished about 1490–1550, producing some remarkable 'portrait' dishes and vigorous decoration of a broad and simple kind not made elsewhere. Specialised in a colour range dominated by orange, yellows and blue, often in combination with iridescent yellow or pearly lustre. Was probably the first Italian area to produce lustre of any kind, about 1500. Declined after about 1550.

Gubbio   Produced pottery from the fourteenth century onwards. Became important from 1498 onwards with the arrival of Giorgio Andreoli, who specialised in lustre of ruby red and pearly silver, and whose family continued working at Gubbio until the mid-sixteenth century. Gubbio developed moulded and gadrooned forms specially for use with lustre from about 1530 onwards. Still a pottery town today.

Casteldurante and Urbino   A pottery area from medieval times, made famous in the sixteenth century by the pottery-painters Giovanni Maria, Nicola Pellipario, Orazio Fontana, Francesco Avelli and by Cipriano Piccolpasso, author of the *Arte del Vasaio*. By the mid-sixteenth century these two adjacent towns made an immense quantity of pottery, rivalled only by Faenza. They were famed particularly for grotesques and elaborate classical *istoriato* dishes. About 1550 Urbino developed a highly elaborate ware with moulded decoration and intricate polychrome painting.

Venice   Produced pottery from about 1500 onwards. Middle and Far Eastern influence shows in designs based on flowers and foliage rather than on classical imagery, notably in the patterns known as *alla porcellana*, often on a glaze stained soft blue or mauve (*berretino*).

Palermo   Produced luxury wares in middle and later sixteenth century, often derived from Urbino originals, but with a provincial vigour which makes some of the examples remarkable. Continued throughout most of the seventeenth century.

Castelli   Produced pottery from the sixteenth century onwards, becoming famous in the seventeenth century for a revived form of the *istoriato* style in a light and cool range of colours. A prolific source of elegant and formal decorative pieces, somewhat limited in their aesthetic range.

Montelupo   A centre for common wares from at least the fifteenth century onwards. By about 1600 Montelupo was producing a tin-glazed ware of rather rough quality, interesting for its vigorous, sometimes wild figures from popular life.

Apart from special pieces wholly carried out by a master painter, the *stile bello* usually resulted in pottery painted with a dominant theme or subject that occupied the centre of bowls and dishes, or a proud position on vases, jugs and pitchers and other hollow wares. Around this theme was a carefully contrived border which emphasised the principal scene. The convention lent itself best to bowls and dishes, such as the *tondino*, made in great quantity in Faenza, particularly at the beginning of the sixteenth century. The small rounded well of this type of dish was a perfect setting for small subject-paintings, and the broad, flat rim invited elaborate border patterns [66]. The *tondini* of Faenza were mostly painted in deep blue and tin-white over a tin glaze stained with cobalt which thus provided an opaque medium-blue background [69]. As a rule, subject-painting was less happily applied to vases and other hollow shapes, because the medallion or lozenge painted with the subject was distorted by the roundness of the vessel, except when seen directly from in front. The painted ornament could not be seen all at once and the more elaborate the decoration the more it was at odds with the form.

Collectors' pieces of the early sixteenth century were chiefly shallow platters and dishes with plenty of scope for painted decoration [71]. Most were meant to hang on walls and were never intended for use. The more important the painting became the more the features of the form tended merely to be a nuisance. For this reason the late dishes for full-scale *istoriato* painting were shallow, concave shapes without pronounced rims, over which the subject could spread uninterruptedly.[11] Except for tile panels, the forms of Italian maiolica were still derived from serviceable pottery even when they were used as a 'canvas' and intended only for ornament. No new forms were devised specially for ceramic painting, although this would have been natural. It was a result of the division of labour in the potteries between the artisans who made the pots and 'artists' who painted them. The artists were seldom concerned with the working of the clay. They worked in a place apart, using bisque ware which was selected from the general production. Standard painted designs were worked out to agree with the established shapes, but the unique designs of master-painters were often at odds with them.

It was no accident that the fine ceramics of the High Renaissance were dominated by architecture, painting and literature, with engravings and book illustrations as intermediaries. It does not reflect servitude on the part of artists and craftsmen to their patrons nor does it indicate any weakness in ceramic traditions. Rather it was a sign of their adaptability. It was an essential part of the 'ennoblement' of ceramics in the contempor-

11   It is strange that rims continued, even though again and again they were obviously a nuisance to the painters.

ary climate of thinking. The thrill of being able to translate a story or a picture into a painted dish still lives on in some of the finest work of the period, as in the Faenza bowl painted with the Death of the Virgin, based on a famous engraving by Martin Schongauer (1445–1491) [Colour Plate I]. This perfect and delicate piece is an appropriate tribute to the master-engraver whom the Italians called 'Bel Martino'. The painted dish seems to have existed eternally rather than to have been fashioned by human hands at some point in time, the more so because all the materials have been transformed by fire since the painter laid them on.

The transformation of materials by fire is part of the appeal of all ceramics, whether seen in the hard scorched clays and fire-bitten surfaces of some modern work or, at the other extreme, in perfect and almost indestructible line and colour in Italian maiolica. The obliteration of the making process in the transformation by fire fascinated people. Indeed, the 'concealment of the art', a concealment which belongs essentially to ceramics, was more fully in accord with some Renaissance ideals of art even than painting itself.

Incidentally, this may be in part the motive behind Luca della Robbia's transition from marble to tin-glazed sculpture about 1440, a time when the Florentine potteries were sensing the possible future of tin glaze as an artistic medium. The della Robbia figures and reliefs retain such a feeling of freshness and transformation to this day. Many people have stood before a della Robbia glazed statue in a reserved state of mind, because the material is unfamiliar on a big scale and stone is conventionally considered preferable. Slowly the strangeness has been replaced by a real response to the figure as it actually is: it has a unique clarity and radiance, to which the key lies in the sense of transformation. Luca della Robbia and his nephew Andrea have an important place in the tin-glaze tradition as the first and finest artists to use the material for serious sculpture [61]. Others tried to follow their example in the seventeenth and eighteenth centuries, but no-one else achieved statues of the same commanding artistic, technical and spiritual standing. Under Andrea's sons the workshop also made a number of apothecaries' vessels, as well as statues and tile reliefs. The pottery was mostly covered with the blue-stained *berretino* glaze, whereas the statues were given the densest possible white.[12]

The special pieces made at Cafaggiolo, Siena, Casa Pirota in Faenza, Casteldurante, etc., were labours of love, made possible by dependable patronage. The special pieces made before about 1535 are generally unique in conception and are finished with craftsmanship of the highest standard. The assurance of the finest pieces sometimes disguises the skill and forethought which went into them. The difficulties which were mastered only become apparent in works of second quality, where defects of composition or drawing spoil a complex idea, or the irregular laying-on of colour, roughness of texture, or imperfections of glaze or firing remind one of the vigilance that the finest work required at every stage.

Not until around 1540 did the *stile bello* begin to belie its name. It was becoming too popular for the old standard to be maintained. This was most evident at Urbino, which from this time forward started to dominate the market for pottery with classical subjects. Under Orazio Fontana and his sons and the gentleman-ceramist, Xanto Avelli, a

12   J. Giacomotti, op. cit., pp. 9, 11, 41–42.

team of subject-painters worked up a market for battle scenes and dramatic events of
ancient history and mythology, the death of heroes, the fall of cities, the martyrdoms of
saints, the rivalries and romances of classical deities. Avelli's own work is lucid and defined, with a personal style and a pronounced interest in the subject-matter,[13] but the
productions of his followers were uninspiring; their routine palette of colours allowed
little feeling for the atmosphere of the subject and little individuality of idea, so that the
themes become difficult to recognise and remember, for it was not they so much as the
general effect and its associations that mattered. Some of the *istoriato* pieces of the mid-
century are memorable largely for their pretentious absurdity, the bulging thighs of
generals in unreliable armour; overweight winged messengers of victory; Roman
noblemen and matrons gesturing dramatic clichés to very blue skies. However, greatly
improved *istoriato* wares, with the figurative painting lightened by a design combining
subject-themes and grotesques, came from the workshop of Antonio Patanazzi in the
last quarter of the century [72].

About 1550 Urbino began to add elaborate modelling to the urns, tureens and chargers and other vessels that were by now so famous. Since the modelled as well as the
plain surfaces were usually painted, the effect was often overwhelming, and sometimes
amounted to little more than a display of ceramic dexterity, such as occurs frequently in
the history of ceramics and glass when great technical skill is not guided by real feeling
or a new idea. Lack of vitality is never really disguised by contrivance, yet almost every
ceramic style resorts to this expedient in its decline.

As has been said, the ceramics of the High Renaissance depended a great deal on
imported suggestions from architecture, painting and literature, especially on engravings of the works of Raphael, Mantegna, Lucas van Leyden and Dürer, and on book
illustrations. Some of these derivative themes were impressive as, for example, the
Pesaro dish painted with a battle between the Israelites and the Amorites [71]. There
was nothing wrong with borrowing from other works of art; borrowing, knowingly or
unaware, acknowledged or secret, has been general practice in all the arts from time
immemorial and is an essential part of all human activity. The danger was that ceramists should be content simply to imitate, to lean on the imagination of others instead of
heeding the suggestions of their own medium. In a general sense this is what happened,
but the work of lasting importance came from individuals who responded imaginatively
to ceramic forms and materials, who did not merely translate ideas into ceramics but
were able to think in terms of ceramic materials. From many examples it is only possible
in the scope of this chapter to mention a few workshops and individuals[14] who achieved
this in different ways.

Giovanni Maria probably served his apprenticeship in Faenza, and then moved to
Casteldurante, where he was working when he completed and signed his famous dish
with the arms of Pope Julius II.[15] A number of other dishes in the same style, with the

13   E.g. his large plate in the Wallace Collection (No. 82), representing a Marine Triumph, dated 1533
and signed *Fra: Xanto A. da Rovigo i Urbino.*
14   See Liverani, op. cit., p. 43 *et seq* and Rackham, op. cit.
15   Now in the Metropolitan Museum. New York. (See colour frontispiece in Liverani, *Five Centuries of
Italian Maiolica.*) This dish is the only one which actually bears the name of Giovanni Maria.

I. Dish painted with the Death of the Virgin. About 27 cm wide. Faenza, about 1510–15. The composition comes from an engraving by the Bavarian Martin Schongauer (1445–91), known in Italy as 'Bel Martino'. The development of new blends of pigments, and above all the slowly-acquired ability to control tone-values, made possible the 'elevation' of ceramics to the status of a minor Fine Art. Whoever rendered this engraving in maiolica was not only a superb copyist but also a ceramic painter of phenomenal skill, for he had to allow for the considerable change the tones and colours would undergo in the firing. *British Museum. See page 95.*

L. Small jug with a strap-like handle. About 10 cm high. Faenza, late 15th century. Everyone loved maiolica : the showpieces which are the pride of collectors today are only one of its faces. One and the same workshop might make sophisticated dishes decorated with ancient mythology and also simple jugs like this, which are now rare because they were used until they broke. The Faenza colours are as important here as anywhere else. *Fitzwilliam Museum, Cambridge (Leverton Harris Bequest). See page 83.*

M. Large dish painted with the Adoration of the Magi. About 45 cm wide. Probably Nevers, about 1660. A showpiece in which the dish is treated like a canvas, with a composition based on an engraving, but considerably simplified, so that the painting has a feeling of its own and does not just imitate oil painting. The leading Nevers *faiencerie* belonged to Italians, and prided itself on working in the Italian grand manner, even long after that vein ceased to be fashionable. *City Museum, Hanley, Stoke-on-Trent. See page 113.*

N. Large oval dish with dragon handles. 50 cm long. Rouen, about 1730. Elegant tableware was needed for use as well as for ornament, and it challenged the pottery-painters for something impressive but essentially trivial, appropriate to a banquet. From this need developed the idea of 'decoration' as a fanciful and traditions of decorated pottery. This joyful and humorous dish makes good use of the high temperature colours developed by Rouen potters about 1720, and manages to be ephemeral yet still vigorous. The dark *trek* or contour-drawing of the lovers in the landscape is just detectable through the camaïeu blue. *Victoria and*

O. Tureen painted in enamel colours. 46 cm long. Marseilles,
Veuve Perrin or Bonnefoy factory, about 1770. Enamels painted on
the fired glaze made possible a finer line and closer control of tone
than could be achieved by painting on the unfired glaze. They also
offered a more generous range of colours, especially reds, pinks
and crimsons, such as the 'purple of Cassius' which appears on
this example. Enamelled vessels had to be fired a third time in a
muffle-kiln, and all enamelled wares of any size were essentially
luxuries. Several factories in Marseilles specialised in marine landscape and still-life decoration. For those who had no need to count
the cost, fine pottery was essential to gracious living. *Victoria and
Albert Museum. See page 123.*

P. Plate. 24 cm wide painted in high temperature and enamel
colours. Mark in blue, VE, for Lambert van Eenhoorn. The back of
the plate is painted with flowers and scrollwork. Delft, early 18th
century. Nothing has been spared to make this piece exquisite. For
years the Dutch had been challenged by Chinese achievements in
porcelain. Now they responded to Japanese porcelain also, and the
centre of this plate shows the influence of both *famille verte* and
kakiemon enamels. The mark is surprising: only a few factories
used the enamel and gilding techniques, and the van Eenhoorn
factory, the Metal Pot, is usually thought not to have done so.
Museum für Kunsthandwerk, Frankfurt am Main. See page 135.

same mannerisms, can reasonably be attributed either to Giovanni Maria personally or to his workshop. He had a dramatic sense of composition which belonged much more to the tradition of pottery painting than to painting and sculpture. He could build up ingenious structures of figures and grotesques and other classical emblems without losing touch with the overall form of the vessel. In some ways his style was conservative, for he emphasised the silhouettes of figures and only suggested the third dimension. It gave his figures a certain stiffness but strengthened their symbolic or emblematic importance [70]. His decorative sense enabled him to bring together features of different size and scale as if a mysterious wind were supporting and animating all the elements in the design. His colour was traditional, too, following the old ceramic convention of local rather than representational colour. The colour was sometimes very restrained, chosen to create a mood, not simply to make a decoration. He went beyond tradition in creating compositions with an atmosphere of magnificence based on human figures and Renaissance emblems, and yet his work was essentially a ceramic mode of expression.

In contrast to the grand manner of Giovanni Maria, Sienese pottery was usually painted with decorative drawing filled in with restrained colours, combined with subject illustrations so fine that they are virtually ceramic miniatures. They were usually carefully worked and the glaze and the forms of vessels still played an important part in the overall effect. It was pottery-painting rather than painting-on-pottery. Sienese workshops seem to have followed a unique course, avoiding the heavyweight style of subject painting and much of the repertory of classical themes that became customary in other centres. Religious imagery was used more than in other places, mostly in simple compositions with a few figures or a single figure against a lightly suggested background. Sienese pottery painting has much in common with manuscript illumination, the circular thrown vessels being a kind of three-dimensional frame around the principal painted subject. Some beautiful decoration was done in the *alla porcellana* style. More often the ornament was of light grotesques and garlands which, seen from a distance, made a series of repeating rhythms, and if examined in detail were found to be full of engaging fantasy. Such a mode of ceramic painting is associated with Maestro Benedetto, from whose workshop, possibly by his own hand, came the small blue and grey dish of St. Jerome [65].

There is not enough evidence to show whether this light style was Benedetto's own personal invention, later adopted by neighbouring workshops, or whether he was simply the best-known of a group of master potters who evolved together this form of ceramic painting, characteristic of its age and yet true to the nature and traditions of their craft.

The names of the painter-potters of Deruta are not recorded. Their individuality is shown in a number of works of different style. From these can be inferred at least three master painters, each original in design and technique, yet well-versed in the tradition of pottery painting.

Deruta produced a great variety of grotesques, floral and garland patterns, histories and heraldic designs [64], but amongst them a large number of pieces which were curiously different from all other Italian ceramics of the same period, because of the frequent use of yellow and pearly lustre, the restricted colour schemes, usually yellow, orange, grey-green and blue, the simplicity of its drawing and the clear, large-scale patterns that were used to surround its subject-painting. The pottery of Deruta and Siena could hardly be more unlike. Yet both were essentially ceramic versions of the art of the Renaissance, and such borrowings as were made from other arts were fully assimilated into the pottery tradition of each place.

From Deruta came a number of fine dishes painted with the bust of a beautiful young woman accompanied by an inscription on a scroll. Most of them are painted in lustre, and they are fully evolved successors of the ceramic drawings of the late fifteenth century [Colour Plate J]. Another Deruta painter seems to have specialised in classical subjects, carefully drawn bold designs painted so as to emphasise or even exaggerate the sense of relief in subject themes and ornament, a mannerism that can all too easily conflict with the form of the vessel, but here done with such mastery that it succeeds.

Deruta potters dared to work large and use simple emblems and strong border patterns without 'refining' them by the use of superficial detail. The result is a strong, consistent style in each piece which is, as a whole, often more truly 'refined' than work with much more polish and sophistication. Its merit was evidently recognised by the Medici, for there are a number of Deruta pieces with their coat of arms.

Lustre was regularly used only at Deruta and Gubbio, and although Deruta lustre owed more to Hispano-Moresque wares than any other kind of Italian maiolica, the Italian use of lustre was different from that of Spain. Because Italian ceramic painting was based on line-drawn profiles, lustre was not used except for colouring or filling in patterns and representations that were already outlined, or for making a background. As a result the lustred dishes are relatively formal; the mind readily perceives the plan and the eye tends not to explore the design as it does Spanish work. Although the Italians got the idea of lustre from Spain, the beautiful silver yellows of Deruta and the pearly-silver and ruby lustres of Gubbio were very different from Spanish effects and must have been made from different recipes, and were possibly fired differently.

Nicola Pellipario worked at Casteldurante in the period 1516–1528 and later at Urbino. In his work the *istoriato* style reached the extreme of three-dimensional drawing and colour, the shallow bowls and dishes being used as miniature canvases for the painting of pictures [66]. Pellipario's drawing was sometimes weak and his themes were frequently derived from engravings, a special favourite being an edition of Ovid's *Metamorphoses* published in 1498. He achieved a control of tone and a richness of colour which have never been rivalled, and with it a mood of nostalgic enchantment all his own.[16] The rich hues of his receding landscapes and evening skies, the columns and architraves of classical buildings which often appear in his composition, seem almost impossibly unsuitable subjects for painting on concave ceramic forms, and it is strange that Pellipario managed to render them at all. Only his extraordinary skill could overcome the inevitable conflict between the natural depth of pottery vessels and the illusionistic depth achieved by painting. However, his best work was done when not undertaking a *tour de force*. Some of his smaller, simpler pieces are perfect and satisfying because of their very restraint and the mastery of what is left out as well as what is depicted.

The painted pottery of Venice was affected by her imports, especially by Isnik ware

16   e.g. the dinner service made for Isabella d'Este, now scattered, and the Ridolfo service in the Correr Museum, Venice.

from Turkey, but also to some extent by pottery from Persia and the Far East. The monumental idea of pottery which had led to derivations from painting and sculpture and architecture had less force in Venice in the sixteenth century than elsewhere. Some exquisite *alla porcellana* painting in blue on a softly blued *berretino* tin glaze was made in Venice in the 1520s and 1530s. Venetian workshops developed some strong ornaments in which freely painted fruit and leaves predominated, with deep blues and greens and a palette that was unusually restrained [67]. Piccolpasso includes a sketch of a fruit-design in his book with the comment: 'These are really Venetian styles of painting, very pretty things, and cost 5 lire a hundred'. The best-known Venetian workshops were those of Iacomo da Pesaro and Maestro Lodovico which flourished in the period 1540–60. The Venetian potteries concentrated on decorative rather than pictorial ornament, and even when pictorial themes and landscapes were borrowed from engravings they tended to be reinterpreted into the light, mobile brushstrokes of the pottery painter, and into ceramic rather than naturalistic colours.

From about 1560 the mood of Italian maiolica changed. After so much emphasis on painting and subject-matter a reaction was almost bound to follow. The new styles depended on elaboration of refined forms, often derived from metalwork, covered with a very fine, white tin glaze called by Piccolpasso 'Ferrara White', with light brush decoration and quickly sketched figures, known as the *stile compendiario* or 'abridged style'. This may have reflected some change in the taste of patrons but it was equally a result of the conditions in pottery workshops. Many of the elaborately painted vessels required skilful work that could not be hurried. In some Urbino work of the mid-sixteenth century the painters were obviously under too much pressure. The market was now large and no longer restricted to wealthy people and connoisseurs, and the established conventions of maiolica could only be produced slowly.[17] Responding to the challenge of the large market, designers turned their attention to the forms rather than the painting. By using moulds for vessels with undulating surfaces, ribbed sides, shell-edges, relief ornament, openwork sides or modelled lids and handles, a workshop could produce large numbers of pieces from a single, carefully designed prototype, and since the interest resided largely in the form the painting could be light and rapid.

The workshops of Vergiliotto Calamelli and Leonardo Bettisi at Faenza led the way with these white so-called *crespina* wares about 1550. Similar work was soon afterwards produced in Rome, and the Ligurian potteries, especially Albisola and Savona, were famous for it in the following century. At first the brushwork was meaningful and careful; it was at its best in deftly sketched figures, grotesques and coats of arms. The calligraphic style of painting was spirited but it easily became facile. The drama and enterprise which lay behind the original pictorial work of fifty years earlier were soon to be found only in the popular pieces made in relatively unsophisticated workshops such as those of Montelupo [74, 75]. Elsewhere they were replaced by the manufacture of congenial ornaments for interior decoration. Though the fundamental technique of tin-glaze ware remained the same as ever, these later productions no longer had the magnanimity of the

17   One of the latest exponents of the Renaissance spirit in pottery painting was Antonio Lolli of Castelli, who painted *istoriato* dishes in the early seventeenth century and still managed to give them the time and attention they needed.

best maiolica; they had a slighter mood which eventually became associated with a new name, *faience*, rather than *maiolica*.[18]

This chapter cannot close without paying homage to the writer of the charming and unique book, *The Book of the Potter's Art*, in which the 'secrets' of the tin-glaze potters are unforgettably recorded.

The *Arte del Vasaio*[19] of the Cavaliere Cipriano Piccolpasso, the earliest detailed manual on European pottery, was written about 1558. Composed in an engaging and highly personal style, sustained by a gale of enthusiasm for the famous pottery industry of his homeland, it describes the methods and recipes used in making fine, painted pottery in the writer's native city of Urbino. It is based on first-hand observation and discussion, and is lovingly illustrated. It is a unique sounding of the state of Italian pottery manufacture of the time [173–177].

Piccolpasso's professed aim is to reveal the technical basis of a craft which had hitherto been passed on by demonstration and word of mouth from master to pupil, father to son, and whose 'secrecy' had been too closely guarded. Some masters, he says, will only 'at the point of death call to themselves their eldest and wisest son, and publish to him this secret amongst the other goods which they leave behind'. Piccolpasso claims that his book will open the craft to new ideas and wider scientific knowledge, enabling it to achieve new greatness.

The art has remained amongst persons of small consideration. . . . Now it will pass into courts, amongst lofty spirits and speculative minds.

Despite his enthusiasm, Piccolpasso underestimated the depth of traditional knowledge passed on and increased generation by generation. Like many others, even in our own day, he did not fully appreciate that skill of hand and experience of materials may be harder to acquire than theoretical knowledge or new ideas. He also seems unaware that the great age of Italian maiolica was already over, and that the prosperous potteries of Urbino were by this time producing rather decadent, commercialised versions of vessels which had been pioneered by the 'lofty spirits' of the previous generation. From a technical point of view, however, his book is more valuable for coming at the end of a period of rapid development rather than in the middle, for by his time many new methods and recipes had become normal practice in the Italian potteries.

Piccolpasso describes first the digging of the chalky clay that was specially needed for tin-glaze wares, a clay which, because of its high calcium content, fires almost white, is light in weight and shrinks in cooling so that glazes do not easily craze on it. Kitchen pottery, he says, is made of coarse, red clay which is heavier and (though he does not say so) will cause crazing in most maiolica glazes because it shrinks relatively little as it cools. He describes the construction and operation of potters' wheels, driven by direct action of the foot on the fly-wheel as is still usual in much of the Continent of Europe. He illustrates the convex wheelheads known as *scudella* and *mugiolo* that allow the potter

18   For later Italian maiolica see Oreste Ferrari, *Maiolica Italiana del seicento a settecento*, Milan, 1965.
19   *Li tre Libri dell'Arte del Vasaio*, facsimile edition with the original Italian and a translation by Bernard Rackham and A. van der Put (London, Victoria and Albert Museum, 1934).

to shape the underside of vessels right down to the foot, and, surprisingly, are now almost unknown. He shows the turning tools and wire bows used for trimming and cutting clay, ribbers for shaping or smoothing vessels as they are thrown on the wheel, and a variety of potters' tools, many of which have changed little in four hundred years and still have a place even in modern factories.

He describes the building, packing and firing of the up-draught kiln, which resembles some kilns used today in Spain and the Eastern Mediterranean area [175]. The fire enters a long chamber whose perforated arches form the floor of the kiln itself. In the fire-chamber are placed the earthenware jugs of glaze materials for calcination or 'fritting'. The pottery is packed for glazing in saggars (circular clay boxes which protect it from the flame) that are stacked over the arches up to the beginning of the vault. Large pieces each have a saggar to themselves; plates and small bowls are placed upside-down, with their rims supported by spurs which protrude through triangular holes in the sides of the saggars. The corners of the chamber and the spaces above and between the saggars are filled with raw unglazed pots for biscuit-firing, and with cheap vessels which are glazed only on the insides. The flames enter the kiln through the holes in the floor, rising around the saggars, and the draught escapes through holes in the vault. These holes can be blocked or opened to direct the heat to one or another part of the kiln, for there will always be variations in temperature because of the uneven distribution of the ware in the kiln. The temperature of the kiln and maturity of the glaze is judged by the degree of reflection or 'brightness' of the glaze when a burning stick is held alongside the pots on the end of an iron rod.

'Maiolica', by which Piccolpasso means lustre, is fired in a small kiln 'because the art is so uncertain that often out of a hundred pieces of ware hardly six are good'. The kiln is constructed to allow smoke to pass amongst the painted pots in the last hour of the firing when the fuel is changed from willow to broom [176, 177]. Broom creates a reducing atmosphere that breaks down the maiolica pigments to reflecting metal. 'When these wares are good', says Piccolpasso, 'they are paid for in gold'.

The book describes, too, the preparation of glazes from lead, tin, wine lees, salt and sand or flint, and the mixing and calcination of pigments. For both Piccolpasso gives various recipes that have evolved in different pottery centres. The pigments he mentions are all derived from the following metals: tin, antimony, copper, lead, iron, manganese, cobalt and mercury, the last being used only for 'maiolica'. The tin metal, whose oxide was the vital whitening agent for all the painted wares, was purchased from Flanders but originated in Cornwall. Considering the cost of tin as well as the labour involved in preparing the glazes and pigments, it is not surprising that all through his book Piccolpasso is keenly aware of the big distinction between white painted wares (*vasi*) and common domestic pottery (*pignatti*), unpainted and finished only with clear glazes (*marzacotto*).

At the end of the book Piccolpasso shows drawings of some of the best known types of designs for painted dishes which had, by this time, evolved into familiar conventions with fixed prices, which he also gives [174]. He uses the current trade names: 'trophies', 'arabesques' (*rabeschi*), 'oakleaves', 'grotesques' ('which have now been almost discarded, I do not know why'), 'leaf-pattern', 'flowers', 'fruits', 'landscapes', *porcellana*, 'strapwork', *bianco sopra bianco*, 'quarters', 'knots' and 'candelabra'. It is interesting that he does not mention subject-painting, heraldry or portraits—probably because these were special pieces painted only by specialist masters and were outside the normal pottery production.

Piccolpasso's book shows the high level of organisation and technical ingenuity that had become customary in Italian potteries by the middle of the sixteenth century, and many processes strikingly close in principle to modern industrial methods. Already, by his time, potteries occupied a middle place between the personal workshop and the factory; the source of power, of course, was still primitive, and the muscular Renaissance artisans, the donkeys and the waterwheels which milled the materials add greatly to the interest of Piccolpasso's illustrations. The book is a fascinating glimpse of details of pottery-making which had existed for centuries but had never before been recorded; for instance, the cross-laminated boards of the fly-wheel which the throwers worked with their feet, the shapes of the irons on the vertical shaft to which the wheelhead was fixed, the manner of making brushes, the various shapes of ribbers and turning tools, the calcination of wine-lees and the stirring of molten lead and tin to make 'tin ash' for the glazes, the construction of cranks and mill-wheels for grinding glazes and pigments, the manner of holding vessels for applying glaze by dipping or pouring and a host of other details that call immediately on the personal experience of any practising potter and remind him that there are few new things under the sun.

Piccolpasso's second book closes on an even older subject:

I am seeking in these last years of my youth to free myself from the trammels of love and I act like the bird that has caught its feet in the snare which, thinking to free itself, gets entangled in it with wings and feathers. . . . The more I have sought to rise above thoughts of love by compounding a lead and tin, full often in my mind the well proportioned limbs of my fair beloved compounded themselves; not any colour could I find that for lustre or brilliance can be compared to her fair tresses. . . . When I came to the Duke of Ferrara's mixture, resembling silver, it appeared to me black, rough and harsh beside her soft arms and dainty hands . . . Love causeth a man to disobey him who counsels to prudence. He nourisheth thee ever on hopes and unpleasing pleasures and giveth thee for guide and leader, vain desire; and yet with all this I am not able to discern a more beautiful state than that of love . . .

7

THE SPREAD OF MAIOLICA

Maiolica from Italy was traded to most of the large cities of Europe and sold without difficulty because it was quite different from the brown earthenware people were used to. The so-called Italian colours, cobalt blue, copper green, Naples yellow and orange-ochre, impressed Northern Europe as Islamic pottery had impressed Spain: maiolica was a new idea as well as a new kind of pottery. The colours and pictorial decoration belonged less to the kitchen and the beer-house than to the world of books, pictures, tapestries and wall-paintings, and a high proportion of the early exported pieces found their way to palaces or merchants' houses and were either ornamental or for ceremonial use.

Where their work found a good reception, the potters themselves soon followed. Just as the ceramists of Faenza had left their crowded workshops at the end of the fifteenth century and spread over half of Italy, so, during the next fifty years, the Italians dispersed into Europe.[1] The commissions which were being offered by the patrons of the northern countries were more easily satisfied by craftsmen and designers on the spot than by dealings at a distance. True, the Venetians carried on a considerable trade in commissioned pieces with Nürnberg and South Germany through most of the sixteenth century,[2] but the cities had close connections anyway, and the special pieces were fairly small. There were great advantages in being on the spot, and many of the things desired by patrons would have been hard to transport. They were interested in tiles for walls and pavements, and most often sets of jars for pharmacies, hospitals, monasteries, private houses and apothecaries' shops. Pharmacy vessels needed to look clean and they had to be marked reassuringly with the names of their contents, and often they had to bear the arms of the donor or of the institution they belonged to. A well equipped pharmacy needed hundreds of vessels. Such work assured the enterprising maiolica craftsman of a reasonable chance of a livelihood from the start, and the market was likely to grow.

Thus, until the late sixteenth century the making of tin-glazed earthenware was dominated by Italian styles, and in most places by Italian artisans and artists.[3] Only by

1 For the diffusion of the maiolica technique generally, see J. Giacomotti, *La Majolique de la Renaissance* (Paris, 1961), chapters V and VI.
2 e.g. a service dating from about 1520, some pieces of which are now in the Kunstgewerbe Museum, Berlin, bearing the arms of two Nürnberg families, Imhof and Schlaudersbach. Other examples are in the Wallace Collection, London.
3 Bernard Rackham, *Early Netherlands Maiolica* (London, 1926), gives detailed information about the spread of maiolica in Flanders, Holland, and into Germany. On p. 49 he quotes the application of one Johannes Guldens for privilege in starting a maiolica pottery explicity in the Italian manner. 'Italico more', in Hamburg in the late sixteenth century. 'The applicant is without equal in Antwerp or any region of Lower Germany in the making of wares either white or decorated with stories or figures in colours.'

the later part of the century did regional styles begin to develop, and even then they emerged from a groundwork of Italian example. From Italy the new movement spread out in four principal directions: to Spain first of all; then to France, where several pottery centres grew up by 1570; thirdly to Flanders, and thence to Portugal, Holland and England; fourthly to Switzerland and from there to South Germany, Bohemia, Moravia, Slovakia and eventually even to Russia. In each locality the Italian conventions met with different conditions, and eventually developed in different ways.

A full account of all the changes that the tin-glaze tradition underwent in each land would require an encyclopaedic treatment which is out of place here. Furthermore, it would overemphasise the later history of tin glaze, since no such detail is available for the earlier periods. Yet the earlier eras were at least as creative as the later. To keep the values of each in proportion, the following chapters aim to describe merely the principal changes, enlarging only on certain points of special interest. Many of the variations of style were really a matter of different emphasis rather than a fundamentally new impulse.

Some of the emigrant potters may have enjoyed direct patronage from influential men in the countries of their adoption. It was their best hope if it could be arranged. In England the making of tin-glaze ware 'was so acceptable to King Henry VIII, that he offered to the same Jasper's Father [Jasper Andries of Antwerp] good Wages and Houseroom, to come and excercise the same here; the which then came to no Effect'.[4] Most craftsmen, however, had to establish themselves entirely by their own wits. Once they had proved what they could do, they might be lucky enough to be granted a privilege of manufacture for a number of years (a temporary monopoly), in recognition of the expense incurred in establishing a new industry.

Setting up a maiolica workshop in a strange country required the conjunction of a number of talents. The man in charge had to be an experienced practical craftsman, able to demonstrate techniques to his principal assistants and to train and supervise apprentices. He would need to make prototypes, to design, to paint, and to draw. He would have to know all the detailed requirements of workshop practice. He had also to be something of an engineer, capable of devising mills for glazes, tanks or 'backs' for filtering and blending clays, as well as the design and construction of kilns. He needed some knowledge of natural clays, to select the right chalky clays to make the special body for maiolica. He would have to begin compounding glazes from unproven materials, some of which might have to be imported.[5] Many trials would have to be made before anything could be made for sale.

All this preliminary work meant the outlay of a good deal of time and capital. In addition, the master-potter must have been able to negotiate personally the terms of commissions with his patrons, and to present them with designs and samples before starting anything like a large pavement or a scheme of wall-tiles. He must also have been

4   From Stow's *Survey*, quoted by Anthony Ray, *English Delftware Pottery* (London, 1968), p. 33.
5   Rackham, op. cit., p. 39, quotes the following record from the transactions of the Société Archéologique de Bordeaux, vol. III (1876), p. 125. 'Olivier Roland, master after God of the vessel named the *Marie* of Crodon in Brittany, acknowledges receiving on board, on behalf of Jehan Lacombe, merchant of Bordeaux, five barrels of charred wine lees, which he undertakes to deliver at Antwerp to one Antoine, maker of images, dwelling at the Dial *à la Camermorte*, or, in his absence, to a Venetian, master of drug vases, dwelling in the rue de Crambeporte facing the Golden Lion'. The record is dated October 15, 1531.

a good enough businessman to calculate costs and profit margins on contracts that might represent the work of a dozen men over a whole year. Lastly, he needed to be a good manager of people, or his best men would either be enticed away by rival businesses, or leave to set up on their own account after taking good note of his methods. New work-shops have always been bedevilled by this risk: again and again a promising workshop would be endangered by the loss of a few key men, and both men and designs and recipes were constantly being stolen.

One of the first pioneer-craftsmen was Guido Andries, known also as Guido da Savino. He was probably trained at Casteldurante, one of the most prosperous and versatile of the Italian potteries. He established his own manufactory in Antwerp in 1512, and made tiles and pavements and apothecaries' jars, painted in an unusual dark, slate blue, orange-brown, lemon-yellow, and copper-green. Some famous tiles at the Vyne in Hampshire were probably made to special commission in his first years at Antwerp [78].[6] He also produced decorated vases and bowls and dishes; these were repeated in quantity and usually had simple patterns based on leaves and scrolls, or symmetrical geometric devices. Only a few examples of his work can be recognised with certainty, and they are less assured than Italian work of the same time, but they were appreciated by a public which associated Italy with the best modern taste and design.

A rival factory belonged to the Floris family and is known particularly for its strap-work 'ferronerie' designs and geometrical painted motifs. Some of its work was taken to Spain and was soon afterwards imitated at Talavera and Triana [76]. Some tiles beautifully painted with Renaissance grotesques and strapwork, from the Antwerp fac-tory of Jan van Bojaert, were installed in the palace of Vila Viçosa, Portugal, in 1558.[7]

From Antwerp the tin-glaze technique soon spread further afield. Members of both the Floris and the Andries families are recorded as making tiles in Spain in the 1560s. Other craftsmen moved to Portugal and others to Holland and England, attracted to these two Protestant countries for religious reasons as well as for their commercial opportunities. In England the making of tin-glaze pottery (or gallyware, as it was first called), was dominated by Flemings and Dutchmen until the middle of the seventeenth century.

Italian potters began working in France in the 1520s. One of the first signs of their presence was the installation of a large tile pavement in the church of Brou in 1530, ordered by Queen Margaret of Savoy for the monument to her late husband Philip the Fair, and probably made by Italians working at Rouen. Amongst the Frenchmen working with them was probably Masseot Abaquesne, a craftsman who had already worked on architectural tiles with Girolamo della Robbia in Madrid. A few years later he was the master of a pottery at Rouen which completed tiles and an important pave-ment for the Château d'Ecouen in 1542. Several of Abaquesne's business records survive, including his contract with an apothecary, dated March 24 1543, to make four thousand drug-jars, some of which still exist.[8] They are painted with profile heads and a leaf and

6   See Rackham, op. cit. The Vyne tiles were the chief impulse behind Rackham's researches, and his whole book is connected with them. See also Henri Niçaise, *Les modèles italiens des faïences néerlandaises au XVIe et au début du XVIIe siècle* (Brussels, 1936).
7   Now in the Madre de Deus Tile Museum, Lisbon (ref. 222–225).   8   Giacomotti, op. cit., p. 112.

scroll background pattern. The idea was wholly Italian but the general feeling and the heads themselves were definitely French.

Maiolica was being made by Italians at Lyon soon after 1550 [77]. Some of them were under the patronage of the powerful Cardinal Archbishop Tournon, whom Piccolpasso met briefly at Urbino in 1557. The earliest accredited Lyon pieces are some dishes painted with subjects from the Old Testament, based on Bible illustrations published by the Lyon printers Jean de Tournes and Guillaume de Rouillé.[9] Dishes of this type had been tentatively attributed to Lyon for some time, when another was discovered, about 1950, which confirmed the matter. This dish, now in the British Museum, is painted with Moses and Aaron before Pharaoh and is marked on the back 'Lyon 1582'. The idea of such dishes came from Urbino, but at Lyon the colours were cruder, the drawing was less fluent, and the overall effect less sophisticated. Incidentally, it is surprising how slowly the Renaissance idea developed in French pottery, compared with the marvellous work of Pierre Reymond and other master-enamellers at Limoges.

After 1600 Lyon was overtaken by Nevers, where the Italians Giulio Gambin from Lyon and Agostino Conrade from Albisola started making maiolica about 1580, in a heroic *istoriato* style based on Urbino models. From the start Nevers made many moulded dishes and aimed at a kind of artistic pottery which went far beyond the shapes which could be directly thrown on the wheel. A number of oval dishes are known, painted overall with classical subjects, of which the most famous is the *Triumph of Galatea* in the Louvre, marked on the back 'fesi a Nevrs 1589'.

Further South, Nîmes, Montpellier and Narbonne began producing tin-glaze pottery about 1570–80. Nîmes is known especially for the Huguenot potter Antoine Syjalon, who made some fine, ornate drug-jars, 'in the manner of Pisa', and plates and vases with subject-decoration satirising the Catholic Holy League. A characteristic of his work is the solid-coloured deep blue background: almost every part of his vessels was painted, leaving the original white of the glaze only to give lines of emphasis [79]. Montpellier is known for apothecaries' pots, *albarelli* and *chevrettes* (spouted pots with a handle, for storing liquids) painted with busts of the kings of France. Some of these are preserved in the hospitals of Arles and Narbonne. Moorish craftsmen fleeing from persecution in Spain found refuge in Narbonne, and brought with them something of the ingenious Islamic geometrical ornament, and a liking for stronger patterns and colour than were favoured in Italy.

In Spain, Italian influence took a different course, probably because of the Hispano-Moresque pottery tradition, which was hard to displace.[10] The sculptor-ceramist Niculoso Pisano was working in Triana from before 1500 until his death in 1530. He and his son, and the Spanish sculptor Pedro Millán, worked mostly in architectural tiles with relief ornament and modelled or low-relief clay figures. The best-known works are the Visitation panel made for the Alcázar in Seville (1507), and the elaborate, monumental doorway in the Convent of Santa Paula in Triana, modelled by Pedro Millán and glazed

9 Ch. Damiron, *La faïence de Lyon* (Paris, 1926), shows woodcuts used by painters of early French maiolica.
10 See generally Ainaud de Lasarte, *Ars Hispaniae* vol. X (Madrid, 1952), and especially Alice Wilson Frothingham, *Tile-panels of Spain, 1500–1650* (New York, 1969).

by Niculoso, marked with the artist's name and dated 1504. These works indicate the nature of the first impact of Italian maiolica on Spain; for some time it was confined to architectural tiles modelled or painted with representational figures, a category of work distinct from anything in the Hispano-Moresque pottery tradition, and which was much appreciated by the Court, and above all by the Church. Until 1560 most of the foreign ceramists in Spain were engaged in some kind of architectural work.[11]

Not until after about 1565 did Spanish pottery itself begin to respond to the Italian conventions, in the wake of a campaign against Moorish customs. The influence came both from Italy and from Flanders, which provided many of the craftsmen who worked in the new manner. The Italian *istoriato* convention dominated the prolific potteries of Talavera from this time onwards until the Napoleonic wars, and is seen in dishes, jars, vases and showpieces with elaborately painted hunting scenes and *fêtes champêtres* and other noble pastimes [80].[12] The long-famous potteries of Aragon and Catalonia were now superseded by Talavera, Puente del Arzobispo, Toledo, and Triana, in all of which the pictorial Italian manner predominated. Elsewhere, Italian styles had but an indirect influence, and they led to a hybrid, popular convention with patternwork that still retained a Moorish flavour, and strongly stylised pictorial figures that remained as much Spanish as Italian [81]. Many varieties of this kind of ornament developed in different regions of Spain and Portugal, and much of the popular work is more alive than the charming but stereotyped scenes painted for the ruling classes.

The tin-glaze tradition of central Europe began in the latter part of the sixteenth century, when groups of Italian and Swiss craftsmen settled in Moravia and Slovakia, fleeing from religious persecution. The remarkable story of this movement is recounted in chapter 10, and leads into a description of the popular and folk pottery which came into being in the eighteenth century and lasted until modern times.

Tin-glaze vessels were made in Germany from about 1520 onwards, but only in small quantities. The fine wares date from the second half of the seventeenth century, when Nürnberg, Frankfurt, Ansbach and Hanau began to produce beautifully finished pottery in tin glaze, but then the inspiration was from Oriental-Dutch examples, not from Italian wares.

German wood-engravers played an important role in providing figure compositions and ornament for early Italian illustrated books. The pictures were valuable to painters on pottery, for they enabled them to get their classical mythological and Biblical subjects right, and in particular they presented subjects in terms of line drawing, a predigested form which painters could use without having to depend overmuch on their own original designs [82]. The practice of working from engravings became common in the sixteenth and seventeenth centuries. It enormously increased the scope of pictorial decoration on pottery, in a way which had scarcely existed in the Hispano-Moresque tradition, for instance. It was a natural short cut to the execution of showpieces; however, in the long run it did as much harm as good to the tin-glaze tradition. At its worst it led to neglect of forms, which could be considered only as carriers of subject-painting, and it sometimes led to pedestrian copies of engravings on to pottery, as if the highest possibilities of ceramic painting lay in imitations of engravings and easel pictures.

11 Ibid.   12 See Alice Wilson Frothingham, *Talavera Pottery* (New York, 1944).

From Venice and Faenza the maiolica technique travelled to Switzerland, the Tyrol, and Nürnberg early in the sixteenth century. The earliest dated German piece is a dish painted with the figures of Samson and Delilah, dated 1526, a free rendering of an engraving. Nürnberg produced small quantities of maiolica from about 1530 onwards, mostly decorated with leaf and scroll patterns of Venetian type, with centre designs of figures and busts borrowed from wood-engravings.

Soon after 1500 tin-glazed tiles were being made for pavements and especially for stoves. This work was somewhat separate from the manufacture of pottery vessels, being essentially a matter of high relief work in modelled, applied and stamped clay, with extensive use of elaborate moulds. It was specialist work and the making of vessels was only a side-line. Generally stove-tiles were glazed in plain green and brown lead glazes, which showed the relief to advantage. The use of tin glaze with painting on surfaces which were modelled already involved an awkward compromise between naturalistic and purely decorative colour [83, 84]. Tin glaze was really more satisfactory with flat tiles, such as became usual in the late seventeenth century. Winterthur in Switzerland became an important centre for painted stoves from about 1570 onwards. The famous workshop of the Pfau family continued for some two hundred years [87].

The *Eulenkrüge* or owl-jugs of Switzerland and the South Tyrol were thrown forms with elaborately modelled surfaces representing details proper to owls, but also including coats of arms and allegorical figures as well [86]. The similarity between some of these figures and those of stove-tiles suggests that the owls came from tile-makers' workshops rather than from potteries. Deplorable though the owls have seemed to some modern purists, they have a grotesque attraction and a deliberate humour which can only be resisted by those who are being too solemn. They were really better suited to hard stoneware than to earthenware clays. They were mostly painted in blue under the glaze, and some examples have traces of other colours added in oil paint with final touches in gold leaf. Such impermanent treatment was perhaps quite appropriate to the whole bizarre idea.

The German tradition of applied and moulded relief ornament prevented the maiolica technique from achieving popularity in Germany as it did in most other countries of Europe. The hard Rhineland stonewares were a superb material for this kind of ornament; the German stoneware tradition naturally tended towards figurative decoration and intricate ornament without needing colour. Thus the suitability of tin-glaze pottery for emblems and inscriptions and coloured painting, was not of much interest in the homeland of salt-glaze stoneware. The clean whiteness of tin glaze only began to appeal generally in Germany in the later seventeenth century, as part of the vogue for Delftware and oriental porcelain [155, 156]. Even so, tin-glaze ware (or faience as it came to be called) had only a short future in the country which discovered and perfected the first European true porcelain and enamel decoration.[13]

All the new tin-glaze potteries of Europe experienced the same technical difficulties. At first the quality of the glazes was distinctly coarse compared with those of Italy. The frits were either less soundly composed or less finely ground than the Italian, and tended to give a fired glaze with an 'orange-peel' texture, resulting from small pinholes and

13   See generally S. Ducret, *German Porcelain and Faience* (London, 1962).

bubbles in the surface. The glazes were also more liable to 'crawling', a common tendency of tin glazes to draw away from certain areas leaving naked patches of clay. The pigments were less finely milled, which meant that the fired colours were sometimes rough and often had a rapid transition from dark to light tones.

These defects were not strange in view of the experience and equipment needed for producing fine tin-glaze ware. In the absence of analytical chemistry and any fundamental explanation of the behaviour of materials, continuity of tradition and rules of thumb were especially important, and it was much harder to establish a workshop in a new place than it would be today. Since all emigré potters had to contend with similar technical problems, a short account may now be given of the basic materials they had to produce. A fuller description will be found in chapter 14.

To make white glazes, lead and tin metal were melted together in proportions of about three to one. The molten metals were agitated, and as the surface oxidised the white scum was scraped off until the whole mass had turned to 'tin-ash'. A second mixture or 'fritt' was prepared, consisting of ashes of wine lees or seaweed, or sea salt, or some other source of potash or soda, and this was fused with silver sand in proportions of about one to three parts. Both preparations were finely ground and were measured out to make a third mixture, consisting roughly of equal amounts of 'tin-ash', 'fritt', and silver sand. This final mixture was melted in shallow trays in the fire-chamber of the kiln, broken up and re-ground and sieved, to form the insoluble powder which was suspended in water, becoming the liquid glaze into which the biscuit ware was dipped. The clay absorbed the water of suspension, leaving a dry powder on the surface of the pot. On this the painting was done.

The pigments had to be prepared with great care from metals or natural minerals, and were calcined and ground, sometimes three or four times. Cobalt blues were made from 'zaffre', an impure cobalt oxide made by roasting cobaltite ($CoAsS$) with quartz or sand. Copper pigments for greens were prepared from the acetate or carbonate resulting from the action of vinegar on copper. Manganese pigments were obtained from nodules of impure oxides, notably from the natural mineral pyrolusite (MnO_2) which is fairly common. This colour was used especially for drawing contour lines which were then filled in with stronger colours. Yellow and orange were made from mixtures of ferric oxide (from natural haematite nodules) and antimoniate of lead. Antimony itself was obtained from the sulphide, present in certain volcanic rocks in Italy. Until about 1700 no reliable red pigment was available for pottery. Vermilion (mercuric sulphide), the strongest red available for ordinary painting, was too volatile to be used in ceramics. The nearest approach to red was obtained by preparing a very finely levigated iron oxide (usually known as Armenian bole) with a flux of litharge.

Suitable clays might be hard to locate. The desirable clay was a chalky marl-clay, known to Piccolpasso as *genga*, and in England known as white gault. Almost always it had to be blended with other clays. Red clays, which were far easier to obtain, were seldom used with tin glazes because the soft glazes usually crazed over them but they could be used for cooking-pots, which the chalky clays could not. Unfortunately, the chalky clays were not only relatively uncommon; they also needed careful screening to eliminate particles of free lime, which would otherwise cause the glaze to flake off as the particles, converted to quicklime during the firing, were reached by moisture seeping up from the unglazed base or footing.

Maiolica was only practicable in certain areas where suitable clays and glaze materials were available or could be brought in by boat, as happened in Holland and in most of the English potteries.

Given time, the new potteries established in northern Europe might have perfected their materials so that they could work as finely as Urbino and Faenza, and imitate the elaborate decoration and scenic pictorial wares for which those cities became famous. Before they could do so, they encountered a new influence which proved even more powerful than the classical example of Italy. It was also more digestible, being already a mature ceramic tradition in its own right, independent of the fine arts and of architecture. This influence was, of course, the arrival of Chinese porcelain in Holland in 1603.

8

FRENCH FAIENCE

The most successful of the French tin-glaze pottery centres which began in the sixteenth century was Nevers. The Conrade brothers flourished to such an extent that, for the first half of the seventeenth century, virtually all French faience of any significance was from their factory. A few other pottery centres persevered, Montpellier, Lyon and Rennes, for example, but with no special repute. Such was the success of Nevers that the great *Encyclopédie* of 1756 states flatly that 'the first faience in France was made at Nevers by an Italian',[1] as if Abaquesne of Rouen and the makers of the Lyon Bible-dishes had never existed.

The Conrade (Corrado) family had a royal monopoly that lasted till 1630, so they were free to produce ideas and techniques and expend capital without the anxiety of rivals snatching their profit by setting up business a few streets away. Although after 1630 a number of other potteries started, the Conrades held the advantage of their early start and their connections. In 1644 Antoine Conrade was appointed 'faiencier ordinaire' to Louis XIV.[2]

The Conrades were particularly known for the showpieces in which they continued their native Italian tradition of *maiolica di pompa*, especially for platters and oval dishes, ornamental jars, vases and gourd-like oval flasks, elaborately painted with pastoral, classical and Biblical themes, nearly all painstakingly translated from engravings [89, 90]. Many works by Van Dyck, Poussin and others were published in 1640 by the engraver Michel Dorigny, and this book became almost a standard source-book for Nevers. In many ways it was a pity that everyone expected pottery to reflect the Fine Arts so faithfully, for a man with the ability to render engravings could surely, in a slightly different climate of feeling, have achieved something worthwhile in his own right. To borrow is natural, but few men are faithful copyists by birth. The most agreeable Nevers pieces are those for which the original engraving was adapted or simplified, and where the painter was obliged to contribute something of himself. To expect him to improvise on his own initiative would perhaps be asking too much, for the engraving was his touchstone, his ideal, as much as it was his patron's, and once a man has been trained to copy, it becomes hard for him to do anything original. When the painter improvised, or departed from the engraving, he did so at his peril. Occasionally one comes across a really bad piece of Nevers pottery painting, which looks as if the painter had lost his engraving or lent it to a colleague and was desperately trying to remember it for fear of having to use his own imagination.

1 *Encyclopédie*, ed. Diderot and d'Alembert (Paris, 1756): article 'Fayence', p. 494.
2 For the information contained in this chapter, see generally Arthur Lane, *French Faience* (London, 1948), and J. Giacometti, *French Faience* (London, 1963).

Map 5.   France, showing the chief faience centres.

To do so, in that age, he would have had to be a man with an unusual cast of mind, for fine painted pottery was admired principally for the degree to which it reflected the Fine Arts, and this was all the more important to people because the ideals of the Fine Arts themselves were largely associative rather than deeply established, having been absorbed fairly recently from Italy.

The Conrade factory also made a number of large ceramic figures in the della Robbia tradition, but with more sentiment. They were a superb technical achievement; however, the thick white glaze deprived them of the precision of stone-carving, and the half naturalistic colouring limited rather than enhanced their dignity, emphasising that there was no strong idea behind them. They were ceramic equivalents of something else.

The four 'Italian colours' began to change around 1620 to a softer palette of muted grey-blue, purplish-brown, light green, and soft yellow, with an effect very different from the Urbino *istoriato* wares that attempted to render pictures on pottery in full colour. On the whole, the softer colours brought together the forms and the glaze and the subject-painting and produced a more unified effect. The colour qualities were probably not altogether deliberate: the shiny, milky glaze of much Nevers pottery had a way of bubbling as it melted; it distorted the finer painted lines and left white specks in areas of solid colour, a characteristic of tin glazes containing a fairly high proportion of lime. Possibly this was the result of altering older glaze recipes with the aim of making a glaze which looked more like porcelain. The speckling of the glaze is apparent in a fine large dish painted with the Adoration of the Magi, but it does not spoil the piece. It merely gives it qualities different from those of oil paintings, and it is no defect that the pigments can be seen to have fused with a glass, slightly changing the painter's strokes as they did so [Colour Plate M].

'Bleu de Nevers' pottery has a glaze of opaque deep blue (a tin glaze stained with cobalt), and overpainting of white tin pigment. The technique had been used at Faenza and other Italian centres, and was occasionally used in England and Slovakia, but it was used more continuously at Nevers than anywhere else. It started about 1630 and lasted until about 1700. The forms of the pots and the painted motifs were inspired by oriental models, though there was no intention to imitate literally. 'Bleu de Nevers' is almost entirely ornamental, intended for walls, alcoves, shelves, to grace an interior decorative scheme. At its best it was most elegant; it needed verve and a fine sense of composition, however, and could easily go wrong. Many examples catch the eye but appear crude and awkward when looked at closely. The blue glaze is flat and dense, and the white is often bubbled and rough. It had to be thickly applied to avoid being stained by the blue glaze, and often the designs seem to suffer from this technical difficulty, becoming hard and static.[3]

Oriental porcelains and Dutch *chinoiseries* affected much of the work of Nevers throughout the second half of the century, and led to a palette dominated by cobalt blue [91]. Variety of colour gave way to variety of tones, known as *camaïeu*. By this time other potteries were in production and the work of the Conrades is often indistinguishable from that of rival concerns. The Nevers potteries responded uncertainly to the

3 Some rare examples of this ware have a base glaze of antimony yellow instead of cobalt. See Giacomotti, op. cit., p. 18.

oriental influence which conflicted with their own Italianate traditions. It was not followed wholeheartedly as in Holland. The forms are often a weak hybrid of Italian and
oriental prototypes, painted with lightweight strokes of a vaguely oriental kind but often
depending on a structure of bands, medallions and other geometrical setting-out, which
came from Italy. Nonetheless, the Nevers kilns were busy enough to endanger the forests
of the whole area from which their fuel came and by 1743 the government had made an
order limiting the number of factories.

By the middle of the seventeenth century faience had become widely fashionable for
ceremonial and decorative wares such as large wall-plates, dishes, vases and large jars,
and of course for tiles and pharmacy vessels, though tableware was still usually silver or
pewter. Competition between factories was fierce. The founder of a factory might be
lucky enough to be granted a monopoly for some years to enable him to start with some
security, but once his privilege expired other enterprises were almost certain to grow up
nearby, stealing designs and technical knowledge, and, if possible, enticing away the
craftsmen and artisans by offering slightly better pay. This happened to the Conrades,
and their factory survived it. However, many of their designs became diffused into a
general Nevers style. Eventually, the chief threat to their standing was to come not from
any of their neighbours, but from Rouen, where in time a faience tableware was to
develop so successfully that the Nevers potters of the next century were obliged to
imitate it.

A privilege for a *faiencerie* at Rouen was granted by the King in 1644. Within a year
or two the business was acquired by Edmé Poterat. At first the designs were in the
Italianate manner of Nevers. By the 1660s, though, fashionable French taste was turning
to the exotic, to oriental porcelain and Dutch *chinoiseries*. The famous 'Trianon de
Porcelaine', built by Louis XIV for Madame de Montespan, was really a 'Trianon de
faience', an entire building walled and furnished with faience at a prodigious cost.[4] The
Poterat factory attracted the attention of Colbert, Louis XIV's Minister of Finance, a
man deeply interested in the advancement of the fine and applied arts. In 1663 Colbert
penned the memoir 'protect and reward the faience-makers of Rouen and district, that
they may work hard. Send them models and commission work for the King'. In 1673
Louis Poterat obtained a licence to make 'porcelain like the Chinese' and 'violet faience
painted in white and blue with other colours as is done in Holland'.[5] Some fine, rare
early porcelains are attributed to the Poterat factory, small vases, cups and saucers, and
small pieces for the table,[6] but apparently the process was not mastered sufficiently
to allow large-scale production and the Poterat workshops followed up the less challeng-
ing, expanding market for faience banqueting services.

Faience tableware was already coming into fashion towards the end of the seventeenth
century when its manufacture was given vast momentum by a series of decrees. As a
contribution to the costs of the War of the Grand Alliance and the War of the Spanish
Succession, the nobility were required to send their gold and silver plate to the mint, at

4   Lane, op. cit., p. 15. The building was inevitably wrecked by frost within a few years.
5   Giacomotti, op. cit., p. 32. 'Violet faience' refers to the slight staining of the white glaze which was
customary in Holland at this time.
6   Hubert Landais, *French Porcelain*, trans. I. and F. McHugh (London, 1961) (3 plates).

first as a patriotic obligation, and later under penalty of a heavy fine. Decrees to this effect were issued in 1689, 1699 and 1709. Faience-makers awoke to the prospect of fortunes. In the famous remark of Duke Saint-Simon in 1709, 'every table in the land of any importance was laid with faience within a week'. Largely as a result of these decrees, France became the dominant force in European faience throughout the eighteenth century. Factories large and small were started all through the land to reap the rewards of manufacturing tableware. The acquisition of tableware started as a necessity: within a few decades it had become also a fashionable pastime. A number of factory owners were themselves noblemen, who were thereby able to provide both the banqueting service and the banquet itself from within their own estates. However, the King himself was no longer greatly interested in faience: he and Madame de Pompadour were patrons and protectors of the Vincennes-Sèvres porcelain factories.[7]

Naturally, this interest in faience and the enormous market for tableware had a far-reaching effect. Manufacturers were open to the full weight of the demand for large services of pottery, many of which had to be made to special order incorporating coats of arms or monograms, and all of which had to match the tastes of noblemen who had never before given much attention to pottery, but now found in it a recreation and diverting field for the exercise of judgment and sensibility. The makers of pottery were therefore now strictly craftsmen and artisans who responded to 'models' or ideas proposed by their patrons, as Colbert had assumed in the memoir already quoted. More and more the craftsman's job became a matter of working out the technicalities of design and manufacture, and perfecting the materials: he was scarcely expected (as he might in earlier or later times) to have new ideas of his own.

The manufacture of the new tableware was dominated by the factories of Rouen until about 1730, and from about 1690 onwards the effect of the new market became apparent in Rouen work [92, 93]. A new category of pottery was coming into being. Until the late seventeenth century fashionable faience was generally, throughout Europe, a ware for decorative purposes and occasional use, not made in extensive series, nor with long runs of repeated patterns. Now it had to be made in large services with plates and dishes exactly matching in size and painted ornament, and replacement pieces had to be available. Also, types of painted decoration had to be worked out that could be used with variations on all the pieces of a single service, plates and platters, sauce-boats, water cisterns, urns, vases and tureens, be they never so diverse. That, too, was virtually a new requirement.

A natural consequence of this need was the use of moulds for an ever-increasing number of pieces. Not only were moulds essential for the making of vessels whose forms derived closely from plate, with cusped, scalloped and lobed edges, or panelled and gadrooned sides, but only by working from moulds could sets of dishes be made exactly to size and repeated. Even simple, round plates were best made on moulds. From this time onwards factories became less and less dependent on the potter's wheel. The thrower still made bowls, jugs and the taller shapes, and the largest vessels, many of which were later fluted and modelled by hand, but his importance was steadily waning. The use of moulds freed the factory from total dependence on skilled labour, for once a

7   Landais, op. cit., p. 19.

mould was made, articles could be produced from it by semi-skilled artisans. 'Throwers' could die or fall sick or move to a better-paid job without upsetting the flow of work. The key craftsman was no longer the chief thrower, but the sculptor or modeller who made the prototype for the moulds.

The intricate, lace-like patterns of the Rouen 'style rayonnant', with its curling bouquets of close-wrought baroque flowers and leaves and its painted 'lambrequins' [Fig. 25], reflects the same regard for precision and production in quantity in the pain-

Figure 25. *Lambrequin* ornament.

ters' workshops [92]. The rendering of figure-subjects, even from engravings, and the painting of controlled, generous, large strokes requires a talented painter. The repetition of the units of a small design requires more application but less verve, and is relatively easily taught and supervised. Further, a design of small-scale units is readily adapted to varieties of shape, and is thus more suitable for the decoration of banqueting services than a design which needs reinterpretation from piece to piece. As a result, most of the French faience of the eighteenth century was painted with designs whose units were basically small in scale, and this was especially characteristic of the early Rouen table-ware. Again, the key man was the designer of the prototype. After him, the factory needed men and women who could learn set patterns and repeat them attentively, and prevent them changing as they became familiar. Only one or two inventive painters were needed: indeed, any factory which depended much on the individual talent of its painters for repetitive work would have been seriously vulnerable.

Other changes were also brought about by the demand for tableware or 'faience noble'. The system of packing and firing kilns had to become more effective to accommodate large numbers of small units such as plates and cups, whereas the older kilns had had a larger proportion of big pieces and used kiln space less economically. Glazes had to be as sound and fine as possible to withstand scratching by cutlery, which had hardly been necessary for showpieces. They had also to meet as well as possible the comparison with porcelain, and some faienciers boasted—Jacques Chapelle of Sceaux, for instance— that their material was indistinguishable from porcelain itself. Rouen glazes were not particularly good in 1700. Over the reddish Rouen clay they tended to craze quickly, and were fairly often pinholed and rough, and looked slightly green and sombre. With regular manufacture of tableware they improved fast and by the 1720s had become much whiter and finer.[8] Some of the faience glazes being used in France by the middle of the century were virtually perfect and imply a considerable amount of research and experiment and a high standard in the preparation of raw materials and frits.

At the beginning of the eighteenth century the art of colour-making remained as it had been in Italy a hundred and fifty years earlier. The first Rouen table services followed well-known Chinese examples and were painted entirely in blue, the strongest and most constant of all pottery pigments. Profit and fashion alike encouraged the development of additional colours and the range grew steadily all through the century, backed by a good deal of experiment. About 1715 the Poterat factory started using a dark red pigment which was probably learned from Dutch potters. Sparingly used in blue designs, it was an immediate success, despite its tendency to remain rough after the glost firing, because of the high proportion of red ochre in its composition. Red has always been a difficult ceramic colour and it has always been popular. The Rouen red (from hematite) was similar to the brick red (Armenian bole) of Isnik wares, and was hardly improved on until the development of chromium-tin reds in the early nineteenth century. Rouen also developed a good yellow ochre and an olive green, and from about 1725 most Rouen tableware made use of these four colours. The 'style rayonnant' of early Rouen tableware was copied with variations by many of the smaller pottery centres of Northern France. At Lille the painting of detail was reduced to a miniature scale, reaching the size of fine lace or embroidery. Large plates decorated in this way are impressive. However, the disproportion between the piece entire and the detail can make the painting look more like something lying on the plate rather than a design which really is part of it.

At Rouen itself in the 1720s the 'style rayonnant' merged into a lighter and more airy kind of pattern with formal scrollwork, strapwork, pendants and festoons, drawn together by strongly emphasised vertical features. Small figures of children or vaguely classical fawns and nymphs were sometimes included in these designs which were derived from Jean Bérain and his son, court designers to Louis XIV. The Rouen wares of this kind were simply a ceramic version of an adaptable, decorative style which descended from grotesque and strapwork Renaissance ornament. The style belonged equally to book engravings, metalwork, jewellery, fabrics and bas-relief work.[9] The Bérain mannerism was ingenious and appeared a good deal in the work of other potteries also from about 1710 until at least 1750. It had a powerful mood, a mood of elegant lassitude (emphasised by the vertical, falling forms), of vague longing or nostalgia, and suggestions of a timeless, abundant, ideal world; yet it was not altogether without some feeling of wizardry, danger and forbidden fruit. The designer could play endlessly with its forms and the languishing mind could enjoy its images and their associations [96].

The Guillibaud family, also of Rouen, were not only commercial rivals of the Poterats. Their factory specialised in a painted faience of almost opposite character. In place of

8   The 'Fayence' article in the *Encyclopédie* of 1756 mentions coating the biscuit ware with a thin layer of unfired white clay to fill pinholes and act as a bond between clay and glaze, a practice which may have started at Rouen, whose clay was redder and coarser than potters would have wished.

9   See Peter Ward-Jackson, 'Some main streams and tributaries in European ornament from 1500 to 1750', Victoria and Albert Museum *Bulletin*, vol. III, No. 3 (1967).

the limited colour combinations of the Poterat factory the Guillibauds used as many colours as possible on each piece: where the former specialised in symmetrical, radial designs, they adopted asymmetrical compositions already tending towards the later rococo style: where the one concentrated on small-scale patterns with minimal representations, the other made a name for its Chinese figures, dragons, birds and insects and garlands. The patterns *à la corne* and *au carquois* were particularly favoured, cornucopias bursting with fruit and flowers or quivers filled with flowers and leaves. The mood was frivolous but the shapes and painting were so well devised and were carried out with such verve, that they achieve a quality beyond fashion and well deserve the place in the pantheon of fine faience which has long been given them by collectors.

The factory flourished from about 1720 to the middle of the century, when some of its best pieces resulted from the merging of its *chinoiseries* (which had never been very Chinese) with the rococo style and the last shreds of the Italian arcadian themes. Most notable are some of the Guillibaud trays and ceramic baskets with dragon handles, painted with cornucopias of flowers and fruit, and polychrome baroque borders surrounding humorous courtly pastimes and idealised landscapes. All this was done with vigour and fantasy and was perhaps a bit too much for the best taste of its own age and ours. It did, however, evoke a world of poise and gaiety where nothing, no one, needed to be taken too seriously [Colour Plate N].

Not all Rouen work was aristocratic. Many of the potteries also made simpler faience, often wheel-thrown jugs, bowls and dishes for the provincial bourgeoisie. Amongst these pots came the narrow-necked Normandy cider-pitchers, which were often inscribed with initials and dates and figures to commemorate weddings and other family occasions [93]. Small wine-flasks of oval or flattened shape were also popular, and many of them carried appropriate inscriptions:

> j'aime le vin et ma maîtresse
> j'oublie son nom quand je suis sou'
> pour me resouvenir de sa tendresse
> Son nom est écrit cy desous.
> 1733.

Some of the most elegant of all *faience noble* came from the Clérissy family factory at Moustiers at the foot of the Alps in the south-east of France. The family came originally from Italy and had run this factory since the early seventeenth century. Faience manufacture was started there by Pierre Clérissy about 1670, while his brother Joseph worked in close association with him at the factory called St. Jean-du-Désert, in Marseilles. Moustiers enjoyed an advantage that Rouen always lacked, a fine natural earthenware clay which fired hard and pale in colour, and was therefore able to make vessels which were thinner and stronger, covered with a rich white glaze. The brothers had the fortune to employ François Viry, an exceptionally talented ceramic painter, who first made the factory famous with his large dishes painted in blue with elaborate hunting scenes taken from the engravings of Antonio Tempesta. The subjects had the appeal of sporting prints, perenially fashionable, from Kashmir to Donegal, and must have found their way to many halls on that account alone. They had also the associations of Italian culture behind them, and were impeccably carried out. Biblical subjects were also done from engravings by Matthieu Mérian.

In the early eighteenth century the Clérissy factory adopted the Bérain style which they developed, from the point it reached at Rouen, to a larger and more dispersed kind of overall design, with more emphasis on figures and fantastic architectural and land-scape settings, connected by devices of draperies, garlands and twining stalks and leaves [96]. The style was taken up and changed further by Joseph Olerys, who is thought to have been trained at the Clérissy factory and set up his own factory in 1738.

Olerys had also worked at Alcora, on the East coast of Spain, where the Count of Aranda had started the factory which was probably the best equipped and most enter-prising of all the faienceries of the century. There Olerys appears to have learnt technic-alities of glaze preparation and colour-making which were in advance of French methods, and he also absorbed something of the Alcora decorative style—a style in which the free compositions and light, balanced pattern-groupings of oriental pottery were at last fully integrated with European subject-matter and traditional European decorative features —formal flowers, garlands, and medallions of deities and heroes from classical myth-ology. Olerys produced a great deal of pottery painted in a soft lime green and a fine orange-yellow, a colour-scheme new to French faience, and which agreed perfectly with the airy, feminine decorative style in which his factory excelled. It is hard to conceive of 'decoration' in the usual sense of the word as an elegant surface embellishment, being taken much further than it was in these exquisite, highly mannered pieces which were imitated by many of the smaller faienceries of the South of France. With Olerys, faience tableware reached its extreme. He made few imposing showpieces; beside his work, showpieces look vulgar and self-assertive. Every item of an Olerys table service was restrained and well-nigh perfect—a showpiece in miniature.

Another kind of decorative ideal was perfected at Strasbourg under the Hannong family. Their faience factory was started in 1724 and made mostly tableware decorated in *camaïeu* blue in the manner of Rouen, but in 1740 Paul Hannong began to experiment with *petit-feu* (enamel) colours, which were already in use at the porcelain factories of Meissen, Vincennes and Chantilly. These colours could achieve a much wider range than the *grand-feu* pigments, especially reds, crimsons, purples and some kinds of orange. The difference between the two types of pigments was this: in the *grand-feu* faience tech-nique (the traditional method of applying colour to the glaze) the pigments were painted on the unfired glaze and glaze and pigments were fused together in the glost firing at temperatures around 1000°–1040° Centigrade. Only a small number of pigments could withstand this heat, notably the long-familiar cobalt, copper, antimony, manganese and iron. However, many pigments could survive a lower firing or *petit-feu*, and could give colours unobtainable in the *grand-feu*. In the *petit-feu* method the pigments were mixed with fluxes and were painted on the already-fired glazed surface of the vessels. At temperatures around 850° Centigrade the fluxes melted and the pigments adhered to the glaze.

About 1744 Hannong introduced Japanese *Kakiemon* designs and 'Indian flower' patterns into his tableware, following the example of German porcelain manufacturers. The *petit-feu* colours came into their own with this kind of decoration. At about the same

time, still looking towards the manufacture of porcelain, Hannong obtained the help of
the brothers Von Löwenfinck, who were specialists in enamel painting, and of the Lanz
brothers, who were sculptors and modellers. In 1751 Strasbourg began to make porcelain, but was prevented because of the monopoly of Vincennes, and this could not be
evaded because the King himself was a patron of Vincennes. The sole solution was to
make the porcelain at Frankenthal, beyond the reach of the royal monopoly, while
continuing faience at Strasbourg. For nine years the Hannongs made both porcelain and
faience, but after Paul Hannong's death in 1760 the inheritance was divided between his
sons. Joseph managed the porcelain factory at Frankenthal and Pierre the faience work
at Strasbourg. However, Pierre was so extravagant that within six months he went
bankrupt and Joseph returned to Strasbourg to save the original factory. Thwarted in
his devotion to porcelain, Joseph Hannong had to realise his ideals in faience earthenware instead [97, 98].

Joseph Hannong was a good administrator as well as a ceramist. He got the specialists
he needed, but he also seems to have regarded his personnel not simply as operatives but
as people whose talents could be developed by the right mixture of training and challenge. He saw that the general aristocratic enthusiasm for faience was leading towards a
showy, pretentious pottery without lasting qualities—exotic forms borrowed from metalwork, sculpture and other alien media, painted with borrowed pictures and second-hand
ornament. Under him the forms of Strasbourg wares were simplified and purged, and he
set up schools of painting to devise floral decorations from life instead of deriving everything from botanical engravings, and the painting on the pottery became softer and
more sensitive. He was also a fine technician and brought enamel-painting on faience
to the highest point it had yet reached. As with many ceramists, his enthusiasm consumed
funds which could ill be spared. Despite his gifts, indeed partly because of them, he
went bankrupt in 1781 and died in poverty and exile in Munich soon after 1800.

Strasbourg faience represents an extreme of the elegance which was sought in French
ceramics of the eighteenth century—the refinement of mould-made forms, the pursuit of
charming decoration, realised by acute control of drawing, colour and tone. It is as near
to porcelain as faience could be. Almost everything from Strasbourg was well designed
within the aesthetic language of the time, and Hannong sensed well not only how to
'refine' but also when to stop, unlike Baron Beyerlé and General Custine who successively
owned the offshoot, rival factory of Niderviller, whose production included some exquisite, some clever, and some dreadful things. Strasbourg shapes and painted decoration were done with a sincerity and judgment which kept them free of the meretricious
extravagance which the market invited, with the exception, perhaps, of some of the
fantastic and half-humorous tureens made in the shape of a turkey or boar's head, the
eighteenth century's equivalent of the old German *Eulenkrüge*. At the other extreme,
Joseph Hannong produced a very fine white faience decorated only in gold, a minor
miracle of restraint at that period.

Even so, the pursuit of perfection can be limiting, and the perfection of Strasbourg's
naturalistic 'German flower' designs, painted in enamel colours and disposed in seem-
ingly casual sprays over the surfaces of tableware was a narrow ideal, even in its own day.
Despite their flowing softness, these decorations are not easeful, and one has only to find

some good examples of oriental ceramic flower-painting to realise that once specialisation reached this point a whole world of possibilities had been overlooked. True ease, real spontaneity, can only come from deeper roots, and it is hard to trim its impulses to the obligations of factories. This is no reflection against Joseph Hannong, merely a comment on the direction taken by ceramics in his age, and the processes at work in the whole of European taste. Specialisation and perfection of technique are bound to become exclusive, and ultimately to narrow the imagination through which new things are discovered.

Rouen, Moustiers and Strasbourg were sources of ideas and models for a very large number of small potteries which sprang up in all parts of France during the century, most of which were short-lived and unoriginal. Twenty-three potteries existed in Franche-Comté alone around the middle of the century, producing 'robust and unpretentious faience' derived from Strasbourg designs [95].[10] A good many such factories were started by craftsmen and specialist technicians who had been employed in larger establishments; having gained inside knowledge of glaze and colour recipes and seen the whole process of faience-making, they could not resist what seemed an opportunity to make a fortune by producing fashionable tableware on their own account. The designs existed: the market existed. All that seemed necessary was a good modeller and mould-maker, a few competent painters and some local artisans to attend to the kilns and the clay production. By a certain amount of intrigue. the leading spirit was usually able to persuade some of his colleagues and workpeople to break away with him.[11] The growth of specialised techniques, especially of moulded pottery, made the prospect of success seem all the more plausible, for it only seemed necessary to make a small range of moulded shapes and then go into production.

Considerable capital, leadership, technical skill and mutual trust was required to survive even a few setbacks, and the only really stable small potteries were those which were owned or supported by men of wealth, such as Sinceny, a pottery established by the Lord of Sinceny in 1734 in his château, with Dominique Pellevé of Rouen as manager. This factory specialised in *chinoiseries*, big Chinese landscape designs with figures, and decoration with birds and foliage, some of which are remarkably bold and free, though still within the conventions of the age [94]. The Meillonas and Aprey potteries were likewise founded by noblemen on their estates. Aprey produced moulded faience tableware, decorated with miniature birds and flowers with radial panels like striped ribbons in pink, said to be derived from Louis XVI silks. Perhaps the interest of a nobleman bore fruit in occasional fresh ideas such as this, undertaken with sufficient confidence to go beyond the known types of saleable designs.

Niderviller is perhaps the best known of all the seigneurial potteries. It was started about 1754 by Baron Bayerlé and his wife, who staffed it mostly with workmen lured away from the Hannongs at Strasbourg nearby, from whom they also enticed away the Anstett brothers, famed for their landscape paintings in enamels. The Baron and Baroness

10 Giacomotti, op. cit., pp. 84–86.
11 Giacomotti, op. cit., p. 150, referring to the period 1770–1800, wrote, 'Artisans from Montauban and Ardus were constantly lured away to work for small local factories which sprang up everywhere along the valleys of the rivers Aveyron, Tarn, and Garonne.'

took a close interest in the designs of the factory and a good many of the pieces were made to their suggestions, resulting in a certain amount of over-contrivance and excessive sophistication, which were well received in the artistic and literary circle of their friends. The whole estate was later purchased by the Comte de Custine, under whom were made, amongst other things, the plates and dishes decorated with *trompe l'oeil* effects—engravings on curled paper, pinned to grained wood, the kind of transient, smart idea which has so often arisen in pottery and glass when technical skill has become divorced from constructive imagination.

Marseilles had many pottery factories all through the eighteenth century, and in contrast to the well-endowed seigneurial potteries first mentioned, those of Marseilles were mostly run by men (and surprisingly often by their widows) who succeeded only by their talent, wit and hard work. The many diverse workshops of Marseilles included something of every kind of pottery form and decoration current in the rest of France, and also pioneered styles of their own. Full of ideas and activity and uncertainties, Marseilles must have been a fascinating place for a potter to work in.

The St. Jean-du-Désert factory, rented by Joseph Clérissy from 1679 and later by his widow and her chief painter and business associate, François Viry, worked in much the same vein as the main Clérissy factory at Moustiers, and remained under the management of the family until 1773. A grandson of Joseph Clérissy, Louis Leroy, managed the Heraud-Leroy factory from 1731–1778, working in a variation on the *style rayonnant* of Rouen and later in rococo wares with floral decoration. Amongst Leroy's own personal work are some strongly designed painted decorations of grotesques with backgrounds of fantastic plant forms, a style which never became generally current, but which produced some of the most original ceramic painting of the age. Amongst the many conventional set pieces of the time, these stand out as originating in some deeper level of imagination, too insistent to be refined or trimmed to suit the fashions of the moment.[12]

The Pentagon factory was run by Joseph Fauchier and his nephew of the same name and under them it lasted from the second decade of the century until the Revolution. They were known for elaborately moulded rococo wares, some of which have affinities with the Guillibaud pottery of Rouen. They also made pottery painted with flower decoration over a yellow base glaze, a convention which was apparently very popular in the Midi, but not elsewhere in France. The factory of Gaspard Robert, started in 1759, produced amongst other things delicate *chinoiseries*, flower decorations and rococo tureens painted in *petit-feu* colours with fish and shell-fish and other marine ornament— one of the most engaging types of Marseilles pottery. The factory of the famous Veuve Perrin and her associate Honoré Savy excelled in such pieces, painted on yellow or white glazes in enamel colours with incredible finesse, a type of decoration which agreed perfectly with the highly contrived tureens and dishes on which it was artfully disposed [100]. *Ars est celare artem.*

The painters of the Veuve Perrin factory were technically at least equal to those of Strasbourg, and their varied compositions of 'still lives' of local fish and crustaceans, or fruits and vegetables of the Midi, are not only rich sources of forms and textures, far more interesting than sprays of German flowers, but have the added merit of being

12   Leroy's pattern-book is in the Cantini Museum, Marseilles.

essentially connected with the food inside the vessels [Colour Plate O]. They whet the appetite, and one longs to lift the lids and smell the soup. The Veuve Perrin started in business about 1754, and died in 1793. The business was highly successful and her son continued it through the revolutionary era into the nineteenth century. The Marseilles potteries always tended to be more flamboyant than those of the rest of France; they used both moulded forms and *petit-feu* enamels with uninhibited verve, where others did so only with care, and the wares of the Veuve Perrin factory are their most exquisite and distinctive products.

Most of the potteries producing fine faience started at the end of the seventeenth century or later. As was mentioned at the beginning of the chapter, Nevers had been producing pottery for much longer, and was less able to adapt itself to the new fashions which accompanied refined tableware. In the eighteenth century most of the potteries depended on the patronage of the provincial bourgeoisie. Their painting techniques still derived from the illustrative Italian tradition, and as this type of work fell from favour the touch became coarser and broader, and tended to abandon the exalted world of classical mythology for themes of a more recognisable kind, local townscapes, rivers, bridges and barges or allegories of a moral or comical kind with obvious relevance to everyday life and compositions commemorating family or civic occasions [101]. Because these pots were often inscribed with commentaries and explanations, they are known as *faiences parlantes*. In comparison with some of the conventional fine faience, they seem crude and provincial but a number of them are really more imaginative and alive. Delicacy can be a parody of 'refinement': there can be more sensibility in a spontaneous stroke or drawing than in the dutiful following of a pattern-book design, and Nevers retained a vigour which some potteries lost and paid dearly for, and others never began to have. During the Revolution *faiences parlantes* became extremely popular; they were simplified into stark renderings of the tricolour, the guillotine, the Bastille, and the shovel, emblem of the Third Estate, and other patriotic symbols with brief mottos: '*Droits de l'homme*', '*je garde la nation*', '*vivre libre ou mourir*' and the like. They are not fine pottery, but they are not mere curiosities. After so many years of decorative convention, the painted images once again became a language of deep associations, stark, and full of conviction [99].[13]

Most of the factories made modelled and moulded objects as well as pottery vessels, from very large constructions such as the extraordinary celestial globe made by Pierre Chapelle of Rouen and his enormous bust of Apollo, to lifesize pottery hounds with long horse-hair ears (Jacques Chambrette of Luneville, *c.* 1740), turkey tureens (Strasbourg and others), tiles and fantastic water-cisterns and drug jars which are part vessels, part sculptures (Niderviller, Fauchier of Marseilles and Fauquez of St. Amand-les-Eaux), clock-faces and cases, figures of saints and shepherdesses, huntsmen and birds and animals, and a multitude of toy-pieces, figures, fruit and vegetables, pin-boxes, pen-rests, inkwells, knife handles, chess-boards, mirror-frames and so forth, decorated with an 'appeal to the artistic sense which disarms the intelligence,' as Dr. Hannover described it. The mould-making techniques which had been perfected to make banqueting services

13   See P. Huillard, *La Faience en Bourgogne Auxerrois, 1725–1870* (Paris, 1961), a generously illustrated account of revolutionary and provincial faience.

on the basis of scalloped metal shapes were used to multiply every kind of fantasy, and enabled the modellers to spend care and time over their work since it could be reproduced for extensive sale.

Despite the skill and patience which is evident in very many of these pieces, and their high cost,[14] their general character is ephemeral. While one is in their world, accepting the convention they belong to, their ingenuity is captivating, but if the spell is broken by looking elsewhere or remembering something else, one becomes aware of much that they are not, of dignity and lasting qualities that they do not have. One recalls the conviction and emotional force found in some oriental figures, and in some crude European peasant figures, which is not found in those elegant figures of the eighteenth century, even on the most monumental scale. Why this deficiency? Perhaps it comes of an attitude of mind which led people not to expect to go beyond an established range of utility or ornament, not to try to make things except in response to an already existing taste, to base their intention on 'models', rather than risk getting lost in the unknown. Perhaps it stems from the specialisation of work in the new potteries and the authority of a manager who could no longer be also a practising craftsman. The faience potters had courage for almost any technical challenge, but their enterprise did not extend to the exploration of uncharted realms of style and feeling.

The market exaggerated the tendency to be trivial. Once ceramics were associated with ornament and diversion, it became undesirable to have something too serious in the wrong place. It would undermine the proprieties, or improprieties, which the occasion required. The ceramic work of this century, whether Italianate, *chinoiserie*, Germanic-floral, rococo or neo-classical, expressed the new European attitude to 'design' as something contrived rather than evolved or discovered, an attitude whose inadequacy only became quite clear in the following century and has not altogether been abandoned even in our own time, despite a better understanding of Far Eastern craftsmanship, and despite the effects of the Bauhaus, and other influences, all recognising that creative design lies deeper than the rational mind.

All the French faience potteries were eventually reduced to dire straits, some by the Revolution, some by the competition of porcelain, which faience came to resemble closely in any case, but which was finer, harder, and had the added beauty of translucency. Others were ruined by the importation of the new white English earthenware, to which France was exposed by the disastrous Free Trade agreement of 1786. This ware was stronger and far cheaper to produce than faience, and resulted in some of the potteries actually being taken over by Englishmen and converted to the new methods. Even if the agreement had not been made, however, the English manufacturing methods would sooner or later have been adopted by the French factories in the natural course of competition amongst themselves.

In any case, the sequence of changes in French faience, with its emphasis on a care-

14 Giacomotti, op. cit., p. 178, quotes a record of a faience dinner service from the Samadet factory, bought in 1775 by Baron Samadet for 267 livres. It included 120 green plates and 50 green dishes and several modelled pieces, one of which was an oil and vinegar cruet in the form of a horse and rider, which together with the modelled salt cellar, was valued at the large sum of 19 livres. The service is now in the Museum of Lourdes.

ful contrivance, and detail and fine finish, pointed towards more and more specialised, and ultimately mechanised, production. Mould-made forms became general in the early eighteenth century and though they did not entirely replace the use of the wheel and other methods of forming clay, they did establish many of the shape-making practices which are used in the modern industry. Most of the eighteenth-century factories had cause at one time or another to regret their dependence on skilled painters because they could abscond and work for competitors. If the painted design could only be printed in some way this recurring difficulty would be overcome, and so also would the problem of finding and training suitable work-people. The application of printed designs was already current in England by the 1750s and was bound to be introduced into France eventually. In fact, the repetition of shapes from moulds meant that, sooner or later, the decorating would also be done mechanically.

One of the advantages of the siliceous white clay body which came into use in the later eighteenth century was that it remained white when covered by a transparent glaze. It led eventually to the practise of underglaze painting, and above all to the application of printed designs to biscuit ware before glazing, which meant that intricate designs could be applied to pottery without requiring skilled labour. A significant moment in the history of French faience was the publication in 1830 of *L'Art de fabriquer la faïence blanche, rècouverte d'un èmail transparent*, by the ceramist Bastenaire-Daudenart. The author cited all the deficiencies of the traditional tin-glaze technique, the softness of the buff body, the tendency of the glazes to craze or to be easily scratched, the cost of the glaze materials, the expense of handpainting, and the difficulty of repeating designs, all of which could be overcome by working in the new English white earthenware technique, for which his book was a practical manual. From early in the nineteenth century the use of the old tin-glaze technique continued by habit rather than from choice, and progressive manufacturers changed to newer and less expensive materials.

Craftsmen of recent times often point out the evil effects of industrialism on ceramics. They seldom realise that industrial methods had become inevitable and necessary some time before they were fully developed. They were necessary not only because of the enormous market which was opening up as the population of Europe expanded, but also because of the technical difficulty of satisfying fashionable European taste by any other method.

Bastenaire Daudenart regretfully counselled his colleagues to look to England:

The English manufacturers have an attitude very different from our own; they consistently aim at the production of articles of general utility; they look with malignant smiles at the efforts we have made over thirty years or so to achieve the finest possible perfection in porcelain; they have perceived, rightly, that these efforts were being lavished on articles which could never satisfy more than the highest classes of society . . .[15]

His remarks applied as well to tin glaze as to porcelain.

15   F. Bastenaire-Daudenart, *L'Art de fabriquer la faïence blanche, rècouverte d'un èmail transparent* (Paris, 1830), p. 15.

Map 6.   The Low Countries, showing the centres of Delftware manufacture.

9

THE NETHERLANDS

Delftware was but one expression of the potential of tin-glaze pottery. However, the popular association of tin glaze with Delft is reasonable because of the enormous output of the Delft factories throughout the seventeenth and eighteenth centuries. Delftware reached every corner of Europe, and even China and Japan, and the Chinese and Japanese made porcelain versions of Delft forms and decoration specially for the European market.

Despite the differences between Delftware and Italian maiolica, the fact remains that the one grew from the other, cross-fertilised, so to speak, by the impact of oriental porcelain. The tin-glaze technique was established in the Southern Netherlands early in the sixteenth century, and its beginnings were wholly Italian.

From the time of Guido da Savino's first pottery at Antwerp in 1512 for about a hundred years the Netherlands tin-glaze potters worked in a provincial version of the Italian manner. Apart from some tile panels and pavements, such as a tile-painting of 1547, supposed to commemorate Guido himself or his sons,[1] their work consisted mostly of small, serviceable vessels, thrown on the wheel and decorated with repeat patterns and pictorial motifs in the traditional Italian four colours, copper green, blue, yellow and ochre. The patterns were seldom difficult to follow, and were often painted quickly; and the inner throwing rings show that the pots were rapidly fashioned from soft clay and smoothed with a ribbing-tool on the outside, with occasional use of templates for the foot and the rim. Useful domestic pieces were certainly made, but few survive because things of this kind were used till they perished. Pharmacy vessels lasted longer, the examples ranging from squat containers for pills and ointments to attractive spouted jars and tall drug-pots of the *albarelo* type.[2] Small altar vases and decorative dishes were also made. Most of the decoration consists of geometrical patterns or formalised Faenza flowers and leaves, drawn in a strong, structural outline and filled in with colours. A few examples have heraldic ornament. A feature of the early Netherlands wares was the absence of manganese brown and the common use of a dark slate blue, from impure cobalt.

A considerable number of these everyday vessels, mostly damaged or fragmentary, have been excavated from the City of London and ports on the North Sea coast.[3]

1 The tile panel represents the Conversion of St. Paul and was designed by the ceramist Frans Floris. It is now in the Vleeschuis Museum, Antwerp.
2 The standard work is Bernard Rackham's *Early Netherlands Maiolica* (London, 1926), with many illustrations, including examples of pottery in paintings.
3 Examples are in the Guildhall Museum, the London Museum and the Victoria and Albert Museum.

A fascinating compendium of Antwerp patterns of about 1520 is to be found in the tile pavement in the chapel of The Vyne (near Basingstoke, Hampshire) [78]. The pavement has been reassembled from scattered tiles found in the house and grounds. They include intriguing faces and 'portraits' of great men and goddesses, and amongst them is the unmistakable face and hooked nose of Federigo da Montefeltro, Duke of Urbino. There are spirited animals and birds, an ingenious variety of flowers and intertwining leaf-and-stem patterns, garlands, roses and geometrical ornament, stock designs done by painters whose skill varied from a very high standard to the level of apprentices.[4]

The manufacture of painted pottery must have spread from the south to the northern Netherlands sometime during the 1560s. One of the Andries family was making pharmacy vessels at Middelburg before the explosion of the arsenal in 1570, and the names of individual *plateelbakkers* are recorded from Haarlem in the 1570s and Amsterdam in the 1580s.[5] To this period belongs a unique pewter-mounted flask painted in blue with roundels of St. John the Evangelist and the Annunciation with landscape backgrounds, with the monogram HE and the date 1570 on the shoulder. If the idea is typically Italian, the brushwork and detail appear to be Dutch [102].[6]

There exist a few examples of Flemish and Dutch maiolica of about 1600 or soon after, before the Italian polychrome tradition gave way to blue-and-white [103]. Small drug-pots were decorated simply with zig zags or wavy bands. More important pieces still followed the Italian pictorial convention, seen in dishes painted with a centrepiece of the Virgin and Child or a military scene. Jars were mostly decorated with bold flower and leaf designs, or pomegranates and other fruits, and similar motifs appeared on tiles.[7]

The oriental themes for which Delft became famous later in the seventeenth century were introduced by events that had no essential connection with pottery. The fortunes of the new Dutch Republic depended chiefly on its trade overseas, and its ships had to battle for their right to the high seas from Canton to the Hook. Their principal enemies were the Portuguese, and if a captain were lucky he might intercept a homeward-bound Portuguese merchantman. Some of these ships carried Chinese porcelain, as did the carrack *Catherina*, whose cargo was sold in Amsterdam in 1604, and the *Sanjago*, captured in 1602. The porcelain acquired a special name on the Dutch market, *kraakporcelain*.[8] After the formation of the Dutch East India Company in 1602, porcelain was

4 See Rackham, op. cit., for illustrations and historical background.
5 E. Hannover, *Pottery and Porcelain*, trans. B. Rackham (London, 1925), vol. 1, pp. 230–1, and Rackham, op. cit., pp. 39–49.
6 This piece was sold at Sotheby's in 1969 after belonging for a long time to a Dutch noble family—a further indication of Dutch origin. The only pieces I know of which are similar are blue-and-white painted pots made by Netherlandish emigrants in Triana, Seville.
7 See C. H. de Jonge, *Delft Ceramics*, trans. Marie-Christine Hellin (London, 1970), pp. 22–23 and plates. This book is the most concise and comprehensive survey of Delftware available in English and the whole of this chapter derives substantially from it.
8 T. Volker, *Porcelain and the Dutch East India Company, 1602–1683* (Leiden, 1954), p. 22. More than three million pieces of Chinese porcelain were shipped to Europe by the Company between 1602 and 1657 (*ibid*, p. 227).

obtained direct from the Far East, and a steady business developed through the Company's offices at Batavia. One of the Company's import offices was at Delftshaven, the port of Delft.

Ming blue and white porcelain was by no means unknown in other parts of Europe. The Portuguese had it and their pottery was influenced by it [88]. Yet they never followed it up systematically in their own work. Why not? Part of the explanation is probably that their local pottery traditions were already mature and settled, whereas the Dutch potteries were still small and open to new ideas, and the taste of the purchasing public was still free of tradition and the influence of past achievements and old possessions.

Porcelain was not immediately imitated by Dutch potters, though it impressed them by its strength and its perfect glazes, and by the strangeness and maturity of its painted designs. After the death of the Emperor Wan-Li in 1619, the supply of porcelain was interrupted by civil disturbances in China, but the demand for it persisted and soon the Dutch potteries began to respond. They began to derive border patterns from Wan-Li originals, and finally to make pieces with centrepiece and border painting taken directly from the Chinese conventions, some of which could stand beside porcelain without looking very different. The Dutch called this work 'porcelain' because it replaced it, although it was actually made from an off-white earthenware clay. At that time the name referred to the general appearance of the ware, not specifically to its material.

The potters who imitated the Chinese decorations were already used to deriving pictorial themes from copybooks and from engravings. It was less difficult for them to respond to oriental prototypes than it would have been for people with long-established traditions of their own. For a time the Dutch potters were unable to equal either the Italian or the Chinese originals; but they were gradually assimilating Chinese design ideas and freeing themselves from the structural decorative forms and picture themes of Italy. They also refined their throwing and their materials in response to the new possibilities that porcelain revealed to them.

This endeavour raised the quality of their clays and glazes to a superb level, as fine as anything known in Italy itself. During the years 1615–1630 they began to coat their pots completely in white tin glaze instead of covering only the painting surface and giving the rest but a transparent varnish glaze. They also adopted the use of *kwaart* (a name derived from the Italian *coperta*), a transparent overglaze applied by flicking with a brush over the powdery tin glaze after it had been painted, but before it went to be fired. In the firing the *kwaart* and the tin glaze melted, the former remaining as a semi-transparent film, giving depth to the finished surface and smoothing and deepening the blue pigment. By the skilful use of *kwaart* Dutch potters were able later in the century to achieve glaze finishes looking astonishingly like porcelain. The difference it made to the glaze and colour can often be seen by comparing the overglazed surface of a pot with the underside, where the *kwaart* was not applied.

Responding to porcelain examples, the potters began to develop tin glazes which were slightly stained with copper and cobalt, giving a cool white, but which unified the blue painting with the form as a whole by making a slightly blue ground. This practice was quite well known in Italy; however, it became customary at Delft because it helped the earthenware to resemble Chinese porcelain, and was especially effective with light and asymmetric kinds of decoration. Some of the less advanced pottery towns continued to use a plain white tin glaze all through the seventeenth and eighteenth centuries, and their painted decoration tended to stare out of the glaze rather than to harmonise with it.

The glazes that were developed to simulate porcelain were probably kept secret and passed down only amongst families or business associates. By the time recipes were published they were in all likelihood fairly widely known already. Some were published by the German chemist Kunkel in his *Ars Vitriaria Experimentalis* in 1679; some were included in the French encyclopaedia of 1756; some were published in the *Proefkundige Verhandeling* of A.F. in 1774; and Gerrit van Paape recorded some in his book *De Plateel-bakker of Delftscheaardewerkmaaker of 1794*. (See Appendix D.)

Experiments were made with the clay body of which Delftware was thrown and moulded, too. As explained elsewhere, few natural clays are satisfactory for the whitish body generally required for tin-glaze pottery. A good clay had to be plastic enough for forming, but not too plastic or it would probably crack as it dried. It had to be pale if it were to resemble porcelain, and it had to mature without warping at temperatures not far beyond 1000° Centigrade to be capable of taking any strong colour other than blue, and it needed to shrink more than most clays as it cooled in the kiln; otherwise the over-lying glaze would be liable to craze or crackle. The usual body of Delftware was a blend of three natural clays, one from Tournai, one from the Rhineland, known as 'black clay', and one local clay.[9] Some recipes advised English clay imported from near Bristol, which cost more than Tournai clay but was said to be better.[10]

Forms and painted decorations of Chinese inspiration predominated in Delft from about 1630 to the middle of the eighteenth century. European themes were also used all the time. Italianate picture compositions, usually taken from engravings of battle-scenes and hunting-pictures, appeared on showpieces in the 1630s and 1640s. Hannover calls them 'inartistic and unintelligent', 'overloaded with painting'. Nevertheless, some of them are skilful and impressive, although they have a pretentiousness that easily arises when alien styles are imitated by one seeking effects without really understanding a convention or enjoying the work for itself. In the painting of seascapes and buildings and scenes from popular life, the painters rendered things they knew and cared about, and then their work was often more delicate and natural. This convention lasted with variations until the end of the eighteenth century, when most of the Delft potteries closed down [107].

The great development of the potteries of Delft and of Holland in general occurred between about 1640 and 1730. The growth of activity can be inferred from records of the admissions to the Guild of St. Luke, to which painters of every branch of the art had to belong. Between 1610 and 1640 only ten master-potters were enrolled, whereas in the nine years 1651–1660 no less than twenty are recorded.[11] The potters began to use personal monograms and distinctive factory marks from about 1640 onwards—an

9   G. van Paape (1794), op. cit., p. 77, gives the proportions used in his time as Tournai clay 6, Rhineland clay 3, Delft clay 2.
10   F. W. Hudig, *Delfter Faience* (Berlin, 1929), p. 69 et seq.
11   E. Hannover, op. cit., vol. 1, pp. 233 and 236.

indication of the personal reputations that were being gained. From that time onwards the Dutch pottery industry was dominated by the town of Delft.

In 1654 a ship loaded with gunpowder exploded in the port of Delft destroying a large part of the city and many of the potteries, at a period when most of them were expanding. The old Delft brewing industry was in decline and many of the former breweries stood empty. Having access by water for heavy materials, they were suitable for conversion into potteries, and within a few years most of them were once again active. The apparent calamity probably helped the potteries considerably at a moment when they needed larger premises. As pottery factories, the names of the old breweries became famous throughout Northern Europe: The Double Tankard, the Peacock, The Young Moor's Head, The Three Golden Ash-Barrels, The Rose, The Three Bells, and many others.

Some of these premises were characteristic of Dutch town-building, in that space was available upwards but not sideways, and they developed an ingenious division of work between the various levels. In the remarkable tile-picture of the Bolsward pottery in Friesland, dated 1737, the kiln is shown extending upwards through each floor of the building [178].[12]

Another reason for the rapid advance of the Delft potteries was that the town was already a centre for painters and engravers.[13] Thus it already possessed many of the basic skills for producing the most expensive kind of pottery. Without this reserve of human skill, the town's industries could never have developed so fast. A number of painters worked both in oil on canvas and on pottery, as was done by Abraham de Kooge and Frederik van Frytom.[14] Pottery painting was not yet the repetitive drudgery that it became in later times, and it was accepted as an art in its own right, not just as a resort for the unsuccessful.[15]

The simpler painted wares of Delft were a by-product of the fine pieces for which the town became famous; they were profitable kiln fillers and were useful training pieces for apprentices. Repeat decoration was marked on the pots by means of pattern-papers in which the design was pricked out with small holes. A pounce-bag of powdered charcoal was dabbed against the paper as it rested against the pot, marking the composition on the powdery glaze. The outlines of important features in the decoration were usually painted with a fine, dark line called *trek*. Then the details and tone-washes were added within them. Master-painters occasionally completed entire pieces alone, but usually they only painted the *trek* and important details.

For the most part the simpler, utilitarian decorated pottery came not from Delft but from other centres such as Gouda, Rotterdam, Amsterdam and Dordrecht. If some of it was second-rate, there are some interesting pieces with strong polychrome brush decoration in which is seen the last of the old Italianate tradition, lightened by the freer

12   See illustration. The panel is in the Rijksmuseum, Amsterdam.
13   Peter de Hoogh, Jan Steen, Vermeer and Karel Fabritius, for example, were all citizens of Delft.
14   See A. Vecht, *Frederik van Frytom* (Amsterdam, 1968).
15   Sir James Thornhill, father-in-law of Hogarth, painted a series of dishes with allegorical classical figures of the signs of the Zodiac when he visited Delft in 1711. One is shown in *World Ceramics*, plate 471.

sense of space and asymmetric composition that had been gained from oriental examples [112].

Even at Delft, not all the pottery was painted. Especially around the mid-seventeenth century a good deal of white ware was made for domestic use and for ornament: jugs, small plates, large dishes, bowls, butter-dishes, drug-pots, jugs and pitchers for wine and beer, and the like [104]. Moulded vessels, such as the 'shell-rim' bowls and dishes with cusped or wavy rims, and jugs with ribbed or wavy surfaces were particularly attractive in plain white, and the dense, satin-surfaced white showed well on them. The edges and modelling of plain white wares showed slightly amber-colour, because the glaze was thinner, and the glaze was the more attractive for not being quite opaque. In the eight-teenth century, toys and figurines were made in plain white, too.

More potteries were founded during the period 1660–1680 than at any other time, when imports of K'ang Hsi porcelain were interrupted by Civil war within China itself. After 1680 the number of new foundations decreased steadily, for new proprietors were usually able to take over factories whose owners had grown old or run into difficul-ties.

Most of the factories appear to have been owned by a small group of businessmen who financed their purchase and provided the working capital and managed the commercial dealings. The practical management had to comply with the rules of the painters' guild and be in the hands of a master-potter. Such a man was known as the 'shop-keeper'. He might be the owner or part-owner of the factory, but frequently he was simply the owners' delegate, appearing for official purposes to be the owner.[16]

The factory units were quite small, and were fairly often bought and sold and changed their speciality with change of ownership. Detailed records of separate factories are published in C. H. de Jonge's *Delft Ceramics*. Skilled craftsmen-painters, throwers, modellers and alchemists or arcanists (glaze and body technicians) were often not permanent members of a factory staff, but moved freely from one to another by special contracts. Businessmen were sometimes part-owners of several factories. Wouter van Eenhoorn (d. 1679, father of Lambert and Samuel) was the founder or co-owner of no less than five; he seems to have started his career as a businessman and to have become also a master-potter as his interests expanded.

Although nearly all the Delft potteries had individuality, based on the special talent of the shopkeeper or owners, the distinctions between them were frequently fine and shifted continually, for they all worked in similar materials within a small range of recognised styles. Their imaginative potential was held in check by trading considera-tions, and they borrowed ideas readily from each other.[17] Unlike the seigneurial fac-tories of France, Germany and Italy, the Dutch potteries were not controlled by a single

16 See de Jonge, op. cit., p. 33–34.
17 Consequently Dutch pottery marks are important for attributing pieces to particular factories. How-ever, the marks are not always reliable. Factories sometimes copied each others' marks from about 1650 onwards, and even in 1764 the Guild of St. Luke found need to impose a fine of 200 florins for the pirating of marks (A. Vecht, op. cit., p. 21). The pottery marks are confusing also because some factories had a factory mark which lasted a long time; some changed their marks when they came under new ownership; some used the monogram of the owner; and some allowed pots to be marked with the personal monogram of the painter, who might or might not be the factory owner as well.

wealthy man whose purse allowed him to follow up his own ideas; they were commercial businesses, raising money on interest and paying dividends, and the price of a mistake could well be bankruptcy.

The principal categories of Delftware were common to nearly all the potteries: *Wit Goet*, or plain white earthenware, including apothecaries' vessels on which the decoration was confined to an inscription within a cartouche; *wapengoet en porcelejn*—wares with heraldic decoration; Italianate compositions and decorative motifs were known as *Straets goet*, that is, they were derived from pottery imported from Italy via the Straits of Gibraltar; there were in addition many varieties of oriental designs with leaf and flower patterns, landscapes and figure-compositions, derived from late Ming or K'ang Hsi originals, as for example the *Kaapsche schotels* (plates from the Cape), ceremonial dishes with delicate decoration in the style of Wan-Li porcelain. Shortly before 1700 came the enamel-painted and gilded wares, nearly all derived from Oriental models, *famille verte*, and others from China; Imari and Kakiemon enamels from Japan. Lastly there were the landscapes, seascapes and scenes of popular life; these were related to both the Italian and the Far Eastern traditions, but were a Dutch invention distinct from both, and appeared on almost all kinds of shape and, of course, on tiles.

Chinese porcelain was the dominant influence. It introduced a new kind of ceramic painting into Europe, together with new conventions of shape which amounted to an aesthetic language which took European taste by storm [106]. As technical 'pacers' Chinese porcelain continuously challenged the Dutch ceramists to find equivalents for Far Eastern methods and materials.

Something must be said here about the sequence of painting techniques used at Delft. From the end of the era of Italianate polychrome, that is about 1620 to around 1670, almost all Delftware was painted in blue monochrome or in varying tones of blue, under the influence of Chinese blue-and-white porcelain [108]. About 1670 polychrome began to return to favour under the inspiration of Chinese enamels. The traditional palette was extended considerably by blending pigments; manganese brown and a deep red ochre became important [109]. The colours were still fired at high temperature in the glaze firing and are called 'high temperature polychrome'. The brilliance and variety of the colours were limited by this high temperature. Purple, vermilion, orange and turquoise, for example, were virtually unobtainable. Yet the example of imported enamel wares from China continually challenged the potters to improve the range and brightness of their colours.

During the 1680s and 1690s, research was being done on new pigments and by about 1700 several factories were using enamel colours and gilding very effectively. The enamels had to be fired at low temperature. Therefore the pottery was given the traditional high temperature glaze firing in the course of which the blues, browns and greys were fused into the glaze, and afterwards it was painted in enamels and fired at about 760°C. in a muffle. A muffle is an enclosed chamber from which the fire gases are excluded, in which an oxidising atmosphere can therefore be maintained throughout the firing. Without it the enamels would have become rough and discoloured. The gold leaf was fixed to the fired glaze in a later firing at still lower temperature. The combination of high temperature polychrome with enamels and gilding produced pottery whose colours still had the deep 'bite' of high temperature colour, and yet had also the brilliance and variety of enamels and gold [110].

After about 1710 a few potteries went over to all-enamel decoration with gilding, abandoning the high temperature technique. Because the enamels adhered only to the surface of the glaze instead of permeating it, they could be used with the utmost delicacy and precision [Colour Plate P].

The discovery of new techniques did not mean that they became generally current. Many of the potteries used the long-established high temperature method all through the eighteenth century, avoiding the high costs and the retraining of painters necessitated by the enamel technique.

Despite the difficulty of distinguishing between the work of the various factories and individual masters, the work of certain master-potters stands out from the rest.

Samuel van Eenhoorn (mark SVE) managed the Greek A factory from 1674 to 1686. He is known especially for his large decorated dishes, some of which are as much as thirty inches wide, painted with intricate leaf and flower ornament in slightly purplish blue with Chinese floral motifs and baroque pattern-work. He also excelled in freely drawn oriental figures.

Rochus Hoppesteyn (mark RHS) shared with his mother the management of the Young Moor's Head from 1680 to 1686 and was then sole owner until his death in 1692 at the age of only 33. He specialised in high temperature polychrome painting which was derived, though seldom copied, from 'five colour' Ming enamels and K'ang Hsi porcelain, and he used a fine blue-white glaze which resembled porcelain very closely. Hoppesteyn was an assured draughtsman and designer and he became as much at home in oriental conventions as the Chinese themselves, but he earned a personal fame which would have been incomprehensible in the Far East. He was the first ceramist of importance to use fully the newly developed technique of gilding. It was not his invention: the work was contracted out for firing at The Hague by the potters named Van der Lith and Godtling, who had found out how to do it. Gilding meant applying gold, either as gold leaf or powder or in solution. It had nothing to do with the smoked lustre techniques of Spain and the Middle East, which seem to have been unknown in Holland. From Van der Lith and Godtling, Hoppesteyn obtained a remarkable deep red pigment made from finely levigated bole, and a bright green.[18] Hoppesteyn's work shows the curious natural affinity between Chinese decoration and European baroque. He also worked from Italianate engravings, a convention which survived at the Young Moor's Head well into the eighteenth century and was later associated with the painter J. van Haagen.

Adrianus Kocks (mark AK) managed the Greek A after Samuel van Eenhoorn. He purified the cobalt blue and achieved a colour close to the clear deep blue which had been developed at the Chinese imperial factories of Ching-tê-Chêng and appears on K'ang Hsi porcelain. Starting with designs borrowed from Chinese porcelain, Kocks also used European baroque decoration and adapted landscapes and figure scenes from engravings. The three elements appear together on many of the masterly pieces made for Queen Mary's Dairy at Hampton Court in 1695. Under Kocks and his son, Pieter

18   de Jonge, op. cit., p. 71.

Adrianus (mark PAK), the Greek A made some of the most impressive and perfectly finished of all Delft pottery, but much of it is so highly contrived that it is easier to admire than to enjoy. The younger Kocks is credited with some of the first *delft dorée* —blue, red and gold decorated pottery based on the Japanese Imari wares which were imported from the 1690s onwards.[19]

Frederik van Frytom was an oil painter and engraver as well as a painter of ceramic tiles and plates. He specialised in idyllic country scenes of wholly European character, painted in blue *camaïeu* with a subtle control of tone which can only amaze anyone who has ever painted on tin glazes. He produced effects of light and recession and a poetic feeling which makes his work quite different from the conventional landscapes painted by his successors [105]. To van Frytom are attributed many wall-dishes with broad, plain rims which act like circular frames to concentrate the picture. The blue and the thick, satin-textured 'dubbelwit' glaze are of the finest quality, and within the limited range of the convention these dishes are minor masterpieces. Van Frytom worked at some time with Lambertus Cleffius of the Metal Pot. He seems to have been a specialist 'outworker' working mostly from his own designs in his own house, and occasionally carrying out specially commissioned work.[20] The gild regulations allowed each factory to have a few associate painters of this kind, who presumably worked on pieces demanding exceptional skill, or needing peaceful conditions and perhaps trials if they were to be done properly. On the strength of his 'dubbelwit' glaze some plain white jugs are also attributed to van Frytom. The forms are gracious and the dense, white glaze is extremely beautiful on its own.

Ary van Rijsselberg was in his prime as a ceramic painter during the years 1718–1735. To him are attributed a number of gilded and enamelled faience pieces signed AR, and some other examples with the mark of the Greek A under P. A. Kocks. If the attributions are right, van Rijsselberg was a craftsman painter of astonishing versatility, working in the style of *famille verte* or Japanese Imari and Kakiemon models and absorbing their decorative language so thoroughly that it became his natural form of expression. In this sense he was the outstanding representative of a whole tribe of Dutch pottery painters, whose imagination was lit up by exotic oriental styles more readily than by their own heritage [Colour Plate P]. He did not merely derive, but made fresh and original designs within the oriental convention. Nonetheless, few of these painters had the sensitivity of van Rijsselberg; few could go beyond what they observed in their models, and none achieved anything of strong or fundamental originality.

Most of these men, and many others, were master-potters recognised as such by the Guild of St. Luke, combining technical knowledge with a talent for the organisation of workshops and a grasp of business, at the same time as they worked on prototypes and special pieces themselves. Their workpeople were mostly specialists: throwers, painters, mould-makers, kiln men, glazers and so forth, but they themselves must have known

19   Until recently this type of ware and the mark PAK was usually attributed to Adriaen Pijnacker of the Three Porcelain Flasks. See *Delfs Aardewerk: Dutch Delftware*, introduction to the Rijksmuseum illustrated guidebook (Amsterdam, 1967). For imports, see T. Volker, *The Japanese Porcelain trade of the Dutch East India Company after 1683* (Leiden, 1959).
20   A. Vecht, op. cit., p. 23.

every branch of the work at first hand. Their individuality is most evident in their styles of painting, but they must also have devoted much time to the design of forms. Most of them were born into pottery families, and their judgment of ceramics was activated almost from the cradle. The management and part at least of the ownership of the Delft potteries remained in the hands of such men until about the middle of the eighteenth century. Only after that did the factories become dominated by businessmen without much experience or personal interest in the actual making of pottery.

Certain types of pottery were made by almost all the Delft factories. Amongst the most commonly found were the *kast-stel* garniture sets of five jars which stood on the cornices at the top of cupboards [Fig. 26]. There were three lidded jars of swelling profile, separated by two jars of narrow beaker shape. The shapes were Chinese but the set itself was a Dutch idea; it was so popular that the jars remained a staple product of the factories even though Chinese sets were imported on a big scale by the East India Company.

Figure 26.   Dutch *kast-stel* garniture set.

Pictorial plates for the shelf or wall were, of course, not a new category of ceramics, but they were made more abundantly at Delft than anywhere else in Europe at any time. They became a kind of popular picture gallery for the mercantile community, and were made familiar also in England and Germany [107]. Sometimes they were painted in sets of twelve, with religious illustrations or landscapes or seascape themes, usually in *camaïeu* blue. Towards 1700 many plaques were made with Chinese figure decoration in polychrome, and later in enamel with gilding. Sets of music plates were painted with the theme or part of a song, together with words. The dessert was served on them after dinner, and once the plates were bare the company could start singing. Such plates had been made in Italy a hundred years earlier, but in Holland they achieved special popularity and graced a long-established custom. Inevitably they had a high accident rate.

Flower vases with multiple flower-sockets were made in a great variety of contrived and exotic forms, from towers and pagodas to squat shapes with applied orifices and modelled ornament. They are often ingenious rather than beautiful.

The Dutch East India Company imported the first tea into Europe about 1610, but some years elapsed before special pots were made in Holland for brewing tea. The teapot is said to be descended from the Chinese wine-jug, a tall, narrow necked vessel with a long spout and a handle. However, the Chinese red stoneware teapots which served as models for the Dutch have little resemblance to the wine jugs and were really not unlike the teapots of today, except that the spout was smaller in proportion to the rounded body. The Dutch began to imitate red stoneware teapots about 1670, and Ary de Milde and Samuel van Eenhoorn were granted a patent for their manufacture for fifteen years from 1680. Tin-glaze teapots with blue or polychrome decoration were only made after about 1700, and thereafter remained an established type of pottery vessel, taken up also in France and England as the habit of tea-drinking became fashionable. In Holland they were made not only in white tin glaze, but in tin glaze with coloured stains, giving solid glaze grounds of black and olive green, over which the designs were painted. Some of the pots are very small, and were perhaps used by ladies for sampling different teas at parties. Teapots are amongst the most pleasing of Dutch tin-glaze vessels, trim and self-sufficient, ceremonial and slightly exotic. On them *chinoiserie* seems especially appropriate.

Finally, there were the tiles, which were made in almost inconceivable quantities for two hundred years, and which are still being produced by methods similar to the eighteenth century technique at the Tichelaar factory at Makkum in Friesland, established about 1600, probably the longest-lived of all North European tin-glaze factories.[21] Some tiles were made at Delft, but most of them came from other centres, especially from Rotterdam and Amsterdam factories with large kilns designed to fire them by tens of thousands. The making, painting and firing of tiles on a large scale needed special conditions different from those of pot-making, and in Holland, Spain and Portugal (and perhaps elsewhere) tiles were almost always produced by specialist factories, not by potteries. Tiles were not made of pot clay. To minimise warping in the drying process, and to survive heat around stoves and fireplaces, they were made of a sandy body, usually containing a fairly high proportion of common red clay.

Only in the Middle East had tiles ever been made in comparable quantity, and the difference could hardly have been greater. There, the tiles usually formed part of a large wall space, dome, or tower, or some other architectural feature, covered with specially shaped and decorated glazed blocks, all on a grand scale. Dutch tiles were usually only about fourteen centimetres square (about the span of a hand) and most often each tile was painted as a complete and self-contained unit, with corner-motifs which made a secondary design when the tiles were arranged side by side. From the polychrome tiles of the early seventeenth century onwards the variety of designs was vast, too extensive to summarise here, but included certain favourite types of pattern such as those based on flowers and fruit, some Italianate, some 'Chinese', and some botanical, also many kinds of figures, especially soldiers, Biblical and mythological illustrations, figures in landscapes, and fishermen with boats in seascapes and harbour scenes. Most of such tiles were installed to provide clean, durable and decorative coverings for walls and stoves in private houses.[22]

Large tile schemes designed for specific architectural settings were relatively unusual. Curiously, the largest known tile panels are in Portugal, where there are still a good many

---

21   Ir. P-J. Tichelaar, the present director of the Makkum factory, has estimated that the total number of tin-glaze tiles made in Holland is about eight hundred million.
22   See C. H. de Jonge, *Netherlandse Tegels* (Amsterdam, 1971).

tile pictures in churches and palaces for which they were made to measure in the late seventeenth and early eighteenth centuries. The largest existing Dutch tile composition is probably the series of pictures of the life of St. Theresa, made in Amsterdam about 1690 for the royal Convent of Madre de Deus, Lisbon. Most of the tile paintings, like this one, were of religious subjects and were adapted and enlarged from engravings.

About 1700 decorative tile panels became popular as firebacks. These were usually painted with an immense spray of flowers bursting out of a small vase, surrounded by birds and insects, the whole composition usually covering some forty tiles [114]. The idea could well have come from Turkish tile ornament, in which the vase of flowers had been current for centuries. A number of large tile compositions were made to special commission, as for example the wall-panels of bouquets, birds and oriental landscapes made for the kitchen of the Amalienburg pavilion at Nymphenburg (1734-9). The tiles were probably made at the Flowerpot factory in Rotterdam.

Many Dutch houses still have tiles which were fixed in the seventeenth and eighteenth centuries, including space-fillers that are plain white. The 'white' varies from soft, cool white to whitish amber and even pink, according to the type of glaze and the thickness of the application and the clay of the body. The effect is mellow and gracious, very different from the dead surfaces and stark whiteness of modern white tiling.

Since tiles were made in such great quantities, their painting became economical and extremely fluent, and the repeat patterns have an unselfconscious verve which contrasts with the studied decoration on formal vessels.[23] In this field there were few oriental prototypes to follow, and though the tile painters borrowed some subjects from engravings and laid out the composition with pounces and pricked papers, they became fully their own simply by much repetition. The 'hand-writing' of the painter and the rapid plying of the brush became an essential part of the finished design. Perhaps the most pleasing of all Dutch tiles are the late seventeenth-century blue and early eighteenth-century manganese brown monochrome painted drawings, where the nimble brushwork has the directness of a pen and wash sketch.

The use of muffle-kilns for firing enamels on to the already finished glaze (*petit-feu*) developed rapidly in the early eighteenth century. The combination of high-fired polychrome colours, enamels and gilding reached its finest point around 1720 [Colour Plate P]. The Greek A, the Rose and the Young Moor's Head factories excelled in it. At this time the Dutch factories were technically more advanced than the French, but they lacked the incentive to develop large services of tableware which gave a special impulse to the development of the French potteries. The finest skills in Holland continued to be given to imitating the ideas of others, for instance K'ang Hsi porcelain (in which field the Chinese themselves also imitated the Dutch imitations[24]); also Japanese Imari

23   Special tile-panels painted by individual artists were, of course, a different matter. They were usually signed and were mostly carefully translated from engravings, and were really closer to panel paintings than to wall-tiles.

24   Chinese porcelain imitating Delftware is by no means uncommon and is an amusing counterpart to the efforts of the Dutch to imitate Chinese work. Some examples show heavily bewigged men and women in elaborate European costume, which clearly struck the Chinese as absurd (e.g. porcelain dishes in the Ionides Bequest, Victoria and Albert Museum. The Bequest also includes a blue-and-white armorial plate and a drug-jar with a European inscription).

wares and the delicate, asymmetrical flower and landscape compositions of the Japanese Kakiemon manner. Thereafter followed versions of Chinese *famille verte* and *famille rose* enamels, and by the middle of the century some potteries were working with purely enamel decoration in the style of Meissen porcelain.

A great opportunity seems to have been missed in the early eighteenth century. In human and artistic terms the experience of two generations was to a large extent wasted by the emphasis on imitation and commerical security, while the imaginative potential of master-potters had little scope. It may be all too easy to evaluate the work of this time in modern terms which simply did not exist then, and to regret the lack of individuality and personal experiment which is felt to be important today. This really misses the point, for each era does not so much choose its values as respond to those which already exist. Individuals may accept them or react against them, but in either case they are being influenced by them. Modern attitudes exist against a background of highly evolved industrial technology which was unknown in the eighteenth century. The artist-potter of today tends to react against the perfection of finish and delicacy of pattern which the Dutch valued so highly. To the modern potter, all that has been said. The potters of that time were discovering that it could be said, and for them this discovery was as magnetic and wonderful as is the modern potter's discovery that he can, on occasions, be almost free of precedent and work from himself, alone.

Nonetheless, the Dutch potters eventually paid dearly for knowing so much about oriental porcelain. Their French and English counterparts knew it less intimately and arrived at a kind of *chinoiserie* which was as much European as Chinese. Their very ignorance forced a kind of development upon them. Where the Delft potters worked from Chinese models, the Rouen potters reinterpreted Delft models. The tale changed in the telling, and people began to tell new tales without realising that they were doing so. The Dutch were to some extent held back by their very success. The demand for their work became so large that they had to establish highly organised working conditions to meet it, and to train thousands of people to perfect specialised processes. It is hard to train human beings to do something very well; to re-train them to do it differently is harder still. Modern factories have exactly the same problem: once machinery is set up to produce certain designs, a change in any one part of the process is liable to upset the others, and so the price of change rises perpetually.

About 1750 the Greek A factory under Z. and T. Dextra began to specialise in all-enamel decoration, abandoning altogether the practice of painting direct on the unfired glaze, a technique which had enabled the colour to permeate the glaze in the firing and had given tin-glaze wares their essential character. The enamel technique could be applied to any kind of glaze, and from now on the white tin glaze was only one amongst many coloured grounds, black, brown, blue, green and turquoise, all of which carried enamel decoration. Although from a technical point of view the enamel technique increased the possible range of colour and expression, it now actually limited it, for it was used to dodge certain fundamental requirements of skill, and to produce dependable, foolproof polychrome decoration on ceramic trivialities which quickly caught the eye and lightened the purse.

From about 1750 onwards Delftware became increasingly pretty, contrived and unambitious in all but a commercial sense, with an ever-increasing proportion of cast toy pieces and trinkets, shoes, sledges, figurines of heroes and shepherdesses, cow milk-jugs, baskets, birdcages, miniature urns and vases. Most of these things were painted with clever, ephemeral decoration. Little trace of feeling or originality remained to be lamented when at the end of the eighteenth century the Delftware potteries began to go out of business. They succumbed to embargoes on the importation of their work by neighbouring countries,[25] and in particular to the competition of porcelain and English whiteware. In the nineteenth century there was a commercial attempt to revive Delft-ware in factory conditions by using underglaze painting on a white clay body. The technique could fairly be called a vulgar imitation of the real thing and could never have been a true revival. The working conditions of mass-production could never have led to the same spirit or quality of work as of old. In particular, the priceless thread of master and pupil succeeding one another in a living tradition had already been broken.

25   Mentioned by van Paape, op. cit., in 1794 as one of the chief reasons for the decline of Delft.

1 0

CENTRAL EUROPE

It is said of the great King Matthias Corvinus of Hungary (1440–1490) that even in the midst of his many and long wars his camp was a school of chivalry, his court a nursery of poets and artists. Born to a kingdom confronting the Turks on one side, with the persistent threat of the Habsburg Empire on the other, and beset by the intrigues of the nobility in his own country, he still found time enough to free his mind from the demands of diplomacy and war to attempt to establish a new Italian Renaissance in Eastern Europe. Under his patronage poets, artists, scholars, architects and men of science were established at Buda, and also numbers of Italian craftsmen and artisans. The first maiolica craftsmen and potters probably reached this part of Europe in the King's service about 1476, the year of his marriage to Princess Beatrix of Naples. The occasion is commemorated in a beautiful Faenza dish with the arms of Hungary and Naples painted in the border [116].

The King's dream of Hungarian Humanism died with him. He was followed by a succession of weak rulers; his kingdom was wasted by the machinations of rival groups of nobles, and finally by a series of Turkish invasions which the divided country could not withstand, the first marked by the Turkish victory of Mohač in 1526, after which the Turkish army reached as far as Vienna; later invasions followed in 1540 and 1552. By the 1550s most of the population of southern and central Hungary had been killed or taken into slavery, and their lands remained an obscure province of the Ottoman Empire for the next hundred and fifty years. No trace remained of the Italian immigrants or their work.

The Christian territories bordering the Turkish Empire remained unsettled frontier lands and would never normally have attracted other skilled craftsmen. Yet, within a few decades many Italian and some Swiss craftsmen settled in these very regions, finding there a liberty they could not have in their native lands.

These men were known as New Christians or Habaners. They belonged to an anabaptist sect which claimed complete religious autonomy, beyond the authority of any church, and therefore they were persecuted by the Protestants as well as by the Roman Catholic Church. The movement began in Zürich about 1524 and was joined by many of the ablest craftsmen and artisans—men perhaps without much school-learning, but accustomed to thinking for themselves, creative by disposition, self-reliant and naturally associated by their callings.[1] From Zürich the new teaching spread into Germany and

1 The name anabaptist means 'baptised anew'. The anabaptists abolished child baptism and returned to the adult baptism of the early church. They regarded the Sermon on the Mount as the supreme teaching of Christ and depended on the guidance of the Inner Light, not on the authority of the church or

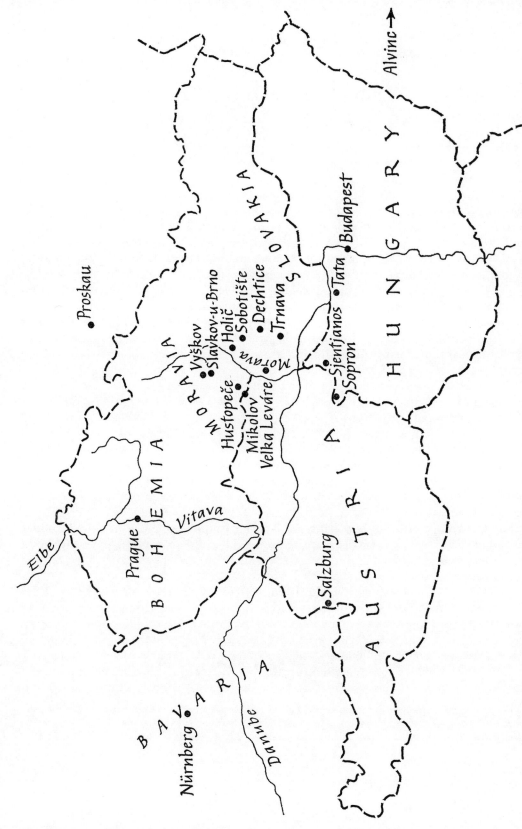

Map 7. Central Europe, showing the chief centres and more important villages where tin-glaze pottery was made.

the Low Countries and to northern Italy, where it found devotees in a number of towns, especially in Faenza, the most important of all the centres of maiolica in Italy, which had been under the rule of the Papal See since being taken by Cesare Borgia in 1501. Here they were methodically persecuted, and at one time the town was attacked and captured by a Papal army in order to extirpate them, but of course this only increased their resolve.

The most determined of the brethren began to seek freedom of worship in other lands. Enduring great sufferings, groups of New Christians began to work their way to the North East and reached Bohemia and Moravia in 1526. Other groups followed in waves which reflected the spasms of persecution. By the 1540s the first settlers were being forced eastward into Southern Slovakia, and from 1546 others settled in western Hungary. In these areas exposed to Turkish invasions the landlords welcomed them because of their industry and technical skills. Penalties were imposed on them by the Catholic kings but were often ignored by the aristocracy who resented the central authority and were themselves often in opposition to the church. The new tenants developed their estates and manufactured things which their protectors valued.[2]

The new Christians, Habanim, or Habaners, as they called themselves, were particularly skilled as physicians, gold- and silver-smiths, potters and weavers. Soon after their arrival they began to group themselves in small, virtually self-supporting settlements known as 'courts', which included their workshops and dwellings in a single enclave where everything was communally owned. Each court was administered by elected elders who took charge of its business dealings and maintained the strict rules of work and prayer to which the people were dedicated. They lived in the utmost simplicity, allowing themselves only the meagre necessities of food and clothing, following an ideal of holy poverty which was intended to be the closest possible following of the life of Christ Himself and the Apostles.

Whatever the Habaners did was done well. Many of their houses are still standing today, virtually unaltered except that the steep roofs are now tiled instead of thatched. Their tools and the articles they made for daily use were always expertly made from the best materials, and were beautiful and ingenious.

The Habaners were prepared to endure conditions which few other men would have withstood, and yet remained competent to develop natural resources and perform skilled work such as few peasants or townsfolk could possibly undertake. The first potter-settlers delved deep for iron-free marl-clays suitable for maiolica, mined lead for their glazes, built their own wheels and kilns, workshops and houses, prepared pigments from local material and used water-power for their mills and simple machinery, and started producing fine, painted pottery in a remarkably short time. A number of settler groups

---

priesthood. Generally, they were peaceable men and avoided any political involvements, but some anabaptist groups preached violence and revolution as the only answer to the persecutions they endured. This conviction led to the forcible establishment of a 'millennial kingdom' in Münster, which came to a bloody and appalling end when the town was retaken in 1535. The anabaptists referred to in this chapter appear to have avoided violence.

2 B. Kristinkovicz, *Haban Pottery*, Budapest, 1962, p. 8, and K. Černohorsky, *Moravská Lidová Keramica* (Prague, 1941), pp. 44–45.

had to move because of Turkish attacks, especially in west Hungary, and had to re-establish themselves again and again.

By the later part of the sixteenth century the Habaner potters were established in three principal areas where raw materials were available.

1. Eastern Moravia, where the chief settlements were at Mikolov, Slavkov-u-Brno and Hustopeče.
2. Western and southern Slovakia, principally at Sobotište (by 1546), Velké Leváre (1588) and Košolná.
3. Western Hungary around Sopron and soon after at Szentjános.

All the Habaner 'courts' appear to have produced plain earthenware and slipware for their own use and for occasional sale in the neighbourhood. Tin-glaze wares were at first made only by the Italian Habaners of Moravia [115]. In the early seventeenth century these potters were driven eastwards by a wave of religious persecution, and from about 1610 onwards western Slovakia was the chief centre for Habaner painted tin-glaze pottery. The potteries produced both tin-glaze ware and coarse red earthenware and the same marks have been found on sherds of each kind. The one was made for sale for the benefit of the community, and the other principally for its own use.

All the areas where the Habaners settled were risky: Moravia because of persecution, and the eastern areas because of the danger of attacks by the Turks. The Hungarian Plain was under Turkish control. The Habaners never settled there, and tin-glaze wares were scarcely made there even after the Turks withdrew around 1700. The chief Hungarian settlements were at Alvinc in Transylvania, where Prince Gabor Bethlen established a court in 1621. This court flourished for over two hundred years. Another court was built at Sarospatak at about the same time, under the patronage of Duke Ferenc Racoczy II.

By an accident of history rather than by choice these potters arrived in an area which was unusually rich in the raw materials they needed. The chalky marl-clay which was virtually essential to them was abundant in western Hungary, the lesser Carpathians and the neighbourhood of Sarospatak. This they blended with common reddish clay and salt. Hungary possessed good mines of lead and copper and was the principal European source of cobalt in the sixteenth century. Antimony, for yellow pigments and glazes, was mined at Szalonak on the Batthyány estates, where most of the miners were also anabaptists. Tin for whitening the glazes originated in England and was bought from Danzig, where there was a strong anabaptist colony. The Habaners added some of the locally available borax as an additional flux to the glazes, a practice hitherto only followed in the Venetian potteries.[3]

Apart from their discipline and personal skill, the settlers had several advantages over the local earthenware potters, whose work was still virtually of late medieval type, made of natural unblended clays, unglazed, or with simple transparent galena glazes and little ornament of any kind. The settlers brought the Italian maiolica practice with them; they could make white glazes which were proof against crazing; they could prepare pigments and make opaque, coloured glazes; they were accustomed to brush decoration and were

3   B. Kristinkovicz, op. cit., pp. 35–36.

quickly appreciated for their skill in lettering and inscriptions. Thus they made a distinctly different kind of pottery from the cheap rural vessels which had so far been known. Their work was suitable for castles and big houses and was fit to take its place on the table or wall-rack with gold, silver and pewter [115; Colour Plate Q].

Habaner sherds are easily distinguishable from common, local pottery by the extreme fineness of the throwing, together with the precision with which all details of lips, feet, lids and handles were finished. The whitish clay which they used for tin-glazed vessels was prepared with immense care from selected deposits of lime-marl clay. It was levigated and sieved repeatedly until it became very fine, so that when fired it was much stronger than other earthenware, even though it was so thinly potted. In co-operation with metal-workers from among their own people, the potters made many vessels for specially fitted hinged lids and bases of silver and pewter; these combined the virtues of metal and ceramics, being elegant, durable, colourful and cleanable. A fine, strong type of vessel which appears to have been made a good deal in the late sixteenth century was a large melon-shaped wine-pot with a long handle springing horizontally from the neck and curving slightly to meet the shoulder. These pots usually had pewter lids and bases and were decorated on the shoulder with simple, carefully devised patterns of interlacing flowers and foliage in blue, brown, green and yellow, reminiscent of the Faenza Gothic floral ornament. [Fig. 27]. They were often dated and inscribed with names, initials or mottoes [115]. A smaller variety served as a table-pitcher [Colour Plate Q].[4] They also made stoves and stove-tiles from hollow, box-like units with relief moulding, usually with Italianate leaf-scroll and shell patterns. These blocks were sometimes covered with plain white tin glaze, and sometimes with contrasting white, yellow and opaque blue glazes. The moulding was not merely decorative: the larger the surface area of the tiles the more effectively they warmed the room.

Figure 27. Habaner *dzbán*, or wine-flask, of various sizes.

Figure 28. Habaner bowl form, of varying size.

The best known of all the Habaner shapes were the dishes with a very broad almost flat rim and a deep central recess, derived from the Italian *tondino*, a form already familiar to the well-to-do who had similar table dishes in pewter [Fig. 28]. In fact, a number of Habaner forms were ceramic versions of metal shapes. This indicates not their lack of

4 K. Černohorsky, op. cit., plates 2–6, dating from 1593–1613. The very earliest Habaner decoration (before about 1500) is in blue, green and yellow only. After 1600 the fine details and outline drawing were done in manganese brown.

invention but the kind of patronage they received: they were making the shapes which already had an established place in a household. The Habaner dishes were probably used occasionally at table, but were valued at least equally for the coasts of arms, commemorations and inscriptions which were painted on the rim [117]. The decoration on the early dishes, up to about 1650, was rigorously simple and effective: two fine bands usually marked out the inner and outer edges of the rim and the centre of the dish. The top of the rim contained arms, name or initials, surrounded by a simple garland. The rest of the rim was divided into three by two leaf-and-flower emblems, and in the centre of the dish was a simple tightly drawn, very delicate floral decoration. This flower decoration with a curved stem and coiled leaf-sprays appears on most early Habaner pottery, with endless variations, all of which are sensitively disposed and painted with controlled verve.[5] It is on their tall pitchers, barrel-vessels with knob-feet for brandy and other distillations, rectangular, hexagonal and octagonal flasks and bottles, drug-jars and spouted drug-pots and tiles [118]. Most of the pots bear witness to the Habaners' special skills, pottery, pharmacy and metalwork, and the close co-operation between the different trades within the brotherhood. Although the Habaners avoided strong drink and tried not to encourage its use, their skill in distilling and brewing was highly valued and, in some areas, they had special licences for this kind of work, and made vessels for storing and decanting beer, cordials and stronger potions, not all exclusively medicinal. Their puritan principles are reflected, however, in the complete absence at this period of drinking bowls, goblets and tankards.

The tradition behind all these vessels, unmistakably Habaner and Central European though they are, is that of the Faenza *bianchi* of the mid-sixteenth century—that is, a pottery with a thick very white glaze which is beautiful in itself, and was sometimes used without any decoration at all, but most often with localised, light decoration whose effect depends on its placing and brushwork and the way the colour and glaze enhance each other. This convention started in Italy as a reaction against the fully-painted *istoriato* ware. It agreed well with the Habaners' austere principles and enabled them to achieve the paradox of a luxury ware without extravagance.

The Habaners of Central Europe followed the Italian custom of marking out areas on their pots with painted bands, and painting the ornament in regular, logically disposed positions within them. In other ways they differed considerably from contemporary Italian practice, in the simplicity of their forms, which were mostly wheel thrown and usually had no applied modelling, or else were simple moulded forms with shell-like ribbing; they also confined themselves to a small range of flower-and-leaf ornament and strictly avoided representations of human figures and animals and any kind of pictorial decoration. Though they were reacting against the social and commercial climate of Italy, in a technical sense their heritage was wholly Italian.[6] Curiously, though, they

5   B. Kristinkovicz, op. cit., p. 25, says that in the seventeenth century the Habaners derived most of their flower and leaf forms from book illustrations, not from life, especially from the *Krauterbuch* of Lonicerus and the *Flora* of Clusius, who compiled most of his work on the estate of one of their strongest supporters, Boldizsár Batthyány.

6   See Gaetano Ballardini, 'Opere di maestri faentini e loro rapporto con le ceramiche *Habane*' (Turin 1932), and Guiseppe Liverani, 'The Revolution of White Maiolica of Faenza', *Connoisseur*, vol. CXLI (1957).

never carried on the Italian custom of covering the painted ware with a film or 'varnish' of transparent glaze, known in Italy as *marzacotto*. Habaner tin glazes are always relatively matt-surfaced.

The Italian background is clearest of all in the reticulated basket-like fruit bowls on a small pedestal foot which were a popular Habaner product about 1600. The idea is directly traceable to Faenza. The originals of these dishes were made by drawing intersecting arcs on a leather-hard clay dish and cutting out the resulting panels with a knife, and sometimes elaborating the reticulations with cusps and hearts and other shapes. The prototype was then fired and pressed into soft clay to make a mould. The mould was then fired in the bisque kiln and the dishes were fashioned by pressing plastic clay into it. These dishes are some of the most pleasing of all Habaner pottery. They were the furthest the potters were prepared to go in extravagance.

Most of the work for which the settlers were admired involved them in a certain amount of compromise; their ideals were strict and puritan and they made a clear distinction between what they would do for their patrons and what they needed themselves. The following extract from some ordinances drawn up in 1612 by the Habaner elder, Andreas Ehrenpreis, of Sobotište, describes their attitude clearly, and is a remarkable instance of craftsmen deliberately sacrificing commercial opportunity for the sake of an ideal.[7] It appears to mark the changeover from the early era of independent craftsmen to the more settled community system under which the Habaners lived for most of the seventeenth century.

Anno 1612. 11th December

First, that our people should give up all bone-white and blue crockery,* and all crockery of similar value mounted in pewter such as can be sold and bring in money; this the potter shall sell, and the remainder, that is anything old and worn out, should be given to the needy.

Henceforth the potters shall not make for themselves, their wives or friends, nor for any of our people, any expensive pottery of this sort (which has become for many a matter of show rather than of necessity), but it shall be and remain totally prohibited.

Our people shall make, as of old, pottery of certain colours, black, yellow, green and red: if our forefathers made do with it (when glazes were not half so dear as they are now) then we can do the same.†

The potters must place all their own glazes, of whatever colour or description, and also their own lead and tin, in the hands of the overseers, and they shall have no power to work for their [private] advantage or to introduce new and different patterns, but must let the overseers give out to them from stock whatever they need.

The overseers must keep firm control and not become slack so that the men make drinking cups fashioned according to vulgar taste like books‡ or boots and such like, as if men did not know well enough already how to get drunk. So also with painted ware (which is made for sale and to earn money) the decoration must not be overdone, and such things as do not appear suitable to us, as pictures of birds and animals and the like, should certainly not be depicted.

7 From the original German text given by K. Černohorsky, op. cit., pp. 247–8.

* i.e. tin-glazed painted pottery with the blue decoration which was not found in traditional slipware.
† i.e. slipware, needing only one firing and an inexpensive glaze.
‡ A number of brandy-flasks shaped like a book survive from later in the century.

Neither should our people make *badern* and *pixen* on the vessels, nor names, for these are needless and are unpleasing to those who come after.*

Our people shall not work for the priest, neither setting the kiln for him nor in any other way, for it behoves us to shun that man.

Also our people should not contract debts or big loans.

The potters' assistants shall not be allowed to distribute any crockery among our own people in the absence of the overseer, with the exception of cooking vessels.

What other people do [only] for money our people should still perform (as ever), right honourably conducting themselves in all their general activities.

And in the sale of goods let there be justice and fair dealing, lest one man ask too much for a vessel while another sells at bargain prices, causing people to speak ill of us.

A typical Habaner pottery workshop consisted of eight or nine men. There was little division of labour, and four or five of these men were probably skilled and versatile craftsmen, able to throw and decorate their work, well-versed in tile-making and moulding, and able to build, set and fire the kiln and, incidentally, skilled in making tools and kiln furniture. Any of them could have organised a workshop on his own account. Women occasionally worked as painters, but the other jobs were done by apprentices. This was probably the smallest viable working unit for a pottery at this period.[8] No one man alone could have produced enough work to live by if he had been obliged to divide his time between the preparation of clay and raw materials and the processes of making, firing and selling of the ware. This applies especially to tin-glaze wares, in which the painting took as much time as the throwing, and all the glazes and pigments needed to be calcined and ground before use.

The ordinances of 1612 were justified in sensing a need to affirm the Habaners' principles and discipline. Their recipes and methods really were secret, and their survival at this time depended on keeping them to themselves. It is even said that the kilns were fired secretly by night, though the purpose of this is obscure. More serious in the long run was the fact that they were puritans making luxury wares, constantly open to the pressure of making extravagant and appealing things which they disapproved of. They remained a people apart, distinguished by race and religion from the rest of the population, at least until 1700, but little by little the decoration of their work became more elaborate, reflecting the local tastes and the preferences of the aristocracy. On the broad-rimmed dishes the three simple flower-sprays began to send out shoots and tendrils and to link up into a continuous elaborate border pattern [120], and on bottles and pitchers it began to embrace more and more of the form as a whole.

The potters' very success must have imposed a strain on their principles. The patronage of royalty (for instance, of the Elector Palatine Frederick V and his son Rupert of the Rhine[9]) was accorded for their fine work, not for their austerity, and as maiolica became

* This requirement presumably applies to pots used by the community; named and dated pots were one of the Habaners' specialities for their clients.

8 I am indebted to Herman Landsfeld of Stráznice, potter and archaeologist, for communicating to me much unpublished material about the Habaners, as well as for allowing me to study his archaeological collection.

9 A dish in the Schweizerisches Landesmuseum, Zürich is thought to have been specially made to Prince Rupert's order. Kristinkovicz, op. cit., p. 10.

better and better known to the ruling classes, it was expected to display its peculiar felicities of painting and colour.[10] Another branch of pottery in which the Habaners excelled was in vessels with an opaque coloured ground glaze of blue, yellow, brown or black, with decoration in tin-white [121]. Much of their work in this field was finer than that of the more famous 'bleu de Nevers', and was especially in demand in the Turkish-dominated parts of Transylvania.

The tendency to elaboration was reinforced, more or less accidentally, in 1669. A series of Turkish invasions had devastated the Habaner establishments of Kosolná and Farkasin and had severely damaged many other 'courts'. In desperation the Habaners sent emissaries to ask help from their anabaptist brethren in the Palatinate and to the anabaptist Mennonites of Holland. The emissaries returned with money, but also with new pattern books and specimens of Delftware and ribbed faience vessels from Germany. These were seed-ideas for the more fanciful kind of decoration which began to emerge at the end of the seventeenth century, when the Turks began to withdraw and the bourgeoisie of the towns to flourish. The first Habaner decoration in blue monochrome dates from this period, and certainly derives from Dutch or Oriental examples. Birds, ferns, insects and animals began to inhabit the coiled plant forms and scrolls, and the first examples of elaborate domed and turreted buildings in pottery decoration probably were a recollection of the buildings in Dutch-oriental landscape ornament, even though the forms of the buildings suggests the Middle East or the fastnesses of Central Europe rather than the pagodas and temples of Cathay [Colour Plate R].

At this same period, roughly the last quarter of the seventeenth century, the Habaner 'court' system began to be abandoned, especially in the urban areas. Although Habaner potters quite often marked their work with personal signs, they had always been members of a closed community. Now they began to earn their livings as independent craftsmen,

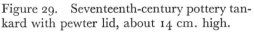

Figure 29. Seventeenth-century pottery tankard with pewter lid, about 14 cm. high.

Figure 30. Slovak *dzbán* or wine-pitcher of the eighteenth century, about 18 cm. high.

10   For example, special commissions are recorded for the Esterházy family in 1641 and 1689, for the Lord Chief Justice Johannes Maholany in 1673, and in 1696 for the Convent of Naháč. See B. Kristinkovicz, op. cit., p. 34.

taking direct private commissions, entering into business partnerships, trading in raw materials, borrowing and lending money and, above all, each drawing upon different aspects of the traditional repertoire of forms and painted designs in his own personal manner, including the pattern ideas newly arrived from Holland and Germany. The staple production of these potters now consisted of wine-pitchers, drinking tankards, and the ever-popular broad-rimmed dishes and, in general, any class of pottery likely to be used on festive occasions, and to grace the wall or dresser when not in use, or when used for storage [Figs. 29, 30]. Cooking vessels were not made in tin glaze; they were made either of iron or in plain red earthenware or slipware.

From about 1700 onwards the Habaners merged with the local Slovak population and their pottery traditions and methods were quickly taken up by native potters. The Habaner-Slovak ware of about 1700–1750 reflects joyfully the mingling of the two strains: the discipline of tradition lay behind it, but the potters were now free to exercise their private fantasy and to supplement the old designs with new material, freely interpreted from books and prints. Above all, they were able to respond to the wishes of private patrons. Many pieces of this period are obviously the potters' or painters' interpretation of some specific request, as the emblems of a trade surrounded by a garland, a pair of hearts transfixed and interlocking within a ribbon tied in a bow, a young hussar in uniform on his rearing mount, or (remarkably frequent) a butcher felling a tethered ox with a vast halberd. The traditional double-bands and flower designs and loop ornament, with a sprinkling of birds and beasts, formed the conventional themes into which the personal requirements were incorporated. These vessels result from the interaction of the buyers' idea on the one hand and the painters' repertoire and imagination on the other.

The period of this fruitful, entertaining interchange is well symbolised by a potter's sign dated 1732 from the small Slovakian town of Velka Levaré, painted in the four traditional maiolica colours [126]. The clay plaque was set in the wall beside the doorway of a pottery in an old Habaner 'court'. The principal figures are the potter himself handing a completed piece to his client, a nobleman in riding habit who is accepting it with satisfaction. Above these figures is something which looks at first like a pattern, but is in fact a formalised picture of a traditional block-wheel, such as was used till about 1750; the vertical side-spokes were turned with the foot. On top of the wheel is a vase; out of the vase springs a bouquet of flowers, and beside the flowers are two birds. The whole thing has a border of diverse patterns, probably samples of the standard range from which a client could choose when making his order. It is signed and dated KRIS-TUS MAG: DIE 23 JULI 1732.

One of the remarkable things about these pots is that the figurative part of the decoration was freely rearranged by the painter even when it was obviously derived from a printed original. Almost everywhere else in Europe, except in England, the use of prints tended to produce studied and literal translations of the original without much life and with no special relevance to pottery rather than to any other applied art. In central Europe the representations were nearly always rapidly drawn, with verve and individuality. Sometimes they were naïve, but they always agreed with the more conventional part of the decoration and harmonised with the shape and proportions of the vessel [122].

The painters remained aware of the pot as a whole, and the form and the painting belong together. Even though the pot is most unlikely to have been formed and painted by one and the same person, it feels as if this had happened, whereas in much maiolica or Delftware of the period the shape and the painting feel as if they were done by strangers at different times and places.

The Habaner work of the early eighteenth century is sometimes called Folk Art. It is not really so. It is the fruit of the collusion between a lively craftsman and the particular desires of his patron. The expansive mood of the pieces associates them with folk art, but each example is freshly conceived; the pottery conventions of the day were constantly being reappraised and combined in different imaginative ways with attention and forethought. Folk Art depends more on physical repetition and the contribution of the material itself with much less control from the mind. A good many Habaner floral motifs did, in fact, become absorbed by Folk Art and appeared in coloured slips over white engobe in the late eighteenth and nineteenth centuries, especially in the Dorond area of Transylvania and around Sarospatak in N. Hungary.[11]

Some of the potters became rich and ceased to be a people set apart from the rest of the nation. Some were re-converted to Catholicism. The Odler family of Dechtice were ennobled. The potter Imre Odler is said by some to have travelled to China and to have introduced new shapes and decorative features as a result of his visit, notably a deep K'ang Hsi blue, a 'bleu poudré' or blown-powder-blue effect, and marble-colour texture resembling cloud-patterns. It is easier to believe that he went there only in spirit, for he seems to have been the proprietor of a lively and prosperous workshop which also produced traditional wares with elaborate painting of flower-and-stem patterns, beasts, birds and fantastic buildings, some of which are probably by his own hand. His working life lasted till around 1710.[12] His descendants worked at Dechtice till 1838.

The period 1680–1740 was also the period in which the French faience tableware services were developed, replacing the gold and silver services which had so far been the customary dishes of wealthy men. Rouen, Strasbourg and Moustiers, Alcora, Meissen, Vincennes, and other faience and porcelain factories grew up in this period, providing the palaces and great houses of Europe with sophisticated tableware and ornaments which had no precedent in ceramic history. Though the Habaners sold much of their work to the nobility, they made nothing like the *faience noble* which was quickly becoming a social necessity for any kind of grand entertainment throughout the continent. The Habaners and Slovaks might have been quite unaware of it for all that can be detected in their production in the very same epoch. Why did they not respond to it? Some of the workshops were perhaps too small, too local, to know what was happening, or too poor to be able to change. But many of the craftsmen were affluent, some even rich, and they could perfectly well have changed had they wished to. The explanation is probably that they had a successful tradition of their own, and were simply too busy to change. Also, factory methods required fundamental change of attitude; for instance, the throwing of clay

11 Also perhaps at Vama and Bicsad in Roumania, where floral coloured slip decoration on a white ground was a speciality—see Gyorgy Domanovsky, *Hungarian Pottery* (Budapest, 1968), pp. 49 and 66.
12 B. Kristinkovicz, op. cit., p. 30.

forms on the wheel is a rhythmic, pleasing activity. It demands energy but it also returns it, whereas mould casting is a technical operation rather than a solace. Even when change is seen to be desirable—and as yet it was not—it is often easier to begin afresh than to change something which already exists.

In the long run faience tableware and ornaments were bound to sweep into fashion in central Europe, for the taste of all the continental aristocracy, and prospective aristocracy, was dominated by France. What could not be obtained at home was bought from abroad; local potteries continued to produce the traditional decorated pitchers, tankards, dishes, drug-pots and wine jars, but services of plates, soup tureens, turkey-dishes, ornaments and the pretty, delicate things came from the faienceries of France and Germany.

In 1745 the factory of Holič was started by the Empress Maria Theresa and her consort, Francis of Lorraine, and began to make faience for the Court in the French international style. Another smaller factory began at Tata in 1758 under the patronage of Count Joseph Esterházy.[13] The name factory may be misleading: neither establishment was very large at first. Holič could accommodate fifty or sixty people, but Tata probably never had a staff larger than that of a flourishing traditional workshop.

Neither factory resembled the dark satanic mills of a later age. The Holič buildings, which still exist, are elegant, two-storey workshops with large, well-lit rooms surrounding a spacious open courtyard, entered by a wide carriageway which goes through the building from the street. The factory lies close by the castle gates and was obviously a source of pride and interest to its royal owners.

The 'factories' differed from the workshops in their methods and their whole attitude to design. As makers of large services they had to be able to repeat shapes exactly, and the shapes which were wanted were baroque and rococo forms with scalloped edges, modelled handles, gadrooned rims, modelled ornament, all derived from beaten metal rather than wheel-thrown pottery [123]. Hence their natural means of shape-making was the mould rather than the wheel, and the natural method of decoration was to work in enamel colours from a precise design which could be learnt and repeated, rather than by permutations of traditional ornament or individual compositions which depended on the painter's personal imagination. The new factories depended on a few key craftsmen and technicians, sculptors, mould-makers, painters, kiln designers and arcanists to devise appropriate pigments, glazes and clay bodies. Once established, a design prototype passed from the studio to the factory for repetition in large or small sizes, as required. The chief difficulty of the new type of factory lay in obtaining, and above all in keeping, the services of the key men. Again and again, eighteenth-century factories were shaken because the chief sculptor (or some other) died, or was bought off by a rival organisation, whereas the craftsmen in traditional potteries were more versatile and the workshop was unlikely to be left high and dry by the absence of one man.

Holič and Tata represented a type of factory which was often established on private estates by noblemen during the eighteenth century throughout the Continent, especially in France, Germany and Italy. Historically they are an intriguing phenomenon. They stood half way between the old hand working pottery and the modern factory. Most of

13   For a succinct account of both, see Akos Kiss, *Baroque Pottery in Hungary* (Budapest, 1966).

them had closed down by about 1820, after which time fashionable pottery was manu-factured on a larger scale with a more consistently commercial intent. In the eighteenth century the factories were analogous to the home farm on an estate; primarily they supplied the big house with its needs and fancies. Their products would be admired at entertainments and occasionally given as presentations, and slowly a general commercial demand would develop.[14]

The initiative for the factory output came chiefly from the owners, who knew what they wanted and selected managers and technicians who knew how to make it. Much of the production consisted of ceramic versions of objects hitherto made in metal, stone and glass, and other materials. As well as tableware there were statues, relief tiles, panels resembling carved stone, clocks and clock-cases, knife-handles, picture frames, figures and a multitude of toy pieces. They worked a great deal from pre-existing models and made direct casts of any shape they wished to copy, including occasionally creatures such as crayfish, whose bodies were cast in clay and painted in vermilion enamel, and disposed on some faience dishes produced at Tata towards the end of the eighteenth century.[15] The Holič factory produced many diverting and finely-made pieces during the eighty-four years of its existence: it followed chiefly the conventions of Strasbourg, where most of the key craftsmen came from, and it borrowed also from Meissen, Castelli, Rouen, Nevers, Moustiers, Proskau, and from Habaner traditions, but it produced little of originality.[16]

Everything from Holič and Tata was well made, though the extravagantly modelled ornament on tureens and other prime pieces was easy to damage. Not everything was made in the elaborate aristocratic style. There are a number of simple, thrown forms, decorated in enamel with relatively careful equivalents of the sort of personalised figura-tive ornament which was being done in ordinary colours by the traditional workshops. There is direct continuity between the two.

There had been three Habaner courts at Holič, and many of the throwers and painters employed in the factory came from Habaner families. Indeed, the presence of these skilled craftsmen may have suggested the whole grand project and made it possible. Through the imperial factory some of the technical innovations which had been brought in from Strasbourg filtered into the traditional workshops which were run by private master-craftsmen.

The fine high temperature red-bole pigment which was much used by Habaner potters from about 1760 was quite new to their tradition and probably originated at Hannong's Strasbourg faiencerie. They also became acquainted with enamel pigments through Holič, but *petit-feu* decoration was never adopted to any extent by traditional workshops probably because of the expense entailed by the third firing. The statues and modelled figurines which the workshops began to produce around 1760 derived from the factory output, as did the rococo features which began to appear in their painted designs and the press-moulded rims of plaques and panels. Generally, the chief stylistic

14   A. Kiss, op. cit., pp. 29–30, gives a short, interesting account of the personalities and working system in the Tata factory in about 1780.
15   A. Kiss, op. cit., colour plate VII (*c.* 1780).
16   G. Savage, *Pottery through The Ages* (London, 1959), p. 137.

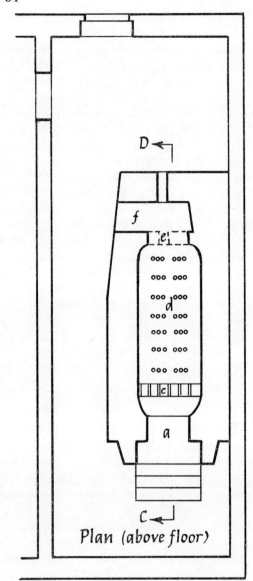

D ←

f

e

d

c

a

Plan (above floor)

C ←

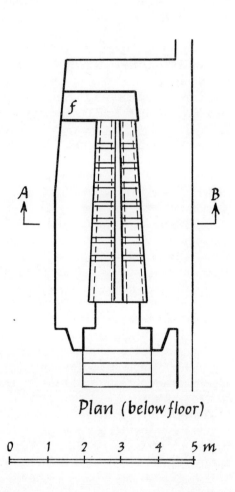

f

A ↑

B ↑

Plan (below floor)

0   1   2   3   4   5 m

a. Firebox

b. Section of kiln floor, showing flues and draught-holes

c. 'Stendr' or perforated baffle-wall

d. Plan of kiln floor showing draught-holes

e. Spy-hole through which trials are withdrawn

f. Doorway leading to chimney and kiln chamber

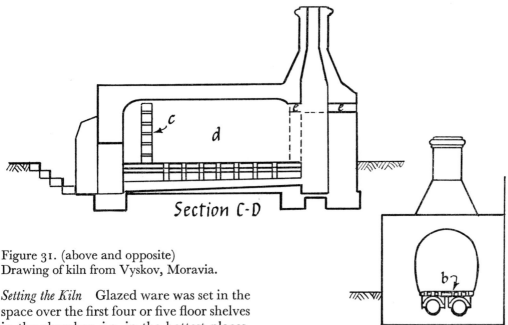

Section C-D

Section A-B

Figure 31. (above and opposite)
Drawing of kiln from Vyskov, Moravia.

Setting the Kiln   Glazed ware was set in the space over the first four or five floor shelves in the chamber, i.e. in the hottest places. The last two or three shelves carried bisque ware, which, of course, required less space as the raw pots could touch or be placed inside one another. The first three rows of holes in the kiln floor were partly baffled to protect the ware from ash carried on the draught. The space by the 'Stendr' (c) was used for the calcination of glazes and pigments, which were twice fired and ground.

Firing   The kiln was fired gently for the first four hours and the tempo was steadily increased thereafter. After eight hours the pull of the draught through the hot kiln and chimney had considerably increased. The pull had to be reduced to make the heat rise through the holes in the chamber floor to reach the ware in the main chamber. This was done by opening the heavy door at the packing entrance (f) to about three fingers' width, allowing a good deal of the draught up the chimney to be taken in from the gap by the door instead of through the kiln. As the heat in the chamber increased the door was gradually opened a little more. The progress of the glazed ware was watched through the spyhole (e). After some fourteen hours small trial pieces were withdrawn through the spyhole with a long rod. After examination they were replaced and repeatedly withdrawn and examined until the glaze was mature—at a temperature of about 980°–1000° Centigrade. The firing usually took sixteen to eighteen hours; once the glaze was mature the fire was left to burn down cleanly, thereby oxidising the ware completely.

Then the firebox was sealed, but not completely, so that a cooling draught passed through the kiln. The kiln was opened as little as twelve hours after the firing.

effect of the factories on older workshops was that they tried to smarten and refine their decorations in a hopelessly misconceived way, and began to lose confidence in the type of work they usually excelled in. By 1780 the effect on decoration was obvious and the elaboration of handles and footrings, and the introduction of flutings to the necks or bellies of painted jugs indicates this loss of confidence, for the new features were at odds with the traditional forms.

One particular innovation deserves comment. Since their arrival in the sixteenth century the Habaner potters had used the long, rectangular kiln which was current in Italy in the sixteenth century and is illustrated by Piccolpasso. It had no chimney; the flames passed up through the chamber, and escaped through holes in the vault. An improved, more controllable version of this kiln became current in central Europe in the late eighteenth century, and is thought to originate from a French design used at Holič.[17]

The kiln shown in the drawing comes from Vyškov in Moravia, and was built about 1800, and was fired with wood. Any solid-fuel kiln needs to be packed correctly and to be fired to the proper schedule to give good results, and often there is no information about these details. This kiln is specially interesting because both the design and the sequence of the firing are on record.

In 1700 the name Habaner still signified a member of a religious fraternity; by 1800 it conveyed little more than the good credentials of pigment and glaze recipes which had once been used by the fraternity. The techniques and styles of the anabaptist potters had by now passed into general use in Moravia, Slovakia, Hungary and Transylvania, and had even become known by the Black Sea coast of the Ukraine.[18] Painted tin-glaze ware was no longer seriously patronised by the aristocracy or the well-to-do: that market had been captured by the French-inspired tableware. The attempts of the pottery-painters to adopt rococo or elegant German-flower patterns only showed how little they understood them, and undermined their natural instinct for spontaneous, improvised pattern-making. Yet there remained an appreciative local market for tin-glaze vessels, and the actual quantity of work produced was probably greater than it had ever been before. Now the tin-glaze potter was becoming a folk artist: he continued to make patterned plates and pitchers, plaques, figures and even children's toys (ancestors of lead and plastic soldiers), but he was also, so to speak, the private artist to the whole community, prepared to draw pictures and make inscriptions to order on his vessels to commemorate anything people felt was worth putting on record. Unlike the private commissions of the early eighteenth century, the personal, illustrative part of the design came now to be added to the other features rather than resolved with them: the illustration itself became of prime importance [124]. One of the commoner products was the *dzbán*, or wine-pitcher with pear-shaped belly and long neck, a handle and slightly splayed foot [Fig. 32]. The *dzbán-sova*, or owl-pitcher, was similar, but was almost closed at the top and was used for the popular *borowička* and other spirits. Usually these vessels were painted with flowers and leaf-garlands appropriate to vineyard country. Often there are found

17   K. Černohorsky, op. cit., p. 37, who also cites Bastenaire Daudenart, *L'Art de fabriquer la faience récouverte d'un émail opaque blanc et coloré* (Paris, 1828).
18   K. Černohorsky, op. cit., p. 45.

amongst the bouquets the figures of the owners or donors of the pot, farmers, soldiers, butchers, inn-keepers, betrothed or married couples, figures of the Virgin and Child or Christ Crucified, and even occasionally alien subjects such as the Three Graces. Churches, guilds and trade associations also ordered special vessels. The activities of butchers, shoe-makers, coopers, bakers and millers, vintners and the potters themselves are all recorded in painted decoration.[19] Scenes from local life are represented, sometimes humorously; teams of horses with carts or at the plough, hunting scenes, country dances, fiddlers and bagpipers, even a parish council meeting, well-armed with beer tankards, and a family seeing a child off for his first day at school; there was also a great variety of decorative beasts and birds and fantastic buildings.[20]

Figure 32.   Slovak *dzbán-sova* or 'owl-pitcher' of the nineteenth century, about 18 cm. high.

It was not great or fine pottery, but it was no less valid than the faience made in the factories for the special purposes of the castle or manor-house, and it often has a more direct emotional quality which places it beyond the judgment of taste or fashion.

Here are the flowers and leaf-scrolls, a continuous decorative refrain descended from Habaner tradition, but now profuse, lavish in colour, as it were representing the recur-rence of the seasons and the vitality of nature amidst which these beasts and diverse persons enjoy their activities, possessions, jokes, love and self-esteem. Occasionally, especially in the later part of the century, the floral devices took on an exaggerated, abstract form, leaving botany far behind, becoming something more like a bursting sun or colour-symbol of some elemental life-giving force [125]. Some have a remarkably modern expressionist feeling. It could be said that one branch of modern painting leapt clear of conventions of beauty by deliberate severance, in search of deeper meaning and power. Peasant art escaped convention by default, by being inadequate, and from time to time it touched intuitively the same deep pulse.[21]

Pictorial decoration on peasant pottery is often inept in detail even though it may in

19 See Joseph Vydra and Ludvic Kunz, *Painting on Folk Ceramics*, trans. R. F. Samsour, Spring Books (London, about 1955), text and many plates.
20 See Vydra and Kunz, op. cit., p. 31, where a page from the sketchbook of a nineteenth-century pottery painter is reproduced, showing sketches of stags and a bird and a basket of flowers.
21 e. g. Vydra and Kunz, op. cit., plates 49, 126, 129, colour plates 113, 139.

total describe a scene or convey a mood. One of the characteristic qualities of these painter-potters was that they were prepared to undertake the awkward problem of carrying out illustrations on pottery vessels in spite of their lack of technical skill. In the 'factories' and larger workshops, and in the prosperous potteries of France, Holland and Germany, painters had clear designs to work from; compositions were laid out with pounces; apprentices learnt certain figures and perfected them. Master painters made sketches for important commissions and might spend days transferring the composition to a large bowl or vase. In fact, the rendering of figures on pottery has always been accounted a particularly difficult aesthetic challenge. The peasant craftsmen of the nineteenth century were obviously quite unaware of all this and did not hesitate to complete in an hour or so a figure composition which more sophisticated painters would have pondered all day. The direct and unpremeditated leap from idea to action gives the special flavour of peasant pottery. A teacher could fault it in a dozen ways, yet it has an engaging vitality which easily vanishes when a craftsman is fully equipped for his task. Not knowing his limits, the peasant-potter habitually went beyond them.

The peasant-potters of the nineteenth century were often poor but they were proud of their skill and their way of life. Whenever possible a potter would set up on his own rather than remain in an employed position, as a provision for his old age; others might think him too old to work, but thus he had at least a chance of continuing and even employing others. Thus there tended to be many small workshops rather than a few larger units, and the potters worked from hand-to-mouth with little room for experiment or innovation, restraint or self-criticism, but they did what they knew directly and unselfconsciously.

Usually the potter's workshop was a part of his house, a single large room housing his kiln, wheel, glaze-tubs and storage racks, and the living quarters opened directly into it. Liquid clay was often sieved into pits in the floor near the kiln, where it would dry quickly, and was stiffened by being pressed up against the wall of the warm kiln. In his yard the firewood and clay were stored alongside his granary and the pens of the livestock. Work began at sunrise. The thrower marked the first ball of clay on the wheel with the sign of the Cross and hoped for good fortune. The market remained small but fairly constant until the end of the nineteenth century, when fairs and travelling salesmen undermined the potters' livelihood by bringing ornaments and industrial crockery into the countryside.

Perhaps because of the hard and messy work they shared, the potters of a district had a strong sense of solidarity, which is expressed in a number of drinking songs. Often these remind the potters that, despite their dirty and ragged appearance, they can do things no one else can do, and in their clean Sunday rig any girl worth knowing will go with one of them rather than with anyone else. One song especially is worth quoting because of its apt comments on traditional patterns, as well as for its character-sketch of the potter himself:

> Here is our potter: fine fellow he is,
> For turning his wheel renowned,
> As God Himself in heaven on high
> Keeps the whole world turning round.

As in the Garden of Eden, God's hand
Made beautiful Adam from clay,
So his vessels arise like flowers of the field,
Hundreds all in a day.

By hundreds they come from the painter's hand,
Decked out in flowers by his art,
Leaves and stems and buds and bells,
Here a bird and there a heart.

One day the potter was hard at work
When the Duke knocked at his door;
Seeing the flowery wares, he smiled,
And lifted a jug from the floor.

'Why so many herbs and flowers?'
Asked he, with ready wit,
'Don't these painted pitchers of yours
Need grazing down a bit?'

The potter scratched behind his ear,
A wily look in his eye,
'These flowery vessels, so please your grace,
Are for poor folk such as I.

I don't like to mention taxes, my lord,
But for folk like us it's meet
To have flowery bowls to feast the eye,
For it's little the food we eat!'

The words of the potter pleased the Duke
And he tweaked the master's ear.
Forthwith he ordered his steward to make
The taxes less severe.

But the master went on painting his work
Just as before, as he deemed right.
Now there's meat in our bowls, but the flowers remain
——To whet the appetite!

Here is our potter; fine fellow he is,
He turns his wheel all day;
He knows the tricks of the tongue just as well
As he knows the work of the clay.[22]

22 Translated from the Czech original in Herman Landsfeld, *Lidove hrncirstvi a dzbankarstvi* (Prague, 1950), p. 289. This book contains a wealth of close description and sketches relating to the life and work of country potters of the nineteenth century.

The houses, farms and cottages of Central Europe had a parlour or 'clean room' reserved for special occasions where the painted pottery was kept. Even poor cottages had at least a 'visitors' corner' in the living-room where painted jugs and dishes stood on racks or hung from the wall.[23] It was all serviceable crockery, but it was also the country-man's picture-gallery. As in a family photograph album, some things came out better than others, but all were important for what they recorded or for their special uses and associations. By no means were all the later tin-glaze wares crudely painted. Some ex-amples stand out as having been painted with special care and forethought, perhaps on the basis of a picture-book or a devotional wood-cut; some have vaguely Chinese scenic designs and figures and are perhaps derived from Dutch or Oriental pieces; and some are labours of love, treasured possessions passed down from generation to generation.

The establishment of factories such as Holič and Tata, and later the domination of the town market by industrial products, squeezed the country tin-glaze potter into a tight corner. If he lost his public there remained to him only the pittance of plain-glazed domestic cooking-pots, and those were usually produced by larger workshops in big kilns at low prices. However, a number of tin-glaze potters managed to survive even up to the Second World War by dint of dividing their time between pottery and small-scale farm-ing, making pots for the parlour and certain special pieces used by the local community, such as the lidded jar with a clay handle reaching right over the top, called *nosáček* [128], and the lidded jars joined together with a ring-handle, called *koutňáček*, which were used for taking food to men out at work.

On the face of things, this was a degeneration but, in fact, peasant art has much deeper roots than may be suggested by its sometimes awkward execution. It is not just a decadent version of some nobler craft; it is a language in its own right with a unique spirit. Like the drawings of small children, it is vulnerable because it can only flourish where it is unselfconscious and where it is really needed. Considerations of 'design' destroy it, and once destroyed it is by very nature almost impossible to revive, for it depends on continu-ity and the secret workings of heart and hand, whereas anything based chiefly on the planning mind can be re-started with relative ease. Thus the various national revivals of peasant art which followed the second world war are little more than a reminiscence of a period of artistic innocence; the outer features survive but without life or inner content.

23   See Vydra and Kunz, op. cit., plate I, p. 19, for a photograph of a Slovakian cottage parlour in 1925, showing the special crockery in place.

Q. *Dzbán* or small pitcher, with pewter lid and mount. 27 cm high. Slovakia, dated 1652. A typical early piece by the Anabaptist potters, who established the maiolica technique in Central Europe in the second half of the 16th century. The restrained but lively cluster of floral decoration was virtually a signature for these crafts-men, and appears on vessels of many kinds. The hollow wares were almost always specially shaped at the rim and the base for the fitting of pewter mounts. Working in very simple conditions, the Habaner craftsmen were quickly recognised for their superb crafts-manship, but their strict principles forbade them to make flamboy-ant or merely decorative objects. *Narodni Museum, Prague. See page 145.*

R. Front view of *dzbán* or pitcher with a handle. 22 cm high. Slovakia, mid-18th century. After the break-up of the 'courts' in which the first Habaner craftsmen worked, the tin-glaze technique was learnt by the native Slovak potters, who decorated their bowls and wine-pitchers with bold, colourful patterns and renderings of men and animals. The castle on this pitcher comes indirectly from Oriental porcelain, but has been turned into a dream-image. The Slovak potters loved strong colours and they developed some intense grass greens, turquoise greens and yellows, and their patterns and gourd-like vessels seem to reflect the fertile country-side they lived in. *Private Collection in Prague. See page 149.*

S. Small dish. 25·5 cm wide. London, dated 1600, perhaps from Jacob Jansen's workshop in Aldgate. The picture seems to represent the Tower and Old London Bridge, showing the sluices which kept the river at a higher level than the tidal estuary. The planned design leaves a good deal to impulse, and the drawing has instinctively been slightly curved to fit the architecture into the circle. The surround of masks and foliage with the strapwork border is typical of the simplified Italianate conventions which reached England from Flanders. *London Museum. See page 164.*

T. Blue-dash charger 42 cm wide. Probably from Lambeth, about 1668. The ship appears to be the royal yacht the *Mary*, flying an English pennant and Dutch ensign. The split-leaf and shell patterns and the pomegranates in the border, and the colour-scheme, come from the Italian maiolica tradition, but the free drawing and the gay, casual atmosphere of the decoration are typical of English work. As usual with these chargers up to about 1700, the back has a thin, clear glaze, probably made from waste glazes and scrapings. *On loan to the Bristol City Museum and Art Gallery from an anonymous collection. See page 168.*

U. Blue-dash charger with tulip decoration. 33 cm wide. Probably from Lambeth, 1680–90. A decorative theme very popular in England between about 1650 and 1720. It could be varied in all manner of ways without losing its general character, and required of the painter only a sense of balance and movement, rather than a skill in drawing. Unlike more pictorial themes, it could not easily go wrong so long as it was done courageously. It is essentially pottery-painting, rather than painting on pottery. *Ashmolean Museum, Oxford. See page 167.*

V. (a) Malling jug with blue glaze opacified with tin, and silver
mount. 19 cm high. Probably from London, about 1600. (b) Plain
glazed ewer with helical flutings and rope-twist handle 26 cm
high. Probably from Ansbach or Nürnberg, late 17th century. Tin-
glaze pottery invited painted decoration, but could also be ruined
by it. The glazes could be very beautiful in themselves, especially
over a fluted surface such as this. *Gerald Reitlinger Esq. See
page 163.*

W.   Large deep bowl. 48 cm wide. Painted in reduced lustre from
copper and silver, by the author. Reduced lustre is one aspect to the
tin-glaze technique which has never been attempted by industrial
methods because it is so variable, but it remains a rich province for
modern potters who work freely, without having to limit themselves
to repeatable effects. *See page 196.*

X.   Large construction by Vlastímil Kvétensk
of Karlovy Vary, Czechoslovakia, 1970. Abou
130 cm high. The 'altar piece' is assemble
from separate slabs with impressed emblem
and figures in positive and negative relief, wit
modelling, slab-building, carving, and piercing
The tin glaze contrasts with the deep blue an
brown glazes and broken surfaces which cove
most of the work, but it also gives dramati
emphasis to certain features, especially th
hanging cloth in the central niche. An evocativ
work with mysterious suggestions, both sacre
and profane. It illustrates incidentally the break
ing down of old distinctions between figure
modelling, pottery, sculpture, architecture an
relief tiles, for they are all involved in this com
manding structure. *See page 196*.

11

THE BRITISH ISLES

In the 1670s and 1680s English Delftware potters submitted to Parliament a number of petitions against the importation of painted earthenware. To one of these petitions the Company of Glass-Sellers replied with the assertion that the pot-makers

never did, neither can they, make such painted earthenware as is imported. There are but six or seven of the said Pot-Makers in England who may employ fifty families or thereabouts . . . Some have had Patents for the making of fine Earthenware here after the manner of Holland . . . but [they] could never make such Ware . . . The importing of foreign Earthenware has been a great Example to the very Pot-Makers themselves, by making their Wares after Foreign Patterns to their great interest.[1]

The Glass-Sellers dealt in imported pottery as well as glass, and the case they put forward in their own interests was not quite fair, but in general it was true of the whole period in which tin glaze or Delftware was made in England, roughly 1580–1790. Up to about 1650 all the known pottery masters working in England were Flemish or Dutch, and their ideas came from Italian or Oriental painted pottery as already recognised in their own countries; and later, when Englishmen became capable of establishing their own Delftware potteries, almost all their motive-ideas can be traced to some Continental example. The highest claim they made was that they could imitate Holland or China ware.

Nonetheless, the products of the English tin-glaze potteries are usually recognised as English and nothing else. The criteria are hard to define: they do not lie in any style or in any particular technique, but rather in a mood, ingenuous, direct, sometimes eccentric, that can be discerned in most of the various types of tin-glaze pottery made in England as they responded to the changes of taste and fashion of the seventeenth and eighteenth centuries.

How satisfactory it would be to be able to show that this character stems from some enduring national trait, a preference for the essential and mistrust of artificiality, which the English tend to attribute to themselves! Actually the slightly naive character of English Delftware was probably a consequence of the humble status of the English potters, who never achieved the aristocratic patronage enjoyed by the French, or the commercial success and technical finesse of the Dutch, or the urbanity of the Italians. The English potteries depended chiefly on the country gentry and the mercantile classes,

1 Quoted by Geoffrey Wills, *English Pottery and Porcelain* (London, 1969), p. 41. Generally for English Delftware, see F. H. Garner, *English Delftware* (London, 1948; new ed. prepared by Michael Archer, 1972), and Anthony Ray, *English Delftware Pottery* (London, 1968) and L. L. Lipski (in preparation).

MAP 2. Great Britain, showing the chief Delftware pottery centres

who had neither the inclination nor the judgment to patronise showpieces or pottery of high expense. With only a vague knowledge of the Fine Arts and of Oriental porcelain, the twin influences which inspired the finest continental pottery, they could not easily admire the reflections of these things. Although pottery manufacture could be lucrative, especially in the first half of the eighteenth century, it was also risky; the indications are that most English potteries worked on a minimum of capital and lived too much from hand to mouth to bring either their artistry or their materials to perfection. In the 'Delft-work law case' of 1748–9, one witness said he knew 'all or most of the Pot-houses in England, which are about twenty-four in number, and of these are, to the best of his knowledge, only six or eight designedly built for the purpose, the rest being fitted up from other old houses.'[2] Rarely was English tin-glaze ware painted with designs fine or delicate enough to attract notice on the Continent. Moulds, which required time and capital and had to be made by a sculptor or professional modeller, were simpler and less usual in England than abroad, and the costly technique of *petit-feu* or enamel painting was only practised in one place for a short period.

The earliest pieces are the Malling jugs, which take their name from East Malling, in Kent, where an example was first recognised. These are small flasks covered with a tin glaze that has been stained or sprinkled with a metallic oxide to give a ground of brown, blue, greenish-blue or black [Colour Plate V]. Most examples are set in silver mounts and have a silver top to the neck, and the earliest known example is hall-marked 1550. The shape follows the traditional Rhineland stoneware wine-pitcher, and suggests that these jugs were made by Flemish emigrés. The stoneware clay and salt-glaze technique of the Rhenish originals were unknown in England at that time, and the mottled coloured glazes may have been used on the earthenware forms to give something of the character of a salt glaze. These rare pieces are charming hybrids. Their coloured glaze grounds have little to do with the main sequence of development of the tin-glaze wares in England, though the idea was occasionally used in combination with brush painting in the first half of the seventeenth century, and reappeared in the coloured-ground and reserve panel type of decoration used at Bristol and Wincanton about 1740.

A more sustained influence on the tin-glaze tradition in England was the arrival of the Italian-French potters recorded in Stow's *Survey*.

About the year 1567 Jasper Andries and Jacob Jansen, Potters, came away from Antwerp, to avoid the Persecution there, and settled themselves in Norwich; where they followed their Trade, making Gally Paving Tiles, and vessels for Apothecaries and others, very artificially. Ano 1570 they removed to London, with the Testimonial of Isbrand Bulckius, the Minister, and the rest of the Elders, and Deacons of that Church; desired by petition, from Queen Elizabeth, that they might have Liberty to follow their Trade in that City without Interruption; and presented her with a Chest of their Handy-work. They set forth in their Petition, that they were the first which brought in and exercised the said Sciences in this Realm, and were at great Charges, before they could find the Materials in this Realm.[3]

The making of paving tiles and various large and small drug-pots was the almost in-

2 See below, and note 24. Admittedly, the same might have been said of the prosperous factories of Delft.
3 Quoted by Anthony Ray, op. cit., p. 33.

variable beginning of all tin-glaze potteries in northern Europe: through these things the
decorative conventions of Guido da Savino's workshop at Antwerp were transplanted to
England. For a hundred years at least the Italianate motifs of Antwerp reappeared
frequently, especially in the borders of dishes and generally in pattern-work on tin-glaze
vessels. For instance, the border of an armorial dish dated 1670[4] contains almost exactly
the same patterns as some of the Antwerp paving tiles which were laid at the Vyne about
150 years earlier. A drug-jar excavated in London, and probably of London origin,
shows the kind of strong polychrome design that potters such as Andries and Jansen
would have used [129]. However, it is virtually impossible to distinguish between the
first English wares and vessels imported from Flanders. All that is known is that Jansen,
anglicising his name to Johnson, was granted a privilege to manufacture tiles and drug-
pots in 1571 and worked at Aldgate in London until his death twenty-six years later
[Colour Plate S].

The Aldgate factory is thought to have lasted into the 1620s. It was probably not the
only factory of its time, for there were already other Flemish potters working in London
when Jansen and Andries arrived. Seven are recorded as living at Southwark in 1571,
and two of them were 'painters of pottes'. Another pot-works was started in Montague
Close in Southwark in 1613, when Edmund Bradshaw and Hugh Cressy were licensed
to make 'all manner of pavinge tyles of all sises, dishes of all sises, potts of all sises . . .
wroughte or made of Earth after such manner as is used in Fiansa and other partes
beyond the seas'. Cressy evidently managed the pottery; Bradshaw was a merchant and
probably put up much of the capital. He disappeared in 1636 after being captured by
Barbary pirates.[5]

From one or another of these factories came polychrome wares with a strongly
Italianate character [131], amongst them dishes with a debased, almost abstract pomegranate and fruit pattern, a theme that probably came to England through Flemish
versions of Venetian originals. The nature of the 'pomegranate' was forgotten in the
process of repetition: the brush-strokes which originally conveyed the roundness of the
fruit became a two-dimensional pattern, turning the fruits into little worlds, each of
which engages the attention and is explored and remade in the mind's eye. The pomegranate dishes were never a fixed pattern; the theme continued to be made with variations almost until the end of the seventeenth century.

The most enduring of the recorded influences on English tin-glaze ware is the work
attributed to Christian Wilhelm, who arrived in London in 1605 and was living in
Southwark in 1618 as a 'member of the Dutch congregation' and as a 'gally-pot maker
and aquivitay stiller'. Wilhelm petitioned several times for a monopoly of the manufacture of *smalt* (cobalt pigment) against a certain William Baker who held the privilege.
He also claimed, impossibly, that he was the inventor of gallyware, as tin-glaze pottery
was called at that time, and in 1628 he was granted a fourteen-year privilege for the
making of this ware at Pickleherring Quay in Southwark. This document refers to him
making 'all kinde or sortes of bottels of all colors basons & ewers saltes dishes of all sortes

4   At Cotehele House, Cornwall. Illustrated in colour by Geoffrey Wills, op. cit., p. 34.
5   See Kenneth Quinn, 'London pottery, 1565–1636', *English Ceramic Circle Translations*, vol. 8, part 1
(1971), pp. 57–68.

drinking pottes paving tyles Apothecaries & Comfittmakers pottes of all sortes & all kinds of earthen works'.[6]

In view of Wilhelm's interest in obtaining the monopoly for *smalt* and his claim to have invented gallyware, it is likely that he devised the blue-and-white painted pottery which started at his time. Two sack bottles dated 1628, painted with designs of a bird on a rock, are thought to be from his workshop.[7] If this is so he can be credited with the first English blue-and-white pottery with Oriental themes, which may explain why he obtained a privilege of sole manufacture such as was only granted to people doing something new.

His designs derived from provincial Ming porcelain, in which the bird in a landscape setting of leaves and rocks was a common decorative theme [130]. The ware had become very popular in Holland by about 1620 and was much imitated by Dutch potters, but it was still new to England. In the English setting, however, the work took a direction very different from that taken in Holland. The Oriental models were not directly imitated in England as they were on the Continent, perhaps because they were still rare. Wilhelm used them but as a starting-point and worked out a type of overall decoration of flowers and ferns, birds, insects, rocks and cloud-patterns that could be used as vertical panels, central devices or borders, as the need arose. Although their antecedents were Oriental, these patterns owe almost as much to Elizabethan decoration as found in embroideries and wall-paintings—overall patterns without groupings or counterpoint in the composition. Often they were associated with inscriptions and dates, names and initials of ownership, a custom which was especially popular in English pottery throughout the next two hundred years. Many of these light and charming personal pieces still survive, including mugs, dishes, pitchers, posset-pots, tall ewers, and a variety of bowls.[8] Wilhelm's factory probably also made larger pieces with more formal painted themes, such as a jug painted with Samson and the Lion (British Museum), but such set-pieces were an established idea wherever tin-glaze work was being done. The decoration he evolved for his smaller pieces was peculiar to England and continued with variations well into the eighteenth century. The early Bristol polychrome of about 1700, for instance, is obviously indebted to Wilhelm's versatile decorative recipe, although by this time the details had changed.

The full range of Wilhelm's productions is not known. Did he also work in the long-established Italian pictorial style, and could some of the surviving dishes of this type be from his Southwark factory? None of them have even a suggestion of the decorative motifs of the bird-on-the-rock themes: had they been from the same workshop some minor borrowings, at least, might have been expected. Furthermore, in a petition made to the King in 1638, Wilhelm claimed that he had 'invented the making of white earthenware pots glazed both within and without, which show as fair as Chinese dishes'.[9]

6   Public Records Office, SP/39/25 No. 42.
7   One in the British Museum and one in the Fitzwilliam Museum, Cambridge.
8   See especially two articles by Hugh Tait, 'Southwark (alias Lambeth) Delftware and the potter Christian Wilhelm', *Connoisseur*, vol. 146 (August, 1960), pp. 36–42, and vol. 147 (February 1961), pp. 22–29. The author shows that many things hitherto attributed to Lambeth potteries were really made by Wilhelm at Southwark in the 1630s and 1640s.
9   Quoted by Ray, op. cit., p. 35.

Most, if not all, the pictorial chargers were tin-glazed only on the upper surface; the backs had a cheaper, transparent varnish glaze, a custom that lasted until about the end of the century. They were therefore probably made in other workshops in the Southwark area,[10] for pottery was made there from about 1613 until the early eighteenth century.

The pictorial dishes are special pieces for decoration rather than use. They belong to a period when Italian art forms were first receiving general acclaim in England, and are a humble reflection of the collections being built up by Charles I and some of the nobility. Amongst them is the earliest known of the large family of Adam and Eve dishes, dated 1635; also a famous full-length representation of Charles I in a dreamlike architectural setting with receding columns and a quaintly checkered floor, dated 1653, and a delightful dish of the Prodigal Son, dated 1657, in a similar interior. These are only a few examples amongst many pieces with a generally pictorial Italianate character. If almost all of them are based on engravings of paintings, the derivation has been made not by faithfully following the original, as would usually have happened on the Continent, but by using it only as a point of departure for a composition which became virtually a new version, and certainly acquired a new mood of its own, whether by accident or intent. A paper silhouette might have been made from the engraving, but most of the translation was done freehand by eye, with simplifications which accord much better with brush-painting than the original engraved lines and modelling. In the process the original engraving became virtually an outline drawing with a colour-wash, a relatively homely image, which other pottery-painters could work from without much difficulty. These were the beginnings of a long-lived and peculiarly English convention of freehand line-and-wash pictorial painting on tin-glaze pottery, taking a middle place between the continental extremes of the specialist *tour-de-force* and the crude imagery of provincial potteries [134].

There are two extraordinary dishes, both dated 1648, in which the reinterpretation of a previous composition (probably a Bible engraving) has gone to great lengths. One dish represents Adam and Eve being expelled from Eden, and the other depicts Susannah and the Elders. The sectional, puppet-like limbs suggest that both dishes are by the same painter, whose lack of competence in drawing is matched by his capacity for vivid expression and the conviction of his bizarre imagination, capable of converting the most conventional subject into his own nearly surrealist imagery, which, once seen, is not forgotten [132].

All these pictorial dishes were special, individual efforts on the part of the London potteries around the middle of the seventeenth century; they were distinct from standard wares, and were probably done by different people. The regular products of the potteries of the times consisted chiefly of wheel-thrown apothecaries' vessels, some plain white or with a name surrounded by a cartouche (equivalent to the Dutch *witgoets*), and some with elaborate decoration; also sack bottles, candlesticks, basins, posset-pots, dishes and small containers for pills and ointments [131, 133, 135]. As in Holland, press-

10 A manufactory existed in the parish of St. Saviour, Southwark, and another Southwark workshop was started about 1642 by a William Bellamy. Excavations in recent years have revealed the sites of hitherto unknown kilns and produced a great many sherds, so there may well have been many Southwark potteries for which no written evidence exists.

moulded ware was often glazed plain white, and on such pieces the tin glaze showed at its best. Most of these pots could probably be obtained at the apothecary's shop, together with the medicines, spices, cordials and preserves which were to be used in them. The close connection between potteries and apothecaries is commemorated by a large number of pill-slabs and other pieces, painted with the arms of the Apothecaries' Company. By 1700 apothecaries were in addition selling tea, coffee and chocolate and probably stocked pottery for them also.

Before the middle of the century two potters who appear to have been employed at Southwark, John Bissicke and John Bennet, started a new tin-glaze pottery at Brislington, near Bristol. Bissicke died in 1659 and Bennet in 1658, but their pottery lasted till 1746. Through them the Southwark designs and techniques were established in the West Country,[11] and were soon afterwards adopted and developed by a number of the Bristol earthenware manufactories. Probably inspired by the success of the Bristol wares, Liverpool citizens followed suit in the first years of the eighteenth century; and by about 1750 Liverpool was, it seems, the largest and certainly the most technically advanced of the English tin-glaze centres. Both cities imported a good deal of their clay from Carrickfergus, in Northern Ireland, and exported much of their finished ware to the West Indies and the American colonies.

In London itself new tin-glaze potteries were started in Lambeth from the 1660s onwards, and at least one other at Vauxhall shortly after 1670.

Because of the movement of personnel between the potteries, it is frequently difficult to establish where any piece originated. The manager of a new pottery took with him the knowledge and designs he had acquired in an older one, so that, apart from small mannerisms, many designs were common to several places. Although excavations have brought up quantities of sherds from Southwark, Lambeth, Brislington and Bristol, the glazes, bodies and firing conditions varied considerably within each centre, and each made a variety of different shapes. Attributions are therefore seldom more than a matter of strong probability.

An especially attractive and peculiarly English type of bowl developed around 1650, and remained popular, undergoing many variations till about 1720, namely the 'tulip charger' [136, Colour Plate U]. It has been associated particularly with the Lambeth potteries, but was certainly also made at Brislington. Whatever its origin, the derivation must come from general recollection rather than by direct imitation, for there is nothing very like the English tulip chargers in any other pottery convention. Generally, the tulip theme consists of three large flowers and some broad, juicy leaves sprouting from a small mound by the lower rim of the dish. The design is usually disposed more or less symmetrically to cover the entire concave surface, and is usually painted predominantly in yellow, orange, brown and green or blue-green, with blue contour lines to describe the leaves and flower-heads. It was a theme rather than a set pattern, and went through many variations during its seventy years of currency, from dense and colourful coverage

11   Brislington pottery is often indistinguishable from London work because the founders came from London workshops. See Michael Archer, 'Delftware from Brislington', *Connoisseur* (July 1969), pp. 152–161. By careful detective work some peculiarities of Brislington are established on the basis of sherds locally excavated, and some well-known vessels are consequently attributed to Brislington.

of most of the glazed surface, to spare and almost abstract versions in only two colours.

From the pottery-painter's point of view it was a wonderfully versatile theme. Covering the whole inside of the dish, the sweeping lines of leaves and stems followed the form as a matter of course. The theme was carried out by a sense of movement rather than by drawing, combining a broad, free structural pattern with localised detail, and line drawing and colour masses which enhanced one another without contrivance. The general mood was strong and lively, and all its associations were joyful. The simple dishes on which it was painted are shallow, and sweep outwards to a thickened, down-turned rim which was frequently painted with the broad, blue dashes which English potters so often used on the rims of dishes. There is a feeling of simple inevitability about the shape of some of these dishes, which may be so nicely balanced that they feel light even though they are thickly thrown. The clay itself seems to have wished to open in just this way, and the throwers were evidently still working according to the mass of their clay and its natural expansion rather than to set measurements and established profiles.

The same strong drawing and polychrome wash appears on a few bowls with individual, illustrative decoration, too, which are probably also from Lambeth. Amongst them are two remarkable bowls showing the yacht *Mary*, presented to Charles II by the Dutch Republic. One of the dishes is inscribed W ^{H} A, the initials of Willoughby Hannon, the ship's captain, and his wife Anne.[12] This triangular arrangement of initials was customary in English pottery painting: normally the upper initial is for the joint surname and the lower are for the Christian names of husband and wife. The other dish was unknown until 1968. Its composition is completely different and there are no initials, but the yacht can be recognised by the flags that appear in both versions [Colour Plate T].

Another peculiarly English convention was the decoration of pottery with the figure or bust of the reigning monarch or his consort, a custom which was well-established even before it became an expression of popular loyalty at the Restoration. It persisted under the Commonwealth and a famous dish depicting Charles I (now at Chequers) is dated 1653. After the Restoration a large number of vessels were decorated with representations of Charles II [140] and some with Queen Catherine of Braganza; later, other kings were represented and occasionally notable heroes, such as the Duke of Marlborough during the War of the Austrian Succession. The popular William III featured especially frequently, dressed in full robes and mounted on a prancing horse, in a landscape indicated by trees, dabbed on the pot with a sponge filled with pigment [141]. Many of the royal 'portraits', especially of Charles II, are affectionate and likeable, and some acquired a quizzical expression by having one eye painted distinctly higher than the other as if the king were sharing some private joke. Queen Anne, however, often fared badly, for by her reign the images were being mass-produced and did less than justice to her bulky form, and by the reign of George I the monarch was sometimes little more than an assemblage of stuffed armour surmounted by a bewigged face and carrying the suggestion of a sceptre, in a landscape of daubs.

12   In the Burnap Collection, Kansas Museum, U.S.A.

A similar degeneration befell the popular chargers painted with Adam and Eve. The earliest, dated 1635,[13] is a free but attentive version of an engraving by Crispin van de Passe, one of a number of religious images that were painted on pottery. The theme happened to be part of the arms of the Fruiterers' Company, but it acquired an immense popularity which is not accounted for by this circumstance. The challenge of rendering the anatomy of Adam and Eve was inescapable, and as the subject became more and more freely repeated by painters of less and less competence, most of the anatomy gave trouble, particularly Adam's abdominal muscles, which eventually became grotesque and could not be wholly covered by his fig-leaf. The subject was especially favoured in the 1680s but remained popular till about 1730, and two examples are dated as late as 1751. By then the images had declined to the level of coloured *graffiti*; Adam and Eve were cave-dwellers, the Tree had become a mere cipher and only the serpent and the fruit proved simple enough to survive debasement.

Armorial tin-glaze pottery was made in every country in Europe because the technique was so suitable for it. The English potteries seem to have produced a larger proportion of small personal commissions than the continental manufactories, and many of these included armorial decoration. Amongst the earliest examples are floor tiles made in London in the 1590s with the arms of the Bacon family. Most of the London armorial pieces were done not for the nobility but for members of City Companies, and showed the initials of husband and wife alongside the arms of the husband's Company. Some of them are obviously based on pewter or silver shapes shown to the potter by his client. When the arms were painted without any other ornament the piece is often very effective for having a localised area of dense design that contrasts with the plain white of the rest, showing well the beauty of the glaze. It is strange that this practice never became customary for other kinds of decoration. In nearly every other kind the painters persistently conceived the painted decoration as an overall pattern or picture. Their decoration might be light or dense, but it remained too unsophisticated to make use of the void until well into the eighteenth century, when it was used in landscape compositions suggested by Chinese models.

Shortly after 1700 the English tin-glaze potteries responded to the same changes of fashion as were felt all over the Continent. Apothecaries' pots and large dishes and paving tiles tended to be replaced by polite tablewares, delicate ornaments and plates and cups, and pottery for tea, coffee and chocolate, carrying a lighter and more informal decoration than before, with delicately sketched pictures and landscapes and themes suggestive of Oriental refinement. On the Continent this change led to the production of large services of banqueting ware and a tendency to work from press-moulds and later from casting-moulds rather than from wheel-thrown forms (see p. 115). In England the pottery industry produced relatively few large, formal services; pewter and silver survived longer on the tables of the wealthy, and before long armorial porcelain services were being imported direct from China. The English tin-glaze potteries enjoyed a less exalted patronage; their main customers were the country gentry and the mercantile section of the community. Their shapes and painting never became so formal as they did abroad; wheel-throwing, though it became finer than in the previous century, remained the

13   Garner, op. cit., plate 14.

usual way of making the majority of shapes except plates, which were formed by a template over a mould which revolved on the wheel.

New potteries were established to deal with the growing demand for tableware and polite domestic pottery. Several potteries had been started in Bristol in the late seventeenth century. The most enterprising was the Temple Back pottery, bought by Edward Ward in 1683, who changed the product from plain earthenware to tin-glaze wares. Redcliffe Backs, owned by the Franks family, appears to have been started in the early eighteenth century. Altogether thirteen pottery sites are known to have been active in Bristol during the century. A tin-glaze pottery making 'clean and pretty' domestic ware existed in Belfast by 1700, but only a single piece from it has been recognised.[14] The first of the many Liverpool potteries began in 1710 with encouragement from the town corporation to make 'all sorts of White and Painted Wares in imitation of China',[15] and it must have done well, for another was established by Alderman Shaw in 1716, and another by Alderman Poole in 1724.

At Wincanton Nathaniel Ireson set up a small and short-lived pottery in about 1730. In Dublin a pot-house on the Strand was managed by a certain John Chambers from 1730 until about 1771, and there were also two other, smaller, potteries. Other Irish pot-houses existed at Rostrevor, Co. Down (1742) and at Limerick (1761-2). The Delft-field pottery of Glasgow was started in 1748 and worked in tin glaze until about 1770.

The commercial possibilities for painted tin-glaze wares were excellent in the early and middle parts of the eighteenth century and much of the production of the Bristol, Liverpool and Glasgow factories was exported to the American colonies and the West Indies. In 1771 the Glasgow Delftfield pottery exported 64,077 pieces of tin glaze and stoneware.[16] Today a mere five well-authenticated pieces survive from its entire output over some forty years. The production of the many potteries of Lambeth, Bristol and Liverpool was very much larger and the vast majority of surviving tin-glaze vessels of eighteenth-century date are attributable to one or other of those centres.

The Continental potteries produced a good many showpieces, objects more or less equivalent to pictures or statues. The nearest English equivalent would be better called parlour-pieces, things which were decorative even when not in service, but were nonetheless intended for occasional use, such as posset-pots, punch-bowls, large jugs, water-cisterns, vases, flasks and a variety of bowls and dishes, tea-caddies, tankards, candlesticks and pottery for serving and drinking tea and chocolate and coffee [137]. Amongst surviving examples there is a fairly clear distinction between the pieces which

14 A pottery shoe. A visitor recorded in 1708 'Here we saw a very good manufacture of earthenware, which comes nearer to Delft than any made in Ireland, and really is not much short of it; it is very clean and pretty and universally used in the North'. Geoffrey Wills, op. cit., p. 60.

15 From an extract from the London *Post-Boy* for August 1710, quoted by Geoffrey Wills, op. cit., p. 57.

16 As might be expected, in course of time the American states developed a Delftware industry of their own. As yet little is known about it. Delftware kilns existed in Pennsylvania and New Jersey, but only one actual site has been located, at Old Salem, North Carolina. The American tin-glaze industry is thought to have flourished chiefly between 1780 and 1820, and its growth may have contributed to the decline of the English industry during those years. The potters seem to have been much influenced by the way of life and the techniques of the Moravian Brotherhood, a branch of the old Habaner movement. I am grateful to Mr. Bradford L. Rauschenberg of Old Salem Inc. for this and other information.

were specially made or painted for a particular patron (or as a 'masterpiece' or proof of talent at the end of an apprenticeship) and those with painted decoration which was learnt by the decorators and often repeated, perhaps with minor variations, or with initials and inscriptions and sold over the counter. Special pieces usually incorporated some kind of characterful pictorial decoration, generally freely derived from an engraving [143, 144]. There was virtually no equivalent of the Dutch special vases with floral decoration or baroque pattern commanding the eye by sheer mastery.

With repeat pieces, however, the English tendency to deviate and improvise produced standard wares that mostly have more vitality than Dutch and other Continental examples partly because they avoided elaboration for its own sake and partly because the discipline of the manufactories either fell short of exact repetition or did not intend it. Thus there are many families of repeat patterns—far too many to describe here—that kept fresh by frequent minor modifications and continually looked to what they might become, rather than referring back to the prototype they were supposed to follow [142].

The Bristol landscape patterns in tones of blue are a good example.[17] They were used above all at Bristol between about 1750 and 1770 and consisted of a delicate landscape with receding horizontal features, reeds, fences, gates, coppices and cottages, intersected by a number of delicate, tall trees with bushy sponge-dabbed foliage and usually a pair of figures, walking together and surveying the scenery [146]. This kind of decoration existed as early as about 1700 but only became systematised into distinct patterns about 1750. It is indebted in a general sense to Oriental or Dutch-oriental models for the play of mass and empty spaces in the composition. However, no surviving example appears to be a direct copy of a Chinese or Dutch original. The general theme was used with endless variations, especially on the outsides of punch-bowls and, even when distinct versions were made in copy-books for the routine painters to follow, nearly every piece has some peculiarity [149]. There must have been a strong preference for following a design freehand whenever possible, rather than resorting to pattern-papers or cut-outs to obtain standardised features. The same principle applies to the Liverpool Oriental designs of about 1750–1770 [147].[18]

The punch-bowl was to England what the tureen was to France, a decorative and partly ceremonial vessel occupying the centre of the table on convivial occasions, a vessel meriting some strikingly individual decoration, often with emblems of ownership and a suitable motto. Many were specially commissioned by private people and for groups of drinkers in inns and clubs. Amongst them, pride of place goes to the two pedestal-footed 'Flower' punch-bowls with decorations borrowed from Bickham's *Musical Entertainer*, a collection of songs and engravings published between 1739 and 1741 [148]. The internal decoration of the two bowls differs significantly: one has a round by Purcell painted along the internal edge and in the centre a drinking group at table. The other has five

17   Often called Bowen Landscapes, because a fine example, now lost, but known from an engraving, is signed '1st Sept. 1761, Bowen fecit'. There is no reason to suppose, however, that this type of decoration, which was current at Bristol for many years, was the personal contribution of Bowen or of any other single painter.

18   Anthony Ray, op. cit., plate 87, shows two Liverpool plates with the same bird and flower decoration, but the placing and proportions and detail differ considerably, showing that the design was followed freehand.

free-standing leaf and flower bouquets and a whimsical centrepiece (surely a personal request) showing two vacant chairs by a table, on which stand the punch-bowl, empty glasses, pipes, and a lighted candle.

Typical punch-bowls of the mid-eighteenth century were about ten to thirteen inches wide, about four to five inches deep; they had fairly steep sides and stood on a deep footring. On the inside was a scene and sometimes an inscription or a coat of arms, and on the outside a continuous landscape pattern, including details appropriate to the owner. A fine punch-bowl in the Bristol City Art Gallery, for instance, has on the outside a landscape showing coopers preparing casks, and a ship sailing out to sea; the inside is painted with the arms of the Cooper's Company.[19]

Bristol and Liverpool potteries, particularly the latter, produced a number of punch-bowls decorated with ships, to commemorate a launching or some commercial enterprise, or the arrival of a ship in the port. Such is the beautiful *Wigilantia* bowl with a Swedish inscription and the initials of the master, made in Bristol in 1765 [150]. A remarkable ship punch-bowl is that recording the docking of the Swedish ship *Magdalena Doratia* in Bristol in 1757, which is signed and dated by a Swedish master-potter, Magnus Lundberg, who was then manager and part-owner of the Redcliffe Backs pottery. Another bowl has a playful device, appropriate to the bowl's use: a border of ships is painted around the inner rim of the bowl, so that when the bowl is filled the ships will appear to be floating on the punch.[20]

In conclusion, something may be said of the technical and social background of tin-glaze wares in England. Until about 1750 English technique appears to have depended on knowledge originating on the Continent. Later in the century there was a good deal of fresh thinking and experiment that began to affect tin-glaze practice, but was soon diverted to the more industrially viable techniques of stoneware and the high temperature white earthenware pioneered by Wedgwood.

From the start English tin-glaze work used technical knowledge coming from Italy via the Netherlands. The use of chalky clays fired by wood in saggars in a rectangular kiln with vents in the arch, as described by Piccolpasso, appears to have been still current at Delftfield in 1748–49. The lead-based tin glazes all resemble those compounded from Continental recipes, and the preparation of pigments first followed Italian and then Dutch practices. It has been surmised that many foreign artisans were working in English potteries in the early eighteenth century,[21] and they were probably welcomed as bearers of the latest inside information about technical matters. About 1700 there came a change of fashion in the conventional colour-scheme of tin-glaze ware. The Italian palette, dominated by yellows and acid greens, was superseded by a fashion for blue, sage-green and red. The Dutch led the way; in France the Rouen potteries developed a rich high-temperature palette by 1720, and the English struggled to keep up. Though blue and

19   Special punch-bowls are too numerous to mention individually. Anthony Ray, op. cit., illustrates several famous punch-bowls very fully.
20   See R. J. Charleston, 'Bristol and Sweden. Some Delftware connections', *English Ceramic Circle Transactions*, vol. 5, part 4 (1963), p. 225.
21   Charleston, op. cit.

green colours were not difficult, the brick-red could not be obtained except by a blend of very finely prepared materials which the English potteries seldom achieved. In most of the English polychrome wares the red is either pale or, more often, raised and rough to the touch. Yellow and orange, which still continued to be used, presented a similar problem, for again the colouring agents, antimony and iron, were refractory, and needed to be carefully balanced with a flux and painted in exactly the right thickness. The recipes and the painting were frequently rather unsatisfactory. Although there are fine examples of English polychrome of the early eighteenth century, on the whole the English painters used the colours naïvely. They seem to have taken a pre-existing type of design and merely alternated the colours as they painted, without rethinking the design as a whole. The effect is colourful only in a fairground sense, and a Dutch painter could have taught them a great deal.

In the 1750s polychrome was mastered by some of the Liverpool potteries, using the so-called 'Fazackerly', colours.[22] These were high-temperature colours, including a deep red, an orange and a lemon yellow and an olive-lime-green, combining a strong hue with a very smooth surface, and they were expertly used. Whoever devised them had realised that the pigment recipe was but half the challenge: the glaze-ground had also to be of suitable composition to bring out the colours. On an unsuitable ground, even the strongest red or yellow would fire pale. The painters also used fine drawing in black, giving precision to parts of the design, and increasing the colour effect by contrast. These colours were used on a good many Liverpool pieces and tiles in various types of designs from about 1757–1770, mostly on a slightly grey-green toned ground.

Enamel colours needed not merely meticulous preparation but a third firing in a muffle-kiln, which entailed higher prices. They were used only at Liverpool from about 1760, and examples are very rare. By this time the enamel technique was already being put to good use for the luxury market by the porcelain painters of Bow, Chelsea and Worcester, and the tin-glaze factories were already sensitive to their own shrinking trade, as the white earthenware manufacturers undercut their prices.

The technique used in Italian potteries in the late fifteenth century, called *bianco sopra bianco*, was much used in Bristol and Lambeth potteries from about 1747 onwards. The method consisted of decorating with a glaze so rich in tin oxide that it became a viscous white pigment. This white could be applied in broad or fine strokes; after the glaze firing it stood out in slight relief over the toned background glaze [145]. Very clean and light effects were obtained with this technique, especially for borders or panels surrounding a piece of formal painting which needed to hold the dominant place, as on ship punch-bowls. The technique seems to have been unknown in England until the middle of the eighteenth century. It may have been introduced from Sweden, perhaps by Lundberg himself, who had known it in the Rörstrand faience factory.[23]

A fascinating glimpse into some of the technical and administrative problems of a tin-glaze pottery is given by the famous 'Delftwork Law-case', heard in Edinburgh in

22   So called because two early examples (destroyed by bombing in 1941) were inscribed T.F. 1757 and C.F. 1758, for Thomas Fazackerley and his wife Catherine.
23   Suggested by Charleston, op. cit., p. 228. The earliest dated Rörstrand example is of 1745, and the earliest known English piece is dated 1747.

1748–9.[24] John Bird, formerly manager of the Delftfield Pottery, sued the four owners of the factory for wrongful dismissal. The partners owned land near Glasgow which was thought to possess good clay. They conceived the idea of manufacturing Delftware and exporting it to the American colonies, where they had business connections, as was being done so successfully from Liverpool. None of the four partners had any knowledge of pottery manufacture. Somehow they became connected with John Bird, who had worked in and helped to manage a pottery in Lambeth, owned by his uncle. Bird investigated the Delftfield clay and pronounced it good; he specified the general layout of the pot-house and kilns, and undertook to find suitable staff for the enterprise. By 1748 the buildings were finished at a cost of some £12,000, a large sum at that time, and about thirty skilled men were brought up from Lambeth to start work.

Unfortunately for the owners, John Bird was unfamiliar with 'burning the kilns'. The first firing, in which all the kiln furniture, 'saggars and sluggs', was being fired, proved calamitous, apparently because the kiln was still damp and the air would not pass properly through the vents. Most of this kiln furniture had to be remade. The first biscuit-firing was a disaster because the supports collapsed, being compounded of a poor clay body. It was then discovered that the Delftfield local clay was unsuitable for tin-glaze ware, despite Bird's earlier assurances that it was good. Clay had to be obtained instead from Carrickfergus in Northern Ireland, at high cost and in secret, because the Liverpool and Bristol potteries already bought this clay and would try to prevent its export to any rival.

One problem tends to call up others. Some of the work-people now criticised the design of the pot-house as being too narrow and needlessly high, 'more like a Church than a pot-house'. Another pointed out that Bird's kiln had 'five vents across the crown' instead of the usual three, and that this might explain the difficulty in firing. In the wet weather the tanks or 'backs' in which the Irish and local clays were blended could not be dried out, and makeshift roofs and fires had to be built to bring the slurry to a plastic state for throwing. Some of the employees murmured that they had never before seen such a procedure, and mistrusted it. (Most potters have a deep-seated feeling that all clay should be slowly 'weathered', despite the fact that few clays really need it.) The complaint was also raised that Bird had chosen the wrong proportion of 'turners' (throwers) to painters. One turner to two painters was usual, but at Delftfield the painters could not get through all the work.

Worse was to come. The millstones for grinding the pigment seem to have been too soft and were bedded in the wrong kind of sand, so that the pigments were mixed with grit and would not fuse properly. Finally, the first firing of glazed and painted pots was a catastrophe. The eleventh and twelfth counter-charges against Bird read as follows:

11. That after he (Bird) had told us he had prepared the Frett (which is a chemical Preparation for giving the Enamel to the Ware) for Burning, and it was burnt, and, when burnt, was sent to be grinded at a Miln, we had erected for that Purpose at a great Expense; and being grinded,

24   See Michael Archer, 'Delftware made at the Glasgow pottery of Delftfield', *Connoisseur* (Sept., 1966). I am also greatly indebted to Michael Archer for his kindness in communicating to me his then unpublished article and notes on the Delftwork Law-case, 'English Delftware: the industry at Lambeth in the mid 18th century', *Connoisseur* (April, 1971).

when the colours were ready our Men went to Work, dipping and painting, not doubting but every thing was justly prepared; but, when the Ware was burnt it came out good for nothing, which was owing to the Frett's not being rightly proportioned; nay, it was not proportioned according to a Receipt he since gave the Company, which is the only one he ever gave them; and which, however, we do not follow, not daring to trust his Receipts.

12. At the drawing of this Kiln Mr. Bird was observed to look at one of the Proof-Pots, and to laugh in a jeering Manner; and then he took one of them away clandestinely to a Person who was no Friend of this Company, who showed it to great Numbers who came to his House, and boasted that none but he could have told it before Hand, and that none but Bird and he knew the Reason. . . .[25]

How else could the owners have proceeded except by employing a man who was supposed to be experienced? Such a man needed to know not only the proper recipes and materials, but a host of small points of detailed practical working. In an established workshop innovations could be introduced gradually, while the regular work was left in the safe hands of artisans who might have little understanding of theory, but knew the practices well. At Delftfield everything had to be started at once, and Bird, who may have been a reasonably competent manager, was found to be ignorant of many practical points which, in his experience, had always been dealt with by workpeople who knew their equipment and materials thoroughly. The absence of a secure basis of theoretical knowledge is striking. There were, as yet, no fundamental principles to refer to when things went wrong. At this very time Wedgwood was establishing those principles for himself at Etruria, and his achievement underlay the rapid success of the white earthen-wares that eventually eliminated the tin-glaze potteries.

Certain points of organisation came to light in the course of the hearing. Delftfield seems to have been a pottery of average size for its period, employing between thirty and forty people. Amongst these were the Manager, with a part-interest in the pottery; he was responsible for running the whole establishment, and was supposed to have a basic knowledge of all recipes for materials, designs of kilns, and to judge the 'proof-pots' and say when the firings should stop. The manager would normally do little or no manual work. He had usually trained as a painter and, like Bird, might 'sometimes sit down and paint the Ware', but he did no routine practical work. Under him was a clerk, who should also know recipes and materials, and how to pack and fire the kilns, and who also acted as the manager's representative in everyday arrangements. The clerk also kept the accounts, and was responsible for receiving, building up and despatching orders. There would be some twelve painters, mostly doing routine work; the foreman-painter had to instruct the apprentices and keep up the standard of painting generally, as well as being the chief artist-painter for special pieces and new designs. At Delftfield there is recorded a 'pot-stainer', who was probably responsible for dipping the ware in the glaze, a position of considerable responsibility, for tin-glaze wares can be ruined by uneven or dribbly dipping, or by glazes applied too thickly or thinly. Then there would be about seven 'pot-turners', who in some factories might also engage in moulding. At Delftfield there was also a clay-cellar manager, who would be responsible for having adequate clay,

25 From the printed record of the Delftwork Law-case in the Library of the Faculty of Procurators, Glasgow, p. 11.

properly blended, in the right consistency for working. In addition, there might also be some 6 or 8 apprentices who entered employment as painters or turners between the ages of twelve and fourteen, on payment of a premium of £5 or £10. They would receive three years' training and a small weekly wage. Thereafter they were committed to a further four years' work in the same employment before becoming free to enter into contracts as independent journeymen. Journeymen usually contracted for three or five years. In addition, a factory would have some ten 'servants' or labourers employed in general work such as clay-preparation, the grinding of frits and colours, preparation of fuel, stoking and unpacking kilns, packing and dispatch of pottery. Normal working hours were from 6 a.m. to 9.0 p.m.

A book called *The Laboratory or School of Arts*, by G. Smith, published in 1740, is one of a number of manuals and recipe books, such as a manager or clerk might have for reference. It includes a number of recipes for tin-glaze and high-temperature pigments, several of which indicate a Continental origin, such as the 'Rotterdam fine Shining White' and the 'Salzburg White'.[26] Unfortunately the manual has many inaccuracies, and some of the recipes must have led people into trouble.

Obviously ideas travelled quickly in the small world of English potters, and in the confines of the turning or painting shop exchanges of ideas and comparisons of workshop practice must have been common. The foreman-painter had charge of prototypes and any copy-books which might be used, but he must have depended also on the personal talents and previous experience of the men under him. For example, the 'powder-ground' technique used by some of the Bristol potteries about 1740, was adopted at the short-lived Wincanton pottery, whose work-people were mostly drawn from Bristol. The technique consisted of placing paper cut-outs around the rims of dishes, and blowing or spongeing powdered manganese dioxide around them so that they made a white reserve shape within a coloured ground. The reserved shapes were then painted or inscribed, usually in blue. Though Wincanton painting was sometimes expert, it showed no sign of originality. The painting on the authenticated pieces from Delftfield, also, depended on ideas and motifs already in existence; perhaps Bird disappointed his employers in this part of the work also.

Once the technical difficulties had been overcome, the Delftfield factory became productive and successful. The owners' anxieties might have been resolved earlier had they been acquainted with Captain Henry Delamain, who bought the Dublin tin-glaze factory in 1752, and whose projects reveal a new approach to techniques and organisation. Delamain was convinced that a few important changes could result in a vastly increased production and he repeatedly sought the assistance of the English Parliament for his projects. He claimed to have devised a new type of large kiln which could be fired with coal instead of wood, which most faience makers considered impossible, because sulphur fumes spoilt the glazes.[27] Volume for volume coal, of course, holds far greater heat value than wood and is easier to handle. Delamain's kiln probably incorporated

26   An extract from pp. 90–96 of this book is published by K. J. Barton in the Post-Medieval Ceramic Research Group *Broadsheet*, No. 2 (Jan. 1965), pp. 21–26.
27   Though a kiln for tin-glaze wares fired with coal seems to have been built for Cressy's pottery in Southwark in the 1620s. Quinn, op. cit., p. 72.

some kind of large muffle-chamber from which fumes were excluded, such as became general practice in Stoke in the nineteenth century. A bowl in the British Museum, inscribed 'clay got over the Primate's Coals', probably refers to Delamain's first success. (His coal came from the land of the Archbishop of Armagh.)

Delamain also claimed that he had 'purchased the art of printing earthenware with as much beauty, strong impression and despatch as can be done on earthenware'.[28] This probably meant printing refractory pigments from engraved plates and applying them over the fired glaze in a third firing, but it could conceivably have meant placing a cobalt blue print on the biscuit ware under the opaque glaze. The cobalt would have penetrated the glaze in the firing, but a clear line would have been hard to obtain.

The few known pieces of Dublin tin-glaze pottery are of fine quality. Had Delamain's plans not been thwarted by his unexpected death in 1757 his grand projects for producing large quantities of faience, as fine as the French wares of Moustiers, might well have succeeded. His plans included training schemes for apprentices and housing areas for the work-people. He appears to have understood clearly that the English tin-glaze factories survived merely by persistent hard labour and a flow of production which undermined high standards and imaginative work. He saw that the best quality of Delftware could only be maintained by a vastly improved factory system, and by introducing new materials and processes, and he appears to have possessed in himself the technical, artistic and administrative qualities necessary to do it. After his death the Dublin factory survived for a few years under his brother, who mistrusted these grand schemes. It closed in 1771.

The mechanical application of designs had long been invited by the elaboration of painted ornament. None but the most successful, important pieces could cover the cost of long and careful painting by hand, after which all might be lost in bad firing. Thus delicacy of design and fineness of painting became to a large degree the hallmark of the 'best' painted pottery. There was a strong incentive to find a surer, simpler way of applying fine decoration, avoiding the need for painters to sustain their attention all through a long series of intricate designs. Transfer printing from woodblocks and copperplates was in use by the 1750s, and was perfected by Sadler and Green at their Printed Ware Manufactory in Liverpool, where they bought in plain glazed pottery and printed transfer decoration over the glaze on many types of ware, including tin glaze. Prints were also used by Henry Stritch at Limerick in 1760–1761, where a manganese printed design was applied and afterwards painted by hand with other colours. This method overcame the chief obstacle to high standards in repetition-work, by solving the placing, composition and drawing of the design. It could not develop anyone's skill in painting, and in the long run it inevitably meant the replacement of personal skill by mechanical methods.

In fact, printed tin-glaze ware is most uncommon, because by the time the transfer technique was developed, the manufacture of tin-glaze wares was already declining. The pottery at Limerick appears to have lasted for only about two years.

There had always been a contradiction between the high expense of glaze materials and of hand-painting and the softness of the chalky clays traditionally used for tin-glaze

28   Anthony Ray, op. cit., p. 78.

ware. When the work was done the pots were very easily chipped or cracked. Surprisingly, little effort was made to devise a stronger body. The clay had in any case to be filtered and blended in slurry form, and could without excessive difficulty have been fortified with flint and frits as had been done in Persia in the twelfth century. The soft-paste porcelain bodies made at Bow and Chelsea were compounded on this principle and became vitreous and slightly translucent at as low a temperature as 1100°C. Delftware clays could have been at least improved by small additions of similar material. Some recipes advocated adding one part in three of calcined flint to strengthen the body, but its effect was undone by the addition of chalk. The chalk whitened the clay and prevented crazing of the glaze, but it made the body soft and liable to chip.[29]

At Liverpool a different solution was tried, which perhaps occurred because of the proximity of potteries making porcelain and stoneware. Tin glaze was applied to stoneware vessels which had been biscuit-fired at full temperature so that they were hard and impervious. The few known examples are mostly small, delicate pots for holding hot liquids. They are beautifully and thinly thrown, and have exquisite handles, such as would have been quite unpractical in earthenware. The difficulty lay in applying the glaze, since the body of the pot was no longer absorbent. The glaze must have been made up very thickly, and the pots must have been heated before being dipped, so that the water in the glaze would evaporate before runs and dribbles developed. Unfortunately, the rim and edges of the handle were almost impossible to glaze adequately, and the glaze could not be prevented from gathering at the bottom of the pot and around the fixings of the handle. It was also difficult to avoid knocking away some of the glaze while the pots were being painted or set in the kiln. Hence, a number of these rare pieces are slightly defective. Once again, the problem was shelved by the changeover to high-fired white earthenware and the ending of tin-glaze manufacture within a few years.

By 1785 most of the English tin-glaze potteries had either closed down or changed to white earthenware or stone-ware. A few pieces with early nineteenth century dates are known. The latest-known piece is from London, dated 1826, but by this time very little Delftware could still have been in production.

29 *Laboratory or School of Arts*, as above (note 26): 'How to prepare the Clay for fine Delft Ware, Take one part of calcin'd flint; one part of chalk, and one part of capital or the cream of clay; mix and work them well to a proper consistence'. A questionable recipe!

12

FAIENCE OF THE EIGHTEENTH
CENTURY

The preceding chapters have traced the passing of the tin-glaze technique from land to land and have indicated how each culture in turn adopted the tradition as it first found it, and then began to use it in new ways. The tradition was sufficiently long-lived to undergo changes that appear to be total transformations. How little there is in common, for instance, between the early tin glaze of Baghdad and Cairo and Dutch gilt and polychrome enamelled wares of the early eighteenth century! Yet the connections leading from one to the other were direct, and the technique itself remained basically the same. If a Cairo potter or painter of 1100 had been reincarnated in Delft six hundred years later he would have been surprised by some of the decorative styles, he would have been impressed by the kilns and the quantity of production, and he would have found the technique itself quite familiar.

So far the tradition has been followed stage by stage up to the dispersion which occurred in the sixteenth century, when Italian craftsmen transmitted the pictorial-decorative conventions of Faenza, Venice and Urbino to many parts of the European continent. The resulting national traditions were too manifold and diverse to be described in any detail within the scheme of this book. The four which have been touched on, in France, Holland, Central Europe and Great Britain, were chosen because each took a different course. In Central Europe and in Britain semi-popular traditions of painted pottery developed, lacking in finesse, but each with a distinct character. Through Holland especially came the immense impact of Oriental porcelain, which spread thence to Lisbon, to Rouen, and to Hanau, Frankfurt and Nürnberg [106, 111, 155, 156]. In France itself occurred the first development of the fine tablewares and prestige pottery and ornaments that became almost obligatory possessions for the aristocracy and upper classes of the Continent in the eighteenth century.

This aristocratic pottery involved a pronounced change of mood, and is distinguished from the earlier maiolica, galleyware and Delftware, by being called by a special name, *faience*.[1]

In the first decades of the eighteenth century there was a second cultural dispersion which diversified the tradition of tin glaze still further, as the ideals of faience were established with varying emphasis throughout France, at Alcora in Spain, in the Italian centres of Doccia, Genoa, Lodi, Nove, Savona, Naples, and at Caltagirone in Sicily, to name some of the most important. In Germany a great many faience factories were set up, amongst the foremost being Kassel, Bayreuth, Crailsheim, Dresden and Abtsbess-

1 The name is of course a French version of Faenza, one of the chief centres from which the tin-glaze technique was introduced into France.

Map 9.   Germany: the chief faïence manufactories.

ingen. Through the factories of Holič and Tata, faience was introduced to what is now Slovakia and Hungary, while it was made in Poland at the short-lived Belvedere factory near Warsaw. The manufacture spread into Schleswig-Holstein, to Kiel, Kellinghusen and other centres, and to Copenhagen in Denmark, Rörstrand, Marieberg, and other places in Sweden, and Herrebøe in Norway. Altogether the faience manufactories of the eighteenth century amount to several hundreds. Many were short-lived, but most had some peculiarities of style or emphasis which are of interest to collectors, but which cannot be described here in the context of the total sequence of tin glaze.

Many of the characteristics of faience stem from changes in the ownership and organisation of pottery factories. Until the mid seventeenth century most pottery factories had belonged to proprietors who were at one and the same time craftsmen, designers, businessmen, and technicians. These men were many of them born into a family business and pursued and developed a family tradition, as did the Conrades of Nevers, the van Eenhoorns of Delft, the Poterats of Rouen and the Guidoboni of Savona. Often they were backed by financiers or helped by the patronage of royal or noble families, but within the business they themselves held the initiative and the power of veto. They inherited a tradition and extended it; they thought and worked within the world of ceramics; they enjoyed the asset of inherited skill, but they were also limited by it.

A considerable number of eighteenth-century *faiencieries* still belonged to men of this kind, but in some of the most influential factories the initiative came from the patrons themselves, the princes, noblemen and merchants for whom the work was being done. Many factories were actually founded and owned by them.[2] They were not conversant with the technicalities of manufacture, but they knew what they wanted and could pay a great deal to get it. Their ideas came as often from outside ceramic tradition as from within, from gold and silver vessels, pewter, sometimes from glass, from paintings and engravings, sculpture and architecture.

Until this time European pottery had for the most part been made and decorated in ways which were suited to the materials and were invited by the nature of clays, glazes and pigments. Some eighteenth-century work is distinguished by extreme difficulty, by ingenuity rather than by craftsmanship and imagination working together in balance. It led to astounding virtuosity in the manipulation of materials, and to finely prepared materials such as had never been known before, but it also led to some ceramic conventions which had little value beyond contrivance, and to an eclectic attitude to design and ornament which was inherited by the industries of the nineteenth century and led to some absurdities. In general, however, and especially in the first half of the eighteenth century, ideas coming from outside ceramic traditions invigorated the potter's craft and produced some pieces which are in their way as perfect as can be conceived [159]. There is after all no such thing as a 'pure' tradition in any art or craft. Ever since clay was first

2   Most books dealing with faience include details of the foundation of the chief factories. For a general introduction, see George Savage, *Pottery and Porcelain* (London), and *World Ceramics*, ed. R. J. Charleston (London, 1968). Amongst more detailed accounts the following are specially useful: J. Giacomotti, *Faiences françaises* (Fribourg, 1963); K. Hüseler, *Deutsche Fayencen*, 3 vols. (Stuttgart, 1956–58); C. Hernmarck, *Fajans och Porslin* (Stockholm, 1959); and G. Liverani, *Five Centuries of Italian Maiolica* (London, 1960).

patterned by being pressed into woven baskets, pottery has continually assimilated ideas originating in other manufactures.

The manufacture of faience and porcelain became in the eighteenth century a fashionable diversion for some of the nobility who founded factories, such as the profligate Karl Eugen of Württemburg, founder of the Ludwigsburg porcelain factory in 1758. For others, such as the Counts of Aranda at Alcora, and the Ferniani family, who owned a factory in Faenza, it was a serious interest, and their attention was reflected both in the quality of the finished work and in the well-being of their workpeople. For all, it was a source of possible profit and certain prestige. It was also the surest way of obtaining the wares they wanted for their own courts and other residences. The appreciation of pottery now became an attribute expected of people of quality: fine pieces and table services were acceptable gifts of state and were objects of admiration and envy. Artistic ladies began to decorate china ware and one of the daughters of George III of England painted the *Triumph of Love* on Berlin porcelain.[3]

For the nobility to have a vested interest in manufacturing pottery was nothing new, but it had never occurred so extensively, nor had ceramic designs ever before been so directly influenced by men of exalted rank.

The most notable establishments were of course the porcelain factories, headed by Meissen itself, which was founded in 1710 by Augustus the Strong of Saxony and Poland. The manufacture of porcelain needed generous financial backing, and the success of many factories depended on capital provided by kings and princes, as at Chantilly and Ludwigsburg. Louis XV acquired a large financial interest in Vincennes; later, the Berlin porcelain works were supported by Frederick the Great, who also increased their fortunes by edicts such as that requiring every Jew to buy three hundred thalers' worth of porcelain at the time of marriage.[4] Many of the more delicate and elaborate things attempted in faience were really better suited to the much harder porcelain material, and the two manufactures were closely connected. Around the middle of the century a number of faience factories undertook the making of porcelain as well, for example, Ansbach, Kassel, Fulda, Niederviller and Ludwigsburg.

By the early eighteenth century even faience could only be undertaken with any pretension to refinement by factories with a good deal of capital behind them. Several *faienceries* got into financial difficulties and were sold by their founders to new owners who took advantage of the hard primary work already done, as happened to Simonet and Fehr's Frankfurt *faiencerie*, and to the factory started at Marieberg near Stockholm by J. E. L. Ehrenreich, the court dentist, in 1758. Factories enjoying the backing or patronage of princes were usually better capitalised and could be given special trading privileges by their royal owners. Such, for instance, was the Kassel factory, founded in 1686 by the Landgrave of Hesse-Nassau, and those of Berlin and Ansbach, founded in 1676 and 1710 by the Margrave Friedrich Wilhelm of Brandenburg. The Proskau factory in Silesia, conversely, was privately founded but ended in princely ownership. It was started by Count Leopold of Proskau in 1763. After his death in a duel it passed to Count

3   See Bevis Hillier, *Pottery and Porcelain, 1700–1914* (London, 1968), p. 42, and also generally, for the social background of eighteenth-century pottery.
4   Ibid., p. 85.

Johann Karl von Dietrichstein in 1770, and in 1783 was acquired by Frederick the Great.

From the very beginning of the century there began an important change of emphasis in the manufacturing methods of tin-glaze pottery. From this time onwards the greater part of the production was not thrown on the wheel but formed by casting, pressing, moulding and modelling [160, 161]. This made possible the repetition of elaborate shapes derived—sometimes even directly cast—from beaten gold, silver or pewter, shapes such as could never profitably have been individually fashioned. It also enabled the factories to produce table services in which each kind of vessel could be repeated exactly to size. The change from throwing to moulding was not merely a matter of alternative method: it involved radically different thinking and planning, and it entailed changes in the organisation of the work-people, and even the selection of people with a different kind of talent. From this time onwards the distinction between the designer or artist and the artisan engaged on repetitive work became greater and greater. The subservience of the artisan was not begun, only intensified, by the industrial system of the next century.

In sympathy with the new emphasis on refined and fashionable shapes, the technique of painting was also much changed. No foolproof method of repeating painted designs was available until transfer prints were invented about the middle of the century, but an ever-increasing use was made of engravings of paintings, and books of engraved designs such as the collection published in 1711 by Jean Bérain, court designer to Louis XIV, which was immensely influential in both French and German faience and porcelain [96]. Part of the chief painter's work was to instruct his people in following his style and his prototype designs, and pricked paper sponces (through which the design was marked out with a charcoal pad) were much used as aids to accurate repetition. The challenge of repetition was eased but not solved by such methods. Much still depended on the individual talent and experience of each painter, and the most far-sighted factories, such as Strasbourg, Castelli, Alcora and the Pentagon in Marseilles, incorporated painting-schools in the establishment, to train and educate apprentices. This was an acknowledgement that the new kind of factory needed a higher level of skill than could be expected of the traditional craftsman. To a greater or lesser degree, most of the factories of the period had to retrain or educate the specialist artisans they employed.

The taste for elegant and refined painting led naturally to extensive use of muffle-fired enamel colours, which gave a wider range of hue and a greater precision of touch than the old high-fired or *grand-feu* colours. The chief obstacle was the expense of the extra firing which enamels required. In France relatively few potteries followed up this technique, and painters managed instead to refine the *grand-feu* palette and brushwork to a quite remarkable degree. In Italy, and especially in Germany, where the enamel technique had originated,[5] enamels were being very generally used by the middle of the century, both for landscape and figure paintings by individual masters, and for repeat ornament on borders.

The fortunes of a factory depended on obtaining the services of virtuoso modellers and

5   The earliest examples are said to be those used on stoneware at Kreussen in Saxony in the 1620s. See W. B. Honey, *European Ceramic Art* (London, 1949), p. 31.

painters, to lead their respective studios and train their assistants, and also an experienced 'arcanist' to devise and prepare glazes, pigments and clay-bodies and to design the kilns. The key men were paid enormous salaries and were always open to the lure of higher offers from rival institutions. The famous porcelain modellers Kändler of Meissen and Bustelli of Nymphenburg could virtually name any price they wished.[6] The restless, brilliant enamel-painter and designer Adam Friedrich von Löwenfinck, for example, left Meissen, where he was schooled, in 1737, worked for three years at Ansbach, helped to establish the Fulda factory for Amadeus von Buseck in 1741, was co-founder of the faience and porcelain factory of Höchst in 1746–9, and later in 1749 he introduced his exquisite flower enamel decorations to the Strasbourg faience of the Hannong family, whence the convention spread rapidly to other *faienceries* in France [97]. Von Löwenfinck remained at Strasbourg, where he became a co-director of the factory.

Once a man had proved his ability the temptation to remove to new areas for greater rewards must have been very strong. The arcanist Johann Buchwald of Fulda, for instance, worked successively at Stralsund, Rörstrand, Marieberg, and then at Eckernförde, Kiel and Stockelsdorff. New factories were always looking for men of proven talent. Joseph Olerys, to take another example, came from France to Alcora when the ninth Count of Aranda was building up the laboratories of his superbly appointed factory. In time Olerys established himself as owner-manager of the former Clérissy factory at Moustiers, where all his previous experience was fulfilled.

Some experts promised more than they could perform. Such perhaps was John Bird, whose fortunes at Delftfield have already been mentioned. Another uncertain character was Johann Wolff, who had been trained at Nürnberg and went to seek his fortune in Scandinavia instead of trusting his luck in the highly competitive conditions of Germany. He persuaded the Danish King to grant privileges for a faience factory, and a company was formed which established the Støre Kongensgade workshops in 1722. In 1725, after many difficulties, Wolff absconded, taking with him some of the best workmen and some precious materials. He next appeared in Sweden, where he was associated with the foundation of the Rörstrand factory, whose craftsmen were drawn mostly from Germany, perhaps on Wolff's recommendations. Within two years Wolff once again had to leave, and his later fortunes are obscure. Both factories prospered after he had left them. Technicalities still depended a great deal on traditional practice and 'secret' recipes, and new enterprises could waste a vast amount of time and money if their first advisers were not really good and given adequate financial backing.

All the principal eighteenth-century factories developed certain specialities according to the particular skills of their key craftsmen and artists. Thus the Castelli factory in the Kingdom of Naples was famed for its delicate figure and landscape decoration, the speciality of the Grue family, who managed it over several generations until about 1750. The Pierre Chapelle factory at Rouen in the 1720s made some of the largest pieces of faience of all time: a celestial and a terrestrial globe standing on pedestals, over four feet high, and some enormous faience statuary. Jacques Chambrette, who founded the Lunéville factory about 1731, made amongst other things large ornamental figures of

6 Bevis Hillier, op. cit., pp. 39–40, for details of the salaries of masters, skilled artisans and labourers. The difference was enormous.

baronial dogs and lions with horsehair manes. Joseph Philippe Dannhöfer was trained
at Vienna and specialised in *Schwarzlot* black decoration of great delicacy, which he
introduced to the factories of Bayreuth, Höchst and Fulda, on both porcelain and faience.
The decorative style of Doccia faience of the mid-century is attributed to the presence of
a French ceramic-painter, Nicola Letourneau, who came from Faenza in 1740 to manage
the studio. The Schrezheim factory produced some large rococo faience sculpture made
by J. M. Mutschele, who came from Bamberg. The Alcora factory seems to have been
particularly well managed, and benefitted from a succession of remarkably talented
painters, technicians and sculptors: Edouard Roux and Joseph Olerys from France, a
Spanish painter Miguel Soliva, and later the sculptor Joaquín Ferrer.

Despite the diversity of individual style and talent, certain characteristics were shared
by almost all the high faience of the period: a finish and perfection of specialised technique, aroused and constantly challenged by the rivalry of porcelain [98]; an emphasis
on elaborate design and miniaturist detail equivalent to those of fine engraving and
chased metal; a strong influence coming from enamelled porcelains from China and
Japan. These porcelains stimulated the production of *chinoiseries*, naturally enough, but
their influence went deep and led to free, asymmetric compositions which merged into
the rococo, and were often used without any obvious oriental associations [158]. There
was also a general derivation from baroque and later from rococo sculpture, from paintings, and from botanical illustrations and other engravings [157].[7] The triumph over
materials and technical obstacles led to the recognition that virtually no challenge of
modelling or painting was beyond the abilities of specialist craftsmen backed by sufficient
money. Oddly, far from bringing a new freedom to ceramics, this technical mastery actually increased the subservience of the craft to other crafts and to the Fine Arts. Since
almost anything could be done in ceramic form, ceramics became a universal borrower
and to a large degree ceased to have any special aesthetic language of its own.

One convention in particular helped to bring this about—the custom of decorating
banqueting tables with elaborate centrepieces representing pastoral landscapes, classical
myths and historical legends, arcadian lakes and temples, and *chinoiseries*. These things
were originally made in sugar by court confectioners. During the early eighteenth
century they came to be made of faience and porcelain, and eventually became larger
and more and more fantastic, reaching an extreme in the period of the rococo, a style
which admirably suited them. Originally the centrepieces had been transient amuse-
ments; now they became durable miniature sculptural compositions with landscape and
architectural settings. The banquet was sometimes simply the occasion for presenting
the latest *tour de force* or ceramic cadenza, which would later receive an honoured place
in the patron's art collection. Some centrepieces were miniature only in a relative sense,
in that they were smaller than statuary: a length of four or five feet and a height of three
feet or more was not extraordinary.

The achievements of the master-modeller in the centrepiece were backed up by the
painters, who embellished these fantasies with a mixture of natural colour and refined
ornament, and sometimes finished them with lavish gilding. The desirability of toned
flesh colours, perennially difficult in traditional tin-glaze pigments, invited the use of

7   Ibid., p. 91, for details of collections of engravings published for the guidance of painters on ceramics.

enamels, which could do justice to the pinks of nymphs and goddesses and courtesans, the amber skin of heroes and satyrs, and to the blushes of young maidens whose lives and loves were frozen by fire into these great fragile compositions. The whole achievement naturally had a return influence on tableware and pottery in general. The centrepiece showed what amazing things could be done, what refined or diverting subjects could be represented, but it also set the tone for the rest of the table service. The centrepiece and the prototypes of tableware came from the same studio, and an idea which worked well in the one case was too good to waste and came naturally to be applied to the other whenever it was relevant. The rococo tureens and cisterns, plates, platters and cruets of the eighteenth-century table look to modern eyes remarkably elaborate, but in comparison with the centrepiece they were merely a restrained reflection of the crowning glory of the board. The eclectic, exotic, flippant perfection of eighteenth-century porcelain and faience was manifest above all in the centrepiece.

The manufacture of faience diminished rapidly from about 1785. In Italy the Nove factory under Giovan Maria Baccin continued to produce rococo faience, and wares of mixed French, Chinese and neo-classical style were made by Cozzi in Venice and Boslli in Genoa and by some others. But in northern Europe the principal factories had either been discontinued or were converted to making porcelain or *faience fine*, which was really a white siliceous earthenware with a clear glaze. Some French and Belgian factories continued until the 1820s, such as Lunéville and Saint-Amand-les-Eaux, which was owned for a time by the ceramist Bastenaire-Daudenart. By 1830 he had changed over to *faience fine* and wrote a book advising other manufacturers to do the same.

England has no manufactories of faience with an opaque glaze, wrote Bastenaire-Daudenart. There is instead the English white-ware with a hard, clear glaze . . . Despite my strong national spirit, I cannot help saying that we should benefit if we could exchange our factories for theirs. One must above all be truthful, and in all pottery other than porcelain I think we have allowed ourselves to be overtaken by our rivals across the sea. Let this not discourage us; our inferiority should increase our competitive resolve.[8]

The same factors were at work in every country: porcelain had become more generally practicable, and satisfied the expensive market. Hard white earthenware had overtaken faience in the market for refined but less expensive tableware and ornaments. Not only was it more durable and much cheaper to glaze, but it could be decorated with transfer prints which laid out the principal features and details of the ornament, and the bright colours could easily be added in enamel by semi-skilled painters. An enormous, urban, middle-class market awaited the manufacturers of this new earthenware, and the factories which made it virtually eliminated the manufacture of faience.

Tin-glaze wares were made after about 1830 only in those areas where it was not worth investing money for the manufacture of *faience fine* or porcelain, and where in consequence the old, low-temperature kilns could still pay their way by firing traditional tin-glaze pottery. These were the backward and rural parts of the Continent. In them an innocent, provincial tin-glaze ware continued to be made throughout the nineteenth and into the twentieth centuries, deriving its themes and ornaments partly from simpli-

8   F. Bastenaire-Daudenart, *La Faience* (Paris, 1828), p. xiii.

fied versions of older faience, and partly from local decorative tastes. Much of this pottery was frankly badly made, but it should not be generally belittled, for the best of it remained vital and generous at a time when European pottery was dominated by the worst artificialities and mock-refinements of industrial wares. Makkum in Holland, Quimper in Brittany, Modra in Slovakia, Talavera and Granada in Spain, Lisbon and Coímbra in Portugal, for example, all produced some very good and genuine work in these late days. But the work came from small and semi-rural potteries, lacking the challenge of new ideas from educated patrons, and lacking the confidence, the time, and the finance, to turn their hands and minds to anything really new. In the absence of strong reasons for getting better, much of their work inevitably became worse. When in time new ideas came to be realised in tin glaze they came from outside this world of traditional pottery, and the old proprietors were deeply puzzled.

13

TIN GLAZE SINCE 1800

Modern jargon sports many fictions, one of which is that industrialism and craftsmanship are in some mysterious way essentially opposed, and another is that the profit motive destroys creative art—as if industries could ever have evolved without craftsmanship of a high order, and as if artists never had any need of money. Despite these obvious facts, people still often assume that craftsmanship is bound to become obsolete in modern societies.

The Industrial Revolution changed the context of the craftsman's work, but it did not eliminate craftsmanship. It intensified the processes of specialisation which had been under way since long before the dawn of the machine age. Specialisation was already well established in the making of pottery when Piccolpasso wrote the *Arte del Vasaio* in 1558, and his drawings show painters, throwers, kiln men and glaze-makers at their different occupations. In the eighteenth century it became more than ever necessary, as refined taste required the repetition of elaborate designs in a greater and greater range of colour and gilding, together with moulded pottery repeated to exact sizes in a great variety of teasing forms. These in turn demanded kilns which could be fired with precision and reliability, and led to a refinement of all the materials and tools with which craftsmen worked.

The tools evolved into specialised machines, but they still needed craftsmen to operate them. Only in recent times has there been a fundamental change, the change from the machine-tool to the automated machine designed to replace skilled labour altogether, and this development is still only in its early stages.

The craftsman-technician and the craftsman-artisan have played a vital part in industry up to this point. The pottery industry, like most others, grew directly out of the practices of the pre-industrial craftsmen, and many of those practices are recognisable in modern factories.

But what of the craftsman-designer, the source of new ideas, new methods, new prototypes, the man in whom the processes of imagination, design, technique and production, traditionally all come together? Did he not vanish with the growth of industry? Perhaps the essential difference between the partial industrialism of the eighteenth century and that of the nineteenth lies in the separation of the functions which originally came together in the craftsman-designer. Perhaps it is in this field, and only this, that there is a real opposition between industrialism and craftsmanship.

As yet the Industrial Revolution is far from complete and during its course the question of the best relation between ideas and design on the one hand and production on the other has loomed large in the whole range of manufactured things which people choose by personal liking and judgement. The importance of the question in the modern world is shown by the multitude of design schools, design research organisations and records of designs, and the relationship between idea, design, technique and production remains ever-changing.

The later story of tin glaze is inseparable from these changes and experiments. It reflects the dominance now of one, now of another of the old functions of the vanished craftsman-designer, as his qualities were split up amongst specialist draughtsmen, artists, technicians and engineers.

Tin-glaze earthenware was the first of all the traditional pottery techniques to disappear at the beginning of the industrial era. The clay-body was soft and was superseded by hard siliceous earthenware. The opaque glaze was costly and was replaced by clear glazes over white bodies.[1] The elaborate faience decoration was slow, chancy and expensive, and was supplanted by the use of engraved designs printed in ceramic inks on fine tissue paper; at first these were applied over the surface of the fired glaze and fixed like enamels in a third firing; later they were placed direct on the biscuit ware and covered by transparent glazes. Thus the popular market was conquered by the new white earthenware or creamware. The expensive market for fine faience with enamel decoration was steadily taken over by the manufacturers of porcelain. The old porcelain monopolies became obsolete during the Napoleonic War, and all the time the processes and materials were becoming better known. Early in the nineteenth century porcelain came within the scope of private companies unrestricted by monopolies; the factories multiplied all over Europe, and most of the faience factories were either converted to the new materials, or were abandoned. By 1800 English Delftware was almost a thing of the past, and in the last fifteen years of the eighteenth century most of the numerous *faienceries* of Holland, France and Germany ceased production. In Italy tin-glaze earthenware lasted longer, and some interesting cast pieces were made at Capo di Monte in the nineteenth century, but the same influences were at work there as throughout the rest of Europe and the manufacture of tin-glaze wares declined markedly.

In general tin-glaze pottery only survived in rural areas where potteries were too poor or too backward to change, and where a local demand persisted for the familiar boldly-painted wares for inns, farms and cottages.[2] In time even this lingering loyalty diminished as pedlars and fairground salesmen brought industrial products even to the remotest areas of Galicia, Slovakia, Calabria, the Tyrol and the Auvergne.

This sounds like the end of the story, the last gasp of a tradition with a continuous sequence spanning almost exactly a thousand years, stretching from the Persian gulf to Spain and Scandinavia. And had men been merely economic animals ravening after cheap consumer goods, it would indeed have been the end. But while the tradition as a

1   The glaze was not always changed immediately. The unpainted, elaborately moulded *faience fine* of Lorraine, for instance, was at first often given a tin glaze. It looks to me much nicer than the yellowish white of the clear glaze, but was presumably discontinued because of its expense, or perhaps because this kind of white was now felt to be old-fashioned.

2   See P. Huillard, *La Faience en Bourgogne Auxerroise* (Paris, 1961). The author shows that many of the designs in rural potteries were taken from sophisticated eighteenth-century faience. The simplicity and easeful directness of country pottery was almost the opposite of the older faience. It is agreeable to touch and use, and people who have any can seldom bear to part with it.

continuous sequence came to an end, the tin-glaze technique itself reappeared inter-mittently in various non-traditional forms during the industrial era, and has done so increasingly in the twentieth century. These appearances have not been part of the general development of mass-produced industrial pottery, but they have been directly the result of the self-conscious preoccupation with art, design and experiment which are as much a consequence of industrialism as is mass-production itself.

Factory-owners are often treated as scapegoats for the ugliness of modern industrial communities. In point of fact the leading industrial manufacturers all over Europe devoted considerable time and money to design, and were often intensely proud of their achievements and of their connection with artists and designers. Ironically, the things which received most care and attention from artists are often the very ones which are most ridiculed or lamented today, whereas some of the simpler, functional and less 'artistic' designs of the same period are clean-lined and satisfying. The attitude to design in nineteenth-century pottery was still dominated by the thinking of the later eighteenth century: refinement was largely equated with ornament and virtuosity, superfluous felicities and demonstrations of technical skill. Because of the association of fine things with elegant living, people tended to look back to the styles favoured by the highest classes of the antique and Renaissance worlds, and to the rococo of pre-revolutionary France. The associations of a style are usually more influential than its formal qualities in themselves. It is understandable that the industrial nineteenth century should have looked back to ages whose virtues had become conspicuously absent in the present. The cultural leaders of the period did more than look back: they tried to recreate the works of those far-off golden days, in so far as they did not undermine the social and industrial structure of their own times.

Thus, while the work-people within factories were taken for granted, the independent artist and designer became an important figure. In England the way was led first by Wedgwood's, and later by Minton's. The latter, for example, had special designs made by the sculptor and architect A. W. N. Pugin, and the sculptor Alfred Stevens amongst many others, and also employed the French artist-designer Théodore Deck, from Sèvres. They also adapted designs and paintings by Mantegna and other Renaissance painters. Many of the leading Continental factories followed a similar policy.

Through the artist-designer some industrialists sought to justify themselves artistically. They were not merely producing functional articles in quantity: they had a sincere desire to achieve the best that was in their reach, and to excel in Art as well as in manufacture.

Art is apt to be frightened away by the direct pursuit; like happiness, it is almost always a by-product. We tend to look back today to Brunel's bridges rather than to the nineteenth century's self-conscious attempts to engender Art. In pottery, the trouble arose to a large extent because factories preferred to have the services of a pure artist rather than of a craftsman-designer, and the pure artist, not thinking in terms of ceramic media, all too easily produced bastard ceramics whose basic attributes were masked by ornament with exotic associations echoing Renaissance painting, Greek sculpture, sug-gesting the perfumes of Araby or the mysteries of the East.

Most of the ideas coming from artists were naturally enough realised in hard, fine, translucent porcelain. A rare venture in the faience tradition, though not actually tin glaze, was made by the French painter, engraver and lithographer Felix Bracquemond in the 1860s. Bracquemond was then a young and successful painter well acquainted with the artistic movements of his day, and a friend of several of the Impressionists. His designs reflect the current interest in Japanese prints and the dramatic asymmetries of Japanese picture-composition. In the strong simplification of drawn line and profile they are also forerunners of *art nouveau*. His designs were printed and painted on a *faience fine* table service made at Montereau and Creil. They were conceived on a generous scale which over-passed the familiar refinements of applied prints and virtuoso enamel decoration. Not for a long time had pottery been decorated with such supple boldness [166].[3]

In England in the later nineteenth century ideas about design and industry were dominated by William Morris and his circle of artistic and literary friends. Their ideas were produced by industrialism, even though they all deplored the Industrial Revolution. In accord with the spirit of his circle, the designer-ceramist William de Morgan had no direct contact with industry. Over a period of some thirty years, in Soho, Fulham and at Lane End in Surrey, his craftsmen-employees carried out his designs and those of his friends in 'Persian faience' and lustre, and he made some use of tin glazes. De Morgan's art pottery differed from industrial ware in spirit and more than in spirit: it used ceramic techniques which were too variable and uncertain to be used industrially. This was especially true of the technique of smoked iridescent lustre-painting for which he is specially remembered. But de Morgan would probably have abhorred industrial methods in any case, for like many of his contemporaries he assumed that Art and Industry were essentially opposed, and that fine ceramics could only come from the labours of independent artists using new technical knowledge with the pure objective of making beautiful things. Once again, here was ceramic technique coming to the notice of men of 'lofty spirit and speculative minds' as Piccolpasso had wished long before. Luckily for himself, de Morgan possessed a small fortune and was able to maintain a high-minded disregard for commercial considerations. What he eventually lost in pottery he regained from the sale of his novels. The craftsmen who served him were less fortunate, and had to find other work when the combined effect of financial difficulties and ill-health put an end to his pottery in 1905.

De Morgan was primarily a draughtsman. His pottery was carefully painted by craftsmen working from his cartoons. His designs have the studied verve of their period, but they can also disappoint because of their contrivances and the absence of any live touch of personal 'handwriting'. Many of the vital juices were used up in the process of translating the designs from paper to pottery. Despite his high ideals, de Morgan was more a designer using ceramics than an artist thinking in ceramic terms. The same applies to the few ventures into tin-glaze tiles by painters in William Morris's own studio: they are faithful renderings of original drawings, but whatever life the original possessed departed as it was copied on to glaze. The English pottery-painters of the

3 Bracquemond's service belongs in spirit to the faience tradition and is often called faience, though it was not actually done in tin glaze, but in an almost colourless clear glaze on very white earthenware. The Victoria and Albert Museum has a few pieces (illustrated in *World Ceramics*), and a larger number are in the Musée des Arts Décoratifs in Paris.

eighteenth century had preferred to work freehand as far as possible, and whether out of wisdom or laziness, or perhaps because they were paid at piece-work rates, they usually avoided this shortcoming.

Whether André Metthey (1871–1920) knew of William de Morgan's work I do not know, but he behaved as if he did, for he avoided the snags attending the translation of designs. While serving as a soldier, Metthey experienced a vocation to become a potter. He began making stoneware at Asnières in 1901. He was as much in love with Art as was de Morgan, but his great desire was to handle and understand the materials themselves in order to work through them, not merely in them. He gave himself an intensive course of instruction, prepared his own clays and glazes, and built his own kiln. Stoneware proved unsuitable for the painted pottery he saw in his mind's eye, and he soon started working in tin-glaze instead. He felt that pottery had a natural affinity with the fine arts, a conviction which has reappeared in France time and again. Metthey's work suffered somewhat from his lack of technical fluency. His pots are heavy and were obviously made with difficulty, but many of them started from a strong idea and were imaginatively worked out, and many were unique.[4] Modestly, Metthey felt unable to fulfil all that he felt was possible, and he invited his painter-friends to share the painting of his pots: Roualt, Dérain, Vlaminck, Bonnard, Signac, and several others. He was still unsatisfied, finding that the opaque white glaze clouded the colours.

From 1908 for the remaining twelve years of his life he worked in the 'Persian faience' technique, that is, underglaze painting on white earthenware paste, covered with clear alkaline glazes. This was really better for the man who has aptly been called the 'Fauve of the Potters', who delighted in strong, luminous colours and colour-contrasts. Nonetheless, while Matthey dreamed in ceramics, his friends only played with it, and returned in their serious work to flat canvas and conventional pigments, which did not have to be fired and undergo change.

Though tin glaze did not satisfy André Metthey, it remains a natural medium for painters, and it has been used by many painters from his time to the present, as a fine art medium rather than for functional pottery. Fernand Léger, amongst others, used it for a number of tile-paintings in the 1920s, working with the ceramist Roland Brice. The Paris-trained Swedish painter Isaak Grünewald used it at Rörstrand, where he painted in the cubist-functionalist manner on vases which in his hands became virtually three-dimensional canvases. Grunewald was not a decorator in the traditional sense; he was a painter working in ceramics, like Pellipario and Avelli long before, except that his idiom was totally different and he used fully the roundness of his 'canvas' in a way which the old Italian painters never attempted.

Visiting England, Dérain introduced Duncan Grant and Vanessa Bell to ceramics, and they both returned at frequent intervals to painting on pottery and tiles over a number of years [167]. A certain amount of tin-glaze pottery was made at Roger Fry's Omega workshops before the First World War, and Duncan Grant has never long departed from the painting of tin glaze ever since, partly for its own sake, and partly, he

4 Most of Metthey's pots are in private collections in France. A few are in the Musée des Arts Décoratifs and the Musée de l'Art Moderne in Paris. An article on Metthey is in *Connaissance des Arts*, vol. 2 (Sept. 1962), p. 22.

says, for its return effect on canvas paintings. Since the Second World War the versatile Danish artist-designer Bjørn Wiinblad has produced much directly-painted tin-glaze faience of his own, and has also designed prototypes which are carried out in his own workshops. In the same period a number of French sculptors also returned to tin glaze, for free-standing figures, bas-reliefs, and tiles and plaques with moulded forms, notably Paul Pouchol, Guidette Carbonelle and Georges Jouve. Most remarkable of all has been Picasso's use of ceramics for painting and modelling from the late 1940s to the present, and much of his work has been done in tin glaze, one of the traditional media of the Ramié workshops in Vallauris where he set up his studio [171, 172].[5] Designs derived from Picasso's work have been made in tin glaze by the Madoura pottery, and many of his ideas have been followed up by his potter-pupil Gilbert Portanier.

The adoption of ceramics by painters and sculptors involves a curious repetition. As in the eighteenth century, ideas once again entered ceramics from the outside: the stranger, taking up the medium, did things with it which enlarged its scope by ignoring all the rules. 'Picasso', said M. Ramié, 'works in a most unconventional way, and would not have obtained employment here as an apprentice'. The artist's use of ceramics often seems to the conventional potter to be a misuse. The work of many artists in recent times has struck potters as wild and arbitrary, and in earlier times artists' work has seemed to be over-elaborate and over-refined. Both deviations have been further queried by traditional craftsmen simply because they are art-forms divorced from use.

By no means all artists' ceramics have been successful. Not all Pellipario's dishes are masterpieces. Gauguin's modelled ceramics proved to be a dead end; the work of Dérain and Vlaminck was merely a holiday, and much of Picasso's ceramic work has been trivial. But a common thread runs through almost all the ceramic work of men coming to it from the so-called Fine Arts: the material is handled, whatever the style or period, with a strong will, a strong idea. The artist makes the material yield to this concept whatever difficulties of form or technique he may encounter. The idea is stronger than the material, and sometimes the material is manipulated in a way which a pure craftsman would regard as crude. But in this way old conventions are shown to be expendable, and new ideas become current, even if the first attempts are not fully satisfactory.

In contrast to the artist, the practising potter, especially the potter working in a definite tradition, can eventually become so familiar with his materials that he comes to depend on the material for his idea, or to work without any idea at all other than to please. And what pleases only the eye cannot please for long. Thus while artists' ceramics often suffer from will or intention overbalancing the qualities of the material, craftsmen's work can suffer from the dominance of habits or dependence on the material itself to provide interest or meaning. This is asking too much. Without an objective seen in the mind's eye, forms, colours, brushwork and other techniques become merely meaningless variations without a theme, as has happened in degenerate peasant work and in some modernistic studio pottery. The ideal, whether a functional vessel or an art-form, depends on a balance of perceptions: the potter can learn much from the artist, just as the artist cannot achieve much in ceramics unless he listens to the potter.

5 Of the many books on Picasso's ceramics, see especially D. Kahnweiler, *Picasso Keramik* (Hanover, 1957).

André Metthey's ideal of the visionary potter working directly with simple, thoroughly-known materials gained enormous impetus during the inter-war period in Northern Europe and the United States especially, from the impact of Japanese traditions which were introduced to the West by Leach and Hamada. Their attitude was that European practices of designing *for* a material or working *with* a given material were inside-out: the artist-craftsman is only worthy of his name when he works intuitively with and through his material, participating emotionally in every part of its preparation and manipulation and in its final trial by fire. Above all they demonstrated that in their tradition the only work of lasting validity was that which was nourished by deeper roots than any personal enthusiasm, ultimately from a reverence for life itself, which made design, and the desire to please or excite, seem trivial. The only lasting aesthetic qualities in pottery or anything else, in their view, were those which sprang from the inner nature and being of the individual. The cultivation of external effects alone was bound to be barren.

Leach and Hamada worked at first in slipware, then in reduced stoneware, and their followers seldom departed from these two techniques, even though what the masters were saying was profoundly applicable to all kinds of pottery, and to many other activities as well. After the Second World War, however, their precepts became so generally accepted that any student-potter in the English-speaking world, and many others also, absorbed the attitude of thinking and imagining in terms of their material from first principles. The ideas which had come from Japan amounted to a philosophy of living: they were not merely artistic precepts. Some of their wider implications were opposed or thrown aside in the West, but the technical consequences were accepted and even extended by others, who were equally convinced, though often for different reasons, that the work of the craftsman-designer has to begin with insight into materials.

These ideas had especially interesting effects in tin-glaze work, because this technique had always tended to a division between clay-workers and specialist painters, a division which persisted as an attitude of mind which distinguished 'form' from 'deocration', even when both kinds of work were done by one and the same person. Now craftsmen came to conceive both these aspects together, to see them as inseparable parts of one whole, and to think and dream in terms of diverse materials unified by fire, rather than regarding them as parts of different processes, or as mere passive servants of their will. Many of the traditional kinds of craft-work, especially those with figurative designs or functional purposes, and tin glaze in particular, seemed to have been limited too much by following only those things which the mind can think out before, and give a rational account of. Modern craftsmen began to make things which the mind cannot think beforehand, things which could only arise from the imagination participating in the material itself during the process of making.

Intuitive ways of working such as this are of course highly unpredictable. The real thing can easily be caricatured and give rise to nothing more than facile imitations of natural forms or vacant modernisms which change with every season. But in an artist or craftsman who is strong enough or lucky enough to be able to follow his own intuitions, they can lead to much that is original and lasting.

Through the long history of tin-glaze ware, most painting and decoration was of the kind which can be thought of before it is done: its general lay-out could be mentally entertained, and it could be rationally constructed, carried out, judged and taught. Modern craftsmen, working directly with their materials, stretched the whole concept of 'decoration' by allowing the special qualities of their materials to render uncalculated forms and textures, half-random shapes, dream-images, and impulses of the moment. Hitherto, most pottery decoration in the West had made use of intelligible forms and images. Now the eye was invited to explore, discover and recreate from what was suggested. Imprecision and deliberate ambiguity were now sometimes as important as the definite image had been in the past. The values of the past were turned inside-out: feeling, rather than finish, vigour, rather than artifice, directness rather than refinement.

Certain techniques of tin-glaze decoration were now followed up for the first time. Theoretically they could have come about long before, but they had not done so because the climate of feeling was not right for them. For instance, fusible, semi-opaque tin glazes could be applied over dark clays and slips so that wherever the glaze is thin it 'breaks' to give colours and textures derived from the underlying clay, not precisely determined by human agency [168]. The same property of certain glazes was exploited for designs incised with a point through the unfired glaze over dark or red clays. Where the point had travelled a fine, variable, textured line developed as the glaze melted in the firing, and some unusual and beautiful effects arose. These methods meant standing traditional tin-glaze practice on its head, for traditionally the glaze should be as white as possible, and cover a light-coloured clay which would not interfere with the enamel-like surface.

Many possibilities of the wax-resist technique were explored. Generally, this technique consists of painting with melted candle-wax thinned with paraffin or light oil, either on the surface of the unfired glaze, to resist a subsequent application of colour, or on the biscuit-ware, to resist the glaze itself, as has been done by Picasso in many of his works at Vallauris. The heated medium has to be applied quickly before it solidifies on the brush, and the technique is unsuitable for formal, repetitive work. There is no room for hesitation, but an artist-potter working direct can do a great deal with this technique [169, 170].

Another recent variant of tin glaze has been the overlaying of one or several coloured glazes on an already-fired tin glaze. The white glazed piece is warmed and a fairly thick coloured glaze is poured or sprayed over it, covering it wholly or partially with a layer which quickly dries. This layer can be scraped, scratched, or rubbed away. When the piece is fired again the overlying glaze mingles with the tin glaze to give areas of mottled and textured colour, set off by the original white. Further glazes can be added in the same way, but each one needs another firing. Thus the method is costly and time-consuming, but it produces effects entirely different from any other form of applied colour, and can be used with abandon or with minute precision. Again, the technique is useful chiefly to artist-potters working direct, free to modify their designs as they proceed.

Tin glaze has usually been thought of as a painter's ceramic medium, but the habit of thinking of glaze and clay together rather than as separate features of separate processes has caused the technique to be taken up increasingly in sculptural ceramics, and used with rough and textured clay surfaces which make the glaze flow from edges and scored areas and gather in pools or runnels elsewhere. The technique can of course be used with many kinds of glaze, but in some pieces the whiteness of the glaze is an important part of the conception [Colour Plate X]. Sculpture-ceramics generally opened up a new field in which the traditional utilitarian properties of glaze and surface are no longer relevant and where rough surfaces and pitted glazes can be desirable.

Traditionally, most painting on tin glaze was conceived as drawn lines with infilled colour. This was essential for many kinds of figurative decoration, but it came also to be used for painted designs even when it was not necessary, simply because it was dependable. A recent use of the medium has involved painting with strong self-evident brushstrokes, sometimes over surfaces which have been deliberately textured or ridged in the throwing, with gradations of colour as the pigment leaves the brush and gathers or runs thin on recessed or raised areas. In a sense, brushwork has always been a record of movement relived by the eye, but except in the Far East it has usually been dominated by representation. This newer brushwork has something in common with the Oriental idea of a stroke being like the note of an instrument: it can be sufficient to itself, or part of a movement, and it may or may not subserve some part of a figurative design. Once again, the technique is essentially informal and depends on intuitively 'seizing the moment' as Hamada has described it. It does not lend itself to routine production [Colour Plate W].

All these are only examples of new techniques which have been followed up in recent times, resulting from a new kind of attention given to materials. Others are also used, and there will be others still. They are all informal techniques which are essentially individual and depend on thinking and feeling in terms of material as well as in relation to an overall plan or design. In most cases the original idea remains open to suggestion and change as it is performed. Things made in this way usually either succeed in a single leap or fail; they are seldom open to judgements of correct or incorrect, better or worse, like older and more formal designs. They depend on a subtle balance between the maker's idea and the material itself. Their danger is that the maker may come to depend so much on the material speaking for itself that eventually he has nothing of his own to say. Once that point is reached the methods become caricatured, and are nothing more than a game of chance.

New techniques are as valid as the old, but they may not last long, just because they depend essentially on the individual touch and imagination. Formal designs can be learnt and passed on much more easily, and may have a long life, lasting many generations. Individualistic techniques can be absorbed by others, but are not easily passed on deliberately. They are also liable to change rapidly according the the impulses of each person, and may be no longer-lived than the well-being of a single man. They may change into something very different over a short period of time. In fact the entire concept of ceramic techniques is changing so rapidly today that it is scarcely possible to regard any as a distinct entity with a life-sequence and special continuity of its own. Ceramics are now increasingly being used with metal, wood, plastics, resins and other materials, and the concept of separate crafts may soon be as much a thing of the past as is the concept of a continuous tradition.

This chapter began with the suggestion that amongst the various kinds of craftsmen the only one to disappear during the Industrial Revolution was the designer craftsman in whom the various aspects of making and imagining came together. He is not as obsolete as was once supposed. Scandinavian factories have for some decades incorporated studios where individual ideas and experiments are carried out, both for one-of-a kind pieces and as a source of design-ideas for the main factory. There is a close parallel with the designer-craftsmen of seigneurial 'factories' of the eighteenth century. It may be significant that factories using this system, such as the Royal Copenhagen Porcelain Company, Arabia in Finland, and Gustavsberg and Rörstrand in Sweden are among the few which have followed up the possibilities of tin glaze in their regular, large-scale production.

Tin glaze was the first technique to disappear when industry began to be mechanised. By 1920 it had reappeared, principally as an artist's technique rather than as a medium for serviceable pottery. After the Second World War its artistic uses were extended, but it also came back into use in certain modern factories, with improved clay-bodies fired at higher temperatures, and once again with hand-painting. By this time the level of industrial prices had risen and the technique was no longer ruled out by the cost of the glazes and the expense of hand-painting. A growing section of the public was able to buy pottery because of its design and character and the individuality of its touch, and in spite of its price. The small handworking studio or small factory unit once again became a practical proposition, and produced many kinds of vessel which were not required in large enough quantities to be worth making industrially.

The output of small workshops is a peppercorn beside that of the highly capitalised factory. The ideas which are developed in small workshops are modest flowers in the garden, or wilderness, of the Fine Arts today. But the small workshop once again comes to have a significance beyond its size, a significance which does not depend only on suggestions of design and technique, which are increasingly being taken up by the main industry. At their best, its products evolve from a perceptive handling of materials and ideas which still remain open to reappraisal and change in a way which becomes impossible for established industrial designs. On the other hand, since most of its work is for use and must be fluent and fairly simple, it is free from the arbitrary experimentalism which often spoils individual artist's ceramics. In a world increasingly polarised between mass-production and wild individualism, the small manufactory once again has an important role, both for its products and for the activities and disciplines which challenge its members. There the creative craftsman can be himself without being self-conscious.

As has been demonstrated again and again over the centuries, unless people are desperate they are seldom satisfied with an object which fulfils only its basic functions. They desire it to speak to them, to remind them of what they know and love, to suggest to them things they love and do not know, to cheer, divert, intrigue, console and uplift them. If it had not been so, the tradition of tin-glaze earthenware would never have come into existence.

At the centre of every vessel thrown on the wheel is a point of stillness, which remains still, whatever forms the clay assumes. The form of the vessel measures movement in relation to this point. The variety of possible forms is endless. So is the possible variety of decoration which gives additional life to the forms. The still point is the beginning of both. The point which exists in the spinning clay but cannot actually be seen is the outward counterpart of the experience of being. Without it, there is no form, no variation of shape, no diversity of pattern, no possibility of any image or dream-suggestion. This book about a certain tradition of pottery can well end with the words of a poet who sensed profoundly the inner and the outer implications of the making of pottery, and the balance of shape and pattern, image and motion.

> At the still point of the turning world. Neither flesh nor fleshless;
> Neither from nor towards; at the still point, there the dance is,
> But neither arrest nor movement. And do not call it fixity,
> Where past and future are gathered. Neither movement from nor towards,
> Neither ascent nor decline. Except for the point, the still point,
> There would be no dance . . .

(T. S. Eliot, Burnt Norton)

I 4

METHODS AND MEN

CLAYS

Until the secrets of porcelain were discovered in the West, white pottery was made either by coating common clays with a film of white clay ('slip')[1] covered with a transparent glaze, or by using a glaze whitened by tin oxide. The particles of tin oxide cause opacity and whiteness because they are suspended in the glaze and reflect light. These two techniques were valued chiefly because they lent themselves to decoration with colours.

As a rule white slipware and tin-glaze wares are quite distinct; the colours are usually different, and have a different texture and edge because the one is under the glaze and protected by it, whereas in the other the colour actually fuses with the glaze and permeates it; but occasionally the difference can be hard to detect.

Except for the remarkable treatise by Abu'l Qasim of Kashan, of 1301[2] there are no direct records of the preparation of materials earlier than the sixteenth century. Even then descriptions and recipes are less significant than they seem, since they refer to impure local materials whose exact nature is unknown, and which cannot therefore be translated into modern chemical terms, and quite often the local names for materials are not intelligible. The point of the recipes was, after all, not to define the material but to enable people to prepare it. No old recipe is of much value alone, but together with examples of the finished pottery, it can provide some glimpse into the practical working background.

Traditionally, tin-glaze wares were made from chalky clay, whose high lime content caused it to shrink considerably as it cooled; this shrinkage put the glaze under compression and overcame the tendency of soft glazes to craze.

You must know [wrote Piccolpasso], that where the soil is white, or contains genga, in all these places clay for making pottery is got . . . and this I understand is called throughout Italy and beyond *Terra Creta*, chalky clay. . . . There is a great difference in Italy between the clay for cooking-pots and that for vases (fine pottery), namely, that one is white and light and the other red and heavy.[3]

In some places chalky clay can be dug in the plastic state. Such, for instance, are the

---

1   The famous painted slipwares of Isnik had a white slip-ground which itself was whitened with tin oxide.
2   The extracts from the treatise which follow later in this chapter are from the translation shortly to be published, by Mr. J. W. Allan of the Ashmolean Museum. I am most grateful to Mr. Allan for generously allowing me to include them.
3   Cipriano Piccolpasso, *Arte del Vasaio*, facsimile edition (London, 1934), p. 8.

gault clays of Kent and East Anglia in England,[4] and those of La Rambla near Córdoba, which are very plastic and which fire to yellow or creamy white colour and are quite hard at 1000°C. In other areas a chalky clay deposit can be collected to mix with plastic clays. The chalky clay is sometimes too rich in lime to harden on its own, but if mixed with a common red plastic clay it lightens it, renders it more fusible and endows it with the cooling-shrinkage which makes for a good glaze fit.[5]

This was the practice in the important pottery-producing area around Valencia. A dark red plastic clay, known as *terra del Pla de Quart*, was mixed with a 'short' or scarcely-plastic earth, called *terra de canter*, and sand, to make the fusible, soft pinkish or yellow-ish plastic clay used by the Paterna potteries.[6] At Manises a redder blend was made, with a smaller quantity of the white clay.

As well as endowing the clay body with a high shrinkage and a capacity to harden at low temperature, the lime also acted as a bleach. At low temperature these bodies may be distinctly pink; at higher temperatures they become yellowish-white. They also become light in weight, owing to the loss in firing of much carbon dioxide from the original calcium compounds. Another of their advantages was that chipped edges did not contrast with the white glaze as red clays would have done. Furthermore, as the French *Encyclopaedia* of 1756 says, 'the whiter the fired clay the less enamel you need to cover it'. Lime clays were usually, but not always, the basis of the clay-bodies used for tin-glaze ware. Italian maiolica from small or undistinguished pottery centres is sometimes distinctly red. Some Rouen faience of the seventeenth and eighteenth centuries had a reddish body with only a small lime content, and at Teruel in Aragon a dark red clay was habitually used with tin glazes [51]. Teruel vessels are almost always badly crazed. Indeed, there are few natural red clays which can be fired with tin glazes below 1020°C. without leading to crazing.

No material is ever without snags. The chief snag of the lime-clay bodies was that the larger particles of chalk would turn to quicklime in the firing. They had therefore to be removed by careful screening. Otherwise the quicklime would lie embedded in the fired clay, protected by the glaze covering, and might remain inert for months or years. Eventually some moisture would penetrate through the unglazed foot of the vessel, caus-ing the quicklime to expand, shaling off the glaze above it. Another snag of these clays is that, being readily fusible, they warp easily and are very sensitive to any unevenness of heating in the kiln [134b]. Traditional updraught kilns were apt to have such irregu-larities, and they produced many wasters.[7]

Although lime clays and chalky deposits are not uncommon, they do not always occur where people wish to make pottery. The Delft potters had to blend their local clays with lime clays from Tournai or even from England; some of their material was imported

4 A Kentish clay of this type is described with analysis and firing-graphs, in *Clay Building Bricks of the United Kingdom* (Ministry of Works National Brick Advisory Council, paper five).

5 Bastenaire-Daudenart, *L'Art de Fabriquer la Faience* (Paris, 1828), p. 20 et seq., describes such deposits near Paris. The chalky-clay or *marne* is found in the plaster-quarries directly above the chalk sulphate.

6 Scals and Aracil, *Cerámica del Museo Municipal de Valencia* (Valencia, 1962), p. 42.

7 A remarkable exhibit at the Bristol City Art Gallery is a pile of no less than 19 plates which got over-heated in a Wincanton kiln in the 1740s, and collapsed to make a solid, fused block like a tall sandwich, in which the clay of the plates is separated by white 'fillings' of glaze.

from Dundry Hill, near Bristol. In England the Bristol and Liverpool Delftware potteries, and the Delftfield pottery of Glasgow, imported clay from Carrickfergus in Northern Ireland. The quest for a blended body combining fusibility, hardness, whiteness, adequate cooling-shrinkage, plasticity and stability for throwing was never-ending and led to many refinements and special local recipes.

The French ceramist, Théodore Deck, recorded several of these recipes in 1870 in his book, *La Faience*, as did Bastenaire-Daudenart in 1828. Each material induced certain special qualities in the final blend. Bastenaire-Daudenart wrote that ideal faience clay would have approximately the following analysis:

$$SiO_2 \quad 58$$
$$Al_2O_3 \quad 30$$
$$Fe_2O_3 \quad 5$$
$$CaCO_3 \quad 7$$

Analyses of older, traditional bodies are given for comparison in Appendix A.
Deposits of such a clay might exist, he wrote, but none is known. Therefore the ideal mixture has to be prepared by blending several natural clays.[8]

Silver sand was often used to make a dense or plastic clay more 'open', steadier on the wheel and less liable to cracking as it dried. Powdered chalk or siliceous pipe clay was sometimes used to whiten the mixture and induce a greater cooling shrinkage. Finely ground calcined flint or quartz helped to harden the clay and made it firmer to throw, but could only be used with a clay which was already very plastic. In Central Europe salt was added to the clay to make it more fusible and shrink more in cooling.

These modifications were made by rule of thumb and could easily be optimistic and defective. Too much lime or chalk, for instance, and the fired body would be white and would be free of crazing but it would chip very easily. Too little lime, and the red common clay would cause crazing of the glaze. Too large particles of sand in the body could lead to pinholes in the fired glaze, especially on the undersides of vessels, where the turning or trimming of the foot had disturbed them.[9]

One of the best clay-bodies ever used with tin glaze was the earliest of all, the fine, yellowish, hard clay which has been known as 'Samarra body', the name given to it by Sarre and Herzfeld, who excavated the Mesopotamian palace of Samarra during the First World War. This mixture was intended to be finely thrown to make equivalents of Chinese porcelain vessels [1, etc.]. It was a superb achievement: a pale, durable body which seems to have been free from warping. The particles were very finely levigated to make the clay fire hard and dense.[10] The spectrograph analysis suggests that it was made

8 He describes the four types of clay which made up the traditional Paris faience clay-bodies, op. cit., p. 20 et seq. The interest of these is rather specialised but since his account gives both a geological description and approximate chemical analysis of the clays, it is probably the most dependable description of the traditional composition of faience clays, with some bearing on traditional faience of other times and places. It is therefore quoted in Appendix B.
9 Partially avoidable by dipping the bisque pot in a thin clay wash.
10 The fusibility of clays is determined as much by the particle size as by the materials they are composed of. A clay whose analysis shows only a small proportion of fluxes may prove easily fusible if its particles are very small.

from a mixture of reddish clay with a dolomite sand; the latter introduced the high proportion of calcium and magnesium.[11] The Mesopotamian alkaline glazes fitted this clay
remarkably well and crazed very little. The combination of glaze and body was a masterly
piece of work, implying a degree of experience and theoretical knowledge in the ninth
century which has never been accounted for.

Lime clays can be hardened by being fired higher, but this may cause severe warping,
for lime tends to act very rapidly as a flux. The only way such clays could safely be made
hard was by adding an alkaline flux to the body and by counteracting the tendency to
warp by adding powdered flint or quartz. Such clay-bodies can be both fusible and
steady. This principle was used by the twelfth-century potters of Kashan and Rayy in
Persia, and to a lesser extent in Egypt.

Abu'l Qasim described the preparation of frit-paste at Kashan as follows:

'To compound a body out of which to make pottery vessels such as dishes, basins, jugs, and
house tiles, one takes 10 parts of the aforementioned white sugar stone (*shukar-e sang*, quartz),
ground and sieved through coarse silk, 1 part of ground glass frit and 1 part of white Lūri clay
dissolved in water. This is kneaded well and left to ferment for one night. In the morning it is
well beaten by hand and the master craftsman makes it into fine vessels on the potter's wheel;
these are left standing till they are half dry. They are scraped down on the wheel, and the feet
are added, and when they are completely dry they are washed with a damp linen cloth to
remove the lines. When they are dry again they are rubbed with a wool cloth until they are
smooth and good.[12]

The tin-glaze lustres of Rayy and Kashan were painted over a body of this type
[Colour Plate C]. The very small proportion of plastic clay in the mixture made it
'short' and difficult to work, but it was hard and durable when fired. Sherds are recognisable by the slightly spongy texture of the section. A consequence of the lack of plasticity was that vessels were often made by throwing separate pieces and then luting them
together when they were half dry. This practice brought about some characteristic
Islamic composite forms with a very pronounced profile; the neck or foot was made
separately and added to the body. Such forms would have been almost impossible to
throw in a single operation from a plastic clay [22].[13]

11   The spectrograph analysis, for which I am obliged to the laboratories of AWRE, Aldermaston, is as
follows:

Titanium	0.20%
Aluminium	more than 5%
Silicon	more than 5%
Magnesium	6%
Iron	4%
Calcium	5%
Sodium	present
Potassium	present
Boron ⎱ Lead ⎰	not detected

12   Translated by J. W. Allan. (See note 2 above).
13   Janet Leach, 'Tamba', *Pottery Quarterly*, Tring, Herts., No. 13, 1957, describes the same practice in
a Japanese village where the clay had little plasticity.

The question naturally arises why tin glazes were not used over impervious stoneware clays, such as are very frequently used for domestic pottery today. Such clays are quite common in Europe, and they fire to a grey-buff colour similar to that of the lime clays used for earthenware. Although high temperature glazes (firing at about 1200–1240°C) would dissolve more of the opacifying tin oxide, such glazes can be whitened in the same way as earthenware glazes,[14] and can be similarly painted, although the colour range is more limited.

I know no satisfactory answer to this question. High temperature clays could have been used, and were not. Stoneware was made in the Rhineland from the fourteenth century onwards, yet hundreds of years passed before other European potters seriously investigated the possibilities of high-fired earthenware clays, even though they tried to make their normal earthenware as hard and durable as possible. They were forced to think afresh by the arrival of Oriental porcelain in the seventeenth century. Even so, although porcelain was achieved by Böttger in 1708–9, hard, high-fired faience only became possible after Wedgwood's development of siliceous white earthenware, two generations later. Wedgwood's discovery was never taken up by tin-glaze potters. His siliceous earthenware was used instead with transparent glazes; it was cheaper and stronger than faience and it became more fashionable. It might have led to an improved faience, but actually it superseded it.

GLAZES

Modern methods of glaze making often turn out to be old methods stood on their heads. The modern ceramist can write down the chemical nature of a substance and calculate its combination in glaze long before he knows how to prepare it. The glaze-makers of times gone by knew what materials to obtain, knew what they would do, without being able to explain why. Hence the enormous importance of inherited experience. 'There are many', wrote Piccolpasso, 'who, till the end of their lives, keep it [a recipe] hidden from their own sons and who, knowing themselves to be on the point of death, call to themselves their eldest and wisest son, and publish to him this secret amongst the other goods which they leave behind.'[15]

The dependence on inherited experience and the absence of theoretical knowledge perhaps explains why high temperature earthenware was not made until fairly recent times. The glass-making powers of lead, potash and soda had been well known by Roman times, but it was not known (nor was it at all obvious) that potash and soda were present in igneous rocks, and that felspar by itself was capable of making a glass over clay fired at high temperature. The nearest that potters came to discovering this was their recognition that certain kinds of sand, such as marble sand and the sand of chemic-

---

14   The ceramist L. Franchet, *La Fabrication Industrielle des Emaux et Couleurs Céramiques* (Paris, 1911), pp. 7–9, says that at this temperature the tin oxide will be totally dissolved. This may be true of some glazes, but not of all. Some eighteenth-century procelain glazes contained small amounts of tin oxide to counteract discoloration of the clay-body.

15   Piccolpasso, op. cit., preface, p. 1.

ally basic rocks, helped glazes to melt, whereas others (such as quartz sand) needed to be melted with larger amounts of lead, salt or potash.[16] In fact, for centuries glaze-making followed the practice of glass-making. It was not understood that the principal modifier of ceramic glazes is alumina (present in all clay), and that the fusibility of a glaze was easily controlled by small additions of some kind of clay. An ordinary low temperature glass contains little alumina. A powdered glass applied to the surface of a clay vessel melts rapidly and runs easily. There is only a small margin of error. Because of this potters were accustomed to a range of temperature in which their glassy glazes would not react too violently. Thus they looked to the fusible low-temperature clays and sought ways of hardening them without having to raise the firing temperature, instead of going beyond the traditional glass-making practices and adding clay or powdered rocks to their frits. The only exception was salt-glazed stoneware. This was a special case, for no glaze had to be prepared. The salt-vapour formed a glass when it combined with the white-hot clay in the kiln.

The earliest Middle Eastern tin glazes were alkaline and depended principally on fluxes of lime and soda and potash in combination with the silica in sand. Consequently, they had a high rate of shrinkage, and on most clays they would have crazed very badly. But glazes were used only for luxury vessels, made of carefully prepared and cleverly blended clays which had an almost equivalent shrinkage. Common vessels were made of natural local clays, modified only by mixing with sand, and these clays were usually left unglazed. There is an immense difference of status between (for instance) the glazed wares of twelfth-century Kashan and the common domestic pottery of the same era. It was not a matter of taking any clay and 'fashioning one vessel to honour and another to dishonour'. Different material was used for each, the one capable of being glazed and the other unsuitable for glazing.

There was a further difference between tin glazes and most transparent glazes. The latter could usually be applied to 'green', unfired vessels, so the pots were completed in a single firing. Tin glazes had to be applied to already fired or 'bisque' ware, partly because they had to form a thick coating and partly because they have a peculiar tendency to draw away from certain areas as they begin to melt, a characteristic known as 'crawling'. Therefore tin-glazed vessels had to be fired twice, and were slower and more costly to produce than other glazed pottery.

In Egypt the methods of preparing materials were extremely diverse. Medieval sherds of local manufacture vary from fine frit-pastes to coarse, soft, sandy clays with glazes which only just manage to adhere to the walls of the pot. Many of the Egyptian pots must have started crazing even before they left the kiln, and the crazing of glazed vessels must have been accepted as inevitable. Crazed and porous pottery was not necessarily considered defective. Glazes have everywhere been employed for their beauty long before they were considered useful. Medieval European pots for instance were glazed outside on the collar and shoulder long before glaze was applied inside them.

16   The famous Décise sand of Nevers has for centuries been well known in France for its kindly influence as an ingredient of glazes and glasses, and appears to contain an appreciable proportion of alkalis. Décise sand and Bacara sand from the banks of the Loire are specially mentioned by Bastenaire-Daudenart, op. cit., pp. 305–7.

Egyptian glazed wares, especially the tin-glazed ware with lustre painting, were certainly not intended for regular domestic use.

The tin-glaze wares of the Fayum followed the Mesopotamian tradition of alkaline glazing. They are almost always badly crazed, and sometimes the glazes melted violently and formed thick pools in the middle of the vessel, reducing the decoration to a blurry fuzz [19]. Lead glazes were less violent in their action, and also shrank less, thereby crazing relatively little. Most tin-glaze lustre is on lead glazes. Ruby-red copper lustre, however, does not develop on lead glazes; to obtain this colour the Egyptian potters used transparent alkaline glazes on white slip.

Abu'l Qasim's treatise includes a vivid but not entirely clear description of the making of tin glazes from three ingredients, a glass-frit of quartz and potash, a calcination of lead and tin, and a calcination of *qamṣarī* stone (probably a limestone) and quartz. These are melted together in a special kiln. The melt was taken out with a large ladle and poured into a pit full of water in front of the oven, to break up into small particles. 'When water and fire meet', says Abu'l Qasim, 'there is a great noise and roaring which one could mistake for real thunder and lightning'.

As the knowledge of tin glazes travelled west-wards, lead became the principal base in the glazes, with relatively small proportions of calcium, potassium and sodium. Alkalis were still introduced into glazes as auxiliary fluxes because fusibility is increased even by small additions of different bases. A mixture of lead, lime and soda or potash combines with silica to form a glass at a lower temperature than any single base can do alone. Common sources of potash and soda were the ashes of wine lees or seaweed, and common sea-salt.

No early recipes seem to have been recorded in Spain. The glazes were similar to those described by Piccolpasso in Italy about 1550. Piccolpasso recorded many glaze recipes from different parts of Italy, but they are all fundamentally similar variations on lead, tin, lime and potash glazes. Through emigrant Italian potters this type of glaze came into general use throughout Europe in the sixteenth century, with only minor variations.

Examples from Piccolpasso's recipes for white glazes and *marzacotto* are given in Appendix B. They are not as informative as they appear, and they are expressed in a somewhat complicated and unsystematic way, probably because they were noted down at different times and places during Piccolpasso's conversations with master-potters. On paper the variations in these recipes appear to be enormous, and one might well doubt that they could ever give similar results. The variations arise from the kind of local materials used—"sand" in one place may be a marble sand containing a great deal of calcium; in another it may mean a granite sand; in another it may be almost pure silica from quartz. To a lesser but still significant extent, the water of different regions would have affected the glaze, according to the concentration of minerals dissolved in it.

Thus, however definite the appearance of an old recipe, it is impossible to express it in modern chemical terminology unless the materials referred to are recognised and analysed. Even then it would be difficult to ascertain how much extra material entered the compound in the form of fragments from frit-crucibles, powder from stone pestles and mortars, and so on.

Until the eighteenth century, glazes were prepared by traditional methods and recipes, slowly improved by the cumulative effect of trial and error and accident. At their
best, the makers of old glazes had an impressive command of their materials. They recognised the effects of their materials and, by adhering strictly to traditional practices,
these effects could be repeated. They may have suffered from lack of theoretical understanding, but modern potters often suffer from not taking adequate account of the
accidental entry of unlisted ingredients when materials are processed. By repeated
calcinations of the materials, slow firings, and a lavish use of tin (equivalent to 20–30
per cent of tin oxide), 'unscientific' potters of old obtained white glazes, many of which
are extremely beautiful and have not been bettered within their chosen field.

Old tin glazes were prepared in a way which appears at first sight needlessly involved,
but which was actually very reasonable. First, a *marzacotto*, or transparent, fusible, glass
frit containing fused lead, soda or potash and silica, was prepared. Each area and each
workshop had its own recipe for its standard *marzacotto*, which was not only an ingredient
for the white tin glaze and a base for cheaper glaze mixtures or transparent "varnishes",
but also a flux for pigments.

To make a tin glaze, tin and lead ash were added to the standard *marzacotto*, and the
whole mixture was then calcined and reground. A Ferrara tin glaze mentioned by Piccolpasso was prepared from equal quantities of *marzacotto* and ashes of lead and tin (in
proportion lead 10—tin 3) and sand.[17] A Habaner recipe from Slovakia consisted of a
kind of *marzacotto* made from one part of quartz sand fused with one part of rock salt.
To this was added four parts of lead-tin ash (lead 3—tin 1). The mixture was calcined,
milled and suspended in water. It was then ready for use.[18]

Marzacotto was also a base for the transparent glaze which Italian and Dutch potters
customarily sprinkled over painted vessels, to smooth and deepen the painted colours,
and to give the white tin glaze the hard shine of porcelain. In Italy this was called
coperta, and in Holland *kwaart*.

Some recipes of the sixteenth and many of the seventeenth century included small
amounts of copper or cobalt to give a green or blue tint to the glaze. This may first have
been suggested by the cool white of Oriental porcelain, and the practice was especially
favoured in the cities where Chinese glazes were best known, Venice and Delft. This
tinting naturally suggested stronger kinds of stainings; the Italian *berretino* glazes of the
sixteenth century were bluish or lavender coloured; they were stained with cobalt and
manganese. The Cairo potters had done a similar thing in the twelfth century by adding
copper to tin glazes to make a green ground for some of their yellow-gold lustres. In
several parts of Europe in the seventeenth century (especially at Nevers and amongst
the Tyrolese and Habaner potters) tin glazes were stained a deep opaque blue; a dense
orange-yellow was made with antimony, and occasionally opaque brown or black colours were produced by additions of manganese or iron, as on some of the English 'Mal-

17 Piccolpasso, op. cit., p. 45.
18 P. Rada, *Book of Ceramics* (n.d., about 1960), p. 52 (translated from Czech). See Appendix B for
several traditional types of *marzacotto* described by L. Franchet, in *La Fabrication Industrielle des Emaux et
Couleurs Céramiques*.

ling' jugs.[19] Similar opaque coloured glazes were used in Andalusia and the Talavera potteries near Madrid, and by the stove-tile makers of the Tyrol.

Manganese, however, was a quiet and sombre colour, and was sometimes added to the glaze in very small quantities to make it whiter, an unexpected property. Diderot's *Encyclopaedia* of 1756 says:

Since some faienciers are unused to mixing manganese into their glazes to make them whiter, they may say that it will make the glaze brown or grey. Let them make trials of it before saying more . . .

A number of tin-glaze recipes from the mid-eighteenth century onwards are given in Appendix B and D.

Glaze defects must have caused many crises for potters over the centuries, as indeed they still do, because of mistakes and misunderstandings. How often over the centuries must this situation, described in 1828 by a great French ceramist, have been painfully re-enacted!

Sometimes it happens that a mistaken sense of economy leads the potter to use tin or lead of inferior quality. Still more often someone adds an extra amount of sand or white clay to the fritt to make the mass bigger. . . . It is idle for people to suppose that, just because a few test pieces happen to have come out well from odd parts of the kiln, the whole mixture has really proved itself, and that a whole kilnful will have the same effect. Then someone takes the risk of making a great quantity of this glaze, with 115 or even 120 parts of sand [instead of 100], and what happens? Very often the only decent, saleable pieces are those which were so placed as to get highly fired, and the rest have almost always to be refired, or else be sold off cheaply. In this way a workshop slides towards its ruin by abandoning sound recipes for supposed economies.

To which Franchet, nearly a hundred years later, added: 'These wise words are, alas, acted on all too seldom!'[20]

The old glazes referred to in the Appendix were intended for use on the traditional marl-clay body, which allowed the use of low temperature glazes because of its high degree of shrinkage. Being whitish, it was assumed to favour the development of opaque white glazes from the minimum quantities of tin oxide, but, in fact, this was only a half-truth.[21]

There is no absolute need to use the light-burning marl clays for tin-glaze pottery. Some red clays are quite suitable, especially those which shrink most in cooling. Many natural red clays can be serviceable, provided care is taken to adjust the glaze to the

19   L. Franchet, op. cit., p. 82, has an amusing comment about the addition of copper tin glazes. 'However, many faienciers, especially the makers of stoves, still trust to the supposed "whitening" effect of copper, although they admit that this causes them serious difficulties. They do not adopt the simple practice of adding cobalt oxide because, on the one hand, habit overrules all other considerations, and on the other, some of these manufacturers regard the use of copper as a special secret.'

20   L. Franchet, op. cit., p. 85, quoting F. Bastenaire-Daudenart, *L'Art de Fabriquer la Faience Récouverte d'un Email Opaque Blanc et Coloré* (Paris, 1828).

21   Because a much more important factor is the composition of the glaze itself. Certain fluid glazes dissolve tin oxide very readily, and need a high proportion of tin if they are to become white and opaque. More viscous glazes, and especially those which tend anyway towards a semi-matt surface, because they favour development of crystals, can become white and opaque with quite a small tin oxide content.

body by increasing the silica and alumina content of the glaze. This probably demands a slightly higher firing: around 1050°C, rather than the traditional temperature of 980°C —1000°C. Over red clays the range of colour on tin glazes is lightly less bright, but tends to be richer and deeper than on the light-firing bodies. Until the end of the nineteenth century, most tin-glaze pottery made from red clay came from places where the lime clays were difficult to obtain. For the most part the red-bodied wares were a kind of economy-maiolica, like the wares of Teruel in Spain, Montelupo near Florence, some of the rural Slovakian potteries, and Morocco. The technique of some nearby centre had been applied to the local clays, but neither the composition of the glaze nor the firing temperature was altered to suit the red clay, and in consequence most old, red-bodied tin-glaze ware is soft and badly crazed.

PAINTING

Tin-glaze pottery is usually painted on the powdery surface of the unfired glaze. A vessel is first given a bisque or biscuit firing, after which it is hard and firm but still porous. When the pot is dipped in glaze (finely ground and insoluble glaze material suspended in water), the water is absorbed by the clay, and a coating of powdered glaze is left on the surface. Once this coating dries it can be painted. Pots are usually given their second firing just as they are when the painter has finished. In some places they are sprayed with a thin film of transparent glaze which, when fired, smoothes the surface and deepens the colours, rather as a varnish deepens the colour of a painting.

Painting on the surface of tin glaze probably only became usual after the introduction of polychrome in the fifteenth century. Some pots and tiles from Málaga and Valencia were undoubtedly painted in cobalt blue direct on the surface of the clay before the glaze was applied. The blue cobalt pigment was powerful enough to penetrate the molten glaze from below [32]. The early green and brown wares of Paterna were sometimes, and perhaps usually, painted in the same way [37, 38, 39]. Some early Moorish pottery from the south of Spain was painted in manganese and other oxides on the bare clay, without any glaze at all [28]. This practice seems to have continued when clear glazes and, later, tin glazes, were introduced. Since Moorish pottery closely followed the practices of the Middle East, it is likely that the oldest tin-glaze vessels were usually, if not always, painted under the glaze. The custom of painting on the glaze surface probably only developed when weaker pigments and colour tones came into use.

Delicate control of tone-values became important in the Italian pictorial convention of painted earthenware in the sixteenth century. It was made possible by the use of subtle, blended colours which were not strong enough to penetrate an opaque glaze [Colour Plate I]. Therefore, the painting had to be done on the surface of the glaze, and from this time onwards almost all tin-glaze vessels were painted in this manner. One of the snags was that the unfired glaze, being powdery, was easily knocked or rubbed away, or smudged by the fingers of men packing the kiln. This is why in Piccolpasso's drawing of maiolica painters at work, each one rests the dish he is painting in a bowl filled with tow, so that he can turn it round without touching the dish itself [173].

In modern practice pigments are based on the oxides of the colour-making metals, cobalt, copper, iron, manganese, antimony, etc. Many of these materials can be used in their pure form provided they are painted thinly enough. This custom only became possible in the early years of the twentieth century, when pure oxides became commercially available. Before that time, ceramic pigments for maiolica painting were produced from mineral ores which contained a good deal of rock as well as admixtures of other metals. Thus they were not fully fusible by themselves. They needed to be calcined with a flux[22] —usually the pottery's standard *marzacotto*—and were then finely milled. Sometimes this process needed to be repeated several times before a smooth-firing pigment was achieved.

Almost every manual from Piccolpasso's time onwards gives recipes for the basic colours and blends of raw materials. The principle of calcination with a flux holds in almost every case, and the recipes are not individually interesting or significant. For one thing, the colour a pigment gives depends a great deal on the composition of the glaze it is painted on: a mixture of iron and copper may produce a green on one glaze and a brown on another. Secondly, since all the raw materials were impure, it is impossible to know the exact chemical composition of old pigments. They contained also the additional impurities introduced from fragments of the crucible and from the granite mill-stones. The hope of old potters was to get bright colours, and the best potteries started with the purest minerals available.[23] Today, when pure metallic oxides are easily purchased, potters realise that chemically pure materials seldom give as pleasing results as the impure, and most pigments are blended from several materials.

The most difficult pigments were reds and orange, and only a few manufactories had sound varieties of these colours. Today red is usually prepared from a combination of the oxides of chrome and tin calcined with calcium carbonate and a lead flux, a pigment which was not discovered until the early nineteenth century. Until then most tin-glaze reds were made from very finely levigated armenian bole (a kind of hematite) fluxed with lead. It was used at Cafaggiolo early in the sixteenth century and was not entirely superseded by chrome-tin reds until the end of the nineteenth century. At its best it could give a deep, warm brick red, but it needed to be applied with great care, or it became either thick and rough or thin and pale. The colour was seldom used extensively for this very reason, but it was a valuable accent colour.[24]

Yellow was obtained from a calcination of antimony and lead, and orange from the same compound with the addition of about 5 per cent of iron rust. These colours tended to burn away in the firing; they had to be thickly applied to give a strong colour, and

22   The mineral was crushed and mixed with the crushed *marzacotto* and placed over sand in an unglazed clay bowl in a hot place in the kiln, usually at some point near the fire itself. In the firing the mixture fused into a rough, spongy mass. Afterwards the bowl was broken and the fused pigment was chipped away from it to be milled. Fragments of crucible-bowls are common finds on old tin-glaze pottery sites.
23   The progressive refinement of the cobalt blue pigments used in Holland in the seventeenth century is a striking example of the development of purer and more predictable colours. At first the 'blues' were often a dark indigo colour. By the middle of the century a brighter but still slightly purplish blue had been achieved. By about 1680 the finest work was done in a very clear blue, in response to the challenge of the clear sapphire blue of K'ang Hsi porcelain.
24   Bastenaire-Daudenart, op. cit., p. 420, recommends a calcination of iron sulphate and potash alum.

well-fluxed to avoid roughness. This is why most strong yellows are detectably raised over the rest of the glaze surface. Antimony yellows are usually egg-yellows. Vanadium oxide gives cooler lemon yellows, but it was not known until the late nineteenth century.[25]

A wider and more controllable range of colours became available from the development of enamels about 1700 onwards, and much of the aristocratic faience from about 1730–1780 was painted only in enamel, especially in the German principalities. Enamels were basically a pigment carried in an easily-fusible glass. They were painted on the surface of already-fired glaze, and had to be fixed to this surface by means of a third firing in a muffle-kiln.

Enamels were important, partly because they permitted the use of pigments which were too volatile to be used at the full glaze temperature. With enamels a range of purple, red, vermilion and orange came within the painters' compass [Colour Plate O]. Because the enamel simply lay over the glaze instead of fusing with it, very fine and delicate painting could be done with it, and also a kind of enamel *sgraffiato*, where lines were scratched through the enamel with the point of a needle. Enamels could be used with a delicacy approaching the limits of human eyesight, and the work of some of the German Hausmaler painters looks as if it had been done with a magnifying glass.

The most important enamel colour was the famous 'purple of Cassius', a pigment developed from gold by the alchemist A. Cassius about 1680, half accidentally, from one of the tests for detecting the presence of gold in a compound. Alchemists played an important part in the development of both porcelain and enamels. The connection is commemorated in the famous tag of Böttger himself, the first maker of true porcelain in the West, who, when put to the making of porcelain by his patron Augustus the Strong of Saxony, is said to have written in disgust above his door: 'Gott, unser Schöpfer, hat gemacht aus einem Goldmacher einen Töpfer.' (God, our creator, has turned a goldmaker into a potter).[26]

Porcelain and enamels both became possible because of alchemical investigations which aimed at the preparation of gold. Ironically, it was only through them that the alchemists actually earned the gold which eluded their direct endeavours.

Although a great deal of tin-glaze ware was produced by painting with enamels, the enamel finish was really best suited to porcelain and it is difficult to see enamelled faience as anything but a substitute for porcelain, whereas the traditional high-temperature tin-glaze vessels had a distinct character in their own right.

The traditional way of painting tin-glaze pottery—painting on the unfired glaze and firing at the full glaze temperature—came to be so generally regarded in the sixteenth century as a poor relation of the Fine Art of picture painting, that it was almost always practised only by direct brushwork, to the exclusion of other methods which were technically just as possible. Thus, once the pictorial convention of pot-painting was established, the possibility of painting certain colours on the raw clay under the glaze was virtually forgotten. The use of wax-resists and *sgraffiato*, and the variety of effects

25 For an excellent condensed description of modern methods of preparing and applying colours to ceramics, see Kenneth Shaw, *Ceramic Colours and Pottery Decoration* (London, 1962).
26 Quoted by Bevis Hillier, *Pottery and Porcelain 1700–1914* (London, 1968), p. 23.

obtainable by scraping or scratching through the pigment with a point, were almost completely ignored, and have only been followed up by artist-potters in recent times. Stencils were sometimes used for cheap repeat-work, however, and mottled areas of colour were obtained by sponge-dabbing and powder-blown pigments. These two last techniques have, rather oddly, been more or less abandoned in the modern era. A technique has apparently to be well buried before it can rise from the dead and be counted new again.

KILNS AND FIRING

There is little direct evidence about old kilns. The idea of a long-lasting kiln is a modern concept. Old kilns were used only a few times before being rebuilt, and in the less technically advanced parts of the world, where labour is cheap, kilns are often reconstructed for almost every firing. Only when the science and structure of kilns became subtle and complex in the early nineteenth century did people consider how to preserve them by building iron bands and frames around them and by using materials which could withstand many firings. Thus virtually all that remains of any old kilns is the hearth and the foundation of the walls.

The amplest evidence of old kilns for tin-glaze pottery comes from Piccolpasso's descriptions and drawings [175, 176]. The idea of the kilns he shows is the same as the traditional kilns of Spain, Persia and the Middle East [187, 188, 189]. but the Italian kilns were probably better constructed and lasted longer. The Spanish-Moorish up-draught kilns were simply a round or oval structure with a perforated floor and a domed vault with holes in to let out the smoke. The walls began well below ground level in order to use the surrounding earth as a buttress. The fire-box was constructed to one side of the kiln, below the level of the floor, and the flames passed into the cavity beneath the chamber, through the floor, passing amongst the pots, and escaped through multiple vents in the roof. The heat was held back in the chamber by the small size of the escape-vents. The traditional kilns of Persia are remarkably like those described by Piccolpasso, except that the fire is directly underneath the main chamber, and the ground plan is more often round than rectangular.[27]

The treatise of Abu'l Qasim mentions briefly the methods of firing current at Kashan in 1301, and is especially interesting for the description of saggars and supports.

'For each vessel is made an earthenware case with a fitting lid. These are placed in the kiln, called in Arabic "shakhūreh" and locally "dam". These are like high towers, and inside have row upon row of fired earthenware pegs, each an arsh and a half long, fitted into holes in the wall. The vessels are placed on them and fired for twelve hours with a hot fire, with this stipulation: that no wood be put on until the smoking has stopped, so that the smoke does not ruin and blacken the pots.'

In all these kilns firing was done with light brushwood, furze or straw. To accommodate the light fuel and ensure complete combustion, the fire-chamber had to be fairly

27 Described by H. E. Wulff, op. cit., p. 159 et seq. Figure 238 shows a diagram of such a kiln. Wulff also describes two variants, both based on the same idea as was usual in Western Europe, very different from the climbing kilns and down-draught ideas of the Far East.

large. It acted as a kind of heat-accumulator from which heat was pulled by the draught of the kiln chamber. No chimney was needed, for the kiln was its own chimney. [Fig. 33].

Kilns of this type have been excavated in Moorish pottery centres in Andalucia and are usually called *hornos redondos*. The *horno quadrado*, of Christian Spain, is similar in principle but is built on a square foundation. It is still used in many small Spanish potteries.

There was no difficulty about firing unglazed pottery. It was simply piled in columns and the heat passed amongst the pots. Glazed ware, however, presented two problems: it had to be set so that each piece was supported but would not stick to anything when the glaze melted, and it needed to be protected from ash carried in the fire-draught. The vessels could either be placed on tiles whose sides were supported by bricks or pots, or they could be placed inside another vessel, such as a jar or a deep bowl. In the course of time specially large and strong tiles were made as shelves, and saggars (clay bowls or boxes) were made to hold the glazed ware. If the bases of the pots were cleaned of glaze, they could safely stand on the shelf or base of the saggar. Otherwise they could be supported on a three-pointed stilt.

These methods have been the principal ways of supporting glazed vessels in kilns without the pots touching each other for well over a thousand years, and until the full industrial development of the hover system, by which the pots are supported on an air-cushion, they will remain so.

Of course, pots do not necessarily have to stand on shelves or inside containers. Bowls and dishes can be supported on stilts and be placed one upon another in a column, as is still done in some traditional workshops. The resulting stilt-mark in the glaze is a pity, but it is understood, and is not a major defect on simple pottery with a thin glaze. On tin-glazed dishes it is less acceptable because it spoils the white glaze and the marks it leaves are the greater because the glaze is usually fairly thick. This method has only been usual in areas where tin-glazed pottery has become traditional enough to be no longer a luxury ware. In Spain large bowls and platters were often fired on edge, thus avoiding the use of stilts under heavy pieces. The early tin-glaze potters avoided using stilts as far as possible because their work was intended for palaces and other important places.

Saggars were customarily used for holding the glazed pottery in the *horno quadrado* of the Christian parts of Spain,[28] and from Piccolpasso's evidence they seem to have been generally used in Italy, but they were used only for what he calls 'fine wares', that is, painted tin-glaze pottery, and mainly for bowls and dishes. The hollow wares (jugs, jars, etc.) were scraped on the rim and on the base so that they could be set in the kiln one upon another. As for the dishes,

'You remember', he wrote, 'that the wares must not touch at any point; now you would take me for a simpleton if I had not shown you that they are not placed in the kiln (unsupported) in the air. You must know that all the flat wares are placed (in saggars) on spurs, which are

28   I am told this by the archaeologist and scholar Luis M. Llubiá. He also says that in the few known medieval sites of the Moorish round kilns there are no signs that saggars were used. Presumably, therefore, the Moorish tin-glaze pots were fired either inside biscuit ware, or on some form of tile or shelf.

made of clay, very small, like chess pawns, and very sharply pointed, for the sharper they are the better; three of these are put in each saggar, and then very gently, with great care, the dish is turned down on them.'[29]

Piccolpasso shows an interesting drawing which he does not explain fully except to say that certain vessels are placed 'upside down on pegs'. His drawing shows a high saggar with rows of triangular peg-holes in the side. This seems to be the first description of a way of firing plates and shallow dishes, which was to become extremely important in the eighteenth century, when plates were needed in large quantity. Three tapered triangular clay pegs or spurs were pushed through the holes in the saggar [182]. They projected just far enough into the saggar to support a dish or plate at three points on the rim. After a plate had been lowered on to them, the next spurs were inserted, and so on, until the saggar was filled. Then another saggar was placed over it, and the process was repeated. In this way a large number of plates could be accommodated in a small volume of the kiln chamber. In later times shallow plates were always placed face upwards, so that the spur marks appeared only on the underside. The method is exactly described and illustrated in Diderot's *Encyclopaedia* of 1756.

The placing of ware in the kiln was a skilled job [181]. It was not only a matter of accommodating as much pottery as possible in a limited space; the saggars had to be so arranged that the kiln draught came up through the floor and spread amongst them evenly. If they were too close together the draught would be blocked and the temperature would not be reached. If they were unevenly spaced, parts of the kiln would get too hot, and other parts would not be hot enough. Anything placed directly in a strong draught would create an air turbulence and lead to local overheating, which was likely to cause the vessels to warp.

Excavations indicate that in many parts of Northern Europe, certainly in France and England, the rectangular kiln described by Piccolpasso remained current until the later part of the eighteenth century.[30] Bastenaire-Daudenart wrote that it was generally used in France until about 1790, and that the usual size was about 4 metres long, 2 metres 60 centimetres wide, and 5 metres high. Robert Dossie describes how to build this conventional kiln in his manual *The Handmaid to the Arts*, first published in 1758 [Fig. 33]. Dossie's kiln differs from older types only in the provision of firebars which keep the fuel free of the ashpit, and a cowl with a short chimney. These help the chamber to retain its heat, and also induce a stronger draught.[31] In theory the heat could be distributed evenly in the chamber partly by throwing the fuel in the correct place under the vault, and partly by opening and closing the vents in the roof. Actually, this was hard to achieve. 'Oh! that this vicious method of firing were totally abolished!', wrote Bastenaire-Daudenart, 'I have watched these kilns in operation; my interest has several times

29 Piccolpasso, op. cit., pp. 67–68, and plate 52a.
30 The excavation of two such kilns of about 1725–50 is described by Brian Bloice and James Thorne in 'London tin-glazed pottery', *London Archaeologist*, vol. 1, no. 4 (Autumn 1969), p. 84, part 2. The kilns were at Lambeth near the area known in the eighteenth century as 'Potters' Fields'. The foundation of the kilns was 12 feet long by 6 feet wide; they were built of red brick and fragments of saggars were found in the ash.
31 Robert Dossie, *Handmaid to the Arts*, 2nd ed., 1764, vol. II, p. 353.

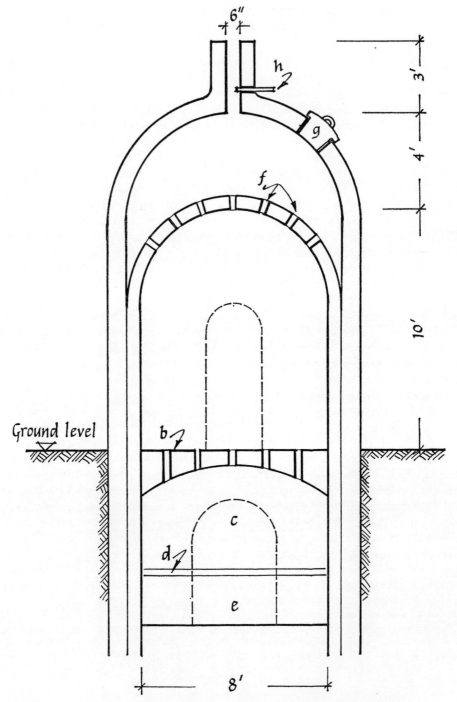

Figure 33.   Diagram of the updraught kiln described by Robert Dossie, 1758.

forced me to stay on for a whole firing, taking between 24 and 48 hours, and I have seen for myself.' His comments describe the sort of difficulties potters had been encountering for three hundred years and more.

How wearisome the whole process can be! Were it only a matter of stoking the wood into the firebox and thereafter obtaining an even distribution of heat throughout the kiln, one could perhaps put up with a structure of this kind, even though the fuel is not economically used. But there are other more vexatious things about these kilns. Sometimes it is the front which heats up too fast, sometimes it is the back; or it may be the left side which gets the heat, or perhaps the right. So then it becomes necessary to throw more fuel under the parts of the kiln which need more flames. The workman suffers from the enormous, almost suffocating heat which comes from the firebox (heat which is completely wasted, incidentally), and because of his fatigue it often happens that the wood falls in the wrong place, and sometimes it falls on the white glaze-mixtures which are being calcined in the undervault, which brings back the lead and tin oxides to the metallic state. . . .[32]

Not only is the firing almost bound to be uneven, he says, but it is wasteful of fuel, and exhausting for the workmen, and the kiln is laborious to build and unnecessarily hard to repair. The right-angle corners are bound to be too cool, because they have two brick-faces to soak up the heat, and they also break up quickly as the brickwork expands and contracts. 'But for the desirability of stacking some transparent-glazed wares on open columns of shelves (en echappade) I would dispense altogether with these square and rectangular kilns.'

He advocates changing over to an oval kiln for wares which are best packed en echappade [180], and to a round kiln for tin-glazed wares, which he considers should always be fired in saggars. Instead of the single firebox he would have one at each end of the oval kiln, and three fireboxes for the round kiln, so that the heat would naturally be more even, and any irregularity could easily be corrected. He would also do away with the undervault because it absorbs a lot of the heat and also restricts the height of the kiln, since it can only support limited quantities of full saggars.

He makes the traditional comment that tin glazes cannot be fired with coal, which is probably correct for any kiln without a complete muffle-chamber, isolated from the fire-gases. The early stages of the firing, he says, are best with hard woods, such as oak and elm which have a short, stabbing flame. Once the bottom of the kiln is red hot the heat is extended upwards with brushwood or light fuel; the firing is concluded with soft wood, such as willow, poplar or pine, which have long, soft flames.[33] Hard woods are never used at the end; they will make the glazes boil and become rough. Despite the long flame of the soft woods, the upper part of the kiln was bound to be cooler than the bottom. The difference of temperature was useful since the biscuit ware had to be less highly fired in order to remain porous enough to gather up a thick coating of glaze when it was dipped or poured with glaze before being painted.

Bastenaire-Daudenart's comments are especially interesting in that he tried to analyse the difficulties which had long been considered inevitable, and suggested solutions which were within the reach of quite modest 'factories' and workshops. It is remarkable, however, that he did not even consider the possibility of the down-draught type of kiln

32 *La Faïence*, p. 83.   33 op. cit., pp. 129–132.

with a side chimney which (with many variants of greater or less complexity) was to become the standard method of firing in most European factories both large and small.[34]

By the time of Bastenaire-Daudenart (who wrote in the 1820s) the old rectangular kiln with an undervault had led to two descendants which differed considerably. One was, in fact, very like the round kiln he advocated, and is represented in the Dutch tile-picture of 1737 [178]. It had several fireboxes and could have been built with or without the undervault. The tile-picture does not show this, but the diagrams in Gerrit Paape's book of 1794 show a similar type of kiln with an undervault [179].[35] The lower chamber was used for the glazed ware, the next for tiles and the upper part of the kiln, which was cooler, was used for bisque ware.

The other kind was the long Cassell-type kiln, of which the kiln from Vyškov is an example. This retained the rectangular shape of the Italian kiln, and the arched passage-way under the kiln floor, but the firebox was set to one end of the kiln and some of the draught entered the chamber horizontally, through a perforated baffle-wall. This could not have happened without the forced draught produced by the chimney at the far end of the kiln, which replaced the relatively primitive vents in the kiln vault. The Cassell kiln largely overcame the perpetual difficulty of uneven heating, by permitting the draught to enter the chamber at different points along its length. It appears to have been especially popular in Germany and the old Austrian Empire, and is still often used by small potteries in those regions. It is usually fired without saggars, the ware being disposed on shelves supported by props. Most Habaner and Slovak tin-glaze pottery was fired in this way.

Tin-glaze earthenware could, of course, have been satisfactorily fired in any of the large and efficient muffle-kilns which were developed in the nineteenth century, for firing at high temperature, but this seldom occurred because by that time the tradition of tin-glaze ware had been out-priced and technically superseded by high-fired white earthenware. Tin-glaze pottery and white slipware remained the only colourful and decorative white pottery which could be fired satisfactorily in old-fashioned kilns at traditional low earthenware temperatures. That is why they continued to be made in many of the less industrialised parts of Europe long after they had been out-distanced by industrial manufacturers producing pottery with printed decoration and inexpensive glazes. In England the tin-glaze technique was wholly supplanted by the white earthen-ware technique by about 1820. In some places it survived well into the twentieth century and in some it retained a continuity of tradition right up to the present day, but usually in the nature of things it survived in areas and in workshops which were conservatively-minded. As a rule they did little more than preserve the general features of the old designs, often in a slipshod manner, and many of them yielded to the temptation of buy-ing prepared glazes from ceramic chandlers. These glazes are usually a cold, hard white, poor carriers of colour, devised without any feeling for the possible unity of body, glaze and pigment.

Care always had to be taken with wood-fired kilns to protect the pots from the ex-cessive or uneven heating resulting from direct play of the flames on the glazed vessel,

34   See Daniel Rhodes, *Kilns* (London, 1969), pp. 36–56.
35   Gerrit Paape, *De Plateelbakker of Delftsch Aardewerk Makker* (1794), plate 4. (See plate 179).

and especially from reduction (or prolonged shortage of oxygen) which could perma-
nently disturb the chemical balance of the glazes and cause a rough, cratered surface.
Saggars surrounding the pots were a fairly fool-proof protection against this, but when the
pots were fired on shelves and exposed to the kiln atmosphere, the kiln gases could only
be controlled by careful stoking of the fire. If the fire were correctly maintained there
would be an alternation between light reduction, with each new charge of fuel, followed by periods of clear burning, as the fuel burnt down with full air supply. This was
probably incidental, rather than planned, but it produced more mature and deeper
colours than muffle-firing and it favoured the development of 'fat' tin glazes with a deep
pearly whiteness which is seldom if ever obtained from electric and muffle-kilns. It probably
explains how some very beautiful white glazes were produced on sack bottles and other
plain white wares in the seventeenth century by quite unsophisticated manufacturers.
In conclusion, the question naturally arises whether there is any future for tin-glaze
wares, or will they eventually become completely obsolete?

I believe that the effects of the high-temperature industrial whitewares have now
passed their maximum, and that tin-glaze wares will continue to be made and may even
increase amongst small-scale producers of pottery, and perhaps even in industry itself.
Other forms of decorated and coloured pottery are now easily available, but none of
them actually supplant the unique colour and glaze qualities obtained from tin glaze.
The difference between old and modern tin-glaze pottery is likely to lie in the type of
clay body and the temperature of the firing.

As has been shown, the potters of old were not obliged to fire at temperatures as low
as 980°C—1000°C. This range of temperature resulted chiefly from a dependence on
past practice and tradition. Today a great variety of strong clays is available, firing
from 1100°C. to high stoneware temperatures, and tin oxide remains an effective opacifier of glazes up to at least 1250°C. There is no reason why high temperature tin-glaze
wares should not be developed, other than the attitude of mind and traditional outlook
prevailing amongst modern potters, which are different from old attitudes, but often
just as limiting. At higher temperatures there is some difficulty in obtaining a wide
range of colours, and many glazes will carry only the most powerful pigments, notably
cobalt blue and colours based on iron. But this limitation is not universal, and with
careful glaze composition it is possible to achieve reds and yellows and orange colours
at temperatures even beyond 1200°C, colours which can be as intense as enamels

My own belief is that, with the increasing sensibility to all domestic articles brought
about by the conditions of modern life, and the increasing feeling for individual work,
craftsman-made pottery, and ceramic sculpture, there will be a return to a much wider
use of tin-glaze wares, just because they naturally possess a quality and character, and
permit an individuality of expression which is impossible in industrial working conditions. Industrially they may also have a future, for hand-painting still exists, even in
large factories, to a much greater degree than is usually supposed. It still exists because
there are so many things that cannot be done in any other way.

APPENDICES

APPENDIX A

BLENDED CLAY-BODIES

F. Bastenaire-Daudenart describes the traditional composition of Paris faience as follows, in his book *L'Art de Fabriquer la Faience* (Paris, 1828). Paris faience was body composed of four types of clay, whose proportions are on average as follows: Each manufacturer has his own special recipe, but all are fairly alike.

Terre blanche	4
Terre verte	3
Terre jaune	1
Argile figuline	1

Terre blanche is a very chalky marl, almost completely soluble in hydrochloric acid. It comes from the plaster quarries and is gathered from directly above the chalk sulphate. Approximate analysis:

SiO_2	34
Al_2O_3	30
$CaCO_3$	20
Fe_2O_3	4
Water	12

Terre verte a clay which induces fusibility because of its high iron content. It also comes from the chalk quarries, and it lies above the *terre blanche*. and is not directly in contact with chalk. Approximate analysis:

SiO_2	57
Al_2O_3	18
$CaCO_3$	10
Fe_2O_3	7
Water	8

Terre jaune is a common, sandy clay, found in many areas near Paris, not necessarily beside chalk quarries. It is yellowish and 'looks like fat sand'. In Paris they call it oven-clay. Approximate analysis:

SiO_2	65
Al_2O_3	9
$CaCO_3$	12
Fe_2O_3	6
Water	8

Argile figuline. This is found deep down where people dig wells. Approximate analysis:

SiO_2	63
Al_2O_3	32
$CaCO_3$ $\}$ Total	5
Fe_2O_3	

The author, an advocate of the then fairly novel methods of chemical analysis of all ceramic materials, did not fully appreciate the importance of the range of particle sizes in the materials he describes, and makes virtually no reference to them, although actually they played as great a part in determining the working properties of the clay as the chemical composition.

About 1800 French ceramist Brongniart made approximate analyses of traditional clay bodies used with tin glazes, as shown in the following table, taken from *A Treatise on Ceramic Industries*, by E. Bourry, 4th English edition (London, 1926), p. 381.

	Silica	Alumina	Iron oxide	Lime	Magnesia	Undetermined
Hispano-moresque faience	46.04	18.45	3.64	17.64	0.87	13.96
Manises faience	54.71	18.80	2.20	19.69	trace	4.60
Luca della Robbia faience	49.65	15.50	3.70	22.40	0.17	8.58
Nevers faience	56.49	19.22	2.12	14.96	0.71	6.50
Rouen faience	47.96	15.02	4.07	20.24	0.44	12.27
Delft faience	49.07	16.19	2.82	18.01	0.82	13.09

The last column includes the alkalis and any carbon dioxide present in the calcium carbonate.

The above analyses differ considerably from the 'ideal' faience clay-body of Bastenaire-Daudenart, especially in the proportions of alumina and lime. The reason is probably that Brongniart's samples were older wares, required to harden at lower temperatures and to carry more fusible glazes than those of Bastenaire-Daudenart.

APPENDIX B

GLAZE RECIPES

Amongst the recipes for *marzacotto* by Piccolpasso are the following:

Marzacotto of Urbino (p. 37)
'sand'   100
ash of wine lees   40–100

Marzacotto of Castello (p. 38)
'sand'   100
ash of wine lees   30–33

Marzacotto of Venice (p. 38)
'sand'   100
ash of wine lees   83

White marzacotto of Ferrara (p. 45)
'sand'   100
tin-lead ash   110
'salt'   60

Page references are to the facsimile and translation of the *Arte del Vasaio*, London, 1934.

Franchet (op. cit., pp. 60–62) gives recipes of several types of *marzacotto*, including the following:

1 Quartz sand   100
   Litharge   300

2 Quartz sand   100
   Potassium carbonate   33–40

Franchet (op. cit., p. 81) gives a traditional recipe from Nevers. Nevers was one of the early centres of tin-glaze earthenware in France and the general practice of Nevers seems to have been followed by many other localities. Here the first two ingredients are equivalent to a *marzacotto*:

Décize 'sand' (with some calcium content)	100 lb.
Alkaline salts (potassium sulphate, sodium sulphate or potassium carbonate)	26 lb.
Tin-ash (from lead 83—tin 17)	60 lb.
Bronze filings	8 oz.

The French *Encyclopédie* of 1756 published recipes for tin glazes from several sources in the article 'Fayence'. The following are extracts from it:

A Nevers recipe:
Lead-tin ash (lead 100—tin 20)	100 lb.
Local sand (containing Ca)	150 lb.
Salt	25 lb.

'English White'
Seaweed ash from Normandy	150 lb.
Fine white sand	100 lb.

Lead-tin ash (lead 54—tin 18)   72 lb.
Manganese   12 oz.

'Holland White'
  'Sand'   50 lb.
  Potash   15 lb.
  Soda   20 lb.
  Lead-tin ash (Lead 20—tin 20) 40 lb.
  Manganese   6 oz.

Many of the old tin-glaze recipes, especially the Italian, Dutch and French, were intended to be used with a thin transparent overglaze (*coperta*, *kwaart*) without which the surface of the tin glaze was rather dry and matt and liable to scrapes and scratches. The fusible coating also helped to avoid 'pinholes' in the white glaze, a defect which almost all tin glazes tend to have. As the overglaze was applied by flicking with a brush, it usually covered only the upper surface of bowls and dishes. The backs and undersides usually have a dense white 'dry' surface, with a good many pinholes.

In places where overglazing was not customary, the tin-glaze recipe was usually more fusible and less rich in tin oxide, and hence rather less white and opaque. This was usually the case in Spain, Germany and England though overglazing was sometimes used in England. The Habaner potters of Central Europe never used over-glazing and the surface of their tin glazes was usually distinctly matt.

During the eighteenth century some magnificent opaque glazes were developed in the best *faienceries*, such as Moustiers, Marseilles, Strasbourg, Alcora, Albisola, Savona, Ansbach, Hanau, Crailsheim, etc. These combined a semi-shiny, satin surface with dense whiteness, and did not need an overglaze.

F. Bastenaire-Daudenart's book *L'Art de Fabriquer la Faience* (1828), is probably the most authoritative technical manual on the subject, for it is based on methodical experiment with proven materials, yet it draws on long experience of the traditional methods of preparing clays and glazes and pigments. One of his

recipes (op. cit., p. 328) is described by Franchet as 'absolutely perfect':

Décize sand   100
Lead-tin ash (lead 82—tin 18)   100
Sea salt   6
Litharge   6

If pure quartz-sand were used instead of Décize sand, the recipe needed more fluxes and the following adjustment was recommended:

Quartz sand   100
Lead-tin ash (lead 77—tin 23)   100
Sea salt   12
Sodium carbonate   6
Litharge   5

Franchet (op. cit., p. 84) and Bastenaire-Daudenart (op. cit., p. 309) say that the chlorine in sea-salt helps to induce a perfect whiteness, the reasons for which are mysterious.

The French ceramist and artist-potter, Théodore Deck, (*La Faience*, Paris, 1870) recommends the following recipe (p. 209):

Lead-tin ash (variable but should   44
contain between 22 and 30 of tin
metal to 100 lead)
'Nevers sand' (containing some Ca)   44
Sodium carbonate ('Sonde d'Ali-
cante')   2
Sea salt   8
Litharge   2

All old recipes and many modern ones have the disadvantage of referring to local materials whose chemical nature is not exactly recorded, and which are not therefore fully repeatable. Greber (*Traité de Céramique* (Paris, 1934), p. 459) says that tin glazes for firing at the traditional temperature of about 1000°C usually lie within the limits of the following formulae:

$$\left. \begin{array}{l} 0.20\,K_2O \\ 0.35\,Na_2O \\ 0.45\,PGO \end{array} \right\} \quad 0.20\,Al_2O_3 \quad \left\{ \begin{array}{l} 2.70\,SiO_2 \end{array} \right.$$

and

$$\left.\begin{array}{l} 0.70\ PgO \\ 0.20\ Na_2O \\ 0.10\ N_2O \end{array}\right\} \quad 0.15\ Al_2O_3 \quad \left\{\vphantom{\begin{array}{l}a\\b\\c\end{array}}\right. 2.50\ SiO_2$$

He recommends this recipe to be fritted and ground, for a good tin glaze.

Litharge	35
Sand	45
Sea-salt	10

to which he equates the following formula:

$$\left.\begin{array}{l} 0.10\ K_2O \\ 0.30\ Na_2O \\ 0.60\ PGO \end{array}\right\} \quad 0.15\ Al_2O_3 \quad \left\{\vphantom{\begin{array}{l}a\\b\\c\end{array}}\right. 2.50\ SiO_2$$

To each of these recipes he recommends the addition of between 6 per cent and 12 per cent tin oxide.

Greber's formulae assume the use of a limy marl-clay body with high shrinkage, and are not suitable for most red clays.

Most general technical ceramic books contain one or several recommendations for earthenware tin glazes, with formulae, and many commercial suppliers of glazes nowadays publish the formulae of their glazes in their catalogues. The practising potter needs to remember that it matters a great deal what type of clay these glazes are used on. They may be sound and craze-proof on one body, and defective on another. In many countries the traditional off-white marl-clay maiolica body is commercially almost unobtainable, and unless a potter prepares his own special mixture, he may be forced to use a red earthenware clay with a relatively small cooling shrinkage, and the ratio of alumina and silica to the bases will probably have to be higher than in Greber's formulae.

Tin oxide is, and has always been, expensive. Cerium oxide, a rare and recent ceramic material, also opacifies glazes but is considerably more expensive still. Today zirconium oxide and its derivatives are often advocated as a cheaper alternative to tin oxide, and they give similar but not exactly equivalent effects. However, as zirconium oxide has to be used in about double the quantity to obtain equal opacification, the saving is less than appears at first sight, and amounts at present to about 30 per cent. Zircon can seldom be directly substituted for tin in a given glaze. To make full use of it a new formulation is likely to be needed. (See F. T. Booth and G. N. Peel, 'The Principles of glaze opacification with zirconium silicate', in *Transactions of the British Ceramic Society*, vol. 58, no. 9, September 1959.)

APPENDIX C

LEAD POISONING

The risk of lead poisoning run by pottery workers was generally recognised throughout the nineteenth century, though it was not always appreciated by the artisans themselves. Bastenaire-Daudenart described a visit to one faience factory where his warning of the dangers of lead oxide was dismissed by the workpeople because, they said, it has such a lovely sweet taste, and could not possibly be harmful. (In Roman times, litharge was occasionally recommended for sweetening wine.)

In most countries today there are stringent regulations about the forms of lead which are permitted, and the conditions in which they are used. Lead poisoning is no longer a common industrial hazard. However, the danger of lead glazes to the user has only become recognised in the last few decades.

It is perfectly possible to use lead in glazes without any risk to health. Glazes whose lead is introduced in the form of lead bisilicate frits fired at 1050° C. and over are normally well within the safety margin, provided that no copper stains are added to them. Soft-fired glazes incorporating unfritted raw lead (white lead, red lead and litharge) can be very dangerous to the user, since some of the lead can easily be dissolved by organic acids in vinegar, wine and fruit juices. Apple juice appears to be particularly active as a solvent. Every year a few cases are recorded of deaths or severe illnesses caused by food and drink stored in poorly made lead glazed vessels.

Few if any of the old tin-glaze potters can have been aware of the danger of lead poisoning, and some of their vessels must certainly have led to trouble, especially pharmacy vessels containing liquid tonics and purgatives. Many of the best tin glazes were fritted, it is true, but the proportion of lead to silica and alumina was usually far higher than would be permitted today.

An article on this subject is 'Lead Poisoning' by Dr. Goldman, *World Medicine*, May 1971.

APPENDIX D

DUTCH GLAZE RECIPES

Blanc de Hollande (from *Encyclopédie* of 1756: article entitled 'Fayence', p. 458).

50 lb. dry sand ⎫
15 lb. potash ⎬ mixture to be calc-
20 lb. soda ⎪ ined, ground and
6 oz. manganese ⎭ sieved.

To the prepared mixture the following are added:

20 lb. lead ⎫ calcined and oxidised,
20 lb. tin ⎬ ground and sieved.

From *Proefkundige Verhandeling*, by A. F. (1774), quoted by F. W. Hudig in *Delfter Faience*, p. 116.

100 lb. white sand ⎫ calcined, ground and
40 lb. soda ⎬ sieved, this com-
30 lb. potash ⎪ pound is called
⎭ *masticot (marzacotto)*

To the *masticot* above are added 80 lb. 'tin-white', made by calcining and oxidising lead and tin metal in proportion 100:33, and also 10 lb sea-salt and 'a small quantity' of cobalt and copper filings to make the glaze slightly blue.

The entire mixture is then calcined three times, re-ground, and sieved, to make the glaze-powder.

From G. van Paape, *De Plateelbakker of Delftscheaardewerkmakker*, Dordrecht, 1794.

500 lb. sand ⎫ calcined, ground and
60 lb. salt ⎬ sieved, making *masticot*.
30 lb. soda ⎭

Lead 3 ⎫ Calcined, ground and sieved,
Tin   1 ⎬ making 'tin-ash'.

The white glaze is made up as follows:

50 lb. tin-ash ⎫ Calcined,
65 lb. masticot ⎬ ground
½ lb. smalt (cobalt ore) ⎪ and
1 *loot* (1/10 lb.) copper filings. ⎭ sieved.

Kwaart, the transparent glaze which is flicked over the pottery after painting, is made thus:

36 lb. masticot ⎫ mixed, calcined,
42 lb. yellow litharge ⎬ ground and
4 lb. potash ⎪ sieved.
7 lb. salt ⎭

APPENDIX E
PRACTICAL COMMENTS

These comments are meant merely as a general guide for anyone starting tin-glaze pottery without having a good adviser near at hand.

Clays. Tin glazes can be applied over any potting clay, but I would advise beginning with earthenware clays which mature within the range 1000°–1080°C. At lower temperatures there will be a considerable difficulty in finding glazes which do not craze, and at any higher temperature there will be difficulty in obtaining a reasonable range of colours.

Dark red clays are best avoided at first, as they need either a glaze with a high tin oxide content, or a glaze devised to 'break' pleasantly over the red body. Light red, buff, or off-white clays are simpler to use. If possible, the same glaze should be tried out on several different clays. The effect will vary considerably, and so will the painted colours. On the whole, light red or buff clays will give the best results, and the glaze will be slightly toned by them. Dark clays are hard to cover, and white clays with an opaque white glaze are boring.

A blend of red and off-white clays can be very pleasing, and may help the potter to arrive at a clay maturing at a certain desired temperature. One must be careful with the light-firing clays, however, as most of the light clays sold by ceramic merchants need to be fired at or above 1100°C.

Ceramic merchants deal mostly in clays suitable for industrial production of high fired earthenware and stoneware. Many good deposits of earthenware clay are no longer commercially dug, and some of these are worth testing, especially in areas where pottery has been made in the past. Almost all natural clays need to be slurried and screened through a 40 or 60 mesh before serviceable pottery can be made from them.

Earthenware clays from chalk or limestone areas are likely to be closest to the traditional tin-glaze bodies. If they are 'fat' and slimy after screening they should be mixed with up to equal amounts of coarser red clay, or stiffened with up to 10 per cent of fine sieved sand.

Some ceramic merchants provide off-white clays which mature at a low temperature (below 1000°C) and are stated to be craze-free. This is because they shrink unusually much as they cool. They are excellent for some purposes, but are seldom very plastic and may be difficult to throw on the wheel.

For tin-glaze work the clay should always be given a biscuit firing before glaze is applied, or the glaze will gather unevenly and 'crawl', leaving bare patches of clay after the firing. Most clays will be good for glazing after biscuit firing at about 900°C.

Glazes. All but very high-temperature glazes will be whitened by additions of tin oxide or zircon, or a mixture of both. The degree of whiteness will vary a great deal from one composition to another, and it is worth making trial of different types of glazes. The colours obtainable from pigments on or under the glaze will also vary: glazes good for iron browns, for instance, will seldom give good copper greens or chrome-tin reds. Any potter who arrives at a good glaze for a wide range of colours early on is lucky. Because of the price of tin oxide, it is advisable to pursue only those glazes which opacify fairly easily. 10 per cent of tin oxide in a suitable glaze can give a deep, opaque white, and there should be no need to add more. Smaller amounts can in some glazes give a pleasant semi-opaque white suitable for use over slips, and which will allow the colour of the clay body to break through in certain places.

Tin glazes usually have to be applied thicker than others, and their consistency should be carefully noted before dipping, pouring, or spraying them. The thickness of the coating is very important. A thin coat will be a mean milk-wash, while too thick a coat will probably be pitted and bubbled, and is likely to run in the firing. Both are bad for any kind of painted decoration. One has to determine the ideal glaze thickness for oneself, and it will probably vary from one glaze to another.

On the whole the best way of applying the glaze is by dipping the biscuit ware in a tub or bowl, when the size of the pot allows it. However the glaze is applied, some runs or dribbles are likely to occur, and these may make the painting run when the piece is fired. With practice, most pieces can be dipped without serious runs developing. The places where the pot is held by the finger-tips must be touched over with dabs of glaze, preferably after the piece has dried thoroughly. Bad dribbles can be pared down with a knife before painting.

About $\frac{1}{4}$ per cent of acacia powder or other powdered gum added to the glaze will make the surface less powdery. The surface will be easier to paint on, and there will be less likelihood of knocking or rubbing away the glaze accidentally.

Three different kinds of lead-tin based glazes are given below as possible starting points. I have not included any alkaline glazes, as these are almost bound to craze unless they are used over a specially devised clay-body. The following glazes are sound for studio use, but may not be acceptable everywhere, since the health regulations of some countries forbid the use of lead in pottery offered for sale. The recipes are only general guides, for the composition of materials varies from one supplier to another, and from country to country.

Tin glaze with a shiny surface; all-round colour range; suitable for oxidised or lightly reduced firing at 1020–1040°C. Good for tableware, etc.

Lead bisilicate fritt	74
China Clay	10
Whiting	2
Flint	4
Tin oxide	10

Zinc-matt tin glaze, good for all colours except chrome-tin red; best in slightly **reduced** firing 1040–1060°C.

Lead bisilicate fritt	56
Flint	8
Hard Purple Cornish stone	10
Borax fritt (1000°C)	8
Zinc oxide	8
Tin oxide	10

Lime-matt tin glaze, good for colours including chrome-tin red; fires at 1060°C. oxidising atmosphere only.

Lead bisilicate fritt	62
Hard purple Cornish stone	15
Whiting	15
Tin oxide	8

If the materials are bought from ceramic merchants, they will probably have been waterground by the manufacturers and will only need passing through a 120 mesh screen before being used. Freshly screened glazes often appear deceptively thick, and since the thickness of the coating is vitally important with tin glazes, it is advisable to leave the suspended glaze to settle for about twelve hours, after which water can be removed or added to make the right consistency.

It is also advisable to leave pots to dry for about twelve hours after glaze has been applied to them, so that the coating becomes completely dry. Otherwise the glaze can be dragged away by certain kinds of brushes and other tools, and blisters of water may form as the loaded brush travels over the surface. These blisters will leave bare patches when the glaze is fired.

High-temperature pigments. A list of the simpler pigments is given below. Nowadays most of these are obtainable ready-ground from most ceramic merchants. They need to be mixed with water and a dab of gum to make them flow, and ground on a tile, to be ready for use. Some of the pigments are very powerful and are more useful if diluted with powdered glaze or china clay; others are refractory and will fire rough unless they are mixed with a flux.

Cobalt oxide. A very strong blue, slightly refractory at earthenware temperatures. Best diluted and mixed with 'impurities' such as clay and other oxides.

Copper oxide, copper carbonate etc. Bright acid green on most glazes, tending to go black and metallic where thickly painted. A volatile pigment which always leaves a soft, fuzzy edge, and is nearly always best when blended with other colouring agents.

Manganese dioxide, pyrolusite. Earth brown or pinkish brown. A gentle pigment which need not always be diluted. No extra flux is needed.

Antimoniate of lead (Naples yellow). Warm egg-yellow on most glazes. A refractory material which will be rough unless well fluxed with a lead fritt. A difficult pigment to use, rough when thickly painted, pale and anaemic if used thinly.

Vanadium oxide. Lemon yellow or orange yellow if mixed with iron compounds. Expensive and refractory, and must be mixed with a flux, but is a valuable alternative to antimony pigments.

Ferric oxide, black iron oxide, ilmentite, crocus martis, and other iron compounds. All give various kinds of brown, depending on the composition of the glaze. Except in reducing conditions, the fired colour will always be rather granular, however finely the materials are ground, and it will vary enormously according to the thickness of the painting. There is no need to add fluxes to these materials, but they will be rough if thickly applied.

Chrome oxide. Various shades of green and olive green, usually surrounded by a yellowish stain on the unpainted glaze. The most important use of this pigment is in combination with tin oxide, to give a chrome-tin-pink or red,

supplied fritted and ground by almost all colour merchants.

All these materials can be blended with one another or with other materials, and the scope for trials is endless. All will vary according to the glaze they are applied to, the thickness of the application, the firing temperature and the kiln atmosphere. Good colours can be obtained without calcining the materials, but they are likely to be more controllable if the mixtures are calcined and re-ground. Many natural ores can also give interesting colours if they are finely ground.

Application of pigments. Pigments are applied by brush-painting, stamping, spraying, dusting, sponging, dabbing, stencilling and other methods on the surface of the unfired glaze. The stronger pigments can be applied to the unfired clay and will come through the glaze from below during the firing. This kind of decoration invites many kinds of incising, scratching, rubbing and other treatments, but the colour-range is more limited than application on the glaze surface.

Enamels. Any of the above materials, and others which are too volatile to be used at ordinary earthenware temperatures (such as selenium), can be applied to the fired glaze surface and fixed by a lower temperature firing. A vast amount of expert knowledge has gone into the preparation of enamels, and every colour merchant and most large potteries have their own recipes, which the amateur is unlikely to improve on. A beginning can be made by blending leadless frit with a pigment, in proportions of about 80 per cent to 20 per cent and firing the enamel at about 860°C.

BIBLIOGRAPHY

D. M. Archer, 'Delftware from Brislington' (*Connoisseur*, July 1969); 'Delftware made at the Glasgow pottery of Delftfield' (*Connoisseur*, September 1966); 'English Delftware, the industry at Lambeth in the mid-eighteenth century' (*Connoisseur*, April 1971)

Dr. Mehmet Bahrami, 'A master-potter of Kashan' (*Oriental Society Transactions*, vol. 20, 1944–5); *Gurgan Faiences* (Tehran, 1949)

G. Ballardini, *La maiolica italiana dalle origine alla fine del cinquecento* (Florence, 1938); *Opere di maestri faentini e loro rapporto con le ceramiche Habane* (Turin, 1932)

E. A. Barber, *Mexican Maiolica in the Collection of the Hispanic Society of America* (New York, 1915)

F. Bastenaire-Daudenart, *La Faïence* (Paris, 1828); *L'Art de fabriquer la Faience blanche* (Paris, 1830)

M. Bellini, *Maioliche del Rinascimento* (Milan, 1964)

A. Berendsen, with M. Keezer, S. Schoubye, J. M. dos Simões, and J. Tichelaar, *Fliesen* (Munich, 1964); trans., *Tiles: A General History* (London, 1967)

E. Bourry, *A Treatise on Ceramic Industries* (4th ed. London, 1926)

A. J. Butler, *Islamic Pottery* (London, 1926)

M. Cardew, *Pioneer Pottery* (London, 1969)

Balbina Martinez Caviro, *Catalogo de Cerámica española* (Madrid, 1968)

Emilio Camps Cazorla, *Cerámica española* (Madrid, 1936)

K. Černohorsky, *Moravska Lidova Keramika* (Prague, 1941)

R. J. Charleston, *Roman Pottery* (London, 1955); *Lundberg and Ljunberg: Give and Take in the Ceramic Industry of the Eighteenth Century* (Stockholm, 1967); *World Ceramics* (ed.) (London, 1968)

Warren E. Cox, *Pottery and Porcelain* (New York, 1966)

Ch. Damiron, *La Faïence de Lyon* (Paris, 1926)

Th. Deck, *La Faïence* (Paris, 1887)

M. S. Dimand, *A Handbook of Muhammedan Art* (3rd ed., New York, 1958)

G. Domanovsky, *Hungarian Pottery* (Budapest, 1968)

S. Ducret, *German Porcelain and Faience* (London, 1962)

G. C. Dunning, 'Trade in early Hispano-Moresque pottery to England' (*Antiquaries' Journal*, vol. XLI, April 1961)

R. Ettinghausen, 'Notes on the *Lusterware of Spain*' (*Ars Orientalis*, vol. 1, 1954)

Lady M. M. Evans, *Lustre Pottery* (London, 1920)

M. Fare, *Céramique contemporaine* (Paris, 1954)

O. Ferrari, *Maiolica italiana del seicento e settecento* (Milan, 1965)

L. Franchet, *La Fabrication industrielle des Emaux et Couleurs céramiques* (Paris, 1911)

A. W. Frothingham, *Lusterware of Spain* (New York, 1951); *Talavera Pottery* (New York, 1944); *Tile Panels of Spain* (New York, 1969)

F. H. Garner, *English Delftware* (London, 1948; new ed. prepared by M. Archer, London, 1972)

W. Gaunt and M. D. E. Clayton-Stamm, *William de Morgan* (London, 1971)

J. Giacomotti, *Faïences françaises* (Fribourg,

1963); *La Majolique de la Renaissance* (Paris, 1961)

E. Grube, 'The varieties of Islamic art' (*Apollo*, September 1965); *The World of Islam* (London, 1966)

E. Hannover, *Pottery and Porcelain* (trans. B. Rackham) (London, 1925)

C. Hernmarck, *Fajans och Porslin* (Stockholm, 1959)

B. Hillier, *Pottery and Porcelain 1700–1914* (London, 1968)

R. L. Hobson, *Guide to the Islamic Pottery of the Near East* (London, 1932)

W. B. Honey, *English Pottery and Porcelain* (rev. R. J. Charleston, London, 1962); *European Ceramic Art* (London, 1949)

F. W. Hudig, *Delfter Fayence* (Berlin, 1929)

T. Husband, 'Valencia lusterware of the fifteenth century' (*Metropolitan Museum of Art Summer Bulletin*, New York, 1970)

Jonkvrouwe C. H. de Jonge, *Delft Ceramics* (trans. M-C. Hellin) (London, 1970)

D. H. Kahnweiler, *Picasso Keramik* (Hanover, 1957)

A. Kiss, *Baroque Pottery in Hungary* (Budapest, 1966)

B. Kristinkovitch, *Haban Pottery* (Budapest, 1962)

H. Landsfeld, *Lidové Hrncirstvi a Dzbankarstvi* (Prague, 1950)

Arthur Lane, *Early Islamic Pottery* (London, 1947); *French Faience* (London, 1948; new ed. 1971)

J. Ainaud de Lasarte, *Ars Hispaniae* (vol. X, Madrid, 1952)

Saul Levy, *Maioliche settecentesche* (Milan, 1964)

G. Liverani. *Five Centuries of Italian Maiolica* (London, 1960); 'The revolution of white maiolica of Faenza' (*Connoisseur*, vol. CXLI, 1957)

Luis M. Llubiá, *Cerámica medieval española* (Barcelona, 1967)

M. Gonzalez Martí, *Cerámica del Levante Español* (Barcelona, 1944 and 1952)

M. Gomez-Moreno, 'La Loza dorada primitiva de Málaga' (*Al-Andalus*, vol. V, 1940)

S. Muratori, *L'Arte della Maiolica a Ravenna* (Ravenna, 1934)

H. Nicaise, *Les Modèles italiens des Faiences néerlandaises au XVIe et au début du XVIIe siècles* (Brussels, 1936)

J. Martinez Ortiz and Jaime de Scals Aracil, *Cerámica del Museo municipal de Valencia* (Valencia, 1962)

Oliver van Oss, 'English delftware in the eighteenth century' (*Transactions of the English Ceramic Circle*, vol. 3, part 5, 1955); 'Some notes on English delftware' (*Transactions of the English Ceramic Circle*, vol. 5, part 4, 1963)

C. W. Parmelee, *Ceramic Glazes* (Chicago, 1951)

A. U. Pope, *Survey of Persian Art* (New York, 1939)

A. van der Put, *Hispano-Moresque Ware of the XV Century* (London, 1904); *Valencian Styles in Hispano-Moresque Pottery* (New York, 1938)

A. Rackham and A. van der Put, *The Three Books of the Potter's Art of Cipriano Piccolpasso* (London, 1934) (translation and commentary)

Bernard Rackham, *Early Netherlands Maiolica* (London, 1926); *Italian Maiolica* (London, 1952)

P. Rada, *The Book of Ceramics* (Prague, n.d., c. 1960)

N. Ragona, *La Ceramica siciliana* (Palermo, 1955)

Anthony Ray, *English Delftware Pottery in the Robert Hall Warren Collection, Ashmolean Museum, Oxford* (London, 1968)

D. Rhodes, *Kilns* (London, 1969)

H. Rivière, *La Céramique dans l'Art musulman* (Paris, 1913)

F. Sarre, *Die Keramik von Samarra* (Berlin, 1925)

C. Scavizzi, *Maiolica, Delft and Faience* (London, 1970)

Kenneth Shaw, *Ceramic Colours and Pottery Decoration* (London, 1962)

Frances Spalding, *Mudejar Ornament in Manuscripts* (New York, 1953)

Ross E. Taggart, *The Burnap Collection of English Pottery* (Kansas, 1967)

Hugh Tait, 'Southwark (alias Lambeth) Delftware and the Pottery Christian Wilhelm' (*Connoisseur*, August 1960 and February 1961)

K. Uldall, *Gammel Dansk Fajansi* (Copenhagen, 1961)

A. Vallardi, *Maioliche italiane del Rinascimento* (Milan, 1964)

A. Vecht, *Frederik van Frytom* (Amsterdam, 1968)

T. Volker, *Porcelain and the Dutch East India Company, 1602–1683* (Leiden, 1954)

J. Vydra and L. Kunz, *Painting on Folk Ceramics* (trans. R. F. Samsour) (London, n.d.)

P. Ward-Jackson, 'Some main streams and tributaries in European ornament from 1500 to 1750 (*Victoria and Albert Museum Bulletin*, vol. III, 1967)

D. Whitehouse, 'Medieval glazed pottery of Lazío' (*Papers of the British School at Rome*, vol. XXXV (new series vol. XXII), 1967)

Gaston Wiet, *Album du Musée arabe du Caire* (Cairo, 1930)

C. K. Wilkinson, *Iranian Ceramics* (New York, 1963)

Geoffrey Wills, *English Pottery and Porcelain* (London, 1969)

Hans E. Wulff, *Traditional Crafts of Persia* (Cambridge, Mass., 1966)

INDEX

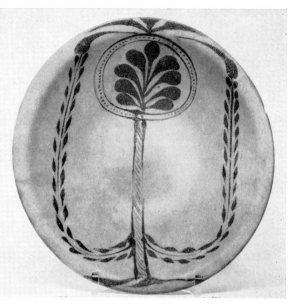

1. Small bowl 14cm wide, with flared rim: a shape derived from Chinese porcelain. Mesopotamia, 9th century. The inscription in soft blue reads *made by Abu. . . .* Luxury ware with white glaze was probably made at first only for the Caliph's court. *Keir Collection. See page 24.*

2. Small shallow bowl with flared rim, painted in soft cobalt blue. 20cm wide. Mesopotamia, probably 9th century. Surely the arresting image has a symbolic meaning. It is the more emphatic for being in no way suggested by the form it is painted on. *Kenneth Malcolm Esq. See page 24.*

Small bowl with flared rim, painted in cobalt blue. 24cm wide. Mesopotamia, 9th century. A beautifully placed device with two contrasting elements, probably painted with symbolical rather than decorative intent. It has been said to represent a fire altar. *British Museum. See page 24.*

4. Small bowl with flared rim, painted in olive green, brown and yellow lustres. 14·5cm wide. The design suggests flowers and leaves and may come from garland motifs in late classical ornament in stone and plaster. The contour lines were drawn first and were filled in with patterns, leaving only the small areas of white to separate the forms. *Keir Collection. See page 25.*

5. Dish with flat base and upright side, painted in tawny lustre 23cm wide. Mesopotamia, 9th–10th century. The leaf-pattern was perhaps borrowed from carved ornament, but the painter's brush has made the curves soft and sinuous. The darkening on one side was caused by exposure to flames in the kiln. *Keir Collection. See page 25*

6. Small bowl painted in tawny lustr 22cm wide. Mesopotamia, 9th–10 century. The formalised bird was fir painted as a strong contour drawing ar was then filled in with colour, leavir reserved areas of white pattern. Th border-pattern of 'eyes' within circl appeared quite often on lustreware. *Priva Collection. See page 27.*

7. Small bowl painted in greenish-yellow lustre, about 22cm wide, and small jug painted in yellow lustre, about 10cm high. Mesopotamia, 10th century. *British Museum. See page 28.*

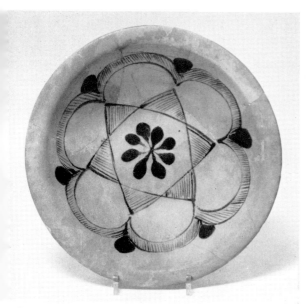

Bowl with turned-out rim, painted in smoky cobalt blue. 27cm ⁻ide. Mesopotamia, 9th–10th century. *The Hon. Robert Erskine. ee page 24.*

9. Bowl painted in greenish-brown lustre. 25cm wide. Mesopotamia, 10th century. Bold images of human beings superseded the earlier 'decorative' emblems. They are some of the most dramatic compositions ever painted on pottery. *Musée du Louvre. See page 27.*

10. Small bowl with slightly flared rim, painted in greenish-yellow lustre. 18·5cm wide. Mesopotamia, 10th century The formalised heads, with long noses, small pointed beards and pointed hats, are typical of the rare Mesopotamian lustred vessels with human figures. This superb formal design is surely also symbolical? The figures seem eager to explain themselves, but the more one looks the more inscrutable they become. *Keir Collection. See page 27.*

11. Small bowl with flared rim, painted in yellow lustre. Inscribed in the base *baraka*: 'blessing'. 23cm wide. Mesopotamia, 10th century. Whereas the bowl shown in Plate 10 is centred on the still rounded shape, here the angular features radiate from the centre and would feel aggressive even if the man were not a mounted warrior. *Keir Collection. See page 27.*

12. Small bowl painted in yellow lustre.
Probably from Egypt, 10th century. About
22cm wide. A half abstract rendering of
a galley with a bank of oars, with a canopy
over the centre of the boat, and flags at
stem and stern. The form of the bowl might
be Mesopotamian, but the fanciful, succulent brushwork suggests that it was
made in Egypt. *Islamic Museum, Cairo.
See page 30.*

3. Small jar painted in greenish-yellow
ustre. 13cm high. Probably from Egypt,
0th century. Scholars still debate whether
ustre painting on tin glaze started in Egypt
or Mesopotamia. The drawing, the con-
our-panels and the border of circles on this
iece have equivalents in Mesopotamian
vork, but the clay is soft and coarse and
he glaze is shiny, which suggest that it is
gyptian. *Keir Collection. See page 30.*

14. Small bowl, 23cm wide, painted in reddish lustre. Egypt, 12th century. The design of concentric circles on the outside of this bowl is found also on Mesopotamian pieces, but the man and woman with fighting-cocks have nothing in common with Mesopotamian formalised figures, and belong to the late classical Mediterranean world. So do the arabesque plant forms, drawn with a suggestion of three dimensions. This bowl is one of a small number of Egyptian lustres with descriptive drawings, all sharing the unusual feature of a solid background. The copper lustre is also unusual; it needs a higher firing than the yellow (silver) lustres, and it involves greater technical risk. *Keir Collection. See page 36.*

15. Bowl about 32cm wide, painted in bright golden-yellow lustre. Egypt, mid-12th century. Gay, secular ornament of the Fatimid period almost every feature is elaborated, the verticals of the Kufic lettering, the cusping of the circular bands, the peacock's crest, wing and tail, and even the branch in his beak. The peacock is a bird of happiness and good omen. This bowl may have belonged to the women's quarters of a rich household. *Islamic Museum, Cairo. See page 33.*

16. Shallow bowl painted in yellow-gold lustre. 23cm wide. Probably Egypt, but possibly Persia, 11th century. Signed on the base. The Kufic inscription repeated round the border means 'blessings to the owner'. What comfortable ceramic drawing! The resemblance to Persian work is not accidental: by the time the Fatimid dynasty of Cairo fell in 1171, many craftsmen seem to have migrated to work under the cultivated Seljuk conquerors of Persia. *Keir Collection. See page 36.*

17. Fragment of a dish painted in greenish-yellow lustre: Christ the King, with the sign of blessing. 11cm wide. Egypt, 11th–12th century. Islam embraced a diverse population, including Greeks, Jews and Coptic Christians. The Copts of Cairo were isolated from the rest of the Christian world; they were not persecuted, and were valued for their craftsmanship. In this fragment, Christian imagery and Fatimid decoration come together. The fine white lines are incised in the lustre pigment, which was painted over the already-fired glaze. *Islamic Museum, Cairo. See page 37.*

18. Small bowl painted with a hare, tawny lustre. 22cm wide. Egypt, mid-12th century. The hare has the same *joie de vivre* as most of the Fatimid decorative animals, in wood-carving, metalwork and pottery, and like most of his kind he gets laced up with the scrollwork and foliage around him. It was probably drawn free, without stencils or pounces. *Musée du Louvre. See page 33*.

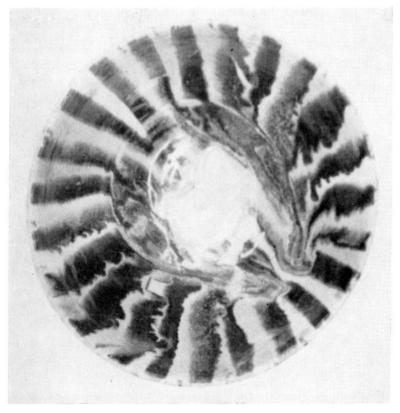

19. Small bowl, 23cm wide, painted in brown and green. Fayyum area, Egypt, 11th or 12th century. The fluid glaze has carried the painting with it. The bowl must have been fired on its edge, or at an angle, making the glaze gather at one side. *Islamic Museum, Cairo. See page 39*.

20. Small bowl painted in deep olive-green lustre. About 19 cm wide. Probably made at Rayy, second half of 12th century. This gem of free drawing and abstract ornament grew from a line-drawing, filled in with areas of solid colour and with some spaces left reserved in white. The idea differs from the pictorial conventions of Egyptian lustre; there is no sense of a picture here, and the painter has enjoyed the freedom to the full. The languishing ladies with faces 'beautiful as moons' were a favourite theme of Rayy painters. *Victoria and Albert Museum. See page 46.*

21. Large bowl painted in lustre. 36cm wide. Rayy, late 12th century. The drawing was probably done with a quill. Arthur Lane suggested that this bowl was decorated by an Egyptian painter who had migrated to Persia. *Victoria and Albert Museum. See page 44.*

22. Ewer for wine, painted in brown-gold lustre. Probably from Kashan, about 1200. 22cm wide. A lovely Islamic shape, based on metal vessels. The placing of the horizontal bands is so right that it seems inevitable. The noble formality of the decoration is deceptive, and the leaf scrolls on the shoulder are more diverse than they seem. The motif on the collar reappeared in Spain three hundred years later. *Mr and Mrs Raymond Ades. See page 45.*

23. Small jug painted in orange-yellow lustre. About 11cm high. Probably from Rayy, late 12th century. The painted design is pattern-recipe suitable for repetition, but it remains free, and the balance of light and dark prevents it becoming facile or static. The unglazed foot ensures that the runny glaze will not stick to the support in the firing. *British Museum. See page 45*

24. Large lustre-painted dish. 29cm wide. Kashan, dated 607 A.H./A.D. 1210. Here the Kashan illustrators have used all their resources: the play between light and dark pattern, diverse scales of ornament, and the contrast between elaborate decoration and artfully simple drawing, building up an image which is earthly, lyrical and meta-physical all at once. *Metropolitan Museum of Art, New York* (*Gift of Horace Have-meyer, 1941, the H. O. Havemeyer Col-lection*). *See page 46.*

. *Minai* dish painted and signed by ɔu Zeyd and dated 584 A.H./A.D. 1187. 5cm wide. Kashan is mentioned in the scription. *Metropolitan Museum of Art, ew York. See page 50*

26A, B. Inside and back of a *Minai* bowl. About 18cm wide. Persia, early 13th century. *Musée du Louvre. See page 49.*

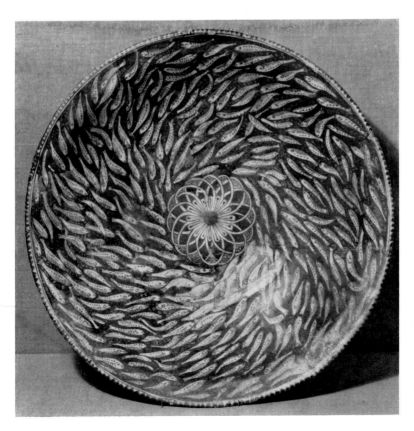

27. Large dish painted in brownish lustre About 45 cm wide. Persia, perhaps Kasha 13th century. Under the Mongols th decoration of pottery became tighter an less intuitive. The central device on th dish has this precision. Though the fishe are arranged spirally they are cunning varied and seem to move, partly becaus the centre is so definite. *Fitzwillia Museum, Cambridge. See page 51.*

8. Unglazed jar painted in manganese. 24cm high. Almería, pain, 13th century. (Much repaired.) Such jars are found on edieval sites in North Africa and Andalucía. Most Moorish tin-laze wares were likewise painted directly on the clay, but with cobalt pigment which penetrated the glaze from below when it was red. *Museo Arqueológico, Madrid. See page 54.*

29. Two *albarelos* painted in lustre and blue. About 27cm high. Málaga, late 14th century. The Moorish albarelo had almost vertical sides. The splayed foot is usual in Andalucían pottery shapes. Similar pots were made by Moorish emigrants at Manises, near Valencia. The shield on the jar on the left is the blazon of the Nasrid dynasty of Granada. *Instituto de Valencia de Don Juan, Madrid. See page 58.*

). Two jugs painted in cobalt blue.
bout 20cm high. Málaga, 14th century.
stituto de Valencia de Don Juan, Madrid.
e page 58

35. Large jug painted in deep red lustre, about 27 cm high. Málaga, late 14th century. The figure of the huntsman is adapted to the pottery form, with a masterly use of background shapes. It has something in common with Mesopotamian figure decoration of several centuries earlier, and the spotted ground is used in a similar way. The white glaze has been slightly darkened by the smoky firing needed to develop the lustre. The vessel is also unusual in that it is made of reddish clay. *Instituto de Valencia de Don Juan, Madrid. See page 64.*

A, B. Large bowl painted in tawny-
own lustre. 59cm wide. About 1400. The
ep, tapering form, the splayed foot and
e multiple rim are features of Moorish
ttery, as is the entire painted design.
hether it was made in Málaga itself, or by
oorish settlers in Manises, may never be
cided. *Victoria and Albert Museum. See
ge 64.*

37. Small dish painted in brown and green. 15cm wide. Paterna, 13th–14th century. Many kinds of abstract designs were used on early Paterna pottery. This one could be of Iberian or even older origin, for the asymmetric movement around the central cross appears also in some ancient rock carvings. *Museo Histórico, Valencia. See page 66.*

38. Dish painted in brown and soft green. 22·5cm wide. Paterna about 1400. The palmettes, mock Kufic lettering, contour-panel and dots and spirals all come from a nobler tradition, but were used at Paterna with a casual, juicy vigour. *Palacio Nacional, Barcelona. See page 66.*

39. Shallow dish painted in brown and green. 20cm wide. The figure holding the fishes by the tail was used long before in Egypt. The Paterna painters depicted it quite often, seldom twice in the same way. It probably signifies prosperity and abundance. *Palacio Nacional, Barcelona. See page 66.*

40. Small bowl painted in brown and green. 15·5cm wide. Paterna, 14th century. The girl's head surrounded with pattern suggesting lace or flowers is the only one known of its kind. Helmeted warriors were often depicted, but the girl seems to be the personal whim of the painter. *Museo Histórico, Valencia. See page 69.*

41. Jug painted in cobalt blue. About 24cm high. Manises, late 14th century. *Palacio Nacional, Barcelona. See page 70.*

42. Jar painted in blue. 31cm high. Probably Manises, about 1400. The design comes from Moorish floriated Kufic lettering, turned into an abstract device. The original contour lines and the strokes of the infilled colour are discernible. *Instituto de Valencia de Don Juan, Madrid. See page 61.*

43. Wide, shallow dish painted in cobalt blue. 34·5cm wide. Manises, about 1400. Both these vessels are old Moorish shapes, and the brush decoration has a dramatic economy quite different from the Paterna tradition. Gradually these and other Moorish conventions were absorbed into the Hispano-Moresque work of the Valencia area. *Palacio Nacional, Barcelona. See page 70.*

44. Dish painted in copper green, manganese brown and iron brown. 22cm wide. Paterna, about 1300. This design was probably well known, for there are three other versions in the same collection. Each is free-drawn and differs in the placing and details, and each has a different coat of arms. The arms here are of de Luna, the lords of Paterna. *Museo Histórico, Valencia. See page 66.*

45. Small dish painted in blue. 14·5cm wide. Paterna or Manises, mid-14th century. Simple and humourous drawing such as this was new in the pottery of Valencia. Cobalt blue had not been used there before this time. Perhaps the new decoration was brought in by craftsmen from Andalucía, where Moorish potters had long been using blue pigments. *Museo Histórico, Valencia. See page 69.*

46. Dish painted in yellow-gold lustre and cobalt blue. 45·5cm wide. Valencia, early 15th century. The ground-pattern is deep blue and the devices with reserved white are lustre, as is the infilling of the ground. The background pattern is based on the Arabic word *alafia,* meaning 'Blessing' or 'Providence', and a figure-of-eight motif which comes from the tree of life design. *Victoria and Albert Museum. See page 70.*

47. Back of a large armorial dish painted in orange-gold lustre. About 48cm wide. Manises, first half of 15th century. Such dishes were made for palaces and castles and large prices were paid for them. They belong to a different world from the small functional vessels, but the leaf-flower and scrollwork is found on both. *Museo Arqueológico, Madrid. See page 75.*

48. Large dish painted in gold lustre. About 43cm wide. Manises, about 1450. The irregularities of the border are probably intuitive, and give variety to what might have been a dull, four-square composition. The palmettes are like those of Egyptian lustres around 1100, and have been used by Moslem decorators ever since. *Museo Arqueológico, Madrid. See page 70.*

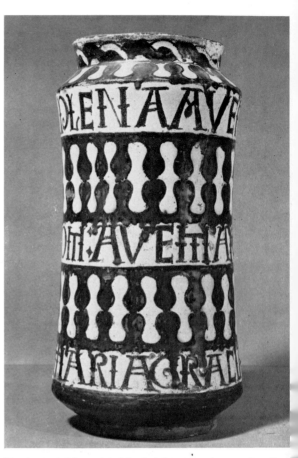

49. Small vase painted in bright silvery-yellow lustre. 22cm high. Muel, about 1500. Muel was a productive minor centre for lustre-ware by the end of the 15th century. The patterns and brushwork are strongly Moorish. Pieces such as these were counted by the dozen. *Palacio Nacional, Barcelona. See page 79.*

51. Large tall jar painted in dark brown and green, inscribed AVE MARIA GRACIA PLENA. 38cm high. Teruel, about 1400. European letters were less often used as decoration than Arabic writing. Here they fit the traditional zoned design of an albarelo made for a convent. Teruel colours are almost always rather dark because of the dark red local clay, which was not the most suitable kind for tin glaze. *Palacio Nacional, Barcelona. See page 80.*

50. Small 'eared' bowl, *cuenco de orejas* painted in silvery-brown lustre. 12cm wide. Muel, about 1500. *Palacio Nacional, Barcelona See page 79.*

61.   The Visitation. Large tin-glaze figures by Luca della Robbia, about 1460. *Chiesa di San Giovanni Fuorcivitas, Pistoia. See page 95.*

62. Spouted drug-jar, slate blue, yellow ochre, green and purple-brown. Florence, about 1450. The powerful split-leaf pattern was used on many drug-pots and vases at Florence and Faenza in the second half of the 15th century, and was taken up by many other factories. *Musée Céramique, Sèvres. See page 85.*

63. *Albarello,* painted in blue, ochre and green, inscribed MIDEA BELL. 31cm high. Faenza, about 1500. The convention of line drawing is still used decoratively, not as a picture in its own right. The popular 'portrait' pieces went in for character rather than flattery. *Musée du Louvre. See page 86.*

64. Satirical plate painted in blue, ochre brown and green. About 35cm wide. Deruta, early 16th century. *Musée du Louvre. See page 86.*

65. Small plate painted in blue and grey-blue: St Jerome in the wilderness. 24cm wide. Siena, about 1510. Inscribed on the back 'fata i siena da m° benedetto'. Early in the 16th century the modelled drawing convention led to picture-painting on pottery. A few painters, Maestro Benedetto amongst them, achieved a new kind of painting specially accommodated to pottery. *Victoria and Albert Museum. See page 97.*

66. Small dish painted with the Rape of Proserpine, grey-green, black and yellow. About 1527. Attributed to Nicola Pellipario, Fabriano. *Victoria and Albert Museum. See page 94.*

67. Armorial dish painted in tones of blue, with orange-ochre, yellow and white hatching on highlights, on a softly blued tin glaze. 32cm wide. Venice, about 1530. The formal appearance conceals the variations and irregularities of the details. The painter has masterfully ignored the inconvenient central recess. *Germanisches Nationalmuseum, Nürnberg. See page 99.*

68. Two-handled urn painted in yellow lustre, blue and ochre, with the arms of a Medici Pope (Leo X or Clement VII). About 27cm high. Deruta, *c.* 1525. *Victoria and Albert Museum. See page 98.*

69. Dish painted with *putti* and animals on a slightly blue glaze in tones of blue with areas of reddish-orange wash. 30cm wide. Deruta or Faenza, early 16th century. *The Wallace Collection, London. See page 94.*

70. Plate painted with 'Cupid Bound', in blue, green, ochre, yellow and purple. 21cm wide. Giovanni Maria of Casteldurante, about 1510. Modelled drawing allied with feeling for flat pattern shows in all this painter's work. He seems to have prepared his own compositions, never to have worked from engravings and the subjects are not mere conventions. This is a careful and disconcerting piece of symbolism, all the tougher for looking urbane. *Victoria and Albert Museum See page 97.*

71. Large dish painted in the full range of maiolica colours, deepened by a clear varnish-glaze. 47cm wide. Pesaro, 1540–50. Full-scale *istoriato,* with modelled drawing at its best, and Joshua on the white war-horse leaping right out of the melée. The subject is from Joshua 10.xii, and the back of the dish is inscribed 'cu Josue bellu esset uicturu E notesceret orationib' solem firmavit'. (When Joshua was winning the battle and night was falling, he stopped the sun with his prayers.) The heroic dish almost does justice to the event. *Victoria and Albert Museum. See page 94.*

74. Polychrome dish, 24cm wide. *Montelupo, about 1630.* Montelupo produced vividly painted popular dishes of ladies, musketeers, bandits, etc in rural settings. Many are crude, but when the lusty painting did not run into difficulties it has a peculiar charm. *Palazzo Venezia, Rome. See page 99*,

72. Small cruet painted in ochre, yellow, green and grey-green. 19cm high. Urbino, about 1570. On the front is an emblem belonging to Alfonso II d'Este of Ferrara. By about 1550 the elaboration of maiolica painting had more or less reached its limit. Thereafter the painting became lighter, while the forms of vessels grew more elaborate. The Patanazzi workshop in Urbino excelled in modelled ornament and delicate decoration. *Victoria and Albert Museum. See page 88.*

73. Heraldic marriage-plate, painted mostly in ochre, blue and yellow with grey line drawing. The arms belong to the families Christell and Siedelman of Nürnberg. About 22cm wide. Urbino, second half of the 16th century. The drawing is witty, as are the strange creatures and their playful liaisons. *The Wallace Collection, London. See page 88.*

75. Large armorial dish painted in soft blue. About 44cm wide. Early 17th century. By this date Deruta no longer furnished pottery to courts and palaces. The fantasy of this dish would not have suited the patrician connoisseur, but it would be enjoyed by a gentleman. The social distinction of the age are exactly reflected in maiolica. *Victoria and Albert Museum. See page 99.*

77. Drug-jar painted in dark and rough blue, soft blue and yellow. About 35cm high. Made by Italian emigrants at Lyon around 1550. *Fitzwilliam Museum, Cambridge. See page 106.*

76. Jar painted in soft blue, grey, yellow and ochre. 33cm high. Talavera, about 1570. The arms are those of the Monastery of the Escorial, and the jar is one commissioned for its pharmacy. The strapwork design is a Renaissance motif favoured by the established order in Spain at the expense of Moorish emblems. It was probably introduced by Italians from Antwerp. This jar is attributed to the master-potter and tile-maker Juan Fernandez, from whom 24,800 painted tiles were ordered for the Escorial in 1573. *Instituto de Valencia de Don Juan, Madrid. See page 105.*

78. Tiles painted in tones of blue, yellow,
green and ochre. The square tiles are 14cm
on the side. Probably from Antwerp, about
1520. These tiles were installed in the Vyne,
Hampshire, about 1520. The whole floor
includes many patterns and 'portraits' of
ladies and nobles, goddesses, emperors
and a large tile of Federigo da Montefeltro.
The names seem to be distributed at ran-
dom and many of them are unintelligible.
*The Vyne, Basingstoke, Hampshire. See
page 105.*

79. Jar or *chevrette* for liquid medicines, painted in deep blue, yellow and ochre. About 24cm high. Nîmes, probably from the workshop of Antoine Syjalon, around 1580. *Victoria and Albert Museum. See page 106.*

80. Dish with drawing in manganese brown, coloured with ochre, yellow, blue and deep green. 39cm wide. Talavera, second half of 17th century. At Talavera, the Italian pictorial tradition changed into a light and freely-drawn mannerism. At first made only for the court and aristocracy, these vessels became very popular and lasted until the potteries were burned down by a French army in the Napoleonic wars. The style has recently been revived. *Instituto de Valencia de Don Juan, Madrid. See page 107.*

81. Plate painted in blue, brown, green and yellow. 33cm wide. Triana or Seville, 17th century. A Spanish version of the Italian idea of profile painting, these plates were popular pieces and were made in large numbers, with many variations. The painters often made a complete mess of the drawing, but this example is unusually good. *Palacio Nacional, Barcelona. See page 107.*

82. Dish painted in soft blue. 41 cm wide. Nürnberg, dated 1530. One of the first examples of German tin glaze with pictorial decoration. The line-drawing with hatched lines indicating relief must have been taken from an engraving. The border is a simplified version of Italian ornament, probably from a Venetian original. *Germanisches Nationalmuseum, Nürnberg. See page 107.*

83. Stove-tile, about 27 cm wide, with transparent green and dark brown glazes, opaque dark blue, and white tin glaze. Nürnberg, first half of 16th century. Many Bavarian and Tyrolese tile-makers used tin glaze with relief moulding. The girl's right shoulder shows the kind of difficulty involved in using white glaze with a hard edge over relief with a soft profile. *Germanisches Nationalmuseum, Nürnberg. See page 108.*

84. Large pitcher of red earthenware, with pewter lid and foot. About 48 cm high. The moulded ornament is coloured with different glazes: opaque blue, clear green and tin-white, with painting in antimony yellow. Annaberg, *c.* 1570. Relief ornament with coloured glazes are much loved in parts of Central Europe, but are not wholly satisfactory to those who are unused to them. *Fitzwilliam Museum, Cambridge (Glaisher Bequest). See page 108.*

85. Dish decorated with coloured glazes, brown, black, green, blue and tin-white. 32cm wide. Bavaria, dated 1607. Stove-tile glazes were also used on flat surfaces, an intriguing return to the *cuerda seca* technique of Andalucía. The Bavarians probably had no idea that it had been used before. *Germanisches National-museum, Nürnberg. See page 108.*

86. Owl-jug with moulded figures and a coat of arms, painted in soft blue. 26cm high. South German, about 1535. This kind of pot was popular in South Germany and it is easy to see why, for it held good liquor and has a likeable face and showed the owner's coat of arms. It has been criticised for not being wholly serious or aesthetically consistent, but the criticism is over-solemn. *Germanisches Nationalmuseum, Nürnberg. See page 108.*

87. Inkwell and pen-rest, painted in grass-green, turquoise purple-brown, yellow and ochre. 27cm high. Winterthur, Switzerland, about 1650. In days when few people had the time or ability to write at all, inkwells were important and somewhat ceremonial and all over Europe tin-glaze potters occasionally made them *Germanisches Nationalmuseum, Nürnberg. See page 108.*

88. Dish painted in blue. 38cm wide. Portugal, early 17th century. The first potters to respond to Chinese porcelain were the Venetians, whose *alla porcellana* designs were based on originals imported through the Levant. The direct sea-trade with the Far East was dominated by the Portuguese and the Dutch, and their pottery was also affected by porcelain. One can feel in this dish a new touch and the release of new ideas. *Victoria and Albert Museum. See page 129.*

89. Vase painted with scenes from the Old Testament, green, yellow, blue, brown and ochre. About 38cm high. Nevers, about 1630. This side of the vase shows the Return of the Prodigal Son. The figures may have been taken from an engraving, but happily, the painter's naïveté prevented him from copying the original. *Victoria and Albert Museum. See page 111.*

91. Pot for some kind of hot drink, painted in soft blue with drawing in manganese brown. 24cm high. Nevers, about 1650. A strange mixture of Italianate decoration with Chinese-inspired detail. *Fitzwilliam Museum, Cambridge (Glaisher Bequest). See page 113.*

90. Very large dish painted with Europa and the Bull. 55cm wide. Blue, green, ochre, yellow. Nevers, mid-17th century. A magnificent example of the Italianate tradition upheld by the Conrade family at Nevers. *Musée du Louvre. See page 111.*

92. Very large banquet-plate painted in deep blue with accents of brick red. About 58cm wide. Rouen, *c.* 1710. A fine example of the intricate Baroque decoration with 'lambrequins' originated by potters in Rouen and later taken up by other centres in Northern France. *Victoria and Albert Museum. See page 115.*

93. Jug based on the traditional North French cider-jug, painted in deep blue and soft blue, inscribed 'Jean Delaland 1729'. 35cm high. A happy mixture of Oriental and baroque motifs. *Fitzwilliam Museum, Cambridge. See page 115.*

94. Jug with moulded lid, painted in blue, green and red. 22cm high. Sinceny, about 1750. Sinceny was one of the most successful of the many *faienceries* established by noblemen on their estates, chiefly to supply the château, but also as a source of income. How completely Oriental decoration had been assimilated by the mid 18th century! *Victoria and Albert Museum. See page 121.*

96.➤ Large oval dish painted in blue with fantastic devices in the style of the court designer, Jean Bérain. 53cm long. Moustiers, about 1740. *Musée Céramique, Sèvres. See page 117.*

95. Teapot painted in soft blue, red and opaque grass-green. 13cm high. French mid 18th century. This piece shows, incidentally, that faience did not have to be showy to be good. The strong spout and handle have the sturdy feel of provincial faience as distinct from porcelain. *Fitzwilliam Museum, Cambridge (Glaisher Bequest). See page 121.*

99. Revolutionary plate, 24cm wide, painted in purple-brown, soft blue and ochre. The door of the bird-cage is open. Nevers, dated 1791. *Fitzwilliam Museum, Cambridge. See page 123.*

97. Pot-pourri vase painted in enamels: crimson, green, etc. About 22cm high. Paul Hannong factory, Strasbourg, 1760–80. The rococo style was suited to techniques of moulding which had already developed enormously because of the demand for table services. Enamel painting with its crisp edge and fine brush-strokes accented the moulded forms. *Victoria and Albert Museum. See page 120.*

98. Plate with trellis rim, painted in enamel colours: purple, red, yellow, blue, green and dark brown. Strasbourg, about 1770. The Strasbourg factory was prevented by monopolies from making porcelain, but its ideals were to a large degree those of porcelain. Despite its appearance this plate is tin-glaze earthenware. *Museum für Kunsthandwerk, Frankfurt am Main See page 120.*

100. Plate decorated in enamel (*petit-feu*) colours. About 34cm wide. Veuve Perrin factory, Marseilles, late 18th century. *Musée Céramique, Sèvres. See page 122.*

101. Puzzle-jug, painted in purple-brown, soft blue, orange, yellow and opaque green. 23cm high. Nevers, dated 1780. Inscribed 'e variste gourde marinier a nevers 1780'. As the neck was full of holes, the liquid in the jug could only be drunk after passing through the handle and being sucked out through the spouts in the hollow rim. The Nevers painters were fond of scenes connected with the busy river-traffic of the Loire. *Fitzwilliam Museum, Cambridge. See page 123.*

103. Large plate, blue, ochre and green, with thick transparent over-glaze. Probably Holland, early 17th century. 35cm wide. Two worlds meet here: the pedestal bowl of grapes and pomegranates is a Venetian idea, while the border was borrowed from the newly imported Wan-Li provincial Chinese porcelain. The colours are traditional Italian polychrome, soon to be abandoned in favour of the blue associated with porcelain. *Fitzwilliam Museum, Cambridge. See page 128.*

102. Flask with pewter mounts, painted in tones of blue. 27cm high. Probably from Holland, dated 1570. An early blue-and-white piece with Italianate scenes in roundels, painted in a non-Italian manner. *See page 128.*

104. Flagon with plain white glaze and pewter lid. 27cm high. Probably Delft, about 1650. Plain white pottery was much used in Holland, but is uncommon today because it was not looked after so well as painted ware. Important pieces were given a special tin glaze called *dubbelwit*. *Victoria and Albert Museum. See page 132.*

105. Plate painted in tones of blue. 24cm wide. Frederik van Frytom, Delft, about 1660. Van Frytom was also an oil painter and engraver, but most of his work was on pottery. His landscapes have a gentle magic which is not explained simply by his superb technique : one seems to see the air itself. Van Frytom appears to have worked in his own private studio, never in a factory, *Gemeentemuseum, The Hague. See page 135.*

106. *Left:* Jug with pewter mounts, painted in blue and blue-grey. Marked on the base GFK (G. Kruyk?). Delft, about 1680. 30·5cm high. *Centre:* Beer jug painted with Chinese figures and landscapes in hazy blue, with baluster body and rope-twist handle. 45cm high. Frankfurt, late 17th century. *Right:* Jug with pewter cover and footring, painted in tones of blue. 29cm high. Probably Hanau, late 17th century. Three decorative-utilitarian pots with Oriental themes, a type made in some quantity by most tin-glaze factories of any standing in Holland and Germany. *See page 133.*

107. Wall-plaque painted in tones of blue, opaque cool green and yellow, with drawing in purple-brown. About 32cm wide. Probably Delft, early 18th century. This scene from everyday life with its intriguing details was probably newly devised by the painter: hence the drawing which is more descriptive than artistic. It was a popular decoration in Dutch houses, and may have been one of a series. *Dr and Mrs A. Fairbairn. See page 136.*

108. Small vase painted in dark and light blue with lotus-flower decoration directly borrowed from Chinese porcelain. About 22cm high. Marked GFK, probably for G. F. Kruyk of the *Porcelain Flask* factory. Delft, late 17th century. *Victoria and Albert Museum. See page 133.*

110. Small bowl painted in polychrome, with gilding. Mark IW for Jacob Wemmerson. Attributed to the Young Moor's Head factory. Delft, about 1710. A charming free-drawn scene with an easy but sophisticated composition. The people are drinking chocolate, the new fashionable drink. *Nijstad Antiquairs Lochem N.V., Lochem, Holland. See page 133.*

09. ◄An unusual wine-cooler, painted in blue, green and red. 49cm long. Mark PAK Pieter Adrianson Kocks of the Greek A). Delft, early 18th century. The mixture of uropean figures with Oriental flowers was uite usual by this date, and the two conentions mingle easily. *See page 133.*

11. Large dish painted in blue. 41cm vide. Mark LVE and MP for Lambert van enhoorn of the Metal Pot, Delft, about 700. The dense decoration suffers from eing reduced into a small photograph. In s true scale the ornament vibrates and is ot fussy. European decoration seldom ade so much use of the byplay between rect painting and patterns of white eserve. Dutch potters learned it from the hinese. *Fitzwilliam Museum, Cambridge. ee page 134.*

112. Dish painted and dabbed with a sponge. 32cm wide. Dutch, 18th century. Vigorous popular painting with succulent strokes in the old palette of Italian colours. There are some clever stratagems, such as the wash colour with overpainting, and the suggestion of movement caused by placing the dark border-motifs diagonally to the buildings. *Fitzwilliam Museum, Cambridge. See page 131.*

113. Large plate, slightly domed in the middle, painted in blue. 38cm wide. Delft, middle of the 18th century. At this period the 'best' decoration was usually carefully and precisely painted. This plate shows that even in the Western world it was still possible to paint freely and yet be sophisticated. *Museum für Kunsthandwerk, Frankfurt am Main. See page 136.*

114. Tile panel painted in polychrome. 169cm high. Probably Delft, first half of the 18th century. *Victoria and Albert Museum. See page 138.*

115. Large *dzbán* or pitcher with pewter lid, and originally a pewter foot-band. 32cm high. Moravia, dated 1593. This may be the earliest dated example of Habaner pottery in existence. The handle cannot be seen, being opposite the emblem on the front. The emblem is an old German potter's wheel. It was turned by hand or foot, by pushing the balusters which join the wheelhead to the weighted rim at the base. The wheel turned on a pivot inside the upper block, and could therefore be tilted when the potter shaped a vessel. The vase and flowers on the wheel remained a popular decorative theme for four hundred years. *Private Collection in Prague. See page 145.*

116. Dish painted in grass-green, blue, ochre, purple-brown, with a *bianco sopra bianco* design between the central device and the rim. 29cm wide. Faenza, about 1476. The arms belong to King Matthias Corvinus of Hungary and his second wife, Beatrix of Naples. *Victoria and Albert Museum. See page 141.*

117. Large plate painted in grey-blue and purple-brown. 31cm wide. Slovakia, dated 1702. The form is based on a pewter dish. The base is recessed and has no footring. The shape is sometimes called the cardinal's hat. The austere decoration was originally adopted for ethical reasons. By the date of this example the convention had lasted for a hundred years and was already on the way out. *Narodni Museum, Prague See page 146.*

118. Pottery cask painted in blue, green and yellow, with drawing lines in purple-brown. 19cm wide. Sobotište, Slovakia, about 1650. The tightly drawn flowers are typical of Habaner decoration. The pigments were mixed with fluxes so they could be thickly applied without becoming rough. The rest of the cask was left white to avoid frivolity, not only for artistic reasons. *Herman Landsfeld. See page 146.*

119. Hexagonal tile with glazes of plain white, opaque blue and yellow, separated by incised lines. Trnava, Slovakia, about 1650. This device with its curious optical illusion was a favourite Habaner tile pattern. *Herman Landsfeld. See page 144.*

120. Dish painted in blue, yellow and green, with drawing in purple-brown. 34·5cm wide. Slovakia, dated 1707. Free, delicate and bold, this decoration has burst out of the traditional puritan flower-motifs, as the desert comes into leaf after rain. Until about this time only the Habaners knew how to make maiolica. Henceforward it was taken up by the Slovak potters and became much gayer. *Victoria and Albert Museum. See page 148.*

121. Small pitcher with blue glaze and decoration in yellow and white. 15cm high. West Slovakia, dated 1667. The application of tin white and other light pigments to a dark glaze was difficult. On the whole the Habaners managed better than the French painters at Nevers, who used the technique for *Chinoiserie* at the same period. *Narodni Museum, Bratislava. See page 149.*

122. Pitcher painted in green, yellow and blue. 26·5cm high. West Slovakia, dated 1775. The garland was an old Habaner motif, but the bows above and below it come from the fanciful Slovaks. The dancing lion is Everyman's coat of arms. Traditionally the design was first drawn in brown and then the colours were filled in. The Slovak painters reversed the process: they painted the design in broad strokes, and used the fine lines to accent it afterwards. *Narodni Museum, Bratislava. See page 150.*

123. Tureen, platter, jug and plate from a service made for the Palffyovsky family: opaque green with purple-brown drawing. Tureen, 28cm wide. Holič, Slovakia, second half of the 18th century. The Holič factory first made faience for the royal residence, and later for general sale. Some Habaner-Slovak potters were employed there. Though the idea of the work was quite different from their hand-thrown pottery, much of the expertise of Holič and some pattern-work (such as the central device on the platter) came about because of them. *Narodni Museum, Bratislava. See page 152.*

124. *Dzbán-sova* or 'owl pitcher', so-called because of the closed top. 19cm high. Painted in dark brown, orange, grey, blue and green. Kosolna, Slovakia, dated 1831, and inscribed NASKA GABOR PAP ERZA. The pitcher is for spirits and the man on the front is its owner. The decoration of swags and leaves is a popular version of the borders of aristocratic tableware. *Narodni Museum, Bratislava. See page 156.*

125. Pitcher painted in blue. 21cm high. Smoleniče, Slovakia, late 19th century. The painted design originated in baroque floral decoration, but in the hands of peasant potters it has lost its prettiness and became dynamic. *Narodni Museum, Bratislava. See page 157.*

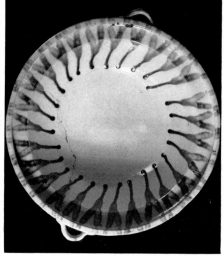

126. A pottery sign from the outer wall of a workshop in Velka Leváré, Slovakia. Painted in blue, green, yellow and brown. 46 by 51cm. Dated 1732. In the lower part of the plaque the potter is presenting a finished vessel to his patron, a gentleman in riding habit. Above is the old-fashioned block-wheel. To either side of the fly-wheel are tools for smoothing and trimming the pots. The vase of flowers and the birds are a traditional feature of the emblem and express the potters' attitude to their work. The border includes samples of different patterns and colours. *Museum of Applied Art, Budapest. See page 150.*

127. Bowl with two small handles, decorated in clear copper-green glaze. About 24cm wide. Modra, Slovakia, 19th century. A similar kind of decoration, using the running property of copper glazes, had been used over tin glaze in Egypt in the 12th century, though the Slovaks are hardly likely to have known it. *Herman Landsfeld. See page 160.*

129. Drug-jar painted in soft blue, green and yellow. 24cm high. Probably made in London or Antwerp, late 16th century. The floral motifs were stock designs of Italian emigrant potters. The abruptly turned-out rim provides for a pig's bladder to be stretched over the top to seal the contents. *W. W. Winkworth, Esq. See page 164.*

130. Mug painted in blue. 16cm high. Southwark, dated 1630. The bird-on-the-rock design with supporting flowers, ferns and insects was adapted from Chinese porcelain by Christian Wilhelm, who had a pottery in Southwark about 1628–40. *London Museum. See page 165.*

128. ◀ Jar with clay handle, called *nosáček* painted in deep blue with lettering in dark brown. 24cm high. Dechtice, Slovakia, dated 1883. This traditional vessel was used for carrying food. *Narodni Museum, Bratislava. See page 160.*

131. Small jug painted in dark and light blue, 12cm high. Probably London, about 1600. The soft edges of the design with the Faenza split-leaf emblem are caused by a thick overglaze, which has also yellowed the glaze on the outside. The ointment pot with the stub handle is glazed plain white. 6cm high, London, about 1650. *W. W. Winkworth Esq. See page 164.*

132. Large polychrome dish. London, probably Southwark, dated 1648. Most painters worked from engravings. The painter of this extraordinary version of Susannah and the Elders clearly had enough imagination to undertake the subject single-handed, and he also improvised a remarkable border. *Colonial Williamsburg U.S.A. See page 166.*

133. Posset-pot with plain white glaze. 14cm high. Probably Lambeth, second half of 17th century. The glutinous posset was sucked through the spout. *Sampson and Seligman, London. See page 166.*

134. Large charger painted in tones of green, yellow and blue over a design sketched in light brown. 47cm wide. Probably Southwark, dated 1657 beside the initials, and twice more on the back. The initials are those of Richard Newnham, a Southwark master-potter, and his wife Elizabeth. The leaf and scroll border is an Italianate design, much used by English potters at this time, but the landscape was probably taken from a Dutch dish. The back is unusual in being covered with a white glaze instead of the usual semi-transparent waste glaze. The dish is intriguingly warped and the glaze is blistered on the back, showing that it was exposed to flames in the kiln. *See page 166.*

135. Wet drug-jar with strap handle (on the far side), painted in blue with a 'label' inscribed S*E* Succo* Mell I.G. 1669. 20·5cm high. *See page 166.*

136. Large dish painted in blue, soft green, ochre, yellow and purple-brown. 44cm wide. Probably Southwark, about 1650. *Bristol City Art Gallery. See page 167.*

137. Large posset-pot with lid, painted in blue. About 40cm high overall. Brislington, *c.* 1670. Possets, sillabubs and caudles were thick drinks made from wine or spirits or ale with egg, milk, sugar and spices, supposed to be warm and sustaining. Large posset-pots like this were probably for convivial occasions and people liked them to be ornate and striking. *Bristol City Art Gallery. See page 170.*

138, 139. Figure of No-Body with a pipe. About 19cm high. Painted in soft green, ochre and blue. Probably Lambeth, dated 1675. The figure with the goblet is about the same size, and is K'ang Hsi porcelain of similar date. It must have been based on some model like the Lambeth figure. A similar figure is shown in a woodcut illustrating a play called *No-Body and Some-Body*, printed in 1606. 138, *Fitzwilliam Museum, Cambridge*; 139, *Victoria and Albert Museum*.

140. Large platter painted in blue and yellow. 47cm wide. Probably Brislington, dated 1682. English decoration was direct and simple compared with Continental practice. The floral border seems to have been painted freehand, for the spacing is irregular and is dense over the King's left shoulder. Charles II was much depicted on pottery, often with a waggish expression caused by one eye being higher than the other. *Bristol City Art Gallery. See page 168.*

141. Blue-dash charger painted in lemon yellow, orange, grey-black and blue wash with line drawing in blue. Clear glaze on back. 27cm wide. Probably Lambeth, end of 17th century. The popular William of Orange was usually shown on horseback in full regalia. This made his image distinctive, and avoided the need to draw his legs. *Reading Museum* (*Blatch Collection*) *See page 168.*

142. Large dish painted in brown, blue, orange and yellow. About 38cm wide. Probably Bristol, mid 18th century. The impulsive brushwork of this Oriental landscape puts it right outside the convention of polite *chinoiserie*. The browns of the colour scheme are also unusual. Perhaps for once the painter was working to please only himself. *Sampson and Seligman, London. See page 171.*

143. Small punch-bowl painted in tones of blue. 27cm wide. Bristol, about 1740. One of three known versions of Hogarth's painting of this subject, which he published as an engraving about 1736. The line and wash treatment with the hop-leaf border is a translation rather than a copy, and the free line is in the long tradition of English cartoons and illustrations. *See page 171.*

144. Plate painted in tones of blue line and wash. About 24cm wide. Probably Bristol, c. 1755. The drawing is of David Garrick and a leading lady, probably Kitty Clive, on an open-air stage. Several similar but differently composed examples are known. *Gerald Reitlinger, Esq. See page 171.*

145. Plate with Chinese landscape in blue, and *bianco sopra bianco* border 24cm wide. Bristol, c. 1760. *Bianco sopra bianco* was used in Italy until about 1600. It was revived in Northern Europe in the mid 18th century. It was a dense white tin glaze painted on a slightly stained foundation glaze. *Sampson and Seligman, London. See page 173.*

146. Plate painted in blue line and wash with sponge-dabbing. 23cm wide. Bristol, about 1760. A charming example of a type of landscape much used at Bristol, indebted to Oriental conventions, but so thoroughly assimilated by English pottery painters that it became more English than Chinese. *Ashmolean Museum, Oxford (Warren Collection). See page 171.*

147. Large jar of Chinese shape, painted in blue. About 35cm high. Liverpool, c. 1770. The crisp Oriental design is characteristic of Liverpool Delft. The painters were probably influenced by the nearby porcelain factories. The ribbed throwing-marks are very strong inside this jar. On the outside they were smoothed with a ribbing-tool. The slight unevenness of the profile results from the pressure of the thrower's palms as he lifted the wet pot from the wheel. *W. W. Winkworth, Esq. See page 171.*

148. The 'Flower' punch-bowl, painted in tones of blue line and wash. 8·75/21cm high, 34cm wide. Signed within 'Joseph Flower Sculp. 1743'. Bristol. The designs around the bowl are from a collection of songs, Bickham's *Musical Entertainer*, first published about 1739. This elaborate bowl was perhaps the painter's 'masterpiece' or proof of skill at the end of his apprenticeship. *Ashmolean Museum, Oxford (Warren Collection)*. See page 171.

49. Flower-brick, painted in soft blue and purple-brown. About 16cm long. c. 1760. Part of the charm of this small piece is the way the glaze has begun to flow, making the pigments look rainy. The 'Flower' punch-bowl (Plate 148) has traces of the same effect. *Reading Museum (Blatch Collection). See page 171.*

150. Punch-bowl painted in blue with yellow on the flags and
with *bianco sopra bianco* border. 29cm wide. Bristol, dated 1765.
This beautiful bowl takes pride of place amongst the many ship
punch-bowls made at Bristol and Liverpool. The Swedish
inscription reads: 'The ship Wigelantia off the stocks Stockholm
1728; in dock Bristol, January 1765'. The initials I.P.C. are those
of the ship's master, for whom the bowl was made. *Manchester
City Art Gallery. See page 172.*

151. Puebla tiles painted in strong blue. Tiles about 13cm wide. Mexico, second half of 17th century. The tin-glaze technique reached Mexico through the craftsmen from Seville. These fanciful designs have already become quite different from Spanish work, and make more use of flat pattern. Oriental influence is clear in some of the flowers and in the odd rendering of the ground. This influence came not only through Europe but also direct across the Pacific. *Victoria and Albert Museum.*

152. Jar painted in raised blue. About 33cm high. Puebla, late 17th century. The tin-glaze potteries of Puebla de los Angeles were started about 1580–85 with the help of the master-potter Gaspar de Encinas from Talavera. About 1630 the Jesuit Padre Bernabé Cobo wrote that the work was as good as that of Talavera, and said that in the last few years imitations of China pottery had been made. This piece owes something to both Spain and China but has a new character of its own. *Hispanic Society of America.*

153. Puebla dish painted in strong blue on yellowish tin glaze. 19cm wide. Mexico, c. 1900. The fuzzed blue is strangely like some very early Middle Eastern tin-glaze pottery. In the hands of Mexican popular potters the figurative decoration has acquired a new mood: the imprecision is as important and suggestive as the definition used to be in the Italian convention. *Victoria and Albert Museum* (*Maudsley Bequest*).

154. Plate painted in brown, ochre and blue. About 27cm wide. Talavera or Triana, late 17th century. A successful decorator's mannerism which was used in Spain for some hundred and fifty years, with a variety of vigorous popular subjects. The glaze on these wares is often poorly prepared and deeply pitted. *Instituto de Valencia de Don Juan, Madrid. See page 107.*

155. Lobed dish painted in blue. 39cm wide. Frankfurt, about 1720. *Germanisches Nationalmuseum, Nürnberg. See page 179.*

156. Large jar painted in tones of hazy blue. 32cm high. Frankfurt, late 17th century. The form is Chinese by origin, but is really universal, for almost any large tall pot being thrown on the wheel resembles this form at some stage of its growth. Frankfurt tin glaze began in 1666. The factory derived a good deal from Chinese porcelain and was partly inspired by the success of Delft, but the designs and the kind of blue were a different interpretation of Oriental mannerisms. *Fitzwilliam Museum, Cambridge (Glaisher Bequest). See page 179.*

158. Tankard painted in enamel green, blue, yellow, deep reddish-brown and black. 20cm high. Ansbach, dated 1736. This is the typical German beer-mug shape, the *Walzenkrug,* which has been made since the early 18th century. The decoration seems to be feeling its way towards porcelain, it is so clear and delicate. Faience was made at Ansbach from 1710, when the factory was founded under the patronage of the Margrave Friedrich Wilhelm of Brandenburg. Porcelain was also made there, but not until 1758. *Germanisches Nationalmuseum, Nürnberg. See page 183.*

157. Two ewers with pewter mounts and *hausmaler* decoration. 26cm and 32cm high. Frankfurt faience, painted in Nürnberg, late 17th century. The piece on the left, painted with the Story of Tobias and the Angel, in *schwarzlot,* is by J. L. Faber. The right-hand piece, painted in green, purple and blue, is signed A.H. for Abraham Helmhack. *Hausmaler* painting was an extreme, specialist way of using the decorative possibilities of white pottery, and flourished chiefly in South Germany. It began on faience, but was really better suited to hard and durable porcelain, which was also used from about 1720 onwards. *Germanisches Nationalmuseum, Nürnberg. See page 185.*

159. Figure of horse and rider in plain tin glaze. 34cm high. Potsdam, about 1740. How beautifully soft and dense these tin glazes could be! *Germanisches National-museum, Nürnberg. See page 181.*

160, 161. Cruet-basket painted in enamel colours with the arms of Breteuil, about 21cm long. Marieberg, Sweden, 1768. Tureen painted in enamel colours. About 35cm long. Rörstrand, Sweden, about 1770.

Two examples, both perfect in their way, of restrained and unrestrained Swedish rococo faience. The natural conclusion of such forms was to be made in porcelain, or at least in very strong siliceous earthenware such as Wedgwood developed. By the mid 18th century the potter's wheel played little part in the making of fine pottery. *Nationalmuseum, Stockholm. See page 183.*

162. Dish painted in deep slate-blue. 40cm wide. Barcelona, mid-17th century. This is one of several popular designs with the *corbata* or cravat-pattern border. It is remarkable how an Italian pictorial motif could be rendered in an entirely Spanish and non-pictorial way. *Palacio Nacional, Barcelona. See page 79.*

163. Jar painted in deep blue and purple-brown. 32cm high. Portugal, late 17th century. *Museu Nacional de Arte Antiga, Lisbon. See page 80.*

164. Very large deep bowl or *barreño*, painted in green, yellow, orange and brown. 62cm wide. Níjar, near Almería, mid-19th century. A type of country bowl regularly made with a variety of designs in the middle, used for preparing dough and for other domestic purposes. *See page 80.*

165. A curiosity—a small Japanese ash-jar, used in the Tea Ceremony. Painted in blue, green, yellow and purple-brown. 11cm high. Probably about 1800. This is a Japanese version of the Faenza split-leaf pattern, and may be unique. I do not know of any other Japanese tin-glaze pottery. European painted ware reached Japan as the property of ship's captains, and was given or bartered by them. It was much admired and many examples are in Japanese museums. The Japanese got tin from Formosa but hardly ever used it in glazes. *W. W. Winkworth, Esq.*

166.   Plate from a service designed by Félix Bracquemond, with polychrome decoration handpainted on a clear glaze over hard white earthenware. 21cm wide. Montereau, about 1864. This is actually not tin-glaze work; the technique and the whole idea are in the tin-glaze tradition, but the materials are those of the new *faience-fine. Musée des Arts Décoratifs, Paris. See page 191*.

167.   Pitcher with semi-opaque glaze, green rim and handles, and painting in dark brown. 34cm high. Duncan Grant, 1911. The pitcher was made by a Tunisian potter and was painted in the workshop by the visiting painter. The drawing borrows a third dimension from the form and becomes a kind of drawn-sculpture. *See page 192*.

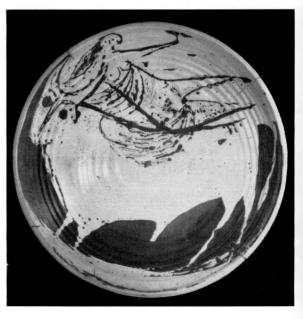

168.   Small pot decorated with cobalt-stained clay slips on red clay, covered by a semi-opaque tin glaze. 7·5cm high. Michael Casson, 1958. The technique exploits the tendency of dark colours to break through opaque glazes from below, the higher the glaze is fired. Several non-traditional practices are combined: high firing, red clay and a motif worked in clay slips instead of brush pigments. *See page 195*

169.   Very large dish painted with Europa and the Bull in tones of brown over wax-resist. 60cm wide. William Newland, 1952. The upper part is painted direct on the glaze, and the lower part is painted over drawing in liquid wax. Some details are deliberately left to chance, such as the way the brush has been deflected by the throwing-marks, and the spots of pigment lying over the waxed surfaces before the wax burnt off. Wax resist needs confidence: all mistakes in tin glaze are hard to alter; mistakes in wax resist are almost impossible to change. *See page 195*.

170. Large dish in tin glaze with wax resist over copper, cobalt and iron pigments. 45cm long. Anne Clark, 1971. Here wax resist is combined with scraping, incising and rubbing, to allow the strong pigments to break through the glaze. *See page 195.*

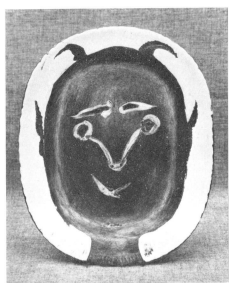

171, 172. Two tin-glaze pieces by Picasso. *171.* 'Mounted rider.' 38cm high, black, red and white, about 1955. *172.* Large dish in wax resist, tin glaze and white slip. Vallauris, 1948. Ceramics appealed directly to Picasso's love of transformations and sleights of hand, by which familiar forms were suddenly turned into something new and strange. It has been said of his honeymoon with ceramics, 'Nothing is searched for, everything is found.' *171. Victoria and Albert Museum London (given by Picasso). See page 193.*

173. Painters at work at Casteldurante, mid 16th century. From *Arte del Vasaio*, folio 57v.* Piccolpasso says disarmingly 'The painting of pottery is different from mural painting because mural painters for the most part stand and pottery painters all sit.' 'Flat ware is held on the knees with one hand beneath it; hollow ware is held with the left hand inside it.' This is being done by the painter on the right. Banding wheels were rarely used. Bowls were placed on soft tow inside a wooden platter, so they could be turned round without roughening the glaze on the underside. On the wall Piccolpasso shows cartoons for landscape and figure subjects. *See page 208.*

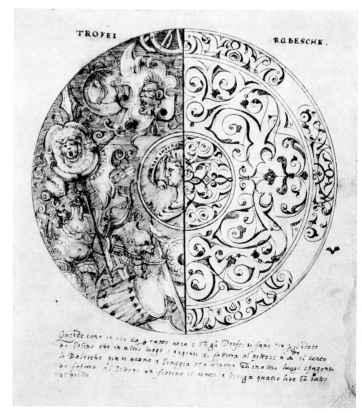

174. Sketches by Piccolpasso showing painted designs of about 1550, from *Arte del Vasaio* folio 66: 'Trophies and Arabesques'. Any competent painter should be able to render these fluently. Like most Italian designs they depend on line drawing. Trophies were usually painted in *grisaille* on a bluish glaze ground, indicated by cross-hatching in the sketch. *See page 101.*

175. *Arte del Vasaio*, folio 32v: the kiln. On the right are spy-holes for watching the progress of the firing. Trial pieces of glazed pottery were withdrawn through them towards the end of the firing. The holes in the roof are vents for the flames and smoke; as the nearer end of the kiln reached the right heat the vents were blocked, forcing the draught to move further along. *See pages 101 and 211.*

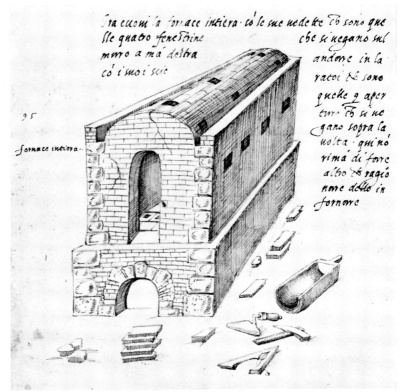

176. *Arte del Vasaio*, folio 49v: the firing of a small kiln for maiolica, by which Piccolpasso means lustre. The kiln is only about three cubic feet in volume 'because the art is so uncertain'. Here he shows the last hour of the firing, when the fuel is changed from willow to broom, reducing the pigments to lustrous metal. The vents in the roof are covered over and there is much smoke. *See page 101.*

177. Inside the lustre kiln is a round muffle with perforated sides, in which the ware is protected from the direct blast of the flames. The drawing shows the section of this muffle, with porringers lying one upon another on the bottom. They are allowed to touch because in this firing the glaze does not melt. *See page 101.*

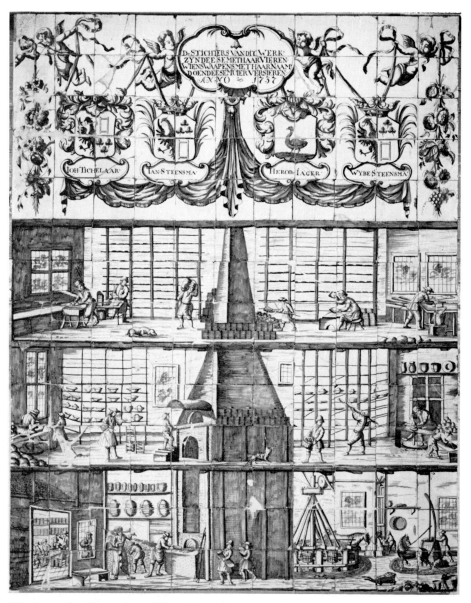

178. Large tile-picture about 195cm high, representing the Bolsward factory in Friesland, dated 1737. At the top are the coats of arms of the owners, three of which include the tilemaker's wooden frame. The heavy work had to be done on ground level. The mules are working two mills, one for preparing plastic clay, the other for grinding glazes. On the far side of the kiln is the decorators' room, on the ground floor, where clients could give instructions, and also because the painted pots should be handled as little as possible before being packed into the kiln. On the first floor are the throwers of bowls and dishes, assisted by a ball-maker who weighs lumps for the thrower, and another man who takes away the thrown shapes on a plank. On the racks are vessels drying, waiting to be trimmed on the underside. The man on the far left seems to be doing this. The men on the second floor are making tiles. The boy is mixing the sandy clay and the porter takes it to the tile-cutters, whose wooden frames are clearly indicated. Around the chimney stacks of tiles are drying.

The firing chamber of the kiln is all in the vertical part with the high door. The arch below the door is the entrance to the firebox. Immediately above it (inside and out of sight) would be a per-forated vault over which the floor of the chamber is built. On the first floor the chimney begins. The aperture under the hood is for removing and replacing the plugs which are in the dome of the fire-chamber. By this means the draught is directed to which ever part of the chamber needs more heat, to make the firing even. *Rijksmuseum, Amsterdam. See pages 131 and 215.*

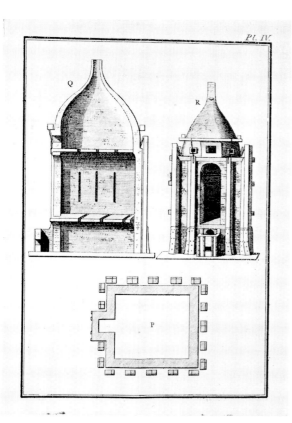

180. Diagram of a similar kiln, from Diderot's *Encyclopédie* of 1756. This picture shows two alternative ways of packing ware in the chamber: *en echappade* with open shelves, or in saggars. *See page 214.*

179. Diagram of a late 18th century Dutch kiln, from Gerrit Paape, *De Plateelbakker of Delftsch Aardewerk Maaker*, 1794. The firebox, fire-chamber, pottery-chamber and cowl are shown. Though two hundred years later than Piccolpasso's kiln, the principle is the same except that the tapered cowl induces a stronger draught. *See page 215.*

181. Spanish potters packing a traditional kiln for glaze firing, 1969. Half the problem is to decide how the saggars can be filled most economically. Everything has to be handled very carefully because at this stage the glaze is powdery and can easily be knocked away from the pot. *See page 213.*

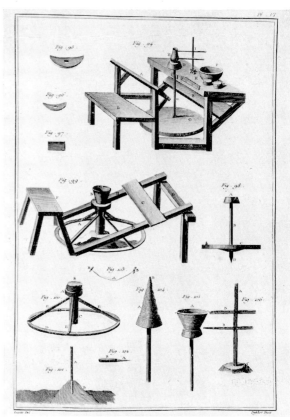

182. Engraving from Gerrit Paape, *De Plateelbakker of Delftsch Aardewerk Maaker,* 1794. The upper plate shows the glazer or *geever* dipping biscuit ware into the tub filled with white glaze. The *geever* was important, for the thickness of the glaze was vital to the finish of good ware, and a careless man could ruin a great value of pottery. His clothes show his importance. The lower plate shows the application of the clear overglaze or *kwaart,* which is sprinkled on with a stout brush. In both pictures the trestle benches rest on saggars in which plates are fired. Pegs were pushed through the triangular holes to support each plate at three points. *See page 208.*

183. Diagrams from Diderot's *Encyclopédie* of 1756. Figure 94 shows the traditional European potter's wheel with its bearing under the flywheel and a brace round the vertical shaft. Figures 95–97 are ribbers for smoothing the clay when it has been drawn up into a pot. Figures 99–101 show the old block-wheel which spins on a single pivot not far below the wheelhead.

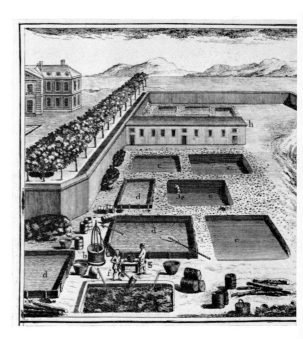

184. Settling tanks or 'backs' used in refining, screening and blending clays. After passing through screens the liquid clay was channelled into the backs to settle. From Gerrit Paape, *op. cit.* 1794. *See page 201.*

185. Tin-glaze painters at work, Puente del Arzobispo, Spain, 1969. They have banding-wheels and some of their pigments are supplied by colour-merchants, but many things remain as they were in Piccolpasso's day. *See page 102.*

186. Workshop at Fostat, 1969, showing the traditional Arab potter's wheel, tilted away from the thrower, which enables him to see clearly the profile of the shape. *See page 58.*

187, 188, 189. Traditional kilns at Fostat, near Cairo, 1969. Two fireboxes, with the main kiln chambers behind them. Two kilns with a generous arrangement of vents in the vault, enabling the potter to direct the draught of flames to one part or another of the chamber. Rebuilding the vault of a kiln. The arch is temporarily supported by biscuit pottery and drainpipes built up on a trestle. *See page 211.*